Capital
Equipment Buying
Handbook

Capital Equipment Buying Handbook

Richard G. Newman
and
Robert J. Simkins

AMACOM

American Management Association

New York · Atlanta · Boston · Chicago · Kansas City · San Francisco · Washington, D.C.
Brussels · Mexico City · Tokyo · Toronto

This book is available at special
discount when ordered in bulk quantities.
For information, contact Special Sales Department,
AMACOM, a division of American Management Association,
1601 Broadway, New York, NY 10019.

This publication is designed to provide accurate and authoritative
information in regard to the subject matter covered. It is sold with
the understanding that the publisher is not engaged in rendering
legal, accounting, or other professional service. If legal advice or
other expert assistance is required, the services of a competent professional person should be sought.

Library of Congress Cataloging-in-Publication Data

Newman, Richard G.
    Capital equipment buying handbook / Richard G. Newman and
Robert J. Simkins.
        p.   cm.
    Includes bibliographical references and index.
    ISBN 0-8144-0369-7
    1. Industrial procurement.   I. Simkins, Robert J.   II. Title.
HD39.5.N482   1998
658.7'2—dc21   97–45962
                                                                   CIP

Printing number

10 9 8 7 6 5 4 3 2 1

Contents

List of Exhibits

Preface

We urge you to read this preface first because it will explain why we wrote certain things in this book and what makes this book different from others. This is a handbook, and we hope it will serve as a reference to you in making some of the most important capital investments your organization must make over the coming years. As a handbook, it is highly unlikely you will read the entire book from cover to cover. There are things you know already about this decision process, for example. You may only want to use the checklists at the end of many of the chapters. You may wish to read an appendix to find out how to locate data on the Internet or who produces a good CMMS (computerized maintenance management system) system. And if you do read it from page 1 to the end, you will see some redundancy because the same subject is mentioned in two or three places in the book. We have used repetition on purpose to facilitate your finding the information you need. Consider the parallel of making a trip to the grocery store to buy grated cheese for pasta. Where do you look? You could try the section with the pasta, and you would find it there. You could try the dairy section, and it is there also. Why? The store manager does not want you to be frustrated and go somewhere else to buy the cheese. The manager wants to make finding it an easy task. We wanted to accomplish the same task. Thus, do not be surprised to find information on spare parts in Chapter 9, on maintenance, and Chapter 11, on total cost of ownership.

We also have tried to bring up some ideas to think about in the process of buying the equipment. Some are new ones; some are tried and tested and still apply. Perhaps the most important message that we attempt to get across is the team approach. No one person knows all the answers to the myriad of questions that arise in the buying process. There must be a good leader in the process, but there must also be the technical experts who come up with some of the answers to difficult questions. Management must understand the complexity of the decision and what the numbers mean. Buying the equipment is not going to satisfy every team member, and there will be some compromising. Yet the function of the team is to bring to bear the best thoughts of each member into the decision. The objective is getting the most value for the funds expended. This does not mean the cheapest or the most expensive, but the one whose output is the best cost per.

This book looks at a wide array of subjects ranging from engineering-oriented considerations to legal factors to purchasing issues to accounting components of the decision process. The focus or orientation will be toward three major considerations:

1. Developing the best possible process to accomplish the purchase
2. Achieving the best decision by looking at the total cost of ownership and cost *per unit*
3. Engaging in the process as a team or coordinated effort reflecting the inputs of many and wisdom from the top to manage the process

In his wonderful book *Alice's Adventures in Wonderland,* Lewis Carroll relates the fall of Alice through the hole. She meets the Cheshire Cat and asks, "What road do I take?" The smiling cat replies, "Where do you wish to go?" Alice responds, "I don't know." Sagely, the cat quips, "Then it makes no difference which road you take."

If you don't know where you are going, you never know when you are there. If you don't know what you want, you never know when you have it. If you do not know what you want in the capital equipment purchase, you will end up buying what someone wants to sell you. You have made the selling job easy for the supplier. All they have to do is convince you their product is better than the competitors. This is easy because you don't really know what you want anyway, or your needs are so vaguely defined that the range of options is almost endless. At the opposite end of the spectrum are requirements for the equipment that are so stringent and demanding that cost escalates beyond all reasonable levels. There must be a balance. The purpose of this book is to help you achieve that balance.

We appreciate your purchase of the book and close with the modern version of the Golden Rule: "He who has the gold makes the rules." It is your organization's money that is going out to that supplier to buy that machine, whatever its purpose. If you don't know what you want, when, and how much it will really cost, do not buy it.

Acknowledgments

Our sincere thanks to our respective spouses, Donna Lou and Helen, for putting up with the husbands who wrote or edited while the grass went unmowed. Any mistakes in the book are ours, but we hope the book will prevent *you* from making any in the buying process. Make a capital equipment purchase error, and your name will be chiseled in the marble of the company. People forget success but always remember failures.

Finally, our sincere thanks to those who really make it happen, the people at AMACOM, especially, Ms. Jacquie Flynn, Development Editor, who did an outstanding job in making the material readable. Her suggestions were greatly appreciated. And to Mike Sivilli, Associate Editor, who "straw bossed" the book to completion. Without these people, there are no books. The errors, if any, belong to us.

Capital Equipment Buying Handbook

1

Overview of the Field

No civilized society can progress without capital equipment. Without it, manufacturing would be reduced to a seventeenth-century level with craftsmen using crude tools and turning out limited output. Thanks to the efforts of a great American, Eli Whitney, the use of capital equipment by limited skill labor was accomplished between 1798 and 1809. Whitney is often remembered for his invention of the cotton gin, but his flintlock manufacturing process is frequently considered his greatest contribution. Although nine years late in completing the contract, Whitney proved mass production was feasible and cost-effective. Using capital equipment, it was possible to duplicate gun stocks and gun parts that were interchangeable, an unaccomplished feat up to that time.

Capital equipment is the lifeblood of manufacturing, agriculture, communications, transportation, medicine, and education. Without it, civilization would be mired in the Dark Ages. Economists have spoken of the three factors of production as being land, labor, and capital. The more modern factors are people, materials, and equipment for manufactured goods; and people, equipment, and processes for services. People and equipment are the common denominators, regardless of what is produced. Since services are not tangible and to a large degree lack the physical characteristics that allow unit-to-unit comparison, the focus of this book is on the goods side of the output. This is not to denigrate services. Equipment purchased for service performance is equally important. The difference is that the measuring of variation in goods is easier and more objective than the service side.

From the decision to buy an office copier to reproduce the 60 copies needed each month to the building of the Saturn plant in Spring Hill, Tennessee, there is a commonality of the capital equipment investment decision: It involves analysis, risk, and coordination. Regardless of the dollar amount or lead time or source, the decision to invest is important to the organization. Likewise, the complexity of analysis is directly proportional to the dollars expended in the decision. As a complex decision, the amassing of the information needed to make the correct choice often lies beyond the capability of one person. It must be a team effort, since there are too many factors for a single individual to consider, resulting in overlooking some elements of the decision. Often the factors evaluated are in conflict from the perspectives of the team members.

Finance people focus on costs and returns. Engineers focus on design elements and quality of output. Manufacturing people focus on the output of the equipment and its reliability. Maintenance people focus on maintainability and an ample supply of spare parts for the equipment. Each comes from a particular discipline, and their input is naturally going to show some bias toward that area. Is that bad? No. This is the reason people are employed in those functions. They are the champions of those areas in a situation where there is a balance to be achieved among a wide array of factors. This is the role of top management. Call it mediator, arbitrator, or simply the boss; there is an important managerial task to preside over these decisions and balance the inputs of the gatekeepers.[1] For example, it may be more economical to purchase the machine overseas on the basis of purchase price, yet if the dimensions are all in the metric system and maintenance does not have metric tools, some of the cost advantage disappears. In addition, if the maintenance manuals arrive and are printed in German or French, there is a communications issue to resolve. These may seem like trivial issues, but when they happen, a machine might stay down and orders will go unfilled. We cannot anticipate every contingency but we can set up or develop a methodology, checklists, or some other device to ensure these factors have been considered in the decision process. This does not mean taking an inordinate amount of time to look at the trivial. It means looking at the list or the schematic for buying capital equipment, checking off the obvious, and moving on to the decision. The process by which it will be done is the issue of this book and its focus. Again, there are significant differences between buying the home copier and the 3,200-ton press. The home copier, purchased at the local office supply store, does not come with the problems of transportation, setup, spare parts, training of operators, maintenance policy, financing, depreciation, and disposal. Yet the decision makers look at these items in the decision process. The process is the important issue of the book.

This book leans toward the team approach to the decision process. Each member of the cross-function team brings input to the decision, and regardless of how the decision is made, the process has had the best collective thinking, the airing of facts, and the providing of the most complete picture possible. For each value received by having the team approach, however, there is a counterbalancing cost to consider. In forming the team, who makes the decision on membership, leadership, or reporting relations? How does one bring about a degree of control to the team processes and avoid a "voting approach," where

---

1. One engineer commented to me that if purchasing had its way, the turbines his company produced would be made out of plastic because it was cheaper. Such a perspective is harmful to the organization.

people are voting in areas where they have no experience and little expertise? Consider the case of supplier selection. Is that a team decision or inputs to the decision maker? While the team approach has gained popularity in this country and as one executive put it, "It takes a team to look at the project because the body of knowledge is beyond the comprehension of a single person," the role of the team must be carefully defined. It is not an opportunity to vote and democratically decide what to buy and which source to buy it from. Consider it more in the context of athletic teams with functional specialists, each bringing a talent to the game. That does not equate to equivalence or one vote per person. Functional specialists bring their talents to the team and consider options for purchase in the light of those talents. It may be an arena of conflict, with financial considerations moving the decision in one direction and quality considerations moving it in an opposite heading. The paramount consideration is to *bring all the issues to the table for informed reflection* on the part of the team so that the decision is the best for the circumstances. It may not be consensus or majority wins. The purpose of the team is not to hold referendums; it is a talent bank that aids in the process, provides information, and hopefully achieves the best overall decision, *not* one that satisfies everyone.

Defining Capital Equipment

Normally capital equipment is defined as any item having a service life in excess of three years and an item that must be depreciated as a capital asset.[2] Capital items appear on the balance sheet of the organization and are part of its fixed assets. It is the equipment of plant and equipment appearing in the financial statements of the organization. This equipment is part of the asset base of the organization, and as an asset must be maintained, protected, serviced, and accounted for in any financial statement. The life of capital equipment is defined in different ways:

1. *The operating life of the equipment.* How long can the equipment function in a serviceable manner with routine care and maintenance? The operating life may be expressed in years or hours of operation. It is a technical consideration. The buyer must look at the operating life and sometimes make simple computations to convert from one frame of reference to the other. For example, a vacuum cleaner manufacturer may warrant the vacuum's electric motor for 5 years. On first glance, such a warranty seems generous. However, when one considers that the average use is once per week for 30 minutes, 5 years from the date of purchase constitutes 130 operating hours, normally never more than

---

2. There are exceptions in cases of high technology such as microcomputers. In some instances, they can be written off as operating expenses in a period as short as one year up to $25,000 in value.

30 minutes at a time with periods between use amounting to 1 week, or 168 hours. The 130 operating hours is less than 1 week of continuous service. Operating life is a function of use, and the operating conditions include the environment in which the operation takes place. Clean room manufacturing equipment will have a service life long after technology has marched beyond that equipment. How long is the equipment serviceable? In one case in the late 1960s, one of us visited a company that was using a milling machine purchased in 1916—surplus from another manufacturer. It still held the tolerances.

2. *The technological life of the equipment.* Technology marches forward, and the new product on the market is quickly supplanted with a still newer and improved model. Technology plays a vital role in the decision process and will be addressed in depth later in the chapter.

3. *The economic life of the equipment.* This is the allowable life for accounting purposes and depreciation of the equipment. A machine, having to be depreciated over 10 years, has no accounting value after that period because the economic value of that asset has been deducted from the balance sheet over the 10-year period according to an acceptable method of depreciation, and the appropriate accounting adjustments have been made to the corporate books. The Internal Revenue Service (IRS) prescribes the period of time over which the item may be depreciated, with the schedule ranging from 3 years to 50 years. In addition, there are several methods of depreciation that may be selected. Some allow for faster write-offs in the early years of the asset life, some allow for uniform write-offs, and there is an opportunity to change methods in certain cases. Does that say the asset has no worth? No. It may still be a revenue producer for the corporation. Indeed, the fact that it is fully depreciated may have no influence over its real worth to its owner or others who may have an interest in it, such as lessors. In some instances, it may even appreciate in value. A 1957 Chevrolet in mint condition is worth far more today than its original cost.

In the capital equipment purchase, the accounting technicalities are left to the accountant, yet these details point to the need to have input into the decision from the accounting people in the organization. The class of the equipment (an IRS term defining the time period over which the asset can be depreciated) and its projected uses may influence the investment decision. Capital equipment purchasing is therefore an accounting decision in some ways, and the financial implications of the decision cannot be ignored. Thus, a member of the decision team is the accountant. Which of the three lives— economic, financial, and technological—is used in the decision process makes a significant difference in the end result. The high-technology machine that will be obsolete in three years is a far different case from the milling machine that will probably greet the next millennium. The shorter the life of the equipment, the greater is the overhead burden it must carry to pay for itself. That return must be recouped through a higher price on the product. Given market forces that influence the price, there can develop significant conflict between those holding out for the newest technology and those seeking the lowest-cost equipment. The conflict becomes one of cost to produce versus competitive advantage gained. If the equipment is costly, the price of the product must rise. Countering this argument is that new equipment produces a product that provides a competitive advantage, which allows the company to charge a premium price. Both arguments may be valid, yet the final decision must balance both views. There must be the opportunity to recapture the cost of the equipment through depreciation, yet there is pressure to move forward with the newest technology.

There is also pressure to extend the life of the equipment. Extending the life may bypass the newer technology or incorporate some of it by allowing expansion or addition. Consider the personal computer, capable of adding units of memory, upgrading the central processing unit, and increasing the operating speed. The decision to upgrade versus buy a new unit must look at all aspects of the decision. The buyer should not rely totally on preformulated decision rules or formulas. The economic life may be determined by a formula. A decision to repair or replace is nominally an economic one and uses some form of baseline. If the cost to repair exceeds 60 percent of the cost of replacement, it is not economical to repair it. The issue is having an array of criteria to determine when the service life is completed and not looking at one measure but at options available. Service life can be extended by overhauls or rebuilding or cannibalizing, if necessary. The issue in the economic life is looking at the total cost of the equipment and developing some rational rule to determine when that life is over.

The converse is also true when equipment value is upgraded by adding sensors, gauges, or in-line test equipment to meet a need and therefore enhance the value of the equipment. It may be more cost-effective to upgrade than replace. Intel Corporation has been promoting overdrives for older computers at a fraction of the cost of replacement of an older model. Does the overdrive make sense? It depends on an array of factors, yet it becomes an option to extend the potential economic life of the equipment. Each case is unique and needs all the expertise it can use.

In the manufacturing field, the process of creating a product can be illustrated in the diagram in Exhibit 1-1. The nominal inputs to the process include people working with material on equipment. The end result is a product that becomes the input (material) for the next element in the manufacturing channel. Eventually the product, in its final form, comes to the user.

Consider the main support rod in the steering column of an automobile. Called a double D bar, it links the steering wheel to the front axle assembly and is essential to the steering of the automobile. If the double D bar is defective, the steering column itself is defective, and the final product, the automobile, has a serious safety deficiency. That deficiency may be totally unknown to

Exhibit 1-1. Manufacturing channel.

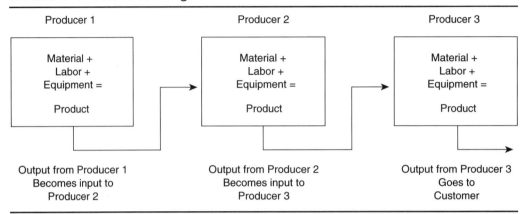

the assembler, yet that assembler bears the brunt of the consequences when the defect causes problems to the user.

In the field of quality, we seek not only adherence to specification from a design perspective but output that is uniform, with minimum deviation from those specifications. In any automated assembly production-manufacturing operation, it is essential that the parts being fed into it meet specification and are within all tolerances. Ideally, parts would have minimum variation between them because variation is the enemy of quality. Variation comes in two forms: **random** or **assignable.** There is not much that may be done about random variation. We know it will occur and how much to expect, but when it will occur is anybody's guess. Assignable variation has a root cause and can be corrected. The sources of assignable variation as measured by the product are the factors of production: material, labor or people, and equipment. Statistical quality control theory tells us to reduce or eliminate assignable variation by having **process-capable equipment**—equipment that is consistently able to produce a product within the design tolerances.

A quality assurance responsibility, process capability testing is an integral part of the final acceptance of the piece of equipment. Consider the act of measuring a finite distance of 1 inch. A common ruler is capable of making that measurement. Reduce the distance measured to ½ inch, and the ruler still is capable. Continue the process until the distance is ⅟32 of an inch, and the variation between measures can be significant. The ruler is now incapable of measuring the distance. A micrometer must be employed. Continue the experiment, and eventually the micrometer becomes process incapable. Process-capable or "good" equipment is a significant contributor to quality output. Thus, the selection and evaluation of capital equipment should be viewed from a quality perspective, and the input from quality assurance should enter into the decision process.

Even in the service sector, equipment can spell the difference between success and failure. It is well known that the IRS suffers the malady of tired and nearly obsolete computers. The failure to keep up with the technology results in slower refunds, lower collections than should be made, and lost opportunities based on the statute of limitations on looking into tax payments. The agency is handicapped in the performance of its function of tax collection.

Capital equipment is purchased to perform functions. The predominant reason is to produce products, yet the service sector is also a purchaser of capital equipment and there is no less a need for good decisions in the service sector. They may be harder to evaluate, yet the success of service sector companies often depends on the quality of the equipment used. Consider a direct mail company that is using outmoded order processing equipment or an airline that loses a flight reservation. Their dependence on equipment is no less important than the manufacturing company that is turning out tires or automobiles or dishes.

Is buying capital equipment a purchasing issue? Yes. Every item purchased contains two sets of specifications: technical and business. Technical specifications describe the product with physical measures such as dimensions, weights, or through drawings or industry standards. An industry standard would be a Rockwell hardness number. Business specifications are terms and conditions of the offer to buy. They would include terms of payment, delivery date, warranties, and indemnification clauses.

The Scope of Capital Investment in the United States

The estimated amount spent on capital equipment in the United States in 1996 is a staggering $570,000,000,000. That is correct. It is $570 billion. To place the figure in some sort of perspective, consider it as equal to:

- Over twice the annual budget for national defense
- $224 for every man, woman, and child in the United States
- About 10% of the national debt of 5.5 trillion dollars
- An amount so large that a person who began spending on July 4, 1776, when the Declaration of Independence was signed, would have to spend $7,250,000 *every day* and only now, 220 years later, would be running out of money

Large quantities of capital resources are being invested daily in working machines, copiers, office equipment, vehicles, computers, and the wide array of other products defined as capital equipment. Such investments demand the finest analysis possible. The investments are dollar commitments for the next 5, 10, or 20 years. The organization will live with the decision, good or bad, for a long time.

To illustrate a small segment of the scope of capital investment in the domestic market, examine the data presented in Exhibit 1-2. It is the capital investment of three Standard Industrial Classifications (SIC) in the United States covering the five-year period 1988 to 1992. The industries represented are:

SIC 3542:   Machine tools, metal cutting type
SIC 3621:   Motors and generators
SIC 3714:   Motor vehicle parts and accessories

These three were selected at random to illustrate the scope of capital investment in any industry.

Two points are clear from this example. First, the investment tends toward being consistent within each of the industries, ranging between 2.0 and 2.78 percent of sales in SIC code 3542, 2.7 and 3.1 percent in SIC code 3621, and 2.8 and 5.37 percent in SIC code 3714. The other point is that investment in capital equipment in each of the sectors is a constant activity of adding capacity, modernizing, or replacing worn or unusable equipment.

Companies allocate significant resources to these investments or purchases every year. They become a part of the capital structure of the company. They also may be unalterable decisions, and can be costly and highly visible. They become more visible when the purchase turns out to be a poor decision, based on incomplete information or faulty judgment. White elephants are not easily hidden.

In terms of just the three industries selected, it is a $4-billion-dollar set of decisions, not counting the recurring costs of maintenance, spare parts, tools, and training. Add to this the associated costs of deciding to lease or buy, use contract or in-house maintenance, customize the equipment, dispose of at the end of the equipment lifetime, and all the other miscellaneous factors that must be considered, and the result is a complex decision. There are no simple formulas. What is available is a process for looking at the purchase in an integrated manner, balancing costs and technology, savings and expenditures, and arriving at a satisfactory decision.

Exhibit 1-2. Capital investment in three selected industries, 1988–1992 (millions of dollars).

Year	SIC 3542 Investment	% of Sales	SIC 3621 Investment	% of Sales	SIC 3714 Investment	% of Sales
1992	$40.4	2.78%	$242.0	3.01%	$3,647.6	4.86%
1991	31.6	2.10	238.1	3.10	3,403.1	5.37
1990	33.3	2.01	238.8	3.11	3,446.0	5.31
1989	39.4	2.78	215.5	2.67	2,964.0	4.51
1988	36.5	2.08	205.5	2.70	1,932.0	2.80

Source: 1992 Census of Manufactures, Industry Series: 3542, 3621, 3714, U.S. Department of Commerce.

The Macro Outlook

The overall picture in Exhibit 1-3 shows an ever-increasing investment in capital equipment. With this rise, there will be continuing emphasis placed on the legitimate analysis of those investment decisions. In reality, there are a series of interdependent decisions.

The purchase of capital equipment by industries is significant and sequential. Machine tools are needed to make the tools to make the products; thus, machine tool sales are bellwethers of the economy. Machine manufacturers sell to other manufacturers and buy from parts and components producers. The interdependency is well established in the economy. The strike at the GM parts-producing facility in Ohio in 1995 provides a vivid illustration. In a matter of days the parts shortage spread and caused eight assembly plants to shut down in less than two weeks. The same situation could be attributed to the lack of a machine. Machine failure or lack of spare parts can cripple an operation, create waste, and bottleneck a company operation.

An implicit dimension of the capital investment decision for equipment is the fact that few equipment manufacturers are totally vertically integrated. Someone else makes some or all of the parts going into the machine, so purchased parts, components, and raw materials must be incorporated into the equipment. This translates to a supply chain for the manufacturer of the equipment. This means business for other companies and a multiplier effect. Company A purchases parts from Company B, which buys from Company C. At the point of transfer, each member of the supply chain covers costs and makes a profit. The ultimate buyer at the end of the supply chain is paying for all of the costs and profits within that chain. Thus, the value derived from the purchase

Exhibit 1-3. Capital equipment spending, 1987–1997 (billions of dollars).

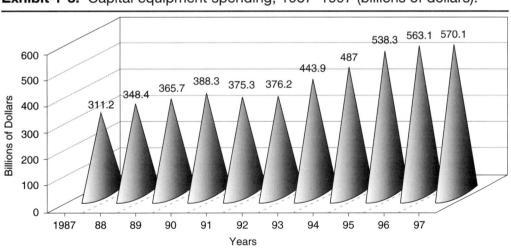

Source: Data provided by the Equipment Leasing Association. Reprinted with permission.

or usefulness of the equipment must justify the expenditure to cover all the costs and profits accrued along the path to reaching the end of the chain.

This lack of vertical integration can work for the buyer as well. Spare parts can be significantly less expensive when they are purchased from the original equipment manufacturer (OEM) of that part as compared with the price paid to the assembler of the equipment. In addition, the ordering of spare parts at the time the equipment is delivered is a way of ensuring the availability of those parts. The spares consideration is important. Are the spare parts available locally? What is available? How long will the equipment be down waiting for spare parts to arrive? What will they cost? All of these considerations are important based on the reliability of the equipment. A company that manufactured poultry processing equipment serviced all its equipment in the field and billed customers for parts and labor. A single bearing cost the ultimate customer $4.75 each; the equipment manufacturer had paid $1.20 for the bearing, thereby gaining a 300 percent markup on the part. In lean times, the spare parts business can mean the difference between profits and losses. Spare part calculations are a segment of the total cost of the equipment and must not be ignored. The lack of the spare parts creates machine downtime and frustration with the decision.

The focus of this book is on the total costs of ownership. The cost of capital equipment is the summation of a string of costs:

1. Preparing the capital request
   - The essential elements of information in the request
   - How the request is developed
   - Who is on the team, what they contribute to the process, and how much weight their input carries
   - How agreement is reached
   - How well the equipment fits the current arrangement
   - Whether the focus is on standardization versus the unique nature of the equipment
2. Sourcing for the request for quotation
   - Source location
   - Lead time considerations
   - Size of the supply base
   - Duration of the contract
   - Terms and conditions
   - What the supplier wants and says
   - Source support
3. Evaluating the options
   - Initial costs
   - Maintenance
   - Spares
   - Productivity

- Prices and pricing policy
- Making sure the comparison is valid
- Sources of bias
- Weighing factors correctly
4. Buying or leasing
   - Advantages and disadvantages
   - Tax considerations
   - Types of leases
   - Maintenance
   - Responsibilities of lessor and lessee
   - Financing the purchase
   - Performance versus payment
5. Financial analysis
   - Payment
   - Retention
   - Different approaches to capital equipment buying
6. Installing the equipment
   - Engineering factors
   - Acceptance criteria
   - Environmental considerations
   - Safety and training factors
7. Displacement and disposal of existing equipment
8. Maintaining the equipment, including spares
9. Modifying the equipment
10. Replacing the equipment
11. Controlling the whole process and keeping it all on time and schedule
12. Overseas buying
    - Unique aspects
    - Caveats
    - Expectations in foreign markets

The focus is always on total cost over the life cycle. Any other perspective will bias the results of analysis. Issues that often arise when comparing options include the following:

- Different effective lives
- Spares consumption
- Capacity
- Maintenance costs for parts and labor
- Downtime
- Maintainability
- Reliability
- Warranty
- Administrative costs of buying

Taking the total cost perspective allows for valid comparison and avoids the bias that may inherently favor the lower initial cost option.

In a midwestern state, the state purchasing agent authorized the purchase of Oldsmobiles as state vehicles as opposed to the usual Fords and Chevrolets. Shocked at the expenditures for the higher-priced autos, state officials questioned the wisdom of the decision. The purchasing agent, however, was not wearing his "price-only" blinders when the decision was made. It was "price per . . ." and thus allowed for comparisons that went far beyond comparing one price to another. It took about four years for the buyer to be completely vindicated: Records finally showed lower total costs for the Oldsmobiles plus a higher percentage still operating in the fleet. The initial cost had appeared more expensive, but the initial cost was deceptive. Hidden behind that initial outlay were four plus years of maintenance. With lower frequency of repair came lower maintenance costs, longer service life, and the true measure of performance: a lower total cost per mile of operation.

The direction must be toward total cost, and the measure must be total cost per unit. Lacking this comparison that levels the playing field, it is possible to provide any number to illustrate the best option. Even the averaging process can be deceiving, since averages tend to obscure wide data variations. Yet it is better than two or three single numbers based on absolute dollars.

Some Aspects of Technology

The buying of capital equipment may have as many philosophical issues as engineering issues present. Technology moves forward at a variable pace. One of the issues faced early in the decision process is that of technology inclusion in the machine: incorporate the existing technology or the technology as it is developed? At the extreme, the CH-47 helicopter, commonly known as the Chinook, is a two-engine cargo/troop carrier and the workhorse of army aviation. From the time it was decided to build a new aircraft to replace the aging and inadequate CH-21 from the Korean War and the time the first unit rolled out at the Boeing Vertol plant, the aircraft underwent over 500 major engineering change proposals, incorporating the newest technology available. Technology developed parallel to the aircraft development found its way into the system. (It goes without saying the cost rose with each engineering change proposal.) This example serves to alert buyers as to the possibility of that same process taking place in the capital equipment buying decision, especially if the machine purchased is custom made. It is analogous to buying the automobile and waiting a month to get the newest accessory. At a certain point, the specifications must become frozen. Waiting for the next innovation can be fruitless effort that simply delays the buying process.

The Boeing 777 aircraft is a two-engine behemoth capable of international travel. Over the next two decades, many improvements and innovations will be made, and the model available in 2018 will be a far cry from its 1998 counterpart. Yet a number of airlines have opted for the 1998 model as opposed to waiting more than 20 years. Waiting for the last increment of technology is a pointless effort.

Another consideration closely allied with the technology issue is obsolescence and finding out where the machine is in its life cycle.

A small printing company was considering the purchase of a press costing over $100,000, a large investment for the company. There was much discussion yet little analysis of the purchase. Once it was agreed that this was the press to buy, the purchase moved forward. The supplier was not particularly responsive to the order and was late in delivering the press. Over the next year, the buyer experienced problems with the press. The seller lived up to the warranty, yet was extremely slow in responding. Finally, the general manager of the printing company asked the repair technician why the whole support process had slowed to a crawl. The technician replied that the seller was busy with new installations of the upgraded version of this press. In fact, the printer had bought the last model of that press ever to be produced. The seller's service staff was excited about the new model and had lost interest in the older version.

Of course, someone must buy the last one, and buying the last one may not be bad per se. Intended use or costs may make buying something less than the cutting edge of technology a better overall buy than the new model. Nevertheless, buying at the end of the life cycle should be compensated for by better prices, and guarantee of spares support and good support during the warranty period.

What is obsolete to Customer A may be the edge of technology to Customer B. At the conclusion of World War II, the U.S. government gave hundreds of C-47s to South American countries. Refurbished in their original configuration as the DC-3, these aircraft became the nuclei of many national and private airlines, replacing Ford Trimotors or Flying Boats or simply being the first aircraft available for starting an airline. One person's castoff can be another's treasure. Were this not the case, garage sales would not be held.

The important issue is finding out where the machine is in the life cycle. Is it new and experiencing all the bugs associated with the new machine, or is it coming to the end of the life cycle? Often with pieces of computer peripherals, the manufacturer will clear the shelves, selling to different channels of distribution or mass merchandisers at a discounted price. The lower price, in the form of a discount from retail, is often the clue that the days of the product are numbered. The question becomes, waiting for the new model to come out or buying the old model at the lower price. Use, support, and spares will tell the answer. Often the newest technology may not be needed or wanted. Buying the new car at the end of the model year is common.

Another key issue is the movement of the technology. Does it crawl at a snail's pace, with the producer making improvements on an incremental basis or simply adding features where the true user could be the only person to determine which is the A model or B model? Is the movement of the technology such that it renders its predecessors almost totally obsolete and robs them of any economic value? Consider the microcomputer a decade ago, when a 286-AT was considered adequate and salespersons were recommending hard drives of no more than 20 to 30 megabytes. A decade later the scene is dominated by the Pentium 100 and above with a recommended 1 GB hard drive. Five years from now it will be the Pentium 600 and a GB hard drive. The price, not discounted for inflation, is about the same (and perhaps even lower for the year 2000 model). This growth in technology is predictable and simply awaits the solution to some technical problems.

Technology advancement has a significant effect on buying strategy and should be a serious point of analysis. When the technology moves so rapidly that the machine is going to be obsolete about the time everyone feels comfortable on it, thoughtful issues are raised. In the case of the personal computer, using the obsolete machine is possible.

Addressing the technology issue, the presence of state-of-the-art PCs in the workplace is a source of fascination. Except in complex engineering or financial applications, the vast majority of PCs are devoted to word processing. Thus, the rationale for having a 166-MHz computer with 2.0 gigabytes of hard drive and 24 megabytes of memory on the board to input information into a machine using technology developed in 1868 (the keyboard) defies description. The "obsolete" 386 will probably work just as well. Buy the equipment to fit the purpose for which it is intended, not to equip everyone with the state of the art to make them feel good. *Technology* is a relative term. Placing too much emphasis on it will result in paying exorbitant sums to capture that latest increment of technology. Here, the marginal cost of that last increment can be very high indeed. That incremental increase in technology may be driven by other factors such as the product itself. Placement of the circuits on the chip closer to each other to reduce the travel time of the signal is going to cause the machine designer to rethink the configuration of the machine. Is the faster transfer speed really needed, and is the cost generated by that transfer speed justifiable in the context of the final use of the product? Only the customer can vote on that issue, and the voting is done with the checkbook.

Transfer that same situation into the $500,000 piece of medical equipment used for a half-dozen procedures before it is ready for replacement with the newer $800,000 model, and the decision process gets very complex and the results costly. Some companies follow the philosophy of incrementing their products and selling the customer on the basis of the incremental value added. In the automobile industry, these are accessories, and they are the real profit makers. Consider the decorative stripe on automobiles. For $35 you obtained 20 cents' worth of paint. (It *was* nicely painted on the vehicle.) The automotive companies are not to be blamed; they are simply trying to cover the costs of capital equipment used to paint that stripe.

Standardization: A Form of Technology Transfer

One of the more ambitious projects in Southeast Asia is power plant construction. Many of these plants are being built under cooperative agreements with various branches of Hopewell Holdings Ltd. of Hong Kong. Many are using 20-year old technology: coal-fired generating stations. Why use a 20-year-old product? The answers are simple. The host countries contain significant coal deposits, the demand for electricity is not being met, the technology is proved, and costs are known. The lead time for construction can be compressed, with the major variation between the plants being the site preparation. It is almost standardization of the whole power plant. Early completion of the plant often means significant bonuses or periods of substantial revenues to the developer of the facility. Compression of the lead time may be a driving force. In addition, reducing the number of unknowns in the operating cost element of the cost equation may have significant value.

Older technology is not necessarily bad or poor technology. Technology is a relative commodity and should be measured in its own environment. Bringing cane harvesting equipment into Barbados in the West Indies would be an economic disaster. Certainly the cane would be harvested in three days, but the number of cane cutters displaced from the workforce might have serious political repercussions. Sometimes pure economics is not enough.

In the examples discussed there are certain common elements: the level of technology in the investment, the cost of the purchase, the support of purchase over its service life, the cost of that support, and the disposition of that equipment through resale or disposal. Readers by now have identified the myriad of different functional entities that can become involved in the decision process.

The ultimate purpose of the purchase is to gain the most value for the dollar expended. Since the dollar in this case could easily be seven or eight figures, the process of defining what is needed, when it is needed, how it will be purchased, and how it will be supported over the 10, 20, or 30 years of its life involves data gathering, financial analysis, source selection, negotiations, cost monitoring, and monitoring the fabrication of the equipment construction and planning for its support.

If one attempts to blend the material needed to make the best decision, the process soon resembles Kipling's famous poem, "Seven Blind Men Viewing the Elephant." Each has a separate perspective. Although that perspective is valid in looking at one part of the elephant, the perspective often rules out other views that must be considered for the good of the entire organization. Any organizational myopia or lack of vision complicates the process by creating a tug of war in the decision process. Is the buying decision a financial one? Yes, it surely is, because the decision involves the expenditure of funds in the acquisition of a capital asset. An adjustment to the balance sheet is going to be made, and finance, in its stewardship role, must protect the integrity of all assets of the organization.

Is it a production decision? Yes, it is, since it may involve the rate at which units are produced and the cost of production.

Is it a marketing decision? It could be if the asset improves the appearance of the product, improves the quality, or lowers the cost to position the product more competitively in the marketplace and give the marketeers a competitive edge.

Is it a maintenance decision? Certainly. Who will maintain, oil, grease or adjust the machine, repair it when it fails, or prevent failure by periodic inspection and preventative maintenance?

Is it an accounting decision? To some extent, the decision may affect standard costs, overhead allocation, and cash flow. The machine must be paid for and eventually disposed of at the end of the service life. Its value as a capital asset is reduced each year through depreciation. Technically the organization sets aside funds to replace the asset when fully depreciated.

Is it a legal decision? Who would make a major purchase without having the legal scrutiny to address such issues as warranty, terms, conditions, compliance with federal, state, and local laws, as well as the ever-present Environmental Protection Agency regulations? Any special terms and conditions must be spelled out in the body of the purchase order.

Is it a purchasing decision? One would hope so since purchasing is the area that must execute the agreement, monitor the supplier's progress, and often act as the intermediary in the complex process of bringing the item from the paper stage to installation.

Is it an engineering decision? Of course, it is. The purpose of the equipment is performing a function of bending, cutting, deburring, crimping, or something else, all within specifications developed by design engineers for the product. Anything less and the product suffers.

If there is no machine in the marketplace, then there are numerous sources that will build one to perform the tasks. Then if it does not work, who is to blame? That becomes a legal issue. Who owns the design? That becomes a purchasing and legal issue. What about the quality of output? After all, that is the purpose of the equipment, and that is a manufacturing and quality consideration. (Quality will be considered in Chapter 9, Appendix A, and Appendix B.)

The process is like the helix. The continuous raising of these questions generates the need for open lines of communication between supplier and buyer and a team orientation in the buying company. The buying company stays on top of the purchase at all times and controls the process. The buyer has assumed a good deal of risk in the process, and the process may backfire if it is not kept under surveillance and control. The other end of the buying spectrum is having the purchase in the form of a turnkey operation where the buyer maintains an arm's-length relationship with the seller and the contract between the two or more parties is a huge legal document that specifically places all the risks on the various parties in the form of liquidated damages that are often very significant and can threaten the economic integrity of the supplier. These are high-risk, high-return contracts or purchases.

Each of the functional areas is a stakeholder in the process, yet there are often opportunities for conflict. The conflicts can have serious impacts on the decision and the results of the decision. For example, one rationale for buying capital equipment is cost reduction through greater productivity. The machine runs faster, produces more units per hour, and is less labor intensive. Yet finance may not want the machine customized since its salvage value or trade-in value drops to zero. However, the customization may increase productivity. Finance may wish to purchase the machine overseas due to the strength of the U.S. dollar. This ardor may be dampened by the need for metric tools for maintenance and repair or the limited availability of spare parts in the United States.

Not to belabor the point, but there are areas of potential conflict, and the purpose of this book is to place the decision process in some sort of perspective. It is not saying who is right or wrong.

How Well Prepared Are We to Buy Equipment?

Many of the people involved in the buying decision have little background in the field. Business schools touch on the subject ever so lightly. Engineering schools approach the subject from the technical perspective. Each company has its own favorite approach to the decision, often mirroring the orientation of the company and its drivers. A financially driven company will look at **payback** (the period of time required for an investment to recoup its original cost), **re-**

turn on assets, or **return on investment,** financial measures of the viability of investments. A company oriented toward manufacturing excellence will look at machine capability. Accountants look at costs. Production looks at output. Engineering looks at technology. Purchasing looks at terms and conditions and suppliers. Where does all this expertise get drawn together in a concise fashion to make the best decision?

Once the capital investment decision is made, where does it get translated into the process of negotiation with the equipment supplier in such a manner that the position of the buying company is seamless in the negotiation process? What should the process look like? As important as the product being bought is the process for buying it. Process is important because good processes ensure a balance in the decision as well as provide a framework for information inputs and checks and balances along the way.

Where are the gatekeepers who open the gate to pursue the next step or close the gate and terminate the process? What are the gates? The internal portion of the process from the company perspective begins at need determination, follows along with specification development, continues with the financial evaluation, the sourcing, the evaluation of proposals, negotiation with the potential supplier(s), writing the purchase order, monitoring the process, arrival, and installation. Acceptance criteria, promises of logistical support, warranty considerations, and the legal system protect against poor or inadequate performance by the supplier. These performance criteria can be backed up with insurance or bonds. The process continues with the disposal of the displaced equipment. In addition, it is necessary to look at the other aspects of the buying process and consider such elements as legal factors in buying equipment both domestically and internationally, buying used equipment, customization of capital equipment (positive and negative considerations), transportation of capital equipment and its special needs, and a total cost approach to buying capital equipment, including disposing of equipment when the time comes to replace the equipment or when it simply ceases operation.

Developing a Frame of Reference

Not every capital investment decision must be treated with the complexities discussed in this book. The purpose is not to provide a prescriptive model for the evaluation process but to explain a pattern of thinking that provides checkpoints or hurdles for the process to clear. Readers can choose the items that fit the needs of the purchase. This book is a guide to buying in the complex field of capital equipment, with the process predicated on a series of fundamental truths about capital equipment buying:

   • *The purchase of capital equipment today lays the groundwork for costs in the future.* As much as we would like the perpetual motion machine or the everlasting machine, there are going to be future costs associated with the equipment. These will be costs of labor to repair and maintain the equipment and spares to replace worn or failed parts. The initial cost of the equipment, in fact, may be the lowest cost element in the service life of the machine. Spare parts are a license to steal. The markup on spares can range from 100 percent to 1,500 or 2,000 percent. There is no upper limit. Is the owner going to idle a $300,000 machine by not spending $5,000 for a bearing? Not likely. Thus, the buyer learns quickly that the initial cost is but the visible tip of the proverbial iceberg. Every equipment purchase generates and is the driver of future costs.

• *Most of the methods used to evaluate capital equipment from the financial perspective are rather unrealistic in nature.* They are rigid in their thought processes and often require information that does not exist. Many of the procedures require projections into the future of savings or revenues from the investment. Often these are carried out for years into the future, yet the ability to forecast accurately is not years but months or even weeks. Thus, when looking at net present value or return on assets, keep a realistic perspective on the data provided in the financial evaluation. Where does this information come from, what are the estimates, and what are the experience factors where the data are based on documented observations? Analysis of good records can often provide the insights needed for good decisions. More often than not, however, once the request for a capital appropriation clears certain levels in the organization, few records are kept to validate the savings projected for the new machine. In some instances, the whole process is one of simply getting the acceptable number in the correct box on the right form. Rarely are the numbers challenged after the fact.[3] Yet challenging these numbers by systematically maintaining the proper records and documentation may avoid making a bad decision.

• *Spare parts purchased today may be cheaper than spares purchased in the future.* Making an extra unit of a part now can be minimal in cost; a future run may involve setup and make-ready costs that exceed the value of the part yet are part of the overall cost. What about the recommended spare parts list? How valid is the list, and what is the difference between these parts and insurance parts? What about unique spares? Can you "horse-trade" spares? What is the relationship between maintaining the equipment and its value in the used equipment market? One trucking company found it cost-effective to dispose of semitractors every 19 months, when heavy maintenance costs were starting yet the value of the tractors was still high. How extensive should maintenance be? At what point is it cheaper to buy a new model since the cost of repair is

---

3. In one company, the magic number was 28 percent. If the section of the capital appropriation request did not have at least 28 percent in the box labeled "Return on Assets," sending the form up the line was a futile effort. Finance would shoot it down. Middle managers quickly learned to play the system and saw to it the right number was always there. It was never checked on an after-the-fact basis.

unreasonable relative to the extension of the service life? Early in the Vietnam War, helicopter engines were getting 1,000 to 1,100 flying hours before requiring an overhaul. The overhauled engines were getting only 600 to 700 hours before needing another overhaul. After the second overhaul, the flying hours again dropped. At what point does one say, "Enough!" and replace as opposed to repair?

• *Someone is going to have to maintain the equipment.* During the first year, it may be the seller. Notice the use of the term *may.* Contracts have been negotiated to waive segments of the warranty for price concessions. This is true where fleet vehicles are concerned. A major public utility negotiated a lower price by waiving a segment of the warranty on vehicles since it maintained its own fleet in the company garage. Taking the truck back to the dealer for warranty work was cost-ineffective. It was easier to put the truck in the company shop. Regardless of when the buyer assumes the liability for maintaining the equipment, the mechanics must be trained, the parts available, and the documentation on the equipment available for repairs. The documentation includes manuals and technical bulletins, all of them in English, a luxury that may not be available if the equipment is purchased overseas.

• *The buying process for capital equipment is expensive.* Visits to suppliers, meetings, developing specifications, more meetings, financial analysis of the proposal, and still more meetings are all consumers of time. Time is money. The cost of the decision process is often overlooked in the overall computation of the total cost of the equipment. A total cost perspective is the correct one. Cost analysis is the route to follow since cost data are normally available in the company. In addition, cost data are easier to adjust for inflation and normally require fewer assumptions or caveats to be placed on them as opposed to projected savings. Total cost of ownership over the life cycle alters the decision by selection of a higher initial cost machine that has lower maintenance costs in the future.

There is also the subtle issue of patience, truly not an American virtue. The concept of lead time, especially on capital equipment, is difficult to implant into the organization. Once the capital appropriation has been approved, where is the machine? What do you mean it may take a year to design, build, and ship? The process is the sum of many subprocesses, and each adds time and cost to reach the final objective of having the machine accepted, in place, operating, and contributing to profit. For no other reason, the use of control tools may be a valuable aid in developing the understanding that capital equipment does not sit on the shelf waiting for the customer. If the desire is to reduce the cycle time, all parts of the cycle should bear proportional share for reduction. Time compression is everyone's job, not just the supplier's. The supplier is only one part of the purchasing cycle and cannot be held accountable for compressing activities that are physically impossible. The buying process encompasses transactions and processes that often can be compressed with careful planning and elimination of duplication of effort. This is another reason for the team to circumvent duplication or allow for concurrent actions that abbreviate the time required for the activity.

• *Unless you are buying for a new "greenfield" facility (i.e., one built on raw land), the incoming capital equipment is probably displacing something on the shop floor.* If you have no trade-in agreement on the new equipment, there is an issue of disposal. Consider the public utilities that purchased transformers and later found the PCBs in them were a hazardous waste. The displacement of existing equipment can be a significant issue and should be part of the capital equipment purchase plan, along with the correct language in the purchase order to ensure compliance with federal, state, and local laws and ordinances, as well as the appropriate indemnification clauses. This subprocess can involve a significant number of steps and can add to the overall total cost of ownership.

• *There must be a degree of managerial control over the project.* Lacking that control, the process can become fractured and disorganized and have schedule implications. In addition, there should be extra funds available for contingency situations to cover such unexpected expenses as visits to the supplier, in-process reviews, and possible cost overruns. Initial cost estimates may be off significantly. A schedule of weekly meetings with agendas offers a way to keep the process on track. Do not bury issues or relegate them to the bottom of the agenda and then adjourn before they have been resolved. Put the tough issues on the top of the agenda and get them settled. Assignments should be made and captured in written form with deadlines and input requirements. The use of control tools is strongly encouraged.

Be knowledgeable about the tools available for analysis. For instance, simple simulation can help in the valuation of a maintenance policy. Suppliers should be able to provide failure curves or reliability data on key components. They should also be able to discuss spares and spares kits, as well as maintenance training. Get supplier input. This may mean having the supplier prototype the machine or "breadboard" a part of it to prove its viability. (Breadboarding involves making a part or assembly, usually by hand as a model, prototype, or experimental unit for test purposes.) In many cases it may be cheaper to spend $50,000 in a demonstration or prototype effort than have a $500,000 lemon in your operation, because the supplier thought he could build what you wanted. Remember that the person supplying the specifications for the machine assumes the risk of performance. Those are the people who make the machine. There will be some puffery here, but they often possess the expertise that will help you in the decision process. Certainly they can provide a list of customers using their equipment.

Start this process early in the need determination phase. Do not allow much of the cost and expense to be wrapped in early in the process. In the case of product design, often 80 percent of the product cost is embedded into the product as it comes out of the design stage. Do not make that same mistake with capital equipment. Consider the purchase as a project, and make provisions for the control of that project with a project manager. Project managers are people with demonstrated organizational skills. This is not the time or place to be testing the person's abilities or skills. One major company, a significant user of project management, often assigns junior or midlevel people to parts of the project under the overall management of a partner. This **mentor approach** allows for the development of the individuals but does not relinquish control.

Failure to have a focal point for the project will likely result in significant delays and raise costs, especially if no one is managing. If the project appears successful, everyone will want to be on board. A failing project is a plague. Remember that success has a thousand parents; failure is an orphan.

As deadlines near, panic sets in, and key steps may be waived or bypassed to meet a delivery date. Managing the project may tell you the train is coming and allow you time to get off the track.

Developing Ground Rules

Over the past decade ground rules have been developed to exclude certain factors that slow the process. One such rule is not to consider salvage value of the equipment. Give it an end-of-life value equal to zero. Adopting this rule allows for customization of the equipment that may reduce the labor content in the product, reduce the cycle time, or allow a single operator to work two machines. The view is on the manufacturing process, which is a machine-human interactive process in many cases. In the unionized environment, the customization for increased productivity, reduced maintenance, or increased maintainability can keep the workforce happy. The addition of the equipment is not only cost centered but worker centered also. This rule also reduces a number of doubtful computations and removes numbers from the analysis that may bias the results. There are multiple reasons for buying a new machine. Some are quantitative and some qualitative, but they can all be good reasons. It is difficult to quantify safety, yet the auto industry spends millions on safety-related equipment with only a vague idea of its return on investment.

Another rule is thinking in terms of families of parts—machines having the capability to produce many parts rather than specialized parts or limited application capability. Manufacturing cells have replaced many traditional production lines, and process flexibility is a key ingredient to stay up with the competition. The primary issue is reducing the amount of labor in the product. This means substitution of equipment for labor.

Consider people as flexible entities in the production process. Moving employees upstream or downstream in the manufacturing process makes sense when making the transition from a traditional job shop to semicontinuous production. One of the most powerful forces today is reduced cycle time. The manufacturing and service environments consider cycle time a competitive advantage. In manufacturing, this translates to reduced in-process inventories and meeting customers' needs more rapidly. This converts to smaller production runs of higher-quality product. The long production run paradigm is being exported to countries where labor costs are very low. Shorter and shorter runs, lesser quantities of inventories at all stages of manufacture, minimal downtime, rapid changeover, and diversity of output will be the criteria for good manufacturing in the future. It will be accomplished with the right equipment for the right job.

Determine at what point the machine will be considered used up with respect to service life. What is the repair-to-replace ratio? Some companies replace machinery when the repair cost is 60 percent of the present worth or value. There may be little point in adding value to a machine whose life is coming to an end.

Determine the rules of maintenance on the machine. Is preventive maintenance desirable, or do we only engage in failure maintenance? The act of assigning someone as an oiler or greaser can have a significant impact on service life. The ground rules limit the options and help in the decision process by reducing the amount of data and information we must handle.

Capital equipment is an integral part of any system—one of the three components of production. The difference is that a poor-quality worker may be retrained or terminated. Poor-quality material may be scrapped or returned to the supplier. A poor-quality machine has a life of its own, and once you own it, it is yours, whether it sits on the line or in the corner collecting dust. You own it.

2

Putting Together the Appropriation Request

There is probably no measure of the variation among methods of putting together the capital appropriation request or proposal for internal consideration. This chapter does not portend to show "the best way," for there is no best way. The chapter does attempt to ensure that all the bases are covered. Achieving that coverage can be aided by the use of checklists or manuals to ensure that the proposal or request conveys all the information needed, is coordinated among the interested parties, and is understood by all concerned parties.

The minimum coverage of the checklist should be:

1. *Customer awareness and support.* Does the person or unit who will receive and operate the capital asset fully understand and support the project as well as the appropriation request? This is the potential user sign-off on the project, accepting the equipment as defined in the proposal or appropriation request. The customer's signature is sufficient to verify the assent. It tells top management that the effort is coordinated and the user is in agreement with the request. This is very important since the ultimate user of the equipment has perhaps the strongest interest in getting the right equipment for the right job.

2. *Project purpose.* Is there a clear understanding and communication of the purpose of the project? The purpose should be easily understood by people who may not be directly concerned with the project. Higher-level approval is often required as the dollar value of the project increases. An unclear project proposal wastes time and creates confusion. It may not be approved as a result or may be returned for clarification because people respond negatively to

We are indebted to Dr. William Feldkamp of Dresser Industries for allowing us to liberally "borrow" many of his excellent ideas presented in his "Project Sponsor's Manual" developed for Dresser Industries in 1995. This outstanding work served as a guide for this chapter. Our use is based on the Japanese philosophy that the sincerest measure of quality of a product is the emulation of that product. Thanks, Bill.

things they do not understand. It is essential that the purpose be clearly communicated. This sounds simple, but it is often not the case. The originator of the request, working on the **appropriation request** (AR), may become so intimate with the details of the project that terms, definitions, and other aspects of the project become second nature to that person. The term, *It is obvious*, is not to the outsider. As the dollar value of the AR increases, more gates must be passed or more tests passed to reach final approval. Each level of approval may generate questions. Clarity of communication is essential.

3. *Changes in operating method.* Are procedures or operating methods going to change with the acquisition of the new equipment? What are these changes, and how will they affect the company? Has there been a comparison of operating methods? If so, what do the results show? This is a key area because the justification for new equipment often comes from labor cost reduction or better feeds and speeds, reducing the cycle time.

In one case, a company purchased a very expensive computer numerically controlled vertical boring mill. Using minimal labor, the machine easily improved the quality of output and required minimal operator assistance. The problem arose because of the unionization in the plant. The most senior operators saw this as an opportunity to observe as opposed to producing. Seniority lists do not ensure the selection of the most competent person for the job; they generate only the most senior one. The labor rate on the machine became the highest in the plant, and much of the cost justification was dissipated by not considering the *who* as well as the *how* of methods changes.

Purchases of capital items nearly always affect the operators in a plant, and the impact that they have on the overall operation can be significant. Introducing a piece of capital equipment with high-speed capability will remove one bottleneck but potentially create many others.

Often the effect on personnel can influence the decision. One company was installing a new supply system through outsourcing. Until it could find positions for five displaced workers, the final approval on the new system was withheld. The company was unionized and did not wish to create an issue that the union could formalize at the next collective bargaining session prior to contract expiration.

4. *Completeness of documentation.* Is the documentation complete, including the comprehensive description of the equipment in the AR as well as the costs? The documentation should include the supplier quotations to show the basis of the cost estimates. In addition, there must be some evidence of the willingness of the supplier to honor the quote during the period while the appropria-

tion is being considered. Normally a period of 60 to 90 days is sufficient to go through the process and get the necessary approvals. If the quotations stipulate "Price in Effect at Time of Delivery," it is important to have a valid estimate of the price or a not-to-exceed price. Management is hesitant to sign blank checks since the approval process is meaningless if no valid cost data are present.

There are methods of establishing upper limits on the projected price by the use and acceptance by both parties of indexes that will place limits on the price or project the maximum price. (See Chapter 10 for details on this process.) Another approach is leaving the appropriation as is and going back for more money when the bill comes in. This is the typical government approach of accepting the cost overrun—after the fact.[1] It is wise for management to establish a cost-overrun policy or allowances, nominally as a percentage of the original cost. The purpose of this allowance is to avoid having to start the appropriation process all over again. The original appropriation should be developed with *all* appropriate costs included in the request to cover *all* the anticipated expenses.[2] The company then allocates an additional percentage for contingency or cost overrun on the purchase. The cost-overrun policy should not be viewed as an automatic buffer for the supplier to be 8 percent to 10 percent above the quoted or anticipated cost. It is present only to cover unanticipated changes or unforeseen events that cause price increases. Such increases should be documented and traceable back to the source of the increase. The causes of cost overruns are changes in the scope of work or specifications after work has begun or fabrication is in process.

Of equal importance is the organization's cost monitoring system. The monitoring system tracks and accumulates the costs associated with the purchase. A good system tracks by types of expenditure or accounts. For example, travel expenses may be related to the purchase and in the final computation of total cost will be part of the total purchase price, but they are allocated in a subbudget as an expense item in the overall budget for the purchase. The tracking is essential since there are always costs that arise in the latter stages of the purchase and installation that must be paid. Sufficient funds should be in the account to cover these. If progress payments are made during the project, it is imperative that such payments be made on the basis of actual progress,

---

1. Government is often accused of "low-balling" the project cost to get the funding and then coming back for additional funds when the project is complete. As one of us was once told, "If we told Congress what it will really cost, they would never fund it." This approach is totally unacceptable in business.

2. Expenses include such elements as plant visits, testing at the supplier's site, and other items classified as expense items as opposed to capital items. This is a matter of truthfulness more than anything else, with the AR reflecting the true cost of the purchase rather than hiding some associated expenses in other budgets. The total amount of money is the same, and it all comes from the same pot, but hiding expenses obscures and distorts the process. It accomplishes little and gives the auditor reasons to fault the organization for poor capital equipment purchasing procedures.

and not according to the calendar. The tracking of progress payments is an accounting function. When an invoice for a progress payment is received, accounting will log in the invoice and attach a sign-off sheet to the invoice listing individuals who are assigned to the project in a monitoring capacity. Normally the paperwork goes to the project leader first and then to members of the team. It is important to have someone responsible for the signature process. It is also important to know where the sign-off sheet and invoice are in the system. This means a log-in, log-out system. Normally the last signature is that of a member of top management. Top management looks at the signatures as an indication that the project is on track. The tracking process can be accomplished as part of the project control process. (See Chapter 12 for information on tracking the purchase using Gantt charts and Program Evaluation Review Techniques.)

In addition, the contract should contain limits on any cost or time overruns beyond the budgeted figures. The budgeted figures are internal documents and are not available to the seller. The purchase order price for the equipment is only a segment of the total cost, but it has an upper limit. Going beyond the original cost estimate or quotation may not be permitted, and late delivery may result in penalties or liquidated damages. (Chapter 5 covers terms and conditions that may be unique to the capital equipment purchase order.) Remember that a contract involves two parties and must be beneficial to both. Getting financial approval and then having to come back for more money is not wise.

The Issue of Disposal

In many cases, new equipment displaces existing equipment. As displacement takes place, a number of issues must be addressed.

The Disposition of the Existing Equipment

Sometimes multidivisional companies can offer the equipment to other divisions of the company via computerized communications with a network program. The "selling price" is an accounting transaction or may involve the transfer of monies from one division to another. This can be a more complex issue than simply an interoperational transfer. These transfers can carry a percentage attached to the actual or book value of the item transferred. In one company, the fee was fixed at 35 percent of the value of the asset being transferred. "Buying" the equipment from Division A for $1,000 would cost Division B $1,350 of its budget, with the $350 going to accounting for handling the paperwork in the transfer of monies. Division B must be wary that the cost inside the company can be as expensive as outside the company.

The Value of the Displaced Equipment

Are there differences between the realized value of the displaced equipment and the book value of that equipment? Does disposal create a loss or a profit? Although this is an accounting issue, it should be included in the initial decision to purchase the equipment. Is the market position such that a higher initially priced piece of equipment may command a premium price on the used equipment market 5 or 10 years in the future, while the lower-priced model may drop in value more rapidly? The answer to this question depends on the situation, but future values should not be ignored or be the drivers of the decision. Awareness toward the issue is important.

Possible Dispositions

Have all the possible dispositions been explored:

• *Trade-in with the supplier to reduce the overall costs.* This option raises a variety of considerations. The trade-in may be a valid method of disposition if the dealer also sells used equipment. It may simply be a sales incentive to make the customer feel that the deal is better than it is. The trade-in allowance may reflect a higher-than-necessary original price, especially if the trade-in is really a discount from the offering price with no cash changing hands. The trade-in may be a convenience for the buyer, allowing the removal of the existing equipment from the premises and elimination of the transactions associated with disposal.

• *Resale as is, where is.*[3] It is essential to factor in any costs associated with moving the equipment off the premises. Thus, *where is* becomes an important consideration. Normally a short period of time of free storage (24 to 48 hours) is permitted before charging the buyer for space rental. From the buyer's perspective, be sure the appropriate transporter has the necessary insurance to be on the seller's property as well as the loading and rigging equipment necessary. Recognize that resale involves the implied warranty provision of being able to pass clear title or notifying the buyer of any liens against the clear

---

3. This issue of "as is, where is" must be approached carefully. There is an implied warranty that automatically follows the piece of equipment. Make sure the selling documentation clearly waives any warranty, implicit or explicit, and the buyer of the used equipment accepts that equipment with no implied warranty and so signifies in writing. If the equipment is a vehicle, make sure that any marking, decals, or paint schemes that may be associated with the selling company or organization are removed. There was a case where a public utility sold a used vehicle but failed to remove or paint over a distinguishing paint scheme. The truck was later involved in a hit-and-run accident. Several witnesses identified the owner of truck by the paint scheme. It was a "Power and Light" truck. The public utility settled the case out of court, even though it was not their specific truck involved in the accident.

title. No disclaimer of warranty can be used to avoid that implicit warranty condition.

• *Auction.* Newspapers and trade publications are awash with advertisements for auctions of capital equipment, and disposition in this manner is a popular method of getting rid of capital equipment. Recognize that selling the capital equipment in an auction often involves costs that may diminish the return from the sales, including the commission to the auctioneer, the transportation of the equipment to the auction site, plus the possibility of no interest in the equipment, which may mean bringing the equipment back or storing it until the next auction. (See Chapter 8 on purchasing previously owned equipment for a more complete discussion of this option.)

• *Rebuild or recondition before sale.*[4] This would involve getting it ready for resale. The issue here is the amount of time and money the company wishes to invest in the equipment, all or a large portion of which may not be recaptured in the selling price. The other side of this coin is that the customization or upgrading of the equipment during the ownership period, coupled with outstanding maintenance, may have a very favorable impact on resale.

• *Sell as scrap for recoverables.* Does the equipment contain anything of recoverable value that may be reprocessed? The recent example of this situation is the massive Cray computer, sold for about $10,000, primarily for the gold in some of its circuits. X-ray film is often sold to recoverers interested in the silver contained in the silver nitrate coating on the film. In the steel industry, the minimills remelt steel. The same holds true for the glass container industry in the charging of furnaces with broken glass. It is a purchasing responsibility to find the scrap dealer. It is also important to have some idea of the metal mix in the equipment. Brass or bronze valves are more valuable than steel valves. Sometimes it is worth the effort to dismantle the equipment and sell different parts to different people.[5]

• *Cannibalize.* The equipment is stripped down, and parts having any value are saved. The rest is disposed of by selling it to a scrap recoverer. In all cases, consider the cost of physically moving the equipment in any form. The value of the parts may be a significant segment of the total value of the equipment. Car thieves often strip stolen autos since the parts are worth more than the vehicle in the open market and often more difficult to identify. In addition, all parts do not have uniform service lives, and if there are several machines of one type on the shop floor, cannibalizing one may supply spare parts for many.

4. This is a possible option that may be used to sweeten the selling price of the equipment. Care must also be taken here as to warranty issues and how the equipment is advertised. Terms such as *rebuilt* or *reconditioned* have legal meaning, and the seller bears a warranty liability when those terms are used.
5. One major city employs a person half-time to deal with sorting and selling scrap. It is sufficient in volume to justify the expense.

Disposal Cash Proceeds

What about the availability of disposal cash proceeds? Once the disposal takes place, additional cash enters the company, so there are accounting issues to consider. In some instances, the company will profit from the sale, but the largest issue is the use of the money as an offset to the purchase price of the equipment. The individual AR should clearly state the impact of disposal of the existing equipment on the total cost of the new equipment. What is the net cash requirement, and when in the purchase cycle is it needed? Higher-level approvals tend to focus on the financial implications of the purchase. Capital is not unlimited and therefore is budgeted. A lesser cost, enhanced by sale or trade-in, can place the AR in a more favorable light.

Adjuncts to Sales

What is done with the adjuncts to sales, such as, spares, tooling, jigs, and fixtures? Often there are spare parts that have not been used that may go along with the equipment. If there is any reason to believe a secondary source of supply is needed for the first critical months of installation, then the selling of tooling, jigs, or fixtures might accompany the sale along with a contract to the buyer to produce a number of the parts required over the transition period. This incentive to the supplier protects the buying company if installation problems occur. The other option is keeping the displaced equipment in place until the new equipment is up and running and then remove it. This is a space and *footprint* issue. The footprint is the physical configuration of the machine, showing size, utility hookups, and discharge points.

Other Equipment Issues

While the process is important and disposal should be considered as part of the appropriation request, there is an array of other issues that should be considered in putting the appropriation request together. Their impact may not be significant, but the role of the appropriation request is to present the most complete picture possible. There is also a credibility to consider. A request that contains gaps, missing elements, or leaves unanswered questions is often suspect as to accuracy. A good project manager will "cover those bases" and indicate that these areas have been considered. If they are irrelevant or do not alter the answer, they still have been evaluated. There are no missing elements in the request.

What is the capacity of the equipment? Ideally, there will be a match between the capacity needed and the capacity of the equipment being purchased. If this is not the case, then either insufficient capacity is present and the wrong machine is purchased, or excess capacity is available.[6] If there is excess capacity,

6. Buying below what is needed is not uncommon. Consider the office copiers that are well below the required speed and output needed. They are still purchased and then "overused."

how will it be absorbed, and what are the alternative uses of that capacity? The number of options are limitless here.

The unique nature of the equipment may afford the opportunity to sell time on the equipment to noncompeting companies to fill in the downtime on the equipment. Since this activity is marketing, the sales function should be carried out by the marketing department. The audience would be local manufacturing managers, and much of this dissemination could be handled by mailing a brochure or flyer indicating availability by month or week and booking procedures. The customer would have to issue a purchase order and provide certain information, as well as insurance for his personnel while on the seller's premises. The other way is to deliver the material and pick up the postprocessed material. The buyer would have to abide by all safety rules of the seller's operation, and the seller would be "job shopping" time on the machine at a specified sum per hour for machine and operator. The excess capacity may offer opportunities to expand the product line or perform subcontracting for customers.

What is the impact of the new equipment on the production line? If the buying company is a process-focused company (job shop), then the machine could become obsolete like other machines or add a significant segment of capacity to the department. The cost per hour charged to that machine could be significant. If the company has a product-focused orientation (assembly line), then the new equipment could require a rethinking of the production line by creating imbalances on the line. This information may not be explicitly required in the AR, but it is important to have considered these possibilities when drafting the document. This is another example of why the project sponsor approach to buying capital equipment is so vital. There must be an organizational focal point for the information in the AR.

The Specific Application

There must be verification as to the anticipated volume of output needed to continue to save money. The issue of sustainability of demand for the product or products has always been an issue in buying capital equipment. It is an implicit assumption in any capital investment decision that the demand for the output justifies the expenditure. If the demand does not continue, the buying company may find the equipment underutilized or even idle. Marketing enters the picture, and signs off on the projected need of the equipment output. There must be assurances of sufficient demand for these parts or products to justify spending the money for the equipment on which to build them. In addition, does this acquisition affect other products? Will it make the inventory obsolete or change the output of existing products to such an extent as to decrease the value of existing inventory? There are accounting considerations if the company finds itself with obsolete or dated inventory whose market value is far less than its costs.

Other Options to Explore

Have other options been explored?

• *Purchasing used equipment to fill the need.* This option offers some cost and lead time advantages. (See Chapter 8.)

• *Rebuilding the existing equipment.* It may be possible to recondition existing equipment as a substitute for new equipment. In some cases this is a viable option, especially with modular components. It is important to consult with marketing when considering this option. If the product line is to be discontinued or altered significantly, buying may be a poor option.

• *Making the equipment in the plant.* This option normally falls outside the range of user expertise. This is not often the core business of the buying company and may create more problems than it solves. Nevertheless, internal manufacture has advantages. It can boost morale by giving people a chance to create as opposed to repairing. Since large amounts of time and money are consumed sending maintenance personnel to schools and seminars to keep their proficiency high, that expertise can be extended to building or retrofitting a piece of equipment.

• *Short term leasing of the equipment.* See Chapter 7 on leasing of capital equipment. A limited-use period that depends on seasonal needs, specific application, or an unwillingness to take ownership could point to leasing as a viable alternative. Construction contractors often lease equipment and expense the lease costs against the job or project on which the leased equipment is used. There can be tax advantages to this approach, and if the equipment is not going to be used for long periods, leasing is a viable option.

Improving the Return on Investment

From the financial perspective, this is the heart of the proposal, and short of shutting the plant down if the equipment is not purchased, it will be the measure or yardstick that will be viewed most closely as the AR proceeds from gate to gate. The scrutiny occurs because return on investment (ROI) is a common denominator and is understood at many levels of the organization. In addition, companies often set a floor for the ROI. Projects that cannot raise the product ROI above that floor will not be approved. Capital is not unlimited, and the AR process is one of capital rationing. The rationing or allocation device is the ROI.

Supplier Quotations

Do the supplier quotations represent what we want to purchase or what the supplier wants to sell us? If the buyer does not really know what is wanted, the seller has an easy job of selling what the seller has to offer. Is the supplier's quotation clear and inclusive, detailing what is really being purchased and the responsibilities of each party to the contract? Are issues such as transportation, testing, installation, and support covered in the quote? Are the distinctions clearly noted, such as recommended spares, warranty information, and logistical support?

The Plan for the Postcompletion Audit

One of the failings of the entire process is to omit a postcompletion audit of the results of the purchase. Did the equipment do what it was supposed to? The audit looks at such items as these:

- Volume of output on the equipment
- Pieces per unit of time
- Scrap and waste factors
- Productivity increases
- Labor hours, both direct and indirect
- Changes in the bills of materials
- Validation of the cost reductions or savings

This is simply monitoring the investment *after* there has been sufficient time to collect the information to validate or invalidate the elements of the proposal. Monitoring is essential to ensure that erroneous assumptions are not reused.

Reconciling the Equipment Life With the Depreciation Schedule

Does the life of the equipment from a pragmatic perspective match the depreciation schedule established for it? The best illustration is the personal computer whose price has fallen rapidly as new models and economies of production occur. The $3,000 200-megahertz computer of last year is now the $1,700 200-megahertz computer of this year. The rapid decline in same unit replacement cost can be a complicating financial factor, especially when setting the depreciation schedule and looking at ultimate salvage value versus book value.

Safety and Environmental Concerns

This aspect remains an essential part of the AR. This is a sticky issue since laws do change, and any changes can generate significant expense for a company to bring its capital equipment into compliance with environmental laws. Issues of emissions, production of hazardous waste as a by-product of the manufacturing process, and the use of hazardous material in the processes must be given careful attention, as must the disposal of these wastes. This issue is doubly significant since two sets of regulations cover environmental issues—state and federal—with both potential civil and criminal penalties associated with hazardous waste. Equipment that is in compliance today may be out of compliance tomorrow, causing the company to move the plant or bring it into compliance. Either can be an expensive alternative.

Although it is impossible to forecast the political whims and wind direction, a proactive approach is far better than reacting to changes. Companies that face these issues in the purchase of the equipment and determine to be not only in compliance but to move to the "better safe than sorry" position stand a better chance of fending off difficulties, or at least being prepared when legislation changes. The environmental issue is as emotionally charged as any other issue on the business scene today. Environmentalists will immediately raise the issue of children being poisoned by the pollution generated by industrial equipment. Extremism knows no boundary when these two groups meet to debate environmental issues.

Ancillary Operating Costs

Normally considered as part of the installation cost, electricity, natural gas, and water are factors to consider as added costs. Although this cost may be minimal or the cost difference can be small, failing to consider it leaves a gap in the proposal. If nothing else, indicate it has been considered in the analysis. In some instances it is a significant cost element and must be given proper attention.

Managing the Effort

There are several schools of thought on the managerial aspects of capital equipment buying. The major issue is continuity of effort. One person or a small group has this responsibility. Some companies, by virtue of their size in numbers and extensive purchasing of capital equipment, have a department or subunit dedicated to capital equipment buying. Some have a capital equipment buyer. For many others, the process is done on a project basis—a project management approach with a champion (or sponsor, or coordinator, or some other title) having a defined procedure and methods for data collection, analysis, and presentation. The project sponsor has this responsibility from the beginning of the project to the point when the postinstallation audit is completed and analyzed. Since much of the role of the sponsor is coordination and information gathering, it can be assigned as an additional duty along with performance of the regular job, or some time allowance can be made for this effort in the work schedule.

This managerial approach to the buying effort has three benefits:

1. *Provides continuity in managing the acquisition.* The management of the project from need generation to completion of the postinstallation audit should

be in the hands of one person to ensure that all segments of the company meet their respective responsibilities. Anything that detracts from this continuity can cause project delays while people are educated on the project or duplication of effort as the new project sponsor backtracks to see that all previous steps have been properly completed.

2. *Provides uniformity in analysis of alternatives or options.* Any project involving forecasts of revenues or costs can have varying levels of depth to them. They may be extensive and elaborate, or rather shallow. Normally, there is enough variation in the forecasts if one person does them. There is no point in introducing more variation by changing managers midstream on the project.

3. *Preserves the history of the project in one place in the organization.* Much of the history of a project contains lessons learned from it—lessons both positive and negative. They can range from acceptance criteria to logistical support to forecasts. Lessons *not* learned are bound to be repeated. There is often much information that can be documented on the project and used to avoid or benefit from previous experiences. This information should not be lost when the project is completed. It can be contained in something as simple as a log or project diary. It can be a summary of project reports or a narrative highlighting the major events of the project. Completing that task is the final assignment of the project sponsor. All the documentation should be kept in the project file.

Duties of the project sponsor include appropriate data collection from all affected areas of the organization using marketing statistics, product pricing data, production requirement, and product cost estimates.[7] This is a very sensitive area, especially the marketing statistics. Since much of the decision to purchase capital equipment lies in the area of expansion of product line, the validity of the market data is critical. Consider two cases of having good data but the intervention of other factors played a significant role in the final outcome.

Case 2-I The Mini-Gauge

The marketing department of a major company identified an area where miniaturization would have potential appeal to customers. The customers who were contacted were very positive and said they wanted the smaller gauges. Data were analyzed and high profitability was forecast. Several hundred units were hand-built and tested. The AR for production equipment was written and approved based on the market potential. When production began, customers realized that

---

7. This assumes the equipment purchase is related to a product's manufacturing process. In the case of support equipment purchases such as copiers and forklift trucks, the data required to justify the purchase may be different, but the overall approach may be quite similar.

their product lines would have to be redesigned and reengineered to incorporate the new unit, a task that would take two to four years. The equipment purchased sat idle, waiting for the changeover to occur. Eventually it did take place, but the returns were not as expected because of the lengthy time needed for the customer to adapt.

Case 2-II Static-Free Carpet

A major carpet yarn manufacturer had developed a static-free nylon fiber in the research laboratory. The market potential was practically unlimited. Funds for production equipment were quickly approved, schedules were developed, and the marketing department went ahead with elaborate promotional efforts, including major advertising plans for trade publications. Manufacturing received the capital equipment but could not make it run due to the tremendous difference in a controlled laboratory versus the atmospheric conditions in a large production facility. The process involved super-heated steam being blasted into the nylon filament through microscopic holes in a jet nozzle. It could not be commercially performed. By the time everyone realized that full-scale production could not be accomplished, the advertising had hit the market. Rushing the process before being sure of the process is dangerous.

The project sponsor has a number of duties besides data collection:

- Evaluating options for meeting the project requirements and developing cost estimates
- Developing the time-table for meeting the requirements on time
- Developing the appropriation request and assuming responsibility for the accuracy of the data presented
- Managing the project by coordinating the activities of affected departments and overseeing the implementation schedule with respect to time and budget
- Supervising the overall project and being responsible for successful project completion
- Compiling the information for the postanalysis performance audit and reports on the project to management

The project sponsor is the responsible party from inception of the project to completion. This person must have an array of available tools, delegated authority from top management to carry the project forward, and cooperation from a wide array of units within the organization, plus the financial and human resources to complete the project. There is not only a capital appropriation involved, but also the cost of that process of bringing it to a successful conclusion. In many instances, this cost is significant and should not be ignored in putting the project together. Among these ancillary or secondary costs, sometimes called **start-up costs,** are the following:

• *Travel costs.* Normally at least three trips are made in the project cycle. Two trips are to customers who have the equipment installed and operating. The purpose of these trips is to observe the equipment in an operating environment and determine issues such as installation, maintenance, spare parts consumption, training, quality of output, and customer applications. These trips are essential to the process, especially if the equipment uses raw materials or components and is related to final output as opposed to support equipment. The third trip will involve the preshipment testing at the supplier's site. There is little to be gained by shipping defective equipment; thus the sample test run at the supplier's site is money well spent. Travel costs can escalate when the buyer insists that a company engineer be present to monitor the in-process acceptance criteria.

• *Project personnel costs.* In the role of coordinator, the project sponsor must have the help of and cooperation from a number of people in the organization. In addition, the sponsor is responsible for the accuracy of the data provided by these others. With the trend toward reduced staffing in many companies, often needed personnel are not available or their workload is such that gathering the data can become a significant addition to an already busy schedule. This is especially true of smaller, growing companies; a seven-day workweek is not uncommon for some key salaried employees. There must be some method used to compensate for the time spent on providing the data. Arguments that this type of work is simply "part of the job" presuppose a degree of organizational loyalty and dedication that is missing in many organizations. The data may be gathered and forecasts made, but they may not be all they should be. In addition, meetings on the project are time-consuming. Costing the meetings can show a significant indirect cost associated with the purchase of the equipment.

• *Communications costs.* These are relatively minimal and include the normal forms of communication, such as telephone, fax, and mailing costs.

• *Change order costs.* Sometimes called ECNs—engineering change notices—or ECPs—engineering change proposals—these are modifications to the original product purchased. Technically, there should be no ECN associated with the equipment; the originator of the AR should have made sure it was clearly specified as to what is being purchased. Yet no piece of capital equipment comes in only one form. There are always accessories or upgrades that are possible.

Components such as motors, pumps, and automatic loaders can be added to the equipment. There are difficulties as well when dealing with the description of what is to be purchased. Does the organization go for the equipment with all the desired accessories—or the stripped-down model? Is there a middle ground? That is the first issue to resolve.

The second issue is the freezing of the requirement. Ordering the machine and asking for options to be added as the machine is being crated for delivery is a sure method of generating a cost overrun. There must be a point where the requirement is frozen and cannot be changed. If changes are desired beyond the design or model freeze date, then the changes may have to be made *after* the equipment is installed and in a production mode. The issues are cost and cost control. Making changes can be expensive, especially if the equipment has passed beyond a certain point in its assembly. Out-of-station or out-of-sequence costs can cause the final bill to soar. In addition, time pressures may be such that there can be no price negotiations on the upgrades, and the buyer pays the seller's asking price for the upgrades.

The ideal situation is no ECNs; however, the project sponsor must be ready to address the issue. This requires some degree of understanding of the schedule and process for assembling the equipment being purchased. Therefore, the travel to the supplier's site is quite important to determine the "drop-dead" dates as they relate to the equipment being purchased and the flexibility in upgrading or changing the original order. Know what you want before you ask for the money to buy it. The key question to ask is, "Is it more cost-effective to have the change done at the factory or when the machine is in production?"

• *Progress payments.* Consider progress payments from a lost-opportunity perspective. The dollars have been paid to the supplier to cover costs during the building phase of the equipment. The use of that money is gone, and the added cost of the project should be the return on that money for the period of time between payment to the supplier and the point at which the equipment becomes a revenue producing asset.

The Approval Process

Every company has its own way of approving the capital appropriation requests. It is crucial for the project sponsor to understand the process not only from the perspective of how the levels of approval are structured but also how the emphasis changes as the document moves higher in the organization. *It is imperative that the project sponsor have a clear understanding of the process in its totality.* What are the gates, and who are the gatekeepers? Often the focus changes as the appropriation request moves up the organization from a technical document in the engineering sense to a financial document. The reason for this shift is based on two considerations. The first is the need for a common yardstick to measure the proposal against other proposals. Capital is not an unlimited commodity for the average company, and not all appropriations will be approved. Yet the competition must be evaluated on some basis that allows for valid comparisons to be made. The second reason is the expertise of the approving parties. As people move up in the organization, more time is spent on management. The totality of technical understanding is often lost over time as the person moves away from these issues. Higher management may not have up-to-date technical expertise to evaluate the request or the AR in the same light as those several organizational layers below. With the number of requests coming in for upper management approval, the signatures of lower-level approvals indicate that these technical issues have been resolved already. These are the rules of the game in the organization—the *hows* of getting the AR approved. This is a matter of company culture and philosophy. Going against the culture or bypassing the procedures is often the best way to sink an AR.

A portion of the approval process may result in the stratification of projects. Certain projects require greater or more elaborate justification than others. Certain projects are necessary items that cannot be absent from the factory floor. In order to allow for valid comparisons, appropriation requests tend to fall into categories or groupings by type of request—for example:

Group 1:   Growth projects
Group 2:   Replacement machinery
Group 3:   Transportation equipment replacement
Group 4:   Transportation equipment additions
Group 5:   Replacement patterns, tools
Group 6:   Miscellaneous projects

The method of evaluation for one group may differ dramatically from another. In the case of Groups 1 and 2, the criteria for evaluation may be return on investment. There may be set rates for ROI, established by the company, that must be met before the AR can move forward. A company may set a floor on the investment of 40 percent on growth projects and 30 percent on replacement machinery based on discounting the cash flow of the project at the appropriate level.[8]

Consider the example of a replacement machine, shown in Exhibit 2-1, having a 10-year service and an initial cost of $300,000.[9] The total cash flow of

8. The financial aspects are covered fully in Chapter 3, but some brief examples are provided here to illustrate how the concept works and how the project sponsor would go about putting the correct information together for a particular audience. Different levels will view the same data differently.
9. With respect to the useful life of investments, consider developing a table of useful lives, with the maximum number of years over which depreciation can be taken under normal operating

Exhibit 2-1. Evaluating the capital investment.

Year	Cash Flow in year (thousands of dollars)	Discounting Factor at 30% Discount Rate*	Present Value of Cash Flow
1	$ 90	0.769	$ 69.23
2	121	0.592	71.60
3	145	0.455	70.00
4	135	0.350	47.27
5	128	0.269	34.74
6	114	0.207	23.62
7	110	0.159	17.53
8	100	0.122	12.26
9	95	0.094	8.96
10	90	0.073	6.53
Total	1,128		357.46

*Arrived at by using the following formula:

$$\text{Discount factor} = \frac{1}{(1 + i)^n}$$

where n refers to the year. Thus, in the first year, the discount would be $1/(1.3)^1$, or 0.769. Continuing the process shows later-year revenues are significantly smaller.

the project is $1,128,000 over the defined useful life, but since revenues in the future have to be discounted at the floor for the investment, the discounted cash flow is $357,460. That value is above the $300,000 initial cost of the replacement equipment and therefore meets the basic ROI criteria. The issue that still remains is the accuracy of the cash flow estimates that must be made 10 years into the future. The reason for setting the discount rate so high may be connected with the issue of accuracy of the cash flow estimates. Make the discount rate high enough, and the cash flows must also be high simply to meet the floor requirements. Cash flow estimates that are high show that either the potential of the product or the machine to generate that cash flow or the estimate is wrong. The higher the estimate, the more justification is needed.

Making the discount rate high will discourage the marginal projects, which will never clear the first hurdle, so the proposed investment will not even be considered. There is no point in taking up executive time with marginal projects. In addition, future ARs submitted will lack credibility.

There are, however, other options to consider: rebuilding existing equipment or purchasing used equipment. The major difference between these two and new equipment is the projected service life. Nominally viewed as half of

---

conditions. Where use is extensive and the asset wears out faster, use a shorter period for depreciation and document the reasons. Also, consider all the costs associated with the purchase and installation process.

Exhibit 2-2. New vs. used or rebuilt equipment.

Year	Cash Flow (thousands of dollars)	Discounting Factor at 30% Discount Rate*	Present Value of Cash Flow	Used Equipment
1	$ 90	0.769	$ 69.23	$ 69.23
2	121	0.592	71.60	71.60
3	145	0.455	70.00	70.00
4	135	0.350	47.27	47.27
5	128	0.269	34.74	34.74
6	114	0.207	23.62	—
7	110	0.159	17.53	—
8	100	0.122	12.26	—
9	95	0.094	8.96	—
10	90	0.073	6.53	—
Total	$1,128		$357.46	$292.84

*See the explanation in Exhibit 2-1.

that of new equipment, the relative merits of used equipment are compared in Exhibit 2-2.

It is easy to see that the used equipment would have a marked advantage over the new equipment. Returning almost 82 percent (292.84/357.46) of the discounted cash flow of the new machine in the five-year period under investigation, the used equipment, if purchased for anything below 82 percent of the price of the new equipment, would be a better financial option. In addition, the lead time for obtaining this equipment would be shorter, and the capital investment would be lower in the absolute dollar value committed. What is forgone is $65,000 in discounted cash flow occurring 6 to 10 years into the future. Given the length of time of the projection, the $65,000 figure may be a great deal less accurate than desired. Accounting plays a vital team role.

The accuracy of the cash flow projections is a paramount issue in developing the justification. Inaccuracies in those numbers create nothing but difficulties in the approval process. In addition to the inherent uncertainties in projecting operating or cost advantages into the future as cash flows attributable to the new or used equipment replacement of existing capacity, the problem of using the numbers becomes more complex as we attempt to be more realistic about the whole process. Consider the following example.

The XYZ Company is considering replacing a 350-ton, Sheridan die cutting press that it bought in 1952. The new press will have a significant economic advantage over the old model, but the question becomes one of how long the old model would continue to last to make the discounted cash flow comparisons. Raising the issue of displacement of existing equipment is very tricky. Once the displacement is accomplished, the operating advantage of the new replacement is gone, and it is replaced by the operating costs of the new equipment. To say that the cash flow is the difference between previous costs or first-year operating advantage versus the old equipment (displaced) is rather tenuous at best if that savings is projected beyond the first year. Would the 1952 model still be operating a decade from now? And the further one goes out into the future, the more tenuous the forecasts become, especially if spare parts are not available.

The whole process is rather like the chicken-and-egg controversy. It is a case of elaborate equations founded on questionable logic. One school of thought is to make the savings or revenue estimates equal for each year, adjusting only for the time period in the first year when the equipment was purchased. Savings or revenues would be 50 percent of expected annual savings if the equipment began operating halfway through the fiscal year. Beyond the first year, annual savings or revenues would be equal each year. Another school of thought says to factor in inflation or anticipated increases in prices of product produced on the equipment. Yet others advise indexing the numbers. It is amazing the number of ways there are to embellish questionable data. Yet index or inflation adjusting is one of the few tools available. Thus, the project sponsor tries to equate the value received from the old versus the new. The saving factor is that these rules of the game apply to all investments and thus allow for comparisons on a relative basis.

Not all capital appropriations can be looked at under the same microscope. In groups 3 through 6, the issue becomes demonstrated need for the investment. Forklift trucks, for example, reach the end of their service life or cost far too much to repair relative to the value of the vehicle. Putting additional monies into repairs may be viewed as a bottomless pit. The simple factor of need, physical deterioration of the asset, inability of the asset to perform its functions properly, or high repair cost may dictate the need to replace the asset. Looking at the financial operating advantage may be impossible, and the data would be nothing more than guesses.

Progressing down the list, it is evident that the dollar values shrink as one drops into the category of patterns, jigs, fixtures, and gauges. If these items are associated with a growth opportunity, they should be considered part of the equipment itself and counted as such. Replacements for existing equipment are nominally limited to a dollar figure.

The purpose of this process of subdividing and categorizing is important. It should help focus attention on the areas of higher-cost risk and dispose of the lesser dollar decisions at a lower organizational level. Any good system will follow this process:

1. Stratify the types of capital investments that can be made. This would be the category approach. In all likelihood, it would restrict category 1 and 2 items to machinery and equipment directly related to new or existing products

2. Stratify these investments within each category by dollar amount.

3. Specify the approval process by type and dollar amounts, as well as the data needed for consideration of the project.

4. Specify the appropriate methodology to be employed in preparing the justification for each of the type of investment. Based on the shortcomings of any capital investment analysis, it is valid to employ several approaches and not be surprised if the answers provided by a particular technique are in conflict. Analysis or analytical techniques do not overcome or compensate for bad data.

5. Specify the time periods over which savings are relevant and the service life of the equipment under consideration. Exhibit 2-3 shows some typical examples of equipment by type and their depreciation periods.[10] The shorter the period, the happier the company is depreciating the asset. Recognize the

Exhibit 2-3. Asset depreciation schedule.

Asset	*Maximum Term*
Buildings	
Permanent plant and office construction	30 years
Temporary or field warehouses	10 years
Mineral processing buildings	15 years
Machinery and equipment	
Heavy duty, durable	16⅔ years
Semidurable	10 years
Rebuilt machinery	5 years
Used machinery	5 years
Furniture and fixtures	10 years
Office equipment	5 years
Autos and pickup trucks	3 years
Lift trucks	5 years
Dies, patterns, and jigs	4 years
Mineral processing equipment	8 years
Mobile communication equipment	3 years
Wet storage tanks and containers	5 years

10. It is essential that each organization have a depreciation policy table or list. What goes into the table depends on the individual company. The table is essential for the computation of residual value from an accounting perspective. A six-year-old rebuilt machine may have a depreciated value of zero but be worth $1,000 on the open market. Selling for $1,000 would incur a tax liability. Sell that same machine in the fourth year, before it is fully depreciated, and there may be no liability or even a loss. While selection of "the" correct equipment to buy should not be made on accounting considerations, they cannot be ignored.

ground rules for reporting the savings or revenue flow. If the policy is to allow first-year savings to represent the average-year savings to be used less any anticipated expenditure such as maintenance or overhauls or increased utilization, then that policy must be uniformly applied to all investments of a particular category.

6. Provide guidance as to how the savings are to be computed, as well as what is allowed in the savings category. This is a tricky area since some savings are readily identifiable, such as faster speeds or feeds that raise machine productivity, and some are cost avoidances that save time but simply reallocate costs from one category to another, such as reduced setup time. Unless reduced setup time translates into more production time for a demanded product, the time savings are spurious dollars since the cost is incurred by having a worker at the machine site and nothing being produced. Tangible savings include feeds, speeds, reduced waste and rework, less downtime, a better production-to-maintenance ratio, as well as better quality and fewer rejects. While quality improvements may occur as a result of better operator-equipment interfacing such as less fatigue, it is important to document the results in a defensible, quantitative manner.

7. Define terminology carefully to avoid bias in comparing proposals. As is often the case, there will be terms used by the financial personnel that are foreign to the engineer, and the quality assurance people may use the term "six sigma" to the frustration of the purchasing staff. The purpose of a single glossary of terms is to facilitate communication in the organization. A few pages devoted to terms can go a long way in ensuring the commonality of the use of terms as well as their understanding by all concerned.

8. Go to the right level for approval. Depending on the size and complexity of the company, the approval process for capital investment items may go all the way to the board of directors. Normally there are levels of approval in any organization, and it is not uncommon to see a positive relationship between the funds requested and the level of approval: The more money needed, the higher the level of approval is required. The issue created by this process is one of orientation of the approving body. Two proposals, equally as good at one level, may be viewed completely differently at the next level.

This process places all potential purchases into categories with a degree of uniformity within each category. It is essential to incorporate this type of information into a manual for project sponsors. The manual should contain an example of each project with a typical analysis that must be followed in developing the appropriation request. A manual may appear to be a good deal of work, but consider the alternatives if the equipment is purchased and sits idle. Tens of thousands or hundreds of thousands of dollars have been spent on a nonperforming asset.

The Manual Format

Putting together a project sponsor's manual or check sheet represents nothing more than an effort to introduce uniformity into the preparation of the AR and the development of a standard by which all ARs are evaluated. The purpose of the manual is to ensure that the correct data go with the request and certain requests that have no data foundation are not biased by creatively manufactured data. Where data are necessary, let them be correct and as accurate as possible. If data are unavailable or sketchy, there is no reason to include them in the analysis. Questionable data, improperly used, cast a shadow of doubt over the proposal.

The Appropriation Request Process

There is no single format to use in developing the AR, and, in fact, often companies use two or three forms to capture the information.

Normally the top or cover form is the executive summary capturing the key elements of the proposal. This is *never* sufficient information to gain approval of a project. It is intended only to highlight the essential elements of financial information, the methods of evaluation used, total project cost in summary form, cash requirements, along with the proposal and its justification. Approvals at lower levels indicate concurrence on the project. Lower-level approval also indicates agreement with the values in the proposal. What else is needed? Again the category method dictates additional information. A request for the replacement of existing equipment would require cash flow analysis, payback period computation, and probably a pro forma profit-and-loss or income statement for the proposed investment comparing it to the current investment to determine the first-year advantage of the proposed investment. This document would then be used for the postinstallation audit conducted after the first year of operation.

There are two options in the AR process. One is full preparation of the AR, with actions to purchase and install the equipment dependent on the final approval of the AR. The second approach is a phased AR, in which the preliminary activities of supplier visits, site visits, and all information gathering for the AR are done on the basis of a lower-approval level of the AR. Once all the data are gathered, the supplier selected, and a clear definition of the equipment to be purchased has been established, the final or equipment AR is moved forward for final approval. Doing the groundwork without an approved AR has some costs but could save considerable time in the buying process. In addition, timing of the process could be made to coincide with preparation of other information such as market forecasts needed for pro forma profit-and-loss statements.

Completing the Appropriation Request

Following is a hypothetical case for the purchase of an automatic screw machine.

These data are available:

Machine cost:	$161,305
Installation and freight:	$5,500
Contingency at 2 percent of cost:	$3,200
Total capital costs:	$170,000
Total cash requirement:	$179,000
Tooling (spares):	$8,000
Factory preparation:	$1,000
Total expense:	$9,000

The project narrative would go into detail concerning the reasons to purchase a new machine as a displacer of the old one. This would focus on the cost and efficiency comparisons as well as the rationale for replacing the old machine. Reasons for replacement can include:

• The inability to get spare parts or the need to have spare parts custom-built or backward engineered in the case of such items as cams, sliders, bearings, spindles, or motors.

• High setup costs as a result of using dated technology.

• Increased machine capacity of the new equipment or the elimination of a secondary operation (the new machine is faster than the old one).

• Inflexibility of the older equipment that creates extensive setup times when converting from one setup to another.

• The need for an operator on the old machine versus an automated manufacturing cell on the new machine.

• Component replacement is not possible and may result in significant costs to replace a whole section of the machine.

• Increasingly higher maintenance costs. Soon the cost of repair will be prohibitive relative to the service life remaining in the machine.[11] This point is extremely important if the company has a good

---

11. Just because the machine has reached the end of its depreciation schedule does not necessarily mean it will be replaced. The usual reasons for replacement include the inability to get spare parts or the cost of maintaining the machine has reached astronomical proportions relative to its value.

maintenance cost tracking system. There are cutoff points where it is no longer economical to put money into an old machine. Since a significant portion of cost is labor in the maintenance field, the value of that labor is often lost when the repair is made. The only real value adder is replacement of parts. Therefore the decision rule of cost-to-repair as a percentage of value should look carefully at the labor going into the repair and the material-to-labor ratio. The labor can accomplish nothing more than to bring the machine back to working order.

• Deteriorating performance that endangers product line through lost sales or loss of market share by the inability to meet demand.

The depth and detail of the request are a function of the approval process. Obviously any capital request in the group 1 or 2 category is going to paint the most positive picture possible. The project must meet the ROI threshold as well as the payback criteria. (See Chapter 3 for the details of computation of the ROI and payback period.) In addition, it involves the expenditure of real dollars.

The important consideration here is the communication process. Does the narrative develop an understanding of the request or leave gaps in the argument? Does it confuse the issue by crowding the justification with technical terms and verbiage that cloud the justification and make it difficult to comprehend?

Securing the Go-Ahead

When the document is complete, the project sponsor should review it with all supporting attachments and data. The AR is then ready to begin its journey. Sometimes it is returned to the sponsor for additional information or clarification. The sponsor has been close to the project, and aspects that are perfectly clear to him or her may be obscure to others.

During this process, the project sponsor must keep the project approvers advised of the progress to date on it. This is simply preselling the project and building up its credibility. As the project moves up the ladder of approval, the greater the number of signatures that appear on the approval lines, the better the chances become for final approval. The signatures show coordination of the project and confidence in the project sponsor; they indicate that increasing numbers of people have seen the proposal and have had the opportunity to review and comment on it, polish it, and make constructive recommendations.

Removing any surprises from the AR is one of the ways to ensure its progress up the ladder toward approval.

The AR is a clear blueprint or road map to the process of not only getting the funding for the equipment but how that equipment is going to contribute to the ultimate profitability of the organization, directly or indirectly, and how that profitability will be evaluated or audited. The project sponsor is the key player on the team, and the selection of the right person is an essential first step. Good people generally produce good results. This is one area where using the best person for the job is essential.

Appropriation Request Checklist

- [ ] Preliminary approval has been given for going ahead with the project.
- [ ] The proposal is written in clearly understood language.
- [ ] Operating changes and expected results are explained.
- [ ] Quotations are attached.
- [ ] *All* associated costs are covered in the proposal and clearly identified.
- [ ] Environmental considerations have been costed.

3

The Financial Dimensions of the Capital Equipment Decision

The financial people in the organization typically are the gatekeepers who have the most influence over the capital investment decision. This is why this chapter appears early in the handbook. There is no point in going into a great deal of discussion if the financial dimensions of the project are not in order. At this point, the organization is looking at the prospect of spending money, internally generated or borrowed, for the capital asset. If the proposal is incomplete or inadequate, chances are it will not proceed further, so this is the moment of truth. The project or machine is beginning to take shape from a resource perspective. An investment will be made of scarce monetary resources, not just for today or tomorrow but years into the future. Capital expenditures are drivers of operating budgets. The equipment must be maintained, repaired, recalibrated, painted, rebuilt, and cleaned over its lifetime. The commitment today obligates future revenues that will be spent years from now. If the decision is a poor one, the potential losses are obvious to all concerned, as one hospital found out.

A staff physician sorely wanted a pricey piece of diagnostic equipment. Because he was a big "producer" for the hospital, the board of directors agreed to spend the $300,000. Not six months later, the newer and more sophisticated model appeared, and the physician insisted on the newer model as a condition of staying on the hospital staff. This one cost $450,000. The "old" machine was now gathering dust in a storage room after being used for three diagnoses. The insurance providers for the patients using the old machine could not be convinced to pay $100,000 per diagnosis.

When a request is made for money to purchase and support equipment, the protector of the corporate assets needs a justification as to the rationale for making the investment. Notice the word *investment* is used as opposed to *expenditure.* Purchasing the capital equipment is an investment of resources in some item that will contribute to the economic well-being of the organization. If that well-being or benefit cannot be identified, articulated, and verified, there are numerous other options for the organization to spend its money. Clearly communications is important.

Most capital requests come from the technical side of the organization. What often happens is that an engineer presents a proposal in totally technical terms to a nontechnical financial person, who fails to understand the technical side and often the benefits. The engineer is frustrated at the inability of the financial officer to grasp the technical significance of the proposal, and the financial officer sees the expenditure of money with no discernible measure of risk and rewards for that expenditure. Each is talking a language the other does not understand.

Communication is the only way we have to make our proposals, needs, or requirements known to others. The success of a proposal often lies in the ability to amass the information over which the decision maker has concerns and present it as objectively and clearly as possible. There should be no surprises in the proposal, and the concerns and issues should be presented with clarity and integrity. These may appear to be obvious points, yet many proposals have bitten the dust because they were not understood, were clouded with technical terminology, or painted a totally unrealistic picture. The negatives were hidden or glossed over, and when they were discussed, weaknesses in the proposals became evident.

Dealing with all of the issues in an objective manner is a balancing act in the preparation of the capital equipment request:

- Being positive but not euphoric about the project
- Being confident in both the depth of the information presented and the accuracy
- Presenting information in a clear, logical way that brings the decision maker to the same conclusion as the presenter
- Talking *to* the decision maker, not above or around or beneath him or her
- Being prepared to point out the impact of *not* approving the proposal without the often used Chicken Little syndrome ("The sky is falling, the sky is falling")
- Effectively communicating so all present understand by speaking in *their* language and understanding *their* communication terms

To understand why some proposals are successful and some are failures requires an understanding of the perspective from the financial side of the organization. How does the financial analyst or financial officer look at the capital expenditure? Look through this person's glasses and you may see what she or he sees.

Financial people are concerned with the stewardship of the financial resources of the organization. They feel a sense of responsibility toward the management of those assets in such a manner as to bring about the highest return at the minimum level of risk to the organization. Most U.S. corporations view themselves as being heavily responsible to their shareholders, who have invested money in the corporation with no firm guarantee of any return on their investment. The performance of the company and, especially, its management in carrying out the activities of that company is the only guarantee. To this perception of fiscal responsibility, add definite attitudes toward risk, and the financial perspective is one of proving the investment meets the criteria for soundness and responsibility.

Consider the example of a staid, conservative bank in a small midwestern town whose lending policy was buying government securities. The lending committee routinely disapproved requests for "frivolous loans" to buy automobiles, renovate homes, and finance capital expenditures. The bank officers were content that they were carrying out their charge. Yet no one who lived in the town under 10 years had the slightest desire to deal with that bank. The bank was dying along with its old-time customers. Yet top management's perception of doing the right thing was accurate (though excessive).

A Look at Risk

Financial concerns often revolve around risk. In the risk situation, there are several possible outcomes, each with a definite likelihood or probability of occurrence attached to it. Some of these risks can be measured. For example, an actuary, a gambler, and a bond trader all have the capability of measuring the risk associated with a portion of their specific field of endeavor. The actuary can tell a 60-year-old man, who is a nonsmoker, the probability of living to age 65. The actuary can answer in probabilistic terms only. The gambler can tell the odds of throwing a 7 on the first roll of the dice. The answer is 1 chance in 6 or drawing a red queen on the next draw (1 chance in 26). The bond trader looks at the rating of the bond and the type of bond and has a good perception of the risks associated with that investment.

Yet there is another dimension of risk to consider: individual perceptions of risk and associated behaviors when faced with risk situations. The decision makers looking at the financial side of an investment will be influenced by their own perceptions of risk and the risk-to-reward ratio—that is, what will occur if the decision results in success or failure. Put another way, How far out on the limb is one going in this decision? What are the rewards that accrue for making the correct decision, and what are the sanctions for making the wrong decision? What is right or wrong depends on the payoffs from the decision. The midwestern bank felt its stringent lending policy was the right decision; it had a real payoff with no risk. Why assume the risk of lending to someone who might default on the loan? The default would be a sign of poor character on the part of the borrower—*and* poor judgment of character by the lender. These lending officers viewed avoiding risk as a noble attribute.

In the main, people tend to be risk avoiders. When faced with options that lean toward certainty or minimize risk, they will tend to go for the sure thing even if there is a possibility of larger payoffs with the riskier situation. One of us has replicated the following experiment with hundreds of graduate students in management science: "Consider the possibility that you have just identified your holding of the winning ticket to a lottery with your payoff at $5,000. You may collect your winnings or trade the winning ticket for another lottery ticket with a payoff of $100,000. What odds of winning the second lottery would you need to be assured of before giving up your winning ticket for the chance to win $100,000?"

The answers always come out the same, ranging from 50 percent probability to 99.999 percent probability to, "Forget it; I am happy with the $5,000." From the mathematical perspective, a probability of winning of 5 percent is sufficient to equate the two sums. Thus, anything above 5 percent tips the scales in favor of the player. Yet everyone who has answered the question wanted the scales way out of balance on their side. Perspectives about risk influence behavior and may bias decisions.

Return now to a decision maker faced with a proposal calling for the expenditure of $500,000. It is not the individual's money at risk, but the result of the investment is a performance measure of that person. Good investments reflect good performance, and poor returns are equated with inadequate or poor performance. What is that financial person going to look for in the proposal, and how will he evaluate it, why? These are the issues addressed in this chapter.

Why All the Signatures?

Since capital projects often entail large sums of money, the usual path is to submit capital requests or proposals prior to putting together the capital budget for the year. Often capital projects require one or more presentations before selected groups of people and detailed proposals as to need, costs, and impacts of acquiring the equipment or postponing the decision. The approval often goes to the highest levels of the company, and certain expenditures require approval of the board of directors. The premise is simple: Exposing the proposal to more scrutiny will ensure a more informed decision. Executives and board members have more experience and may view certain areas with different insight based on their previous experiences. In addition, approval at this level means the proposal has serious financial implications for the company, and a consensus is important from those who have the ultimate responsibility for the health and vitality of the company. This should be far more than a process of affixing signatures to a requisition or cover form. It is an opportunity to train people and gain a degree of uniformity and clarity in the proposal development. It is not just procedure. Each level of approval should add something to the process, and each level of approval should add to the information base about the proposal and its impact.

Often the listeners are those responsible for finding the money used to purchase the capital equipment. They will judge the worthiness of each project, rank it relative to others, and assign the cutoff point above which projects are approved and below which they are delayed or disapproved. These persons see a larger perspective. They will construct elaborate criteria for financial evaluation and set up a series of financial gates or hurdles that the proposal must get through or over prior to final approval. Their job is to see that only the most worthy projects are funded. This is their responsibility, and it should be appreciated. Making the approval process too easy encourages mediocre proposals and may reward marginal performance in preparing the proposal.

The Early Financial Decisions

Any proposal for a capital expenditure must contain the costs and benefits of that investment. (Saying, "I need one of those," became obsolete when one reached kindergarten.) Do the benefits of the investment outweigh its costs? Were it all so simple, there would be no reason to put it in a book.

Because the focus of this book is on total cost of ownership or life cycle costs, we begin by looking at the typical costs that may be associated with each phase of the life cycle or segment of the process.

In the initial phase, the **determination of the need,** an array of decisions is made.

Type of Equipment: Custom Made or Off the Shelf?

Will the equipment be commercial, off-the-shelf (COTS) or custom-made to suit a specific purpose or need?[1] COTS equipment means selecting what the

---

1. The federal government is turning more toward buying off the shelf in many agencies. The costs associated with paying for the development of the item is becoming too expensive in many cases. COTS may be with us for some time.

supplier produces as part of the product line. It can result in shorter lead time, greater availability of spare parts, and greater experience on issues such as maintainability and reliability. Warranty issues are clear as to the liability of the supplier. By accepting the order and selling off the shelf, the supplier warrants the machine capable of performing the task specified by the buyer.

In some cases, there is a need for custom-made or custom-designed equipment. This normally translates into longer lead times, possible limitations placed on the availability of spare parts, reliability and cost issues, and cost control and warranty issues.

Custom built and off the shelf are the ends of the spectrum, with all sorts of areas in between that must be considered also. For example, an injection-molding machine can be off the shelf, but the molds are probably all custom made. This means dealing with at least two suppliers in some cases, and the issue of comparability comes into play.

If the choice is a custom-designed piece of equipment, is the design portion included in the contract? Is the buyer going to design the machine and have it built to specifications, or will the supplier design the machine and then build it? Another option is to specify the design of the machine as one contract and then competitively bid or negotiate the build portion of the process as a separate contract. The mix is important and can have significant implications as to the downstream costs of the equipment. The supplier who custom designs and builds the machine has a total lock on that machine and can build in any level of technology and exclusivity desired. It can almost become an annuity with respect to spare parts and maintenance. In addition, what are the real costs of the design portion of the contract versus the build portion?

One company was buying three custom-built machines. It received a quote from one supplier for $125,000 for the design and the three machines. Prior to contract signing, the buyer decided to break the contract into two components, beginning with the design contract. The final payment of the contract would be contingent on the ability of three suppliers to bid on the construction of the machine. The buyer wanted to avoid the building in uniqueness that would hinder or negate competition. By **splitting the contract,** the company obtained bids on the design and paid $50,000 for the design portion of the acquisition and $15,000 for each of three machines for a total of $95,000, or $30,000 less than the original offer.

How valid the cost estimates are for custom-built equipment is an important issue. They can be high to cover any possible contingency and generate excessive profit for the supplier, or they can be low, and the supplier may run into financial difficulties and need more money to complete the project. The latter situation makes the capital budgeting decision process more difficult since there must be some form of **contingency planning,** with funds set aside to cover possible contingencies in the buying process. Couple this potential cost with the longer lead time, the possible limitations on the supplier's resources such as design engineers and drafting personnel, the supplier's backlog, and the custom-built machine can be an expensive and risky situation.

There are no absolute numbers as to how much should be set aside or budgeted for the contingency issue, yet 10 to 15 percent set aside to cover contingencies can always be returned to the corporate coffers after the project is completed. It is simply a hedge against having to return to ask for additional appropriations.

Supplier Progress Payments

In some cases, the supplier is going to want **progress payments** for building the equipment. Suppliers are hesitant to finance the project by waiting until the completion of the project for payment because their expenses go on during all the stages of the purchase. As a result, the buyer will have funds tied up in the purchase and have nothing to show for the expenditure except progress reports. There is an opportunity cost associated with the progress payments. The funds are no longer available to the buying company, and so the forgone interest that might have been earned on those funds must be added to the cost of the equipment. An opportunity has been lost as well to use the funds in other investments.

Variations from the off-the-shelf or standard will add to the cost, the lead time, and perhaps the complexity of maintenance. In addition, what are the industry practices with respect to pricing? Some industries have price in effect at time of delivery as the standard. Thus, the buyer really does not know what the price will be until something is delivered. This totally protects the seller, and places all the cost risk on the buyer.

Early Costs

Regardless of the decision, there is a cost incurred in the need determination phase. It appears on the operating budget, not the capital budget, yet it is tied to that item of equipment. The cost is the preliminary design time to prepare the proposal and get the relevant data amassed to allow purchasing to begin the process of putting together some of the other costs. The proposal should be as complete as possible. Items omitted from it that arise later and are errors of omission do nothing but raise cost and reduce credibility. What is the cycle time for putting together the proposal? What is the cost per engineering hour?

There are other cost elements beyond proposal preparation and equipment cost that must be factored in:

• *Testing or compliance costs.* It would be foolish to purchase an item of equipment that was not tested at the supplier's facility *before* it was shipped to the buyer. In fact, some companies specify acceptance criteria and testing during the manufacturing or assembly process. The cheapest place to detect problems is in the early stages of manufacture. Nevertheless, there is a monitoring cost associated with compliance or testing in both personnel time and material time. Making the pilot run at the supplier's facility can save money later in the process.

• *Transportation costs.* Capital equipment has one common characteristic: It is usually large in size. This may limit the transportation options and even require special rigging to secure the freight and special handling to ensure its safety during transportation. It will mean loading at the supplier's facility and unloading at the buyer's site. It means there must be sufficient space to get the equipment into the facility and special equipment for unloading. It may require special insurance covering the transportation phase of the process and added costs of unloading by riggers.

• *Installation costs.* Who is going to install the equipment? Is the supplier responsible for part or all of the installation? Is installation included in the cost of the equipment, or does it come under a separate contract? For most large equipment, installation is covered under a separate contract, and therefore costs more money.

• *Site preparation costs.* The site must be prepared for incoming equipment: utilities in place, environmental issues resolved, and the site capable of accepting the equipment with respect to noise, vibration, temperature, weight, and material flows and control. This is part of the cost of the process.

• *Training costs.* Some capital equipment is replacement equipment, and operator training is minimal. But new equipment may require training the operators, and in the case of computer numerically controlled (CNC) equipment, programmer training can be needed. Who provides that training, and at whose cost? Is it part of the purchase price or an ancillary cost? Who will operate the equipment? Do union considerations enter the picture? In one company, the most senior employee bid on the job of operating CNC equipment to machine a high-precision helicopter blade part. The operator simply pushed the start button and stood back from the machine. At $15 per hour, it was an expensive button.

• *Make-ready costs.* With some exceptions, there are costs of installation and pilot runs that go beyond normal installation costs. There is a period of testing: trying the equipment and seeing if it works correctly, plus making minor adjustments. This may consume personnel and materials. It is rare that any machine goes right into production, especially if it is new. There are always some costs incurred in getting the machine on line. If materials are consumed in the process and the output does not meet specifications, the supplier may seek protection under limited liability in the agreement, saying the supplier warranty is limited to defects in workmanship and materials and consequential damages are not covered under the warranty. Look for this disclaimer in the proposal from the supplier. It is a *very important consideration* and could open a door of liability. (This subject is covered in Chapter 5.)

• *Tooling, parts, and supplies.* Although considered a secondary expense, tooling, jigs, fixtures, or support items can be costly. These are not spare parts. They are the operating supplies needed to make the machine work. They may also be viewed as insurance against loss of productive time.

• *Spare parts costs.* Sometimes spares are purchased with the equipment, or they come in a spare parts kit. In one sense, this is the supplier's way of ensuring the necessary spares are available to perform the maintenance during the burn-in period as a hedge against failures. It is a method of reducing downtime by having the spares on the buyer's site and available for immediate use. What is the cost associated with the kit, and is that cost included in the purchase price?

Summing all of these costs gives the buyer an estimated total cost of the equipment purchased, shipped, installed, tested, trained, set up, and ready to move into production. All of these activities have costs associated with them and must be included in the first element of total cost of ownership. Failure to do so simply hides costs and deludes everyone about the real cost of the equipment.

In addition, these costs are often sunk costs and are rarely recoverable. They involve the direct outlay of monies and therefore represent a cash drain on the organization. They are expense items and require coordination, planning, and control with other departments. They require the resources of other departments in getting bids, awarding contracts, and setting up training. These activities must be costed to charge the machine fully with all of its initial costs. From the financial perspective, it is helpful to indicate the amount of money spent on the equipment relative to the total cost. It is the machine that will generate the revenue, yet that machine is covering a financial cost well above its purchase price.

The completed proposal now moves up the line for review at higher levels, depending on the dollar limits within the organization.

The Revenue Side

Cost is but one element of the equation. The other, and the more difficult segment, is that of revenues or cost savings. What will the impact be of purchasing the capital equipment? This is an area of significant discomfort for many people since it involves making projections over future events and justifying those projections to typically skeptical persons who know the alternative uses for those funds and the payoffs from those investments with certainty. Here comes a risk proposal challenging a certainty of return on investment. What are the approaches and the pitfalls of each approach?

Identifying potential revenues associated with a particular machine is a difficult process, and there is no universal approach to the problem. It is somewhat easier if the piece of equipment is stand-alone and therefore capable of being measured by itself—for example, a piece of equipment in a medical practice that allows the prescribing physician to perform the test in the office as opposed to having the patient visit a laboratory. Actually there are three broad classifications that might be used:

1. *Stand-alone item of equipment* that either fully performs the function, such as the medical example, or a multistation piece of equipment that encompasses the whole process or a significant segment of it. This is the case of adding the new machine or piece of equipment where none existed before. This is the classic make-or-buy decision, with the challenger as the make option and the defender as the buy option.[2] It is in-house versus out-of-house comparisons.

2. *An integrated piece of equipment* that is replacing an existing item and may be viewed as superior with respect to speed of operation, capacity, quality of product, lower reject rate, lower scrap or waste factor, user of alternative materials, or something else. This is normally the replacement of existing capacity to improve something, such as productivity or quality. The challenger is the new equipment, and the defender is the old item. In this case, it is a comparison issue, focusing on many of the technical aspects of the equipment. The issue becomes one of translating technical considerations into revenues and the degree of validity in the translation.

3. *A piece of indirect equipment,* such as a copier or fax machine, that is non-production related and supports the operation in a general sense. The operation could proceed without it but it is a necessary convenience. Consider the impact of removing the office copier and having to print copies on the computer or desktop printer as the option. In making comparisons in this area, the seller hopes the buyer sees the need for the equipment as a given. Benchmarks become competitors' products and features, as well as service after the sale. Since there is no direct contribution to revenue generation, the best that can be expected is a cost per unit analysis, downtime reduction, and reliability analy-

2. The terms *challenger* and *defender* were made popular by the Machine and Allied Products Institute (MAPI) in its pioneering work in evaluating capital equipment. Developers of the MAPI system of capital equipment evaluation attempted to allow for comparisons of the displaced equipment and its challenger.

sis. Selling the idea of indirect equipment is very difficult; leasing can offer significant advantages. (Leasing is covered in Chapter 7.)

Revenue is the source of return on investment. What is necessary are the benchmarks to make comparisons.

Stand-Alone Equipment

In the case of the stand-alone equipment, the comparison is relatively easy. The benchmark becomes the buy option or the existing method of doing business with the supplier. Selecting the option of bringing the operation in-house and purchasing all the attendant equipment, tooling, and support for the equipment requires a side-by-side comparison of the options. It is therefore important to have some idea of the price structure of the supplier as well as the attendant costs to produce the item internally.

Case 3-I

The ABC Company is considering purchasing the necessary capital equipment to produce key molded parts for its line of vacuum cleaners. Current estimates on the number of parts are 10, which requires that ten four-cavity molds be purchased. Projected demand is 500,000 parts per year, or an average of 50,000 units of each part. The injection molding process is machine paced, has a cycle time of 30 seconds, and can be operated by one person. Changeover time is 20 minutes, and production runs are normally 10 days in duration before changeover. Shot life[3] on the molds is 200,000, and molds cost $25,000 each. They are considered a moot point, however, since the company would have to supply the molds to potential and existing suppliers now. The bid on equipment cost is $150,000. The process uses reground nylon, readily available and selling for 60 cents per pound. The average consumption per unit is ¼ pound with a 4 percent shrinkage factor. The machine service life is considered to be 10 years. The average wage rate for the operator is $10 per hour (salary and fringes). The average price being paid from the supplier is 50 cents per unit plus the amortization of the molds at 6.25 cents per unit.

Given this information, what added data would be needed for

---

3. Each injection into a mold cavity is called a shot. Shot life is the number of injections a mold can take before it must be reworked or replaced.

analysis, and what would be the approach used to evaluate this make-or-buy decision?

Analysis: The defender is 50 cents per unit with mold costs canceling each other out, regardless of the location of the mold. The identifiable cost elements are direct labor and material. Direct labor costs based on 8 units per minute, or 480 per hour, are 2 cents per unit. On the basis of 15 cents for material, even counting the 4 percent shrinkage, labor and material are 17 cents per unit. Adding normal time allowances of 17 percent for breaks, wash-up time, and fatigue, labor costs rise to 2.34 cents per unit and material is 15.045 cents per unit, giving a total direct cost of 17.385 cents per unit, or $17.39 per 100 units. With the defender's price at 50 cents per unit, the contribution to overhead is 32.61 cents per unit for the supplier. The analyst recognizes that the supplier must use the 32.61 cents to cover factory overhead, sales, and general and administrative expenses, as well as operating income and interest payments. In the make side of the analysis, the analyst quickly recognizes that the buyer's company is making a profit on the final product that contains those parts, not on the individual components going into the product. Thus, profit is deleted from the computation. The next element to consider is the selling expense. Internally manufacturing the part negates any selling expenses. The issue comes down to the degree of coverage of the overhead accounts afforded by 32.61 cents per unit on a volume of 500,000 units per year. This amounts to over $160,000 per year.

There are several different ways this dollar figure can be viewed. If the analyst is trying to portray a favorable picture, an argument can be made for paying off the cost of the capital equipment in about one year, assuming the ancillary expenses are not too great. Another view is taking the normal percentage of overhead the buying company bears and applying it against the make option and treating the residual as a potential direct contribution to paying off the equipment. Assuming the normal overhead is 30 percent of product price, these units would carry 15 cents (30 percent of 50 cents) of overhead burden. This would leave a contribution of 17.61 cents per unit to general expenses, or $88,000 per year, resulting in a payback period of approximately 20.4 months. Payoffs beyond the 20.4 months would reduce costs by 17.61 cents per unit. In theory, the profit margin on the end item would rise.

This can be viewed as a rather quick-and-dirty solution to the problem and is possible because of the definite other option to employ. In addition to a wide array of knowns in the example, there are several underlying assumptions: that the demand is sustainable for the parts at least up to the payback period, that the company is willing to produce the parts and does not mind being in that business, and that the company has the expertise and supervision and could produce the quality required. Space is available, and the addition of the injection molding machine would not disrupt the operation. The lead time is not extensive for the machine, and the installation is also feasible in a reasonable time frame. It is assumed the value of the decision is sufficient to warrant attention to the matter, amounting to some $88,000 per year beyond the payback period and contributing some $75,000 to overhead. It is doubtful that the actual overhead expenses associated with these parts would amount to that much, but the contribution is still present based on formula pricing and accounting allocation techniques. Soon the assumptions become larger than the problem, yet all are potential pitfalls for the analyst. Assuming can be an expensive hobby.

Integrated Equipment

In dealing with the case of integrating a machine into the operation where it is a contributor to the overall profitability, the process options begin to decrease. This drop is based on the inability to differentiate the value of one machine unless we are looking at a replacement for an existing piece of equipment. It is a substitution process, based on a defined set of parameters. Two approaches can be used:

1. *Cost per unit with inclusion of all relevant costs over the life cycle of the equipment.* This approach requires projections on the service life of the machine and allows for comparisons of machines with different service lives and setup costs, as well as different physical characteristics. Reduced cycle time can often nullify the higher initial cost of a machine because of higher productivity, which equates to a lower variable cost of labor. Make the demand high enough, and the productivity can quickly offset higher initial costs.

2. *Total cost comparison between options.* Total cost comparisons are tricky since the issue of service life has to be considered. The lower total cost option may appear better but does not offer unbiased comparisons. The duration of the period of need is a vital consideration. If that period is short, a lower service life is acceptable. Extend that life, and a higher initial cost may be justified based on better performance over the longer period.

In applying these two approaches and reducing the options to a single equation, a decision maker can use the incremental approach to the analysis and apply it to the following problem.

Case 3-II

Two injection molding machines are capable of making part 12345. The 700-ton machine has a 30-second cycle time, and the 450-ton machine has a 45-second cycle time. The shot life on the mold using the 700-ton machine is about the same. One operator is needed for each of the two machines, and a four-cavity mold is used on both. Using the same data from Case 3-I, consider the options available: buying the 700-ton press or continuing to use the 450-ton press.

Analysis: The gain from the 700-ton press, having a four-cavity mold and a 30-second cycle time, is 8 parts per minute. With production time at 93 percent of the production day and with allowances for breaks and fatigue, this equates to 446 production minutes, or 3,568 units per day.[4] If this machine ran for 230 days per year, it would have a capacity of 820,000 parts per year, not counting setup or mold change times. Based on a demand for 500,000 parts, the utilization rate would be 60.92 percent. The 450-ton press would produce 2,377 units per day, or 546,750 units per year. Again based on a demand of 500,000 per year, machine utilization would be 91.44 percent.

Clearly the productivity of the larger molding machine in terms of cycle time reduction is an attribute that the lighter-pressure machine is incapable of achieving. It is a technological advantage. Now the question becomes, Is that technological advantage going to be used? If it is impossible to find some use for the unused 30 percent utilization (allowing some time for maintenance and setup), the extra speed of the heavier press has no offsetting advantage. Looking at cycle time, the argument can be made for an output of 8 units per minute versus 5.33 per minute. Clearly the heavier press has the advantage.

To view the problem in another way, the heavier press has 50 percent greater capacity. Is the incremental cost of the 700-ton press with its spare parts greater or lesser than the 450-ton press? If the total cost difference between the two presses is less than 50 percent and something can be found to fill in the 30 percent time, the 700-ton press would be a better purchase. Exhibit 3-1 makes

Exhibit 3-1. Comparison of two presses assuming a 500,000-unit demand.

Attribute	700-Ton Press	450-Ton Press
Utilization rate	61	91
Capacity per year	820,640	546,750
Labor cost per hour	$10	$10
Maintenance cost per year	$1,200	$1,500
Mold cost per unit	Equal for both	Equal for both

a side-by-side comparison of the options. Clearly neither option will be a clear winner, not an unusual situation. The better choice is not simply a single-factor decision. Being superior depends on cost, utilization, and speed of operation.

---

4. The 34 minutes allow for two 12-minute breaks during the shift and 10 minutes wash-up time. It is a machine-paced operation with little worker fatigue associated with it and lightweight parts to remove on completion of the cycle time. It is also a low-skill-level job.

The analyst looks at the effective cost of each of the options in the exhibit. In the case of the 700-ton press, the cost would be 6 cents per unit less for maintenance, or 2.4 cents per unit, whereas the 450-ton press is 3 cents per unit based on a 500,000-per-year unit output. Since labor, material, and maintenance costs are nearly the same, the issue comes down to overhead analysis. At $60 per hour machine overhead, the 700-ton press is bearing a cost of 12.5 cents per unit. At $45 per hour, the 450-ton press is bearing a cost of 14.1 cents per unit. This means the 450-ton press has a cost of 2.2 cents more per unit when considering overhead and maintenance. To be fair, the utilization rate must be considered. Adjusting for the utilization factor by multiplying the overhead by (100 per utilization rate) gives the following results:

$$\text{700-ton press} = 12.5¢ \times \frac{100}{60.1} = 20.8¢ \text{ per unit}$$

$$\text{450-ton press} = 14.1¢ \times \frac{100}{91.0} = 15.5¢ \text{ per unit}$$

The picture has now changed with the adjustment for utilization. Which is the correct answer? In fact, there are several correct answers, depending on what is to be included in the computations, so the decision maker begins to fall back on some of the qualitative aspects of the decision. Does the company want the extra capacity? Is the demand for the part sufficient to see a future need for the heavier press? Can other products be produced on the 700-ton press that are more costly on the 450-ton press or impossible on it? The list can be endless. The issue is to make the comparisons as valid as possible before entering into the qualitative dimensions.

The effective total cost per unit would be developed from the following factors:

Initial price per unit (*IP*):	Offering price/(service life × capacity)
Maintenance per unit (*M*):	Maintenance cost/(service life × capacity[units per year])
Salvage value (*SV*):	Salvage value/(service life × capacity)
Variable costs (*VC*):	Variable costs (direct labor, materials, and overhead)/unit
Ancillary costs (*AC*):	Mold costs/(service life × capacity)
Utilization factor (*UF*):	100/utilization rate

The final element in the equation is the utilization factor. The greater the rate of utilization, the less effect this factor has on the answer. It is the "penalty" levied on having a press that has the technological capability but is never used. If the 450-ton press is operating at better than 90 percent of its capacity and the 700-ton press is at 61 percent of its capacity, the reduced cycle time of the heavier press has no real advantage. *It is technology without an economic purpose.* The 700-ton press should be penalized for having the capability but not having to use it. It is the analog of the clerical employees' using Pentium chip PCs to perform word processing when "obsolete" 386s would do quite well in their place.

The effective total cost thus becomes:

$$\text{Effective total cost} = IP^*(UF) + M - SV + (VC \times \text{units}) + AC$$

Adding the overhead (effective) and maintenance costs, the 700-ton press, at .1739 cent per unit for labor and material, gives a total cost of $0.406 per unit, still less than the outside supplier. The 450-ton press will cost $0.363 per unit. As production increases, the overhead on the 700-ton press can fall to $0.137 per unit at 91 percent utilization, or a total cost of $0.335 per unit. Both options are better than outside sourcing. The per unit cost can be converted to total cost over the service life of the press by multiplying the unit cost by the service life times the annual capacity.

In the analysis, the key variable is the utilization rate. It forces the analyst to penalize excess capacity and focus attention on buying the right press for the right job. The factor is obviously based on the demand for the products. Should that demand go above the 546,000 level, the 450-ton press is no longer a viable option. Then the choices become the 700-ton press or two 450-ton presses. Why select two presses? There would be less likelihood of maintenance downtime, a catastrophic failure would have less impact, and if demand fell below 500,000, one machine could be declared excess and eventually surplus.

The key issue is capacity and its availability. The lack of that capacity can have a negative impact on the production process and the output of the operation. It is essential to make the best and most informed decision, bringing in as many quantifiable elements as possible and penalizing for buying unneeded capacity as well as disqualifying unavailable capacity.

Ancillary Support Equipment

Ancillary support equipment may be needed for anything from copying to material transportation; it may be copiers, word processors, forklift trucks, or company cars. Although not strictly needed for the core business of the organization, it may be needed to support production or manufacturing.

Let us say that the case for need has been made, and now what occurs is the side-by-side comparison of the options available, the cost per unit, the downtime factor, the maintenance element, and the capacity. The best example is the office copier. There are many models available, and each assembler and manufacturer have built-in features that make their models attractive to the end user. The primary difference between models is the volume of copying that each machine can handle in a given period of time. What is the capacity? Armed with these data, companies invariably purchase the model that is *below* their need level to save money. As a result, the copier is often down for failure maintenance, with the most familiar figure in the office being the repair person sent by the copier supplier.

Why is this wrong decision made? The reason is that too much attention is focused on the initial cost or the monthly lease payment, and little attention is given to the downtime issue: the time consumed waiting for copies to be produced and the attendant loss of productivity in using this machine-paced capacity. (Go to a printing service facility, and see the equipment designed to stand heavy and continuous use.)

The analysis for buying a copier should look at these factors:

- Initial cost
- Rate of utilization
- Downtime analysis
- Maintenance costs
- Availability and costs of supplies

A simple technique is to allow the potential users to test the equipment before buying. (This can be effective too in the stand-alone type of equipment.) Another approach can be that of standardization.

A major midwestern city is considering standardizing its forklift trucks. Standardization will reduce inventories of spare parts, allow for purchasing leverage, and decrease training costs for maintenance personnel. The program runs into trouble because the Water Department balks, saying its use of forklifts differs from that of other departments in the city. The Water Department trucks carry different loads and different shapes and must have greater capability. The city has the following options: (1) pursue the program and tell the Water Department to adapt; (2) scrap the standardization program and let each department buy its own needs; or (3) overbuy (buy the top-of-the-line equipment, standardize, and allow the excess capability to be present but rarely used).

Analysis: There is no simple answer to the question without data to see which is the best possible alternative. In some cases, it is better to have the excess capacity and still have the capability to standardize. The issue is perspective. Look at the life cycle, the total cost, each cost element, and the capacity, with an eye to the chances or likelihood of needing that capacity. Balance the need to the options. *Do not simply buy on price.* It is far from the only key variable in the decision equation.

The three examples show the need to capture all the relevant information that may be useful in the decision process. They show that both quantitative and qualitative factors enter the decision process, that it is possible to reduce the bias in the process, and that the people putting together the information have different perspectives. Where direct labor utilization is very important in the press example, analysts often overlook the time spent by clerical employees' feeding paper into the copier. Yet direct labor in manufacturing today is a small part of the overall product cost. Machine utilization was a key factor for the press and a nonstarter for the forklift.

There is no one answer. The secret is being comprehensive and unbiased. A common set of measures ensures that each option or alternative will be appraised with the same yardstick. This is important as we turn to the financial evaluation methods commonly used.

Standard Financial Tools

In the analysis of the financial dimensions of the decision, the financial analyst has a variety of techniques to employ. Each has strengths and weaknesses; the common denominator is the data employed in the analysis. If the information is faulty, fragmented, or just plain wrong, all the analysis in the world is not going to lead to the best decision. Models act only on the data supplied.

A second consideration is the uniformity of data in the organization. As companies grow, systems begin to emerge that are add-ons to the traditional corporatewide accounting, inventory, and financial systems. This growth of nonuniformity has been aided by the rapid growth of the desktop computer and the user friendliness of programs such as spreadsheets and statistical and financial packages. Add to this the growth of multidivisional units in larger companies, and the proliferation is geometric. The result is different programs on different systems incapable of communicating with each other. In this situation, data must be reformatted or even reentered, exacerbating the problem of communication.

There are efforts underway in many companies to solve this problem and integrate all the information under one system. (The industry leader in this effort is SAP AG in Germany.) Operating from the same database is laudable but expensive. Conversion to the common denominator runs into millions of dollars.

Financial evaluation tools use a limited amount of information, as seen in the exploration of the payback period, the return on investment (ROI) based on either cash flow or earnings before taxes, discounted cash flow, and qualitative or nontraditional models.

Payback Period

Perhaps the simplest of all of the financial models, the payback period's name tells its story. How long does it take to recoup the initial investment in the equipment? How long is the payback period? Simple payback analysis looks at a revenue stream and the initial cost of the equipment and computes the period of time necessary to pay for the equipment fully. It is simple to the point of being naive, yet it is widely used in both analysis and selling the equipment. Its popularity stems from the inability to make long-range revenue forecasts or savings projections or the lack of confidence in these projections.

Exhibit 3-2 compares two possible investments. A glance at the data shows that Investment 1 has a payback period of three years. In that time, the net revenues are sufficient to recoup the initial investment. Investment 2 takes an additional year to bring in the $100,000 in net revenues. From the payback perspective, Investment 1 is superior. Yet the technique has shortcomings: It ignores payoffs or returns beyond the payback period, and it does not address the time value of money.

Other assumptions too have been made in this example—zero salvage value of the investment and no definition of net revenues—but these can be adjusted. The principal shortcoming is the bias that results from looking only at the time required to pay off the investment. This method will tend to favor investments that generate high returns in the early years, and payoffs or revenues in the years beyond the payback period will be ignored. Quick return of capital is the orientation.

Not considering the time value of money is another shortcoming. The $25,000 return coming five years from now is certainly not worth $25,000 today. Even the most simplistic understanding of inflation renders that assumption untenable. By any reasonable measure, there must be some adjustment for inflation, the time value of money, foregone opportunities, or an understanding

Exhibit 3-2. Summary data for two investments.

	Investment 1	Investment 2
Initial cost	$100,000	$100,000
Net revenue		
Year 1	35,000	25,000
Year 2	30,000	25,000
Year 3	30,000	25,000
Year 4	15,000	25,000
Year 5	10,000	25,000
Year 6	0	25,000

that the nickel candy bar is a vague and distant memory in the minds of the middle-aged.

Issues With the Payback Period

So if it lacks sophistication, why is the payback period method used? The answer is twofold. First, it is a simple method of computation, easily understood and communicated. Second, for companies that are short on cash or suffer a liquidity problem, the payback analysis provides the fastest possible return of the cash outlay. From their perspective, there may be only short-run considerations and *no* long run on the horizon. Often the statement is made, "It will pay for itself in *X* months," with the expectation that rapid repayment will be the decision criterion. Repaying itself or generating revenue by cost savings implies that the investment is better than what is being used now. Either the investment generates revenue, or it is an improvement over the existing method. The point is that there must be a basis of comparison. The ATM is superior to the bank teller in speed of operation and information provided. Putting in an ATM without knowing the cost of the same transaction in a manual mode would allow no method for computing the savings. The yardstick must be present to measure one option versus the other.

Another approach with the payback period is the use of a policy that all investments must pay for themselves in a finite lifetime—say, five years. Any investment that will not recoup its initial cost in that period will not be considered. Thus, payback period offers a way to limit the risk by setting a cutoff date for the investment to pay for itself.

Another important issue is when the payback begins. All projects do not begin on the first day of the year. A project that begins paying off on July 1, six months into the fiscal year, and returns $1,000 for the first six months of the project life would be half of that year. If the total project cost is $7,000 and in the second **calendar** or **fiscal year** of the project, the return was $2,000 per year, the payback period would be 3.5 years. Returns during the first year of the project must be adjusted to reflect the period of time covered by that return. Assuming that first year of the project is a full year will lead to an inaccurate payback period.

Evaluating at the Margin

If it is clear the equipment will not meet the desired criteria, the decision is easy. Where the difficulty arises is at the margin (this is true of any investment decision, of course). When the payback period desired is 3 years and the calculations show it will pay back in 3.1 years, the decision maker is sitting on the horns of the dilemma. Is 3 years an inviolate time period? Have the revenues been understated? What happens if the volume of usage increases significantly? All of these factors begin to weigh on the decision. What is the answer?

One approach is to consider the financial analysis as only one part of the decision. It may carry substantial weight in the ultimate decision, but other issues, such as quality, productivity, product appearance, and cost, play a part too. Therefore, the decision is a weighted average of all of the factors that come into play, as in the following example.

A physician is considering purchasing a blood analyzer for her office. The equipment has an initial cost, an operating cost, periodic maintenance and calibration checks, and a residual value dictated largely by the rate of technological advancement in the industry. In computing the payback period, the physician would have to determine the fixed costs present in the investment itself, the fixed cost per year of ownership, the variable costs per treatment, the number of treatments per year, and the price charged for each treatment.[5] There are several approaches to solving this problem; we look at the payback period here.

Analysis: The basic data for the problem are as follows:

Blood analyzer initial cost:	$50,000.00
Supplies per 100 tests:	$1,000.00
Annual maintenance and calibration cost:	$1,000.00
Variable costs	
Taking blood sample:	$3.00
Run time:	$0.25
Review time of results:	$6.00

The results show a variable cost of $9.25 per run. The physician estimates that 300 analyses will be run each year. Allocating the fixed costs of supplies, maintenance, and calibration against those patients would be $3,000 for supplies and $1,000 for maintenance and calibration, or $13.33 per patient. Total cost per patient would be $22.57. Assuming the standard charge that third-party payers would allow for this test is $60, the payback period would be computed as follows:

---

5. This problem is used for a specific purpose. The blood analyzer is as important to the physician as the socket machine to the manufacturing company. Each "industry" has its own capital investments, and the tools are applicable regardless of the industry selected.

Gross revenue per year: 300 × $60   = $18,000
Operating costs   300 × $22.57 = $ 6,771
Contribution to payback $11,229

Payback period = $50,000/11,229 = 4.5 years[6]

The issue now becomes how satisfactory that payback period is. If the physician is satisfied with that period of time, purchasing the machine would be a good decision. Yet it is a physical asset in the practice and subject to depreciation. It will not be worth its original value in five years. Thus, the physician must look at what the depreciation of the asset will do to his/her **cash flow** in the practice. Depreciation can be viewed as the **return of capital** to the organization. If the allowed period for depreciating the equipment is five years, then $10,000 ($50,000/5) can be added to the cash flow of the practice. This would have the impact of lowering the practice's tax liability by allowing funds to be set aside to replace aging assets.

The physician must consider other factors as well—for example:

- The period of planned ownership, that is, the true service life of the equipment
- The revenues generated beyond the payback period, or $11,229 per year after the analyzer has been paid for by treatments
- The ability to perform the analysis in the office, thereby saving patients a trip to a hospital or laboratory to have the same test performed
- The ability to shift some of the costs of operation to the analyzer that might be office overhead
- The prestige factor of having the technology in the practice
- The ability to get rapid results in certain critical patient situations

These and other similar factors would be important if the physician felt that four years was as long as she was willing to go for a payback of the original investment. At the margin or when the decision is a close one, as in this case, the analyst must engage in some what-if analysis. Revenue estimates are just that: estimates. Each additional analysis adds $40.75 to the net revenue stream. Recognize that the $1,000 for maintenance and calibration has been allocated over the initial 300 analyses, or $3.33 per patient. Add back the $3.33 to the revenue less costs $60.00 − 22.58 or an **incremental** or **marginal contribution** of $40.75 per analysis.

Carrying the example further, consider what the data tell the analyst as additional patients have the analysis performed and the relationship between increasing numbers of analyses and the payback period. The numbers, set out

---

6. This example assumes the residual value of the machine is zero and the machine arrives and is in service the first of the fiscal year for the physician.

Exhibit 3-3. Blood analyses and the payback period.

Treatments per Year	Net Revenues	Payback Period (years)
300	$11,229	4.45
310	11,638	4.29
320	12,046	4.15
330	12,455	4.01
340	12,863	3.87

in Exhibit 3-3, show that each analysis above the 300 level will reduce the payback period by approximately five days. This type of analysis, which can be done on any spreadsheet, points out the sensitivity of the payback period to the addition of analyses.

The example was a piece of medical equipment; the substitution of the word *sales* could have easily been substituted since each analysis is the sale of a service. It is the blood analyzer for the physician, the ATM for the bank, and the milling machine for the job shop. All contribute to the profitability of their respective operation and can benefit from the same tools.

Return on Investment

Always considered a popular tool of analysis because of its simplicity and its capability of coming up with a single number, ROI (return on investment) offers an opportunity to make two types of comparisons: ROI based on cash flow and ROI based on earnings before taxes (EBT). The difference between the two approaches is based upon how depreciation is treated. ROI based on EBT looks at the savings in variable or operating costs associated with the new machine over the old one and computes the return on that investment. To illustrate the two methods and the different answers, consider the data from the payback period problem using the second investment with its uniform revenue or operating savings of $25,000 for a 10-year period. (Note that this is extending the operating savings to match the depreciation schedule.) Assuming a 10-year service life using a straight line depreciation of $10,000 per year and zero residual or salvage value, the cash flows would be the sum of the earnings before taxes, or $250,000 plus the depreciation, or $100,000, for a total of $350,000 in 10 years or an average of $35,000 per year. This value is divided by the initial investment of $100,000, giving a value of 35 percent as the ROI on a cash flow basis.

To compute the ROI on an EBT basis, the depreciation is removed from the operating savings, giving a value of $15,000 per year over 10 years, or a total of $150,000. This value is divided by the average investment over the 10-year period. Note that doing ROI on an EBT basis requires looking at the fact that the investment is changing every year. The investment at the beginning of the first year is $100,000; however, $10,000 of depreciation is considered a return of capital, so the *average* investment during that year is $95,000. In the second year, the *average* investment would be $85,000 since the start of the second year saw a value of $90,000 at the beginning of the year and an ending investment of $80,000, allowing for the $10,000 depreciation, or an average value of $85,000. Each year the average investment declines as depreciation reduces the size of the investment. Thus, the ROI on an EBT basis will change every year. It will increase since the size of the investment diminishes yearly as a function of depreciation. A quick-and-dirty method in this example is computing the average investment as half of the original investment of $100,000. The average saving in operating cost less depreciation is then divided by the $50,000 ($100,000/2). This calculation is $15,000 ÷ $50,000, or 33.3 percent.

Note that we have made some simplifying assumptions in the discussion of this technique that would not be present in a real problem. We assumed the investment was made in a single year, giving rise to a capital expenditure of $100,000 in that single year. If this is the case, depreciation can begin in that year, but if the equipment was partially paid for in one year and the remainder paid in a second year, the cash flow would be different. We will illustrate this later in the chapter when we view a single problem using several different methods.

Discounted Cash Flow

Moving to overcome the inadequacies of the payback period and ROI, the financial analysis now considers the issues of the time value of money, the salvage value of the equipment, and the initial cost of the equipment, specifically its components and what costs are sunk costs and what are investments.

In looking at discounted cash flow, two widely accepted models are available: **net present value** and **internal rate of return.**

Net Present Value

The net present value (NPV) approach calculates the discounted value of the revenue stream plus the salvage value less the initial cost of the equipment:

$$\text{NPV} = -C_o + \Sigma \frac{R_n}{(1 + i)^n} + S_n$$

where C_o = initial cost of the equipment
R_n = revenue in the nth year
i = discount rate
S_n = salvage value in year n or the end of the service life

The computations represent the simplest portions of the analysis. Filling in the blanks with the correct data is the key factor.

This tool is complex due to the length of the service life of the equipment and the revenue stream projection. It is made doubly difficult in many cases due to the integrated nature of the equipment on a production line, and pulling out one machine and crediting it with the revenues of work in process is stretching the point to a degree. Nevertheless, it is a tool that can be used.[7]

We will explain the concept of present value in its financial sense and then explore the validity of the data going into the variables. Among the numerous issues to explore is the concept of present value, which means bringing future revenues back to present value by discounting. The term **discounting** is used to illustrate that $1 received some time in the future is worth less than that same $1 received today, for two reasons:

1. The dollar received today and invested at 6 percent will be worth $1.06 in one year. By getting the dollar not today but a year from now, the individual forgoes the opportunity to invest that dollar for the year. Dollars received in the future are worth less than dollars received today.

2. A more pedestrian approach is to look at inflation as the cause. A dollar today will buy more than a dollar received a year from now due to inflation or a general rise in prices over time. The future dollar is worth less than a current dollar. From a pragmatic perspective, the business executive investing in capital equipment today using borrowed funds finds inflation a friend. It is a case of borrowing valuable dollars today and paying back cheap dollars tomorrow.

Because no one can forecast inflation with accuracy, the financial analyst will use the investment approach. If the same dollar were received two years from now, it would be worth even less because the investor would have invested the $1 for a year at 6 percent and in the beginning of the second year invested $1.06 for the one year. The effect of compounding is now beginning to be seen. Thus, to find the value of the dollar received one year from now, with a discount rate (i) of 6 percent, that dollar would be discounted (reduced in value) according to the following equation:

$$\text{Present value (PV)} = \frac{\$1.00}{1 + i}$$

$$= \frac{1.00}{1.06}$$

$$= \$0.943$$

7. For a basic discussion of the tools, see D. Johnson and R. Oppedahl, "Present Value and Internal Rate of Return: A Review and Comparison," *South Dakota Business Review* (September 1995): 1, 7–11.

The dollar received a year from now is thus worth only 94 cents. If the dollar were received two years from now, the equation would be:

$$PV = \frac{\$1.00}{(1 + i)^2}$$

resulting in a value of 88.99 cents. The further out in time the discounting process goes, the less the value of the dollar. This is one of the reasons that banks charge interest to borrow money. Raising the denominator of the equation to the second power allows the analyst to consider the compounding effect. To remove the cumbersome calculations, there are both tables (see Appendix D [P.V. tables]) and numerous computer programs available with every spreadsheet to take the drudgery out of the computational process.

The other elements of the equation are also tricky. C_o represents the original cost of the capital equipment investment. Defining this element with a high degree of accuracy may not be difficult, but the elements that make up the total cost of that equipment may have many factors that are related to the equipment but not part of it. For example, the purchase of a CNC socket machine requires the following cost elements that were paid for to get the equipment into a ready status:

• Transportation from supplier to user
• Space allocation and installation costs
• Test runs at the supplier and on site
• Operator training
• Maintenance training
• Cost of buying the equipment (transaction expenses)
• Disposal of the old equipment

How many of these costs are equipment related, and therefore part of the equipment purchase, and what are operating expenses? Are there any new or extraordinary expenses that occur that directly relate to the equipment such as trips or meetings?

A good rule of thumb is to allocate an extra 10 to 20 percent for the cost of the machine to cover these contingencies, which are real costs and have to be covered somewhere. It is easier to return unused funds from a budget than to find funds that are needed but not budgeted.

One approach is to consider the cost of the equipment as delivered, installed, accepted, and retention paid as the full criteria for ownership. (The issue of retention will be covered in Chapter 11.) Retention refers to a sum of monies, part of the original price, paid only when the equipment meets its acceptance criteria, and title passes from seller to buyer. The purpose of retention, used extensively in the construction industry, is to maintain some leverage over the supplier to fulfill supplier commitments, and ensure the proper installation and performance of the equipment. The issue is the consistency of methodology used. To make valid comparisons, all candidates must be treated the same, and the same cost elements must be included in the analysis to avoid bias in the results. It is not uncommon for some cost element to be excluded from the computations to make the project appear more attractive. Remember, though, that capital projects drive operating budgets, and the total cost of ownership should be the relevant value for the decision process.

The salvage value also presents forecasting problems. What will be the value *n* years from now? Any value put on this variable is merely a guess in most cases. Cases abound where the salvage values have been negatives, meaning it *cost* the company money to dispose of the equipment at replacement time. In some instances, the salvage value equated to what a metal scavenger was able to take out of the machine. The first Cray computer, which originally sold for millions of dollars, sold for $10,000 based on projections of the recoverable gold in the machine. And there are also opposite cases on record, where the salvage value of the equipment turned out to be more than the original cost of the machine. The company actually purchased the machine, used it for 10 years, and sold it for more than it had paid for it. How was this accomplished? Simply by maintaining it well, documenting the maintenance, and using it for what it was designed to do. One does not have to go any further than the automobile that is garaged and well maintained by the owner. At trade-in time, that effort is rewarded.

To overcome the difficulty of trying to predict, a simplifying assumption would be to place a salvage value of 0 or $1 on the equipment. This would accomplish two tasks. It would allow for customization of the equipment without financial concern of some event that may take place 10, 20, or 30 years from now. And it would place all the candidates on the same basis and emphasize the need for the equipment as part of the company's manufacturing strategy now, not as a seller of used equipment in the future. The accounting for profits from the disposal of the equipment is not a difficult matter, and disposal can be carried out in a variety of ways.

The most difficult estimate is the revenue stream into the future because there are all sorts of possible traps the analyst can fall into. There are many arbitrary decisions that must be made as to placing valid numbers on the revenue estimates. For the physician cited earlier in the chapter, the process would not be overly difficult knowing the number of patients needing the analysis, the charges allowed by medical insurance, the operating costs of the equipment, and the capacity of the equipment. Those factors would allow for accurate revenue estimation. Contrast this with the milling machine or punch press or forklift truck that is not a production item but simply a service piece of equipment. Its revenue estimates are just that: estimates. Each case is different. If the revenue estimates are difficult or, worse, spurious in nature, then the present value technique may not be usable.

The important consideration is the validity of the data being used. Do not torture the data to make them conform to the model being used.

Perhaps the most controversial aspect of the equation is the discount rate. At what level should this be set? Some argue that the appropriate rate is the weighted cost of capital for the corporation; others look to the opportunity cost of capital or the return that could have been made by investing the funds in another revenue-producing asset. The theoretical aspects can be avoided by using an appropriate corporate discount rate. This is an individual organizational decision. If discounting is used, the value for the discount rate is a corporate decision.

Internal Rate of Return

In contrast, the internal rate of return uses the same equation but moves the initial cost to the left-hand side of the equation:

$$C_o = \sum \frac{R_n}{(1 + n)^n} + S_n$$

Instead of being given a discount rate, the analyst solves for the discount rate that will equate the original cost with the discounted revenue stream and the salvage value. What is the lowest rate that balances the revenues and the costs? If that rate is as large as the corporate discount rate or greater, the investment is viewed as favorable in the financial sense. Solving this equation for any value involving more than three periods is best left to the computer, since it involves polynomials in the equation.

To illustrate the use of both methods, consider the problem with the two investments as seen below.

Assuming a 10 percent discounting rate, zero salvage value for the equipment, and the revenues represent a full year of operation, the resulting revenue streams are shown in Exhibit 3-4.[8]

Using spreadsheet approximation equations, the IRR (internal rate of return) is computed. Investment B has a significantly higher value. Its difference can be traced to the length of the revenue stream and the total return from it compared with Investment A.

In looking at the same set of investments using the discounting process, the answers are different from the payback period analysis, which directed selection of the first investment due to its shorter period to recoup the initial investment. The difference in results, however, does not negate one technique

---

8. The revenues flowing in payback analysis go to cover the investment. If the revenues cited in year 1 represent only six months operation, the payback period is shortened by six months. If periods of operation are unequal, this must be considered as the payback period is calculated.

Exhibit 3-4. Returns and discounted revenues of two investments (each having an initial investment of $100,000).

Year	Revenue From Investment A	Discounted Revenue for A	Revenue From Investment B	Discounted Revenue B
Year 1	$ 35,000	$31,818	$ 25,000	$ 22,727
Year 2	30,000	24,793	25,000	20,661
Year 3	30,000	22,539	25,000	18,783
Year 4	15,000	10,245	25,000	17,075
Year 5	10,000	6,209	25,000	15,523
Year 6	0	0	25,000	14,111
Total	$120,000	$95,605	$150,000	$108,881
Internal rate of return	7.90%		12.98%	

in favor of another. The use of one technique as opposed to the other depends on these factors:

- The type of investment (replacement equipment versus expansion of the existing product line versus new product production)[9]
- The size of the company and its investment posture
- The resources devoted to the analysis

One study points to the increasing popularity of discounted cash flow techniques coupled with a significant rise in nonfinancial techniques in evaluating competing projects. These techniques include strategy considerations on the project itself, flexibility afforded by the equipment, future potential, as well as response to competition, even if the competition is oneself in the market.[10] Companies often compete with themselves by offering a number of products that perform the same function and have very little difference among the offerings. Product proliferation is one way to increase market share. For example, overdrives for computers being sold by Intel Corporation are do-it-yourself upgrade kits for both 486 systems and Pentiums up to Pentium 100s. The purpose of the overdrive unit is to replace the existing chip with a faster processor unit. The Pentium 90 can be souped up to a Pentium 150 for slightly over $300. Thus, a perfectly good desktop does not have to be replaced; it can be modified instead. This is a new market niche and was probably driven by the sheer size of the potential market coupled with the low cost compared to full replacement of the desktop. The profitability is obvious; the manufacturer's suggested retail price is $379, and discounters sell the upgrade of the Pentium 90 for $318; the names of the distributors are supplied by Intel on the Internet. No doubt, a

9. See S. Chen, "An Empirical Examination of Capital Budgeting Techniques: Impact of Investment Types and Firm Characteristics," *Engineering Economist* 40, no. 2 (winter 1995): 145–170.
10. Ibid., pp. 163–164.

significant portion of the capital investment decision was driven by the market potential of the end product.

Nontraditional Analysis

Nontraditional or nonfinancial techniques will move the analysis into subjective model building and focus attention on such areas as the multifactor evaluation process and analytic hierarchy process.

> **Multifactor evaluation process** (MFEP). A multifactor decision-making approach where the factor weights and factor evaluations may be accurately determined and used in the decision process.

The factors that will be considered are listed according to their importance in the overall decision. Then a weight is assigned to each factor such that the sum of the weights equals 1.00. Each candidate is evaluated on how well it meets the needs of the company purchasing the machine. Let us say that a company is looking for quality of output, low maintenance cost, and minimum downtime. Quality is paramount, and is rated at 0.7, with maintenance cost at 0.2 and downtime at 0.1. It considers three machines—models A, B, and C. The results of the analysis are shown in Exhibit 3-5.

Exhibit 3-5. Results table for multifactor evaluation process.

Factor	Weight	Machine A	A Score	Machine B	B Score	Machine C	C Score
Quality	0.7	0.9	0.63	0.8	0.56	0.9	0.63
Maintenance	0.2	.8	.16	.9	.14	.5	.1
Downtime	0.1	.7	.07	.9	.06	.5	.05
Totals	1.00		0.86		0.76		0.78

Using this approach, machine A is superior to the other two options. This is a very simplistic example used only to illustrate the concept of quantification of subjective estimates. It is a simple scoring and weighting device that ensures consistent comparisons.

> **Analytic hierarchy process** (AHP). A process that uses pairwise comparisons to determine factor evaluations and factor weights in a multifactor decision environment.[11]

---

11. The source of both definitions is B. Render and R. Stair, Jr., *Quantitative Analysis for Management*, 6th ed. (Englewood Cliffs, NJ: Prentice Hall, 1996), pp. 559–571. Also note the availability of software for solution to AHP problem.

AHP is recommended to determine the consistency of the answers provided by the decision maker. For example, comparing three possible machine models on the quality dimension calls for a 3 × 3 matrix. Each factor generates a matrix, with the size of the matrix determined by the number of options (e.g., four machines would generate a 4 × 4 matrix).

The matrix in Exhibit 3-6 shows preference between pairs of options. Consider the factor of interest to be quality of output. A rating of 1 indicates identical preference between the options. At the other end of the scale is a rating of 9, showing very strong preference between a pair of options. The higher the numerical value, the less that option is preferred. The value of 8 in the machine 1–machine 3 cell shows that machine 1 is very strongly preferred to machine 3. Machine 3 would have to show vast improvement in its quality of output before being considered a close quality competitor to machine 1. The first row compares machine 1 to 2 and 3, and the second row compares machine 2 to machine 3. If machine 1 is strongly preferred to machine 3, then the comparison of machine 3 to machine 1 would have to be the reciprocal value, that is, machine 3 valued against machine 1 is only 1/8. The process continues to look at all other variables and develops a measure of the consistency of the decision maker's choice pattern as well as the relative importance of each factor on the basis of paired comparisons.[12] In this example, machine 1 is the choice. This approach, which is not financial, allows for consideration of variables that are not totally quantitative.

Exhibit 3-6. Analytical hierarchy process matrix for three machines.

Quality of Output	Machine 1	Machine 2	Machine 3
Machine 1	1	5	8
Machine 2	1/5	1	2
Machine 3	1/8	1/2	1

Risk analysis is a somewhat different issue. There are numerous ways to approach this area. We discuss only one for illustrative purposes; the model used is derived from a risk model developed for one of the major engineering companies in this country. The idea was simple: The higher the project risk, the higher the level of approval needed to take on the project. Low-risk projects could be approved at lower levels since the likelihood of failure and the resulting losses were small. Higher risk meant potentially larger losses that could be disastrous for the company, so top-level executive review is imperative.

As the integrity of the data come under question, the issue of risk arises. How risky is the project? Is there any way of measuring the relative risk of the investment based on the confidence of the quality or validity of the information provided, as well as the perception of the investment risk itself? The decision

12. For a complete discussion of the technique, see T. Saaty, "How to Make a Decision: the Analytic Hierarchy Process," *Interfaces* 24 (November–December 1994): 19.

maker has a perception of risk or benchmarks against which to measure relative risk.

Say that a company has $1 million available for capital investment. It can invest the money in short-term government securities paying 5.75 percent interest annually for a period of two years. The return will be $50,750 for each year, assuming the first-year interest is not reinvested. The risk level is very low for a variety of reasons, so the financial officer assesses the risk as 1 on a scale of 10. The value of 1 is a qualitative assessment based on the analyst's general knowledge and information. The second element is the quality of information going into that assessment or the probability that the information is totally correct. On the option of investing in the government bonds, the validity of the information is very high, and therefore the probability of getting valid or correct information is 0.99999, or 1.

Analysis: The risk equation is:

$$\text{Risk factor} = \text{Project risk}^{2-b}$$

where b = the probability of the information being correct.

Consider the bond investment. Because of the low risk associated with it, the analyst gives it a value of 1 on a 1 to 10 scale. The information on the bond (e.g., yield, date of maturity, payment date) is all accurate, thus giving the probability of accuracy a value of 1.0. Putting this into the equation yields:

$$\text{Risk factor} = 2^{(2-1)}$$

$$= 2$$

This is a low-risk project.

Consider the case of investing in an experimental machine where the data associated with the machine are judged to be correct but not corroborated or the information relies on best estimates. The risk is high at 10, and the probability of accuracy is 0.6. Now the formulation is:

$$\text{Risk factor} = 10^{(2-0.6)}$$

$$= 10^{1.4}, \text{ or } 25.119$$

The risk level as compared to the preceding choice is roughly 12 times greater.

The growth of risk in the decision is not a linear function. Risk grows exponentially and must be treated as such. Exponential growth is quite common. The steel industry found that cleaning up pollution was relatively easy for the first 80 percent of the pollutants, but the final 20 percent drove costs up exponentially. The borrowing company finds each increment of debt somewhat more expensive than its predecessor, and when it becomes too high, the cost of debt capital grows exponentially. Exponential risk growth is also common.

Other nontraditional approaches can include focusing on several quantitative dimensions of the machine's output. This could include quality as measured by the C_p, or process capability index. A driving force within a company may be consistently producing a quality output. One way of doing that is using the highest-quality machine to perform the job. The **process capability index** is one measure that is used to determine the likelihood of defective products coming off the machine. The index is defined by the following equation:

$$C_p = \frac{\text{Upper specification limit} - \text{Lower specification limit}}{6\sigma}$$

The minimum acceptable level for C_p is 1.00. The upper specification limit minus the lower specification limit would be the tolerance range or the sum of the print tolerances. If C_p were equal to 1, then, algebraically, the sum of the print tolerances would equal six sigma or six standard deviations ($\pm 3\ \sigma$). Assuming the normal distribution for process output, the expected output that would be defective due to random variation is 0.3 percent. Going $\pm 3\sigma$ (standard deviations) from the mean or average value would encompass 99.7 percent of the output. We can expect only 3 units of 1,000 produced to be defective due to random or unassignable causes with a process capability index of 1.00.

Increase the C_p value to 1.5 and the range of the print tolerance would increase to 9σ or 9 standard deviations.[13] As the number of standard deviations increases, a larger and larger portion of the output should fall inside the distribution or "under the normal curve." This means the likelihood of a random defect decreases. In this case the probable likelihood of a random defect falls to 1 in 100,000.

Another way of measuring the process capability is by use of the equation:

$$C_{pk} = \frac{\overline{X} - \text{lower specification limit}}{3\sigma}$$

13. If $C_p = 1.5$, then print tolerances must equal 9 standard deviations, since $C_p = \text{PT}/6\sigma$. If $C_p = 1.5$ then P.T. $= 1.5\ (6\delta)$ or 9.06 (standard deviations).

or

$$C_{pk} = \frac{\text{upper specification limit} - \overline{X}}{3\sigma}$$

This equation allows for comparison of specification tolerance with inherent process variation by looking at the relationship between the tolerance and the process average. Again, the value for C_{pk} must be greater than 1. Is there more than one C_{pk} value? Yes. There will be a value for process capability associated with every critical characteristic in the product, and Lucas and Plinkington suggest that using this approach assists in having clear acceptance criteria as well as lower start-up costs.[14] (More discussion on the quality aspects in capital equipment buying is found in Appendix B.) The important consideration is the consistent capability to produce quality output. If it is not in the machine when purchased, it is not going to appear magically sometime in the future. Therefore, investing in equipment with higher process capabilities than needed can offset costs in the future.

The quality of the output can be both objective and subjective and can be a powerful motivating force for a company to abandon traditional analysis. The issue is one of balance. Does the increased machine cost and its resultant higher quality justify the expenditure for higher-quality or more-process-capable equipment? There is no single answer to that question. It is a company decision that is often based on intangibles or subjective considerations. The company that is manufacturing surgical equipment is quite sensitive to the appearance of the equipment as being "clean and bright." Certainly appearance has little to do with performance, but the user's perception is a selling feature. Disposable staplers are produced under very rigid conditions to ensure their antiseptic qualities, but they also *appear* to be sterile as well as actually being sterile.

Another factor that may be part of the decision process concerns safety and environmental considerations. This is an important issue. There is probably no other area in business that is more regulated than that of hazardous materials and waste. It is a legal issue from both civil and criminal perspectives and imposes cradle-to-grave responsibility on producers of hazardous waste. The ability to avoid fouling the environment has become a selling point for the manufacturers of environmentally friendly equipment. In the cooling tower industry, zero-discharge systems are becoming more popular. The water is used continuously and cleaned as it recirculates; thus, any discharge is pure water, regardless of whether it is liquid or steam. The pollutants are captured and compressed into a solid, and the water leaving the tower is significantly

---

14. For an interesting example of an application of the concept and its value, see T. J. Lucas and R. Plinkington, "Selecting Equipment Using SPC," *Quality* 34, no. 2 (February 1995): 8.

purer than that entering. This is not a financial issue, but it *is* an important consideration due to the possibility of avoiding a real cost associated with the equipment that was not anticipated.

Product appearance can be enhanced by automated or laborless manufacturing processes such as electrostatic and thermal bonding as opposed to painting in the case of coating metals. A desire to be at the leading edge of the technology can be used as a marketing tool to portray a specific company image.

There are many reasons for making decisions that lie beyond the frontiers of objectivity. The analyst has to consider them as possible reasons for a particular decision, regardless of how irrational they may appear.

Tracking the Decision

One survey shows discounted cash flow methods to be the most popular method when purchasing capital equipment, followed by nonfinancial techniques and payback period, with accounting rate of return being the least popular technique.[15] In Canada, capital budgeting practices place reliance on subjective and judgmental techniques in generating the projected cash flows. The techniques most used were internal rate of return and payback period, both of which dominated the NPV technique. As the complexity of the decision increases, discounted cash flow techniques are more often employed. The discounting rate is the weighted cost of capital.[16]

Whatever method is chosen, there is a need for a consistent approach within the organization as well as the need for a postcompletion audit report. All the analysis in the world done before the fact is of little value if the equipment fails to meet the criteria set forth for it. A relatively simple form that looks at the investment after the first year to see how well it did perform versus the proposal on which the decision was made is useful. Exhibit 3-7 contains an example form.

Using the form for the first year of the project will provide some indication if the project is on track and meeting its decision criteria. Knowing that the project is not over until the postcompletion audit report has been completed and accepted should provide the incentive to see that the numbers are correct with respect to savings or variable cost reduction. It should not be the case that a rosy picture is painted, the project approved, and never revised as to the accuracy of the data provided and the ability to meet the desired decision criteria, regardless of the technique used.

The probability of hitting the target exactly is nearly impossible. Variances

15. S. Chen., "An Empirical Examination of Capital Budgeting Techniques: Impact of Investment Types and Firm Characteristics," *Engineering Economist*, 2, no. 40 (winter 1995), 149.
16. "Capital Budgeting Practices," *CMA Magazine* 67, no. 9 (November 1993): 31.

Exhibit 3-7. Financial analysis project format.

		First Year Proposed	First Year Actual	Variance
	Elements of Investment			
	Capital assets			
	Additional working capital required			
	Less disposal of old asset			
A	Total investment			
	Expense items			
	Total cash required			
	Investment beginning of period (line A)			
	Less depreciation or amortization			
B	Balance end of period			
C	Average investment (line A + B ÷ 2)			
	Life of asset			
	Cash flow			
	Earnings before taxes (line F)			
	Add depreciation			
	Other cash items			
D	Net cash flow			.
E	Investment recovered (line D ÷ A)			
	Statement of Earnings (Incremental)			
	Net sales			
	Variable costs			
	Variable margin			
	% to sales			
	Capacity costs			
	Manufacturing			
	Direct charges			
	Selling expenses			
	Administrative & general			

	Engineering			
	Depreciation			
	Total capacity costs			
	Operating earnings			
	Other income (Expense)			
	Project expense			
F	Earnings before taxes			
G	ROI on an EBT basis (line F ÷ C)			

will occur as last-minute changes are made, tooling added, spares increased, or technology advances during the build period. One of management's responsibilities is to set the range or zone of acceptance from a financial perspective. If the ROI desired is 30 percent, then technically, 29.9 percent is unacceptable. Yet 29.9 percent can be rounded up or an assumption made to move the ROI higher. The issue is a realistic floor or window of acceptance of the project. The window concept implies a reasonable range with respect to the decision tool used.

The range concept is important from another perspective. Computing using any of the tools available requires estimates of savings. These savings are the result of decreases in operating costs brought about by reduced setup times, faster machine speeds, better feeds, reduced labor utilization, less downtime, and less maintenance. All of these factors will have an impact on the cost of goods sold, boosting the profits of the products produced on this machine. Therefore, the cost savings are really **profit improvements** generated by that machine, assuming the price of the product is held constant. Profit improvement has a slightly different connotation from cost reduction. If the new machine reduces direct labor cost by $5,000 per year, after the first year, it will be impossible to have an operating budget with that $5,000 in it. After the first year, it would be foolish to budget funds that are not going to be spent. That $5,000 worth of labor has been lost to the department having the machine. Where has it gone? All things being equal or held constant, it has reduced the cost of each unit and raised profits.

What happens if the purpose of the purchase is to reposition the company in the marketplace to become a more competitive producer? If the purchase of the capital equipment is necessitated by a need to become more ambitious in pricing, all of the savings or profit improvement cannot be viewed as ROI or part of the payback period analysis. A decision has to be made as to how much can effectively be used to pay for the machine and how much is needed to regain the position of an aggressive producer. The issue is how much the company recoups from the investment versus giving back to the customer in the form of reduced prices. It is the classic trade-off situation and a weakness in the analysis. Where will the savings flow? Will they be tracked with such care as to identify if they were the result of the investment, or will they go into a general fund, to be lost by pooling?

The percentage applicable or appropriate to the equipment is a managerial decision and will vary from company to company. It is important to keep the process focused in such a way that the numbers are valid and reflect the objectives of the purchase rather than making the process a slave to an equation whose foundation may be questionable and whose true objective becomes obscured in mathematical manipulations. The same data sets can provide different answers. The decision is not simply a financial one. It is a quality issue, a manufacturing issue, a marketing issue, an engineering issue, and a maintenance issue.

A Real-World Problem

A company has decided to purchase a CNC blank machine. We shall return to this machine in Chapter 12 to look at the whole process. For now, we are looking at just the financial data. The company has selected the model from the best supplier, and added the bells, flags, and whistles to the purchase. Now it has to do the financial analysis. Starting on the cost side, the installed cost, with freight and contingency, is $170,000. Tooling and factory preparation adds $9,000. However, these costs are treated as expense items and charged to a departmental budget. The estimated "savings" or profit enhancement over the existing machine is $53,500 per year, coming from decreased labor costs, setup cost reduction, and additional business arising from the capacity available on the new machine. The new machine is significantly less labor intensive, with the labor savings amounting to almost half of the savings and reduction in setup and changeover cost accounting for the remainder. Reduction in maintenance cost is about 4 percent of the total savings.

The numbers are valid taken to four decimal places and counting the number of pieces produced per year as well as the fringe benefits of the operator, who would not be needed since the machine finishes sockets directly from preloaded pallets. The following information is relevant:

- The service life of the equipment is 10 years.
- The residual or salvage value at the end of 10 years is estimated at $20,000.
- The machine being replaced has negligible salvage value.
- The company uses straight line depreciation.

- The contract calls for payment of 25 percent of the purchase price on signing the contract, 55 percent on successful completion of supplier site tests, and the final 20 percent on a net 30-day payment of the final invoice.
- As a result of the timing of the purchase, $60,000 will be spent in the fourth quarter of one year and $110,000 in the first quarter of the next year to purchase the machine, accessories, tooling, and testing.
- The start-up of the equipment in a production environment is due during the last part of April, so the earnings for the first year encompass only 7.5 months of operation.

On the basis of the information provided, certain assumptions are necessary to compare the machine using the various methods. One major assumption is the discount rate. What is the appropriate value to employ to discount future earnings on this machine? The discount rate is set at 20 percent to reflect the company's opportunity costs of capital. Using the information available, it is now possible to set up a table reflecting that information and using the data to compare the various methods. The data table, shown in Exhibit 3-8, looks at the investment, the cash flow, and the statement of earnings on an incremental basis.

The computations show a 28.2 percent ROI on a cash flow basis and a 36.3 percent ROI on an earnings-before-tax basis. Next comes the calculation of the payback period. Looking at the data reveals operating earnings of $23,100 in the first year as compared to $36,500 in each year thereafter. Based on the data provided, it is evident that the machine was not in operation at the beginning of the year, but based on the ratio of 23.1 to 36.5, initial operation began about May 1995. Thus from the period of May 1995, 63 percent of the year remained. During this time $23,100 in EBT was amassed. Add the next four years' earnings at $36,500 per year, or a total of $146,000, plus the $23,100, for a total of $169,100, approximately equal to the initial investment. Do *not* be fooled by the presentation of the data. The payback period begins when the meter starts running, and if the machine did not come on line for five months into the year, the initial year when it went into service is not a full year but a portion of it.

All projects do not start on January 1. If the earnings for the entire year were $23,100, then the payback period would be longer. Payback assumes that the flow of earnings is earmarked for recapturing the cost of the investment. Earnings must be viewed from the perspective of when they occur.

If the analysis called for the use of NPV or IRR, it is best to go to a spreadsheet for this analysis. Using the basic data from the problem and the IRR equation, it is determined that the IRR is 15.22 percent. If the company is satisfied with an IRR of 15.22 percent or less, the machine has a zero or positive NPV. Desiring more than that as a criterion for the investment, the organization would rework the data to find additional savings or look for a cheaper machine. The summary data are shown in Exhibit 3-9.

(*text continues on page 90*)

Exhibit 3-8. Basic data for analysis of the CNC socket machine purchase ($000).

Elements of Investment by Year	1994	1995	1996	1997	1998	1999	2000	2001	2002	2003	Totals	Average
Investment at beginning of period	40	43	156	139	122	105	88	71	54	37		
Additional investments	0	130										
Return of capital	0	17	17	17	17	17	17	17	17	17		
Balance at end of period	40	156	139	122	105	88	71	54	37	20	832	83.2
Average investment	40	99.5	147.5	130.5	113.5	96.5	79.5	62.5	45.5	28.5	843.5	84.4 Average investment
Cash flow by year												
Earnings before taxes	0	14.1	36.5	36.5	36.5	36.5	36.5	36.5	36.5	36.5	306.1	30.6 Average EBT
Depreciation—book basis	0	17	17	17	17	17	17	17	17	17	153	15.3
Other cash items												
Residual value		−130								20	20	
Net cash flow	0	−98.9	53.5	53.5	53.5	53.5	53.5	53.5	53.5	73.5	479.1	47.9 Average cash flow

Statement of Earnings (incremental)

Variable margin	0	40.1	53.5	53.5	53.5	53.5	53.5	53.5	53.5	53.5
Capacity cost—									
Depreciation	0	17	17	17	17	17	17	17	17	17
Manufacturing									
Marketing									
Administrative									
Engineering									
Total capacity cost		17	17	17	17	17	17	17	17	17
Operating earnings	0	23.1	36.5	36.5	36.5	36.5	36.5	36.5	36.5	36.5
Project expense		9							
Earnings before taxes		14.1	36.5	36.5	36.5	36.5	36.5	36.5	36.5	36.5
% ROI—EBT basis (Average EBT/average investment)		14.17%	24.75%	27.97%	32.16%	37.82%	45.91%	58.40%	80.22%

36.29% average ROI EBT basis

% ROI—cash flow basis (Average cash flow/investment)

28.18% ROI cash flow basis

Exhibit 3-9. Summary of the different analyses of the CNC socket machine.

Technique	Result	Comments
ROI—cash flow basis	28.2%	
ROI—EBT basis	36.3%	
Payback period	4.6 years	Less than a full year of operation when going on line
Internal rate of return	15.22%	Using earnings before taxes
Net present value	Positive up to 15.21%	If payments are received at the beginning of the year
Net present value	20%	If payments are received at the end of the year

What is the correct answer? Technically, they are all correct. It depends on the method chosen for analysis, the data collected, the willingness to trust the data, and the accuracy of records on the present equipment coupled with the performance of the new equipment.

Does this leave the analyst in a quandary? Not in the least. Here are five reasonable financial measures all pointing in the same direction. Some are more conservative than others, and some are more complex than others, yet all serve their purpose to direct the analysis toward an informed decision.

Is the process complete? No. A number of options still need to be explored. This segment has dealt with the computational aspects of the numbers provided. Still to be discussed are the values of the numbers themselves, where the money will come from to pay for the machine, whether the $170,000 figure is a firm one, and how will it be paid for and by whom.

The impact of changing any element of the equations can be significant. Any decrease in the machine cost is going to:

• Reduce the payback period.
• Increase the internal rate of return.
• Increase the ROI on a cash flow basis.
• Increase the ROI on an EBT basis.
• Make the NPV more positive.

Accomplishing this by lowering the price of the equipment or getting lower interest rates to finance the purchase or any form of cost shifting is going to make the investment more positive.

Paying for the Equipment

All the financial analysis contained the hidden assumption of the availability of funds to buy the equipment. If the company is rich in liquid assets, the issue of paying for the equipment is a moot point, and the discussion ends with the writing of the check to the supplier according to the terms and conditions of the purchase order. If the situation is one where the buyer needs the equipment but is strapped for liquidity, there are many and diverse options, yet each carries a cost. Here are the traditional options:[17]

- Short-term borrowing or debt instruments
- Longer-term borrowing or debt instruments
- Having the seller finance the sale of the equipment over some finite period
- Having a third party finance the sale, as in the case of equipment trust certificates
- Raising equity capital
- Approaching the state in which the company resides for business retention funds to offset the cost of the equipment or provide tax credits related to the purchase of the equipment.
- Leasing the equipment directly from the manufacturer of the equipment or selling it to a third party and leasing it back from that third party

The traditional sources of funds lie more in the finance field, yet the financial analysis of capital equipment must briefly look at the area. One important reason is that the financial viability of the organization is a key issue in considering how the investment will be paid for or financed. Financially viable organizations with low levels of debt, high levels of cash, or cash-equivalent assets have little problem financing the investments. Cash-strapped organizations often find debt burdens raising the marginal cost of borrowed funds. A second reason is that the accuracy of the discounting process is totally dependent on the use of the correct value for the discount rate. Is it the cost of capital as a weighted average of all capital sources in the organization or a desired rate of return based on the type of capital raising instrument contemplated for financing the purchase?

Numerous sources are available for short- and long-term borrowing, including financial institutions, pension funds, and insurance companies. All seem eager to make investments that raise their income stream and can be viewed as low to moderate risk. Yet the availability of capital does not come without a cost: The longer the period of the loan, the greater the interest paid for the use of the money. The cost of the money borrowed must be considered in any computation of the payback period, rate of return, discounted cash flow, or any other technique used. In the analysis of the blood analyzer, it was assumed the physician had the funds available to buy the machine. If the ma-

---

17. It is not our intent to get involved with corporate finance, a separate subject. Yet any form of financial transaction creates costs that should be allocated to the equipment cost to provide a total cost of ownership perspective.

chine was financed in any way, that stream of repayments would have to be considered from the perspective of the interest on the loan used to finance the purchase.

The financial issue becomes one of addressing how to pay for the investment and then what the best interest rate is that can be secured for the borrowing. If internal funds are available, the second issue goes away with the exception of treating the issue of the appropriate rate of interest to charge ourselves for using internal funds for financing purposes and would outside funding be preferable. If outside financing is sought, what are the options?

What is of major importance here is that there is a policy covering some critical dimensions of the financing issue because they play a significant role in the analysis of the capital equipment purchase. They include such issues as the following:

• What are the cutoff points for internal financing and external financing? How much is present in the capital budget of the company?

• To what extent does the organization want to involve outside entities, such as city or state governments, in the process?[18]

• What is the flexibility offered by the analysis to use different incentives in the computation of the key parameters of the investment decision? As an example, many states have well-defined, aggressive programs for encouraging companies to locate in the state and add capacity and new equipment. The various plans for this business retention offer a wide range of incentives (e.g., tax abatements, income tax credits, tax holidays).

In Illinois in 1995, a manufacturers' purchase credit was phased in.[19] The purchase of manufacturing machinery entitled the buyer to a 25 percent credit on what the taxes would have been if the machinery was taxable. The credit was then used to offset sales taxes on noneligible equipment purchases.

The process of information gathering can be complex, but it may be worth the time and effort to determine the interest that the state or local government has in job development or supporting investment by tax credits. Alabama, for example, allows companies to write off 5 percent of their capital investment costs for 20 years up to the level of their state income tax.[20] There are certain qualifications that must be met, but failing to consider the incentives available might disqualify a projected investment, while considering and counting incentives may turn a marginal investment into a profitable one. This is also the

---

18. One has only to look at the Japanese invasion of the U.S. automobile assembly market in the late 1970s and early 1980s as states engaged in bidding wars to get the plants to locate inside the state boundaries. It was a feeding frenzy, with multimillion dollar commitments for everything from roads to land to training the workforce.
19. L. John, "The Business of Business Retention," CFO 12, no. 1 (January 1996): 35.
20. Ibid., p. 33.

proverbial two-edged sword, and it may work against a company. States may grant concessions in one administration and take them back in another. The average politician never saw a tax he did not love. For this reason, companies should approach these types of concessions warily. There are good ones and bad ones, and the structure of the concession means a great deal.

The source of information on these opportunities is often the appropriate economic development office in the state, nominally headed by the lieutenant governor's office. The local government cannot be ignored in this area of job creation and investment, especially where the community has a profits or earnings tax. Any form of incentive can be a valuable contribution to the possible payoff of the investment. Consider the case of U.S. Steel and the requirement placed on it to build a water treatment facility at the Gary, Indiana, works to treat the water before it was returned to Lake Michigan. The multimillion-dollar pollution control facility had to be financed by bonds. The city of Gary decided to offer the bonds in the market, and U.S. Steel guaranteed payment of principal and interest. As municipally offered securities, they were tax exempt from federal income taxes. They also carried a lower interest rate, some 2 percent below the average 8 percent for taxable bonds. As a result, U.S. Steel saved $53 million in interest payments over the repayment period of the bonds. This same approach was used hundreds of times all over the country until the federal government changed the rules in 1986 and made this type of financing much more difficult and expensive since industrial revenue bonds were nothing but financing schemes.

Making the Case in Your Own Organization

After weighing all the formulas and intangibles, the analyst must make one final determination: What is the decision environment in my own organization? What are the factors that make an investment decision positive or negative in my environment? Are the measures applied equally, or are there organizational biases that place more weight on one factor than another or skew decisions in favor of one approach compared to the other? To admit the presence of these biases is not apostasy in the organization, but the reality of dealing with the culture and orientation of the organization. A good analyst keeps a finger on the pulse of the organization to avoid losing a good proposal due to naiveté. That person must be current on a variety of important issues.

The formal portion of the process begins with the **capital budget,** a document portraying the perceived needs and resources available. The word *budget* implies an allocation process. It is a competition for scarce resources or costly resources. It involves trying to get the funding for the project. It can be looked at in the context of "many come forth, few are chosen." Of those that come forth, some are absolutely necessary, some are nice to have, and some simply look great but do not really enrich. Yet each proposer of a capital equipment purchase views this need as greatest and most worthy of being satisfied. It is reminiscent of the aria sung in the *Mikado* by Pish Tush, who says, "You are right and he is right and everyone is right." The way to avoid conflict is giving everyone what she or he wants. The constraint is the resources available. Decisions must be made whereby some projects are funded and others relegated to the reject pile. Making a decision equates to selecting among alternatives, and the ability to present the alternative in the most honest and favorable light is an art form. Recognize the words *honest* and *favorable*. They may be mutually exclusive terms.

In making the case for the equipment, consider the various elements before submitting the request.

It is fundamental to understand key players in the process and their orientation as well as the orientation of the company as a whole.

- What does the process look like in your organization?
- What are the steps in the process?
- Where are the possible delays in the process? Are those delays due to overwork or a subtle way of killing the project or delaying it?
- What department carries the most weight in the organization?
- Is the decision a financial one?
- Is this the final gate?
- Is it a marketing decision?
- If the equipment will not give a competitive edge in the marketplace, why spend the money?

Some companies favor quick pay-off investments and lean toward projects that offer the fastest possible capital recovery. Some companies pride themselves on being showplaces of technology. Still others are followers and buy only proved and tested equipment. Some companies are opportunity seekers and buy equipment to take advantage of a perceived opportunity and dispose of it when the opportunity has faded.

It is essential to know the time line for the equipment. Using the previous example, the CNC socket machine was off the shelf, manufactured in Japan, and therefore was FOB port of entry. Other parts ordered from the supplier came FOB the supplier's facility in New Jersey. This part of the process required a rigging contract for the machine from the port of entry on the West Coast. Transit time had to be added to the lead time, and the ocean freight documentation in the form of the arrival notice had to be made available to the rigging company. The machine was shipped to the supplier first for the test runs on the purchased machine and then to the customer. These examples may seem like boring details, yet the arrival of the machine, less the tooling, eliminates the value of the machine. It is tantamount to buying a car without tires.

How long does the process take internally? Inadequate lead time for proposal preparation consistently leads to rejection. Company executives are not willing to risk large sums on poorly estimated savings. It is important to know the degree of monitoring that takes place to verify the accuracy of the cost data provided. Were the numbers really correct, or were they developed knowing that they would never be verified or even tracked? Every capital budget has a cutoff point. Lacking that barrier, there is no point in having to budget. All the monies needed would be available. What is the cutoff point? Where are the unacceptable limits on investment? Good, clear language is necessary for acceptance of the proposal.

Understanding the organization's financial environment is essential. Does the company want to know the whole truth with respect to costs, or is it happy to be given an unrealistically low figure that excludes costs that will occur later in the machine life cycle?

In certain weapons systems, costs were made to appear very low or substitutions were made to drive down costs that later were expended to meet the mission requirements. When the OH-58 Kiowa helicopter was first produced, it contained the Allison C-18 engine. The aircraft was underpowered because of funding limitations on the program. As soon as the first units came off the production line, the contractor offered the U.S. Army a "blue-ribbon package" to retrofit the fleet for $250 million to upgrade from the C-18 engine to the C-20, the engine it should have had in the beginning. How does that happen? In this case, the retrofit would come from O&MA funds (Operation and Maintenance—Army), while the original buy came from PEMA funds (Procurement Equipment and Missiles—Army). These are two different accounts and two different budgets. There may be no way of telling what the total costs actually were.

The financial climate is a key issue; how the project or purchase is presented is essential. A higher initial cost may be counterbalanced with lower operating costs or maintenance costs. The important points are good communication and valid data. Good communication is essential to translate technical terms into business terms. For example, consider the list of potential savings below and how these would be translated into the financial perception of the product:

- Fewer people doing the job
- Better use of material
- Less maintenance required
- Lower inventory (or no inventory) of spare parts
- Simpler tools for maintenance

- Reduced setup time leading to greater machine productivity
- Reduced wear and tear on tooling
- Increased in-line gauges that reduce inspection time and cost and decrease the likelihood of unacceptable quality
- Faster cycle time, reducing machine-paced idle time for workers
- Reduced worker fatigue, raising worker productivity on the line
- Reduced downtime
- Environmental issues (does the equipment use hazardous material or create hazardous waste?)
- The technology in the equipment: known, proven, and validated versus unknown, experimental, and estimated

All of these are technical factors that must be converted into cost elements to place the decision in proper perspective. Again it is a communication issue of quantifying, in an understandable manner, data that come from the technical side of the process to the financial side.

Savings: Real or an Illusion?

Remember that the savings are never really accomplished until some action has taken place. Labor savings are not real unless the workforce is reduced by one or more people. Material savings do not take place unless the scrap or waste factor declines. To specify the savings and never follow through on the action that brings about the savings is a smoke-and-mirror savings.

In the analysis of labor savings, consider who will run the new machine. If the saving was computed on the basis of the $16-per-hour operator's no longer being needed and the plant is unionized, forget the integrity of that estimate. There is an animal called bumping rights. It may end up that the $8-per-hour sweeper will go out the door when the dust settles.

Recognize also that when savings occur in the year the investment is made, after the initial investment, they are profit enrichers, not savings. No sharp budget analyst will allow a bloated budget to pass unquestioned. If the unit labor cost drops by 20 percent for a product, the next year's operating budget should have that cut built into it and therefore be smaller. Where the saving appears is the gross margin on the products produced on the machine. There is less labor in the product; therefore the gross margin is higher.

Recognize the needs with respect to the cost accounting system and time standards systems needed to verify those savings. These systems do not appear by magic, and what is measured must be valid and accurate. In the final analysis, all of the justification comes down to the integrity of the data going into that analysis. Regardless of the degree of automation, computerization, and accounting sophistication that companies are able to achieve, honest and complete data have no substitutes in the justification of capital equipment purchases. As it is true in the data processing or decision support area, it is no less true in the evaluation of capital equipment: Garbage in, garbage out. Formulas will manipulate data, not cleanse them.

Finally, there must be postpurchase verification of the savings or margin enhancements. Is this step often omitted? Yes. It is the moment of truth in the analysis, the opportunity to see the errors of analysis or omission made in preparing the request. It is a learning opportunity. But it can also be embarrassing and threatening since it reveals any problems that were not considered when they should have been. Yet it is essential to learn from mistakes made in the past, for mistakes ignored will be repeated, and the buying of capital equipment is no exception to that rule. Keep your data clean and accurate. Be flexible. There are always three ways to add the same number in a column and come up with three totals.

4

Sourcing New
Capital Equipment

Make no mistake. The process of sourcing is complex. There is more to it than simply selecting the lowest quotation or going back to a familiar supplier or distributor who has handled your business in the past. This is especially true in the area of capital equipment buying. The dollar size of the purchase, the service life of the equipment, and the ongoing relationship with the supplier all contribute to the complexity. Once the selection decision is made, the buyer is going to have to live with that decision for a long time. The worst mistake that can be made is to treat the capital equipment decision as routine. Having been through the entire process once does not mean that shortcuts can be taken or steps omitted the second time around. Consider each purchase as the claimant to careful planning and execution using the skills and knowledge gained from previous buys but not skimping on the effort. Errors made in the buying process are long-lived and not easily forgotten.

Unique Aspects of Sourcing for Capital Equipment

There are a number of unique aspects to the sourcing issue for capital equipment.

Competition

In the buying arena, there may be many competitors or few. The competition can be expanded by considering options that not only produce the parts or family of parts, but do away with secondary operations associated with it. Looking at the process of producing the end item or part becomes the key gauge for determining the level of competition.

A multistation machine may incorporate several operations. This would preclude transferring the material from workstation to workstation. But it also compounds the complexity of the decision, requiring the buyer to look at a wide array of factors. The decision now becomes a total product analysis.

A company is interested in purchasing a machining center capable of completely producing a complex brass part. The machine would replace two Browne and Sharpe screw machines, and all the secondary operations on the parts would be eliminated if the new machine were purchased. In this case, it was not a one-for-one replacement but a total system replacement.

Analysis: The buyer must look at the full impact of that machining center. The machining center will displace two machines and free up capacity on other machines due to the capability of performing secondary operations:

- What will be the labor savings?
- What will be the energy savings?
- What will be the space savings?
- What about scrap and rework?
- What about setups?
- What about the output in pieces per hour?
- How is productivity of both equipment and people affected?

The machining center's capacity needs to be considered:

- Is the machining center "too much" capacity?
- Is the buyer trading off costs for one method for a more expensive way of doing the same job?
- Is the buyer purchasing a machining center that has more technology than is needed now or into the future?
- Will its presence make the other equipment in the process technologically obsolete?
- Will the machining center operate at a reasonable percentage of its capacity?

The sources need some thought:

- What are the options open as far as sources are concerned?
- Where are they located?
- What technology are they using?

- Is it proven technology or experimental?
- Is the level of technology necessary, or is it nice but not necessary?[1]

The International Buying Arena

The sourcing of capital equipment will likely bring the buyer into the international buying arena. The sourcing issue then expands to consider both the foreign source and domestic representation. Often with commodities, it is easier to purchase domestically, but capital equipment is international in the range of sources. International purchasing opens an array of factors that must be added to the decision.

Domestic Representation

In all likelihood, the buyer is going to be dealing with the domestic representative 95 to 100 percent of the time after the purchase. If the confidence in that representative is lacking, it is a warning of problems that will occur in the future. Consider the domestic representative as *the source after the source.* Therefore the evaluation is done on two sources of supply: the original equipment manufacturer (OEM) and the domestic representative. If the latter is found lacking, *caveat emptor.* If there is no domestic representation at all, *caveat emptor.*[2] Lacking domestic representation, all future dealings will have to be conducted from afar, which can create a serious workload for a company as well as significant downtime if needed spare parts are not available. Lacking the domestic representation, the buyer must carefully consider the investment in spares with the initial purchase as well as the issue of maintenance training. Sometimes it is difficult to deal with a domestic supplier only 100 miles away. Consider now the foreign supplier 10,000 miles away, separated by distance, language, and legal systems.

Here are some questions to consider:

- Is the supplier represented domestically?
- Who is the domestic representative, and what is the relationship of that representative to the parent company?
- What does representation really mean?
- How do the representatives earn their money? Are they stocking distributors or agencies?
- Is their representation for one foreign manufacturer or several?
- What is their inventory of spare parts?

1. In many instances older technology offers higher reliability and more predictable maintenance expenses. It is often easier to get valid cost data and project future expenses more accurately. In addition, the higher technology may simply not be needed. Why spend money for it?
2. Not having someone representing the supplier should act as a warning to the buyer.

- How are transactions handled?
- Is the purchasing done from the domestic representative who accepts the order, thereby making the transaction a domestic one, or does the representative simply expedite a foreign purchase?
- Can representatives simplify the transaction?
- How well do they communicate with the principal? Do they speak the language of the principal?
- What other expertise do they have?
- Will they be there at installation of the equipment? (Insist that a factory-trained technician be present at the installation and throw the switch. This gets the buyer off the hook with respect to "incorrect installation problems" that may be encountered.)
- Will they handle some of the details of transportation, especially customs issues?
- Do they have technicians to work on the equipment?
- Are they factory trained?
- What was the duration of the training?

Transporting the Equipment From Overseas

This is an area of specialists, fees, commissions, and paperwork. Do not treat it lightly or consider it as part of the order. It can be very expensive by the time the buyer goes through all the steps in the process of buying and bringing goods into this country from a foreign producer. In the issue of transportation, the buyer pays the freight costs and duties in any case. Again, the intervention or presence of the domestic representative is very important. The representation is directly paid by the terms of the agreement or embedded in the price. Keep the transportation aspect as simple as possible by buying from the domestic source in the form of the domestic agency.

Paying for the Equipment

What about payment for the equipment? Will special arrangements be needed, such as letters of credit or purchases of foreign currency? Remember that the letter of credit favors the seller and normally results in the buyer's paying on the basis of documentation. In the case of capital equipment, this should be avoided at all costs. Without retention or retainage until acceptance criteria are met, the buyer may be left with little or no leverage over the supplier and little recourse in having the acceptance criteria met. This is one reason to select a source that has a strong domestic agency presence. That agent must be judged on the overall capability to support the foreign equipment in many ways. The more seamless the relationship appears between the foreign manufacturer and the domestic agency, the less reluctance there should be about buying overseas.

Perhaps the domestic agency can be of help in this area, especially arranging for credit terms from the supplier. Often the data needed by the foreign supplier are more readily available in the country of destination. It is very important for the buyer to know the financial condition of the supplier, especially a foreign supplier. This is more important if progress payments are to be made. In addition, reading a credit report or a balance sheet or profit and loss statement in the United States will be different from the data from comparable companies overseas. The United States is a data-intensive country with an overabundance of financial information. Sellers can look at the customer and make comparisons of the customer to the industry in which the customer is located. In terms of securing credit, there are a number of internationally known companies, such as Dun & Bradstreet, that supply useful credit information. The domestic agency may be of significant help in analyzing the creditworthiness of the buyer. From the buying perspective, if credit is desired, it may be in the interest of the domestic representative to assist the buyer in this process. Because the buyer will have to work with the domestic representative, the domestic representative will have to work with the buyer for a long time. An understanding of the mutual dependency benefits both parties.

Lead Time

If a foreign location is involved, the buyer must factor in lead time. What is the impact of location on lead time? How much does the foreign location add to the lead time? Is that additional time important or simply inconvenient?

Equipment Modifications

Modifications may be needed on the equipment to meet U.S. health and safety standards. Where will these be accomplished? It is probably best to have the shipment go to the domestic representative first for the changes and to do a sample run on the machine.

The Foreign OEM

The foreign OEM must be investigated on the technical capability of the product and history of performance of both product and company. What is their staying power? The relationship between the OEM and the domestic agency must be investigated to see the latitude afforded the agent to act for the principal. How binding is the word of the agent, and what is the scope of authority? The domestic agent is evaluated with the same rigor of a domestic source in terms of capability to perform, financial stability, and customer satisfaction. That agent is the point of contact in the future.

Defining the Sourcing Process

Has the sourcing process been clearly defined by the buying company, and is the definition consistent over all equipment purchases? Is there a clearly defined effort or methodology in place to keep the company up on the marketplace? Good sourcing is an ongoing process. It should not be limited to when the buy takes place. Keeping up with the market may prove highly beneficial, and an ongoing sourcing philosophy can save time and money by spreading the cost in dollars and time over a larger time base. Keeping abreast of what is going on in the equipment market can be accomplished by going to national and regional trade shows in the product area. The cost of sending one or two manufacturing engineers to a major show for two days is minuscule in comparison to the data they can gather. Industrial or trade shows are one of the few places where the buyer can see many models, relatively side by side, and side-by-side comparisons are always the best. The rationale for two attendees is simple: There are two perspectives on the equipment and two sets of observations.

Going to these shows should not be restricted to times when a purchase is contemplated but should be used as part of the overall sourcing process, and the cost should be budgeted on an annual basis. Management should not consider the visit to the trade show as an all-expenses-paid vacation. This is a serious effort to keep up with the changing industrial technology in the field.

It is essential to have an evaluation process in place. Make sure part of the process deals with visiting sites where the equipment is installed and up and running. A user is often the best source of information on the viability of the source of supply.

Sourcing should be a continuous process. It takes place as we routinely amass information on suppliers by visiting trade shows, talking with sales representatives, and observing the marketplace. All members of the team should be alert to potential sources of supply from their individual perspectives. Team members bring more information to the table on potential sources of supply, thereby expanding the options. The more competition present, the greater the likelihood for a good purchase.

"Good" does *not* mean the lowest quote; it means the greatest value for the dollar expended. It is the best cost per unit of output. Lacking that measure, the buyer is left with meaningless cost comparisons. A BMW costs eight times more than a Yugo. That is a statement of fact. Now where do we go from that statement? Exactly nowhere because it does not convey anything other than disjointed absolutes. If we say the service life of the BMW is 10 times the service life of the Yugo, then there is some basis of comparison. Spend 8 times as much but get 10 times the service life begins to make some sense. It is crude, but it starts to bring about relative measures, and relatives are the basis of comparisons.

Finding the Source

Finding a source is one of the difficult parts of the entire process. The difficulty is caused by the avalanche of information available from a variety of sources. The information explosion can probably be matched by the advertising explosion.

Publications

Companies, anxious to make themselves known to the public, are found in a wide variety of places: catalogs, mailers, trade publications, manufacturers' catalogs, and registers such as the *Thomas Register* and *McCrea's Bluebook*. Add to this the plethora of advertising from electronic forms of communication, such as faxes and the Internet, and the average buyer is deluged with data. Note the word *data* is used. *Data* means the raw material from which information is obtained after the data are evaluated or refined. There is no shortage of data in an economy resplendent with multiple modes of communication. The issue is making the refining process as productive as possible.

Consider a long-time purchasing standard, the *Thomas Register*, consisting of 33 volumes with information on more than 55,000 products and services contained in more than 40,000 pages of detailed information. The *Thomas Register* contains the "Products and Services Section," the "Company Profile Section," and the "Catalog File Section." The buyer may consult the register online or use a CD-ROM, which is also available. Literature can also be obtained by fax as well as using ThomasNet on the Internet. A recent development is the joint venture of General Electric and Thomas Publishing Company called TPN Register. It is an Internet-based procurement service for industrial material said to reduce purchasing cycle time by 50 percent, and cost by 30 percent. It allows for rapid transmission of information between buyer and seller, and allows for structured negotiations between the two parties. Information on this and other Thomas Publishing services may be found at the website www. thomaspublishing.com.

The Internet

The Internet can be consulted. In a trial run, "automatic screw machines" was entered into the proprietary search engine. Immediately, 88 sources for the machinery were identified, as well as over 2,000 sources for automatic screw machine parts. The search was then narrowed to six sources in the state of Illinois. In addition, the ThomasNet system showed which supplier catalogs were available. This was a quick-response system to gain information that could take hours to obtain from printed sources. The important aspect of using ThomasNet is the allocation of time. The tedious work is done by the search engine, and when the buyer takes over, it is to work on the evaluation of the potential source. This is the purpose of information automation: to do the busywork rapidly.

We also tested Literature by Fax on the Internet. The response time was less than three minutes from call completion time to receipt of the information requested. It was indeed a rapid response.

Information From Suppliers

The issue was not only the rapidity of getting the information, but how much more information could be gathered by using electronic means as opposed to thumbing through catalogs. Knowing what one wants is essential. After finding out who is out there, the next step is to request information from the supplier. This may come in a variety of ways—via catalog or mailer or even a visit. We do not recommend going directly to a quote at this stage. There is little point in starting the process until the supplier pool has been narrowed down. Responding to a request for quotation (RFQ) can be expensive for the suppliers. There is no reason to begin this process until the requirement has solidified to some degree. Raising supplier expectations and costs to respond to phantom orders does neither party any long-term good. Fishing expeditions should be restricted to the lakes and streams.

This part of the process is still concerned with information gathering through wandering about at machine tool shows, picking up brochures, and examining the equipment. It is a scouting expedition or a fact-finding mission. In the preliminary stages, the Yellow Pages of the telephone book is considered a legitimate source, especially if directories from major cities are available. This does not mean your team is going to base a multithousand-dollar buying decision on a listing in the local telephone book, but it does define who is local.

Sales Representatives

Sales representatives often call on nonpurchasing individuals in the organization, a practice that many purchasing professionals frown on; they sometimes view it as "back-door selling." From the salesperson's perspective, it is trying to talk to the potential initiator of a requisition. It is an attempt to communicate directly as opposed to indirect communication through the buyer.

In terms of how this is handled, there are several viewpoints. If the buying effort is truly a team effort and any attempt to **back-door**[3] the **sale** is a waste of time, the salesperson is doing his or her job of disseminating information

---

3. *Back-door* or *back-door selling* refers to the practice of bypassing the normal purchasing channels, and trying to sell by going directly to the user of the product. By using this approach, the seller tries to convince the user to consider only his product as a viable option, thus eliminating competition for the sale. It is a practice loathed by purchasing personnel.

on the products he or she sells. If the buying company has a history of being the target of back-door selling, such practices can be very dangerous. There are many cases where engineers have made commitments to salespersons that went far beyond *any* authority the engineers possessed. The salesperson was happy to accept what he or she viewed as an order. After all, is it the place of the salesperson to question the authority of the engineer to commit the company? Legally, the salesperson has no ground to stand on by accepting statements and turning them into an order. The law protects the principal from unknown or unwanted agents. Yet the seller is on the buyer's property. If the principal or the duly authorized agent does not disavow the actions of the unauthorized purchase, then apparent authority can be viewed as given to the unauthorized person, now making that person an agent. Engineers and maintenance supervisors become "instant buyers."

Where is the fine line? Discouraging the salesperson from selling the product is not the answer. Having a team approach where the seller is communicating to only one member of that team is a possible answer. Remember that the purchase is not going to be made on one dimension by one person. The authority of the person contacted by the salesperson is limited. In some instances, it may be useful to have the salesperson make a presentation to the team. This can be quite useful because a wide variety of information can be delivered.

Past Suppliers

Frequently buyers return to a supplier they formerly used. Former suppliers represent knowns in all facets of the transaction. Their products are identified with respect to cost and performance. Experiences with the supplier form the basis for selection or rejection, and sometimes the personalities of the supplier's personnel can provide a positive experience, making supplier selection easier. It is dealing with a known quantity. In addition, there is the issue of who will be the interface. In some cases it may be the OEM or the agent representing that OEM. While this interface is very important, remember that it is the machine that is important, not the people.

In the case cited earlier of the multistation equipment, the dealings were made through a domestic agent. The purchase was conducted easily, with no problems encountered. By the time the buyer was ready to make another purchase, three key people had left the agent and formed their own company to represent another international supplier. The engineering department decided to go with the people they knew and trusted. Proving that justification of anything is possible, they justified the new machine over the previously purchased model. Justification is very easily accomplished by simply saying the newer model has "greater flexibility" or "more potential" or choosing some phrase that really says nothing or is so ambiguous that its true meaning is lost.[4] The purchase of the new machine was made and the results were predictable: Selected on the basis of vague generalities and platitudes, the new machine proved to be unreliable and costly to maintain. So much for trust and faith in the general verbiage.

The technical problems were a result of having to make short production runs of different but similar parts. The users who were consulted made the same part day after day after day. The application was different. Different applications may make the machine perform totally differently. The user was bound and determined to get the new machine, and the focus was to justify the new. The user also "slimmed down" the process. It was false economy.

When looking at the process, make sure consideration is given to all dimensions of the purchase. Perhaps some of the steps can be truncated, but not many. A good sourcing process, carefully followed, ensued by good negotiations and completed with a good contract, will go a long way in closing the gap of not having worked with a supplier before.

Buyers in Other Companies

A final source on sources are buyers and purchasing professionals in other companies. It is common practice to be in professional contact with other buyers through a variety of channels. Meetings of local professional associations offer an opportunity to discuss sourcing issues and exchange information. The advantage provided by this avenue is the preliminary screening done for the buyer by a colleague. The buyer can ask questions about the source and feel confident that the information received is accurate. The objectivity present in a buyer-to-buyer conversation is normally high. A buyer who has had a bad experience with a supplier is not likely to recommend that supplier to a purchasing colleague. A repetition of the first bad experience by someone else does not expunge it. This information source should not be overlooked. The network can be a good form of communication.

Evaluating the Supplier and the Offer

Prior to the preparation of the purchase order, the buying team undertakes the complex process of evaluating the proposals received from various suppliers. Sometimes there may be a single proposal since competition may be thin in

---

4. When reading the justification, watch out for sweeping generalities that could fit any situation. If something is better, it is better because of some definable parameter. It produces more

some industries. In addition, existing suppliers may have large backlogs that either prevent their responding to the RFQ or responding with a price that is noncompetitive.[5] Regardless of the number of responses, the task facing the buyer is indeed complex. (The term *buyer* used in this chapter will refer to the buying team.) The complexity is raised by a variety of issues, including adherence to the RFQ, potential limitations imposed by the equipment, cost considerations, and differing perspectives on the equipment itself, again looking at it from an output perspective, a quality perspective, and a cost perspective.

There must be a systematic approach to the evaluation process. This may include developing forms for recording key data, developing some sort of rating scale or factor analysis to weigh the variables, a valid cost analysis of the equipment itself, and consideration of the extras that often accompany the response to the RFQ. How closely does the response match the RFQ? What are the areas of deviation? Are they critical areas such as delivery, price, and operating characteristics, or are they cosmetic aspects?

Recognize that the supplier has responded to the RFQ that your company or organization has developed. If your RFQ was not properly developed, the response cannot be counted on to close the gaps in it. A buyer who does not know what is wanted should not expect the supplier to be a psychic. This is the reason that the RFQ must be written with the idea that it is the communication device between the buyer and the potential sellers. But even if the RFQ is well written, clear, and unambiguous, buyers often undo much of the good already done by allowing deviations or making statements such as, "Suppliers are encouraged to be innovative in their responses to this RFQ." This old ploy for free engineering usually results in deviations from the RFQ that do nothing but complicate the evaluation process. In all likelihood, there *are* going to be deviations from the RFQ; there is no need to ask for them. In addition, there must be some baseline against which the responses are measured. Lacking a baseline, there can be no measurement that means anything.

At this point an ethics issue is raised: How much information from one respondent to the RFQ can be passed on to another respondent? Are the ideas in an RFQ response to be treated as proprietary information? Legally, the answer is no. The supplier is responding to a request. Beyond the legal issue, however, is the ethical issue of confidential information. If it is made known that there will be a sharing of ideas, then the supplier is forewarned. Doing it without that warning is not considered ethical.[6]

---

units per time period. It meets or exceeds specification compared to other alternatives. It requires 40 percent less setup time. The generality is often the tip-off of an attempt to justify without really committing oneself to specific performance.

5. The "high price response" is an old gambit used to keep up the appearance of being a responsive bidder. The bid is so high that it will not be accepted, yet the bidder cannot be accused of ignoring the bid. Ignoring a bid solicitation too often may translate to disappearance from the bid list.

6. This view of sharing information is cultural. The Japanese view copying as the highest level of flattery and therefore share information among suppliers. Cultural differences can create problems.

Starting the Process: Having a Good RFQ

In order to save time and effort and avoid duplication, the data on the technical dimensions of the equipment, developed in the appropriation request, can be used in the RFQ. There are a variety of approaches that can be taken to ensure these technical aspects are correct and reasonable. In some instances, much of the identification of the potential sources has been done before the RFQ is sent out. The candidate list has been narrowed and the specifications prepared with the idea that the selected RFQ receivers can meet them. There are those who would call this "slanted specifications" with the specifications delineated to allow only a limited number of responses. Others would say this is a good purchasing practice to get the information gathered ahead of time and know exactly what is wanted. Whichever way it is done, it is essential to have a clearly written, well-defined RFQ that minimizes the likelihood of misunderstandings and ensures that the respondents quote on what the buyer wants to purchase.

In addition to the technical dimensions and specifications of the equipment, the RFQ is developed to include comprehensive information:

• *Required delivery date.* When putting together the RFQ, the buyer recognizes the degree of flexibility needed in specifying the delivery date from a legal position. Although it is a needed date, realize the implications as to possible breach of contract on the part of the seller by failing to deliver on time. Realize the reasons for being late and consider the possibility of a liquidated damages clause in the RFQ. It is best to place it in the quote and get the issue on the table as early as possible. There will be negotiations on the final form and substance of the contract, but letting the suppliers know the areas of concern early in the process can save valuable time later, when time becomes more important. (This subject is discussed in greater depth in the Chapter 5.)

• *Duration of the quote.* How long is the quote considered valid?[7] Evaluation takes time, and an expired quote is a waste of time to evaluate. The expiration period should be at least *two months after receipt of the quote.* Make sure this statement is in the quote. If nothing is said by the offerer, the Uniform Commercial Code (UCC) is the final authority.

• *Warranty information.* What are the expectations of the buyer on the warranty issue? How long a warranty is provided on the equipment? Is every part warranted for a uniform period, or are the warranties for dynamic components less than static components? What is the coverage from a legal perspective? Is

---

7. Remember that the Uniform Commercial Code (§ 2–205) stipulates that firm offers are open for a reasonable time but in no case can that period exceed three months. If the offerer quotes a longer time period, the offerer retains the right to revoke or withdraw or change the offer after three months.

the warranty a limited liability warranty? Who has the final say in the repair-or-replace decision?

• *Support services offered and prices quoted.* Postsale service information should be solicited from the supplier. This should include a list of services and prices charged for those services, any retrofitting of the equipment, or upgrades.

• *Installation assistance.* What is the nature and depth of assistance offered by the supplier in the installation? Will there be a supplier representative present for the installation as part of the selling price, or is this an extra cost? How extensive will the supplier participation be in acceptance testing, recalibration, and making adjustments? What will these cost? Are they considered to be postpurchase services or part of the original offer?

• *Retrofitting capability of the supplier.* Upgrading in the future is always an option to maintain. Is the supplier prepared to perform that function, or does the buyer have to rely on a commercial retrofitter or used equipment company to retrofit? This is segregated as a separate service because retrofitting is an important aspect of the equipment purchase. The inability to upgrade equipment may make that piece of equipment the bottleneck in the operation at some later time. It should not be necessary to replace the equipment with something new regularly but also have the option of upgrading or incremental modification of the equipment as desirable features become available.

• *Maintenance support and training.* What sort of support and training (manuals, videos, etc.) comes with the purchase? In some instances, the obligation of the supplier may be limited to one set of manuals. This does not mean there is not more available in the form of videotapes for maintenance personnel. The question then becomes the cost of the extras versus the value derived from a different form of communication. One company selling rather expensive upgrade boards for personal computers included a videotape that showed a person installing the card. After the first 10 minutes of the tape, the announcer instructed the owner to bring in his own computer and follow the tape through a repeat of the process. Punctuated at various segments was a view of the installation at stages. The installer could compare a picture to the actual. The installation was easily and successfully accomplished. The dynamic visual was far more effective than the written instructions in the manual. With a generation now raised with VCRs in the home, the supplier who produces videos to supplement written manuals may see a rise in customer satisfaction, and the repetitive use of the video allows for better training at a lower unit cost.

• *Production rate of the equipment.* What is the production rate specified on the equipment? Is that a sustainable rate or maximum rate? If it is a maximum rate, how long can that rate be maintained before a failure or breakage can be expected or some component has to be replaced? What are the Mean Time Between Failures (MTBFs) and Mean Time Between Removals (MTBRs) of the dynamic components?

• *Maintenance schedules.* What is the recommended maintenance schedule for the equipment with respect to parts maintenance and replacement and the frequency of each? What are the cost and availability (particularly lead time) of replacement parts? Are there other sources for replacement parts?[8] Are there operating supplies that are unique to the piece of equipment as differentiated from spare parts? For example, certain pieces of lab equipment may require liquids with very high boiling points. Are the operating supplies or consumables unique to the OEM, or are acceptable substitutes available?

• *Operating requirements for utilities as well as utility specifications,* such as special gases, voltage, pipe openings, and flow rates. Utility requirements on the consumption side should be an integral part of the RFQ, but as important are the unique specifications for utilities that may come with the equipment. Does the machine use 220 voltage or 440? What is the recommended cable for carrying the current? Are there changes that will have to be made at the equipment site to accommodate the equipment?

• *Pricing information with an emphasis on the unbundling of prices to the largest extent possible.* Much of any product cost is consumed in the areas of overhead, selling expense, administrative expense, and operating income to the supplier. A fraction of total product price is composed of direct labor and material going into the product. It can be argued that these other costs are essential and all contribute value to the product, yet the actual material and labor in the product can be small relative to the price. Using the traditional accounting term of *cost of goods sold,* the product may contain only 30 to 35 percent of its price in labor and material and less than 75 percent of its price in cost of goods sold. It is important for buyers to understand what they are paying for and how much they are paying for it. Prices that are quoted in a bundled format often hide valuable information. The buyer is buying the equipment and should have the option of knowing what it will cost for other elements, beyond the equipment itself. The only way this has a chance of being known is to ask for it in the RFQ.

• *Certification of compliance with applicable regulatory agencies and testing laboratory requirements.* How does the operation affect the immediate environment with respect to noise, ambient temperature, dust, fumes, particular waste, and scrap? For example, in the automotive assembly industry, one of the major expenditures is cleaning up the air in the painting facilities. The odors and suspended particulates can pose a health hazard. Equipment to clean the air removes 95 percent of the contaminants before recirculating the air to the environment. The recycled air is cleaner than the air outside the plant. What additions will be necessary for safety or meeting environmental concerns? What impact will they have on operating costs?

---

8. This is a touchy issue. The spares business can be so lucrative as to make the initial price of the equipment almost inconsequential.

A small midwestern college installed elaborate laboratory hoods in its new chemistry building without spending a little extra on sensors. When the fans were turned on and the hoods left open, the force of the fans sucked the heat out of the laboratory. The heating unit responded to the temperature drop and came on, bringing the temperature up, so the fans had that much more hot air to suck out. The resulting natural gas heating bill ran the utility bill up 300 percent in one winter. Much of the increase was traced to the lack of consideration of what was going to occur when the hood motor was turned on. A simple timer would have paid for itself hundreds of times over in unused natural gas.

• *The appropriate ISO (International Standards Organization) qualification.* The requirement for ISO certification may be necessary from the marketing perspective. It may be your customers who are requiring ISO certification on your part. How can one claim complete compliance with ISO principles if the equipment one is using does not come from an ISO-certified supplier? As the ISO requirement becomes more popular, this issue will rise in relative importance to the buyer.

• *The conditions of the order.* For example:

The price to be quoted shall include:
    a. The equipment transported to dock site at the ABC Company
    b. Supplier site testing with tooling and materials furnished
    c. Manuals and or videos for maintenance personnel
    d. Retention terms

The RFQ should be as complete as possible with respect to the commercial side of the purchase in order to eliminate surprises to the supplier and get a price that realistically reflects the requirements of the buyer. Having all the information up front makes the negotiation process easier to plan and allows the negotiation targets to be realistically set. In addition, the RFQ can convey the intent of the buyer. A poorly prepared RFQ may not solicit the desired responses in that the seller may disregard impossible-to-meet specifications or may take advantage of vague requirements. This is not an area in which to play games.

Many of these issues can be avoided by visiting an installed site, observing the machine in operation, and talking with the users and the people who maintain the equipment. This is part of the qualification process and should be articulated in the RFQ as to supplying sites where the equipment can be viewed.

Finally, set a realistic deadline for the return of the proposals. This translates to having sufficient lead time for the entire process. Do not make the supplier respond rapidly or not allow yourself sufficient time to evaluate the proposals. Fighting deadlines for either party often results in mistakes.

Evaluating Proposals

Once you have the proposals, the next step is evaluation. Initially, log in the proposals or quotes, a simple housekeeping chore to note the responsiveness of suppliers. The proposals are then evaluated in two forms: the technical evaluation and the business evaluation. In some organizations, the technical response and business response are kept apart, and the technical evaluators do not see the business portion of the response in order to remove any possible bias that could creep into the decision by being influenced by price considerations. The role of the technical evaluator is just that.

Who meets the technical requirements that are in the RFQ? Notice the term *meets the requirements* is used. At this juncture it is important to make a distinction with respect to requirements. They come in three major forms. In the first case, the buyer's company designs the equipment it wants to purchase, and the RFQs go out to qualified suppliers to respond to that request. The buyer here is the responsible party if the equipment fails to operate properly. The buyer has supplied the specifications, and the implied warranty of suitability lies with the buyer. There is no legal recourse against the seller if the machine fails in essential purpose. The seller was just following instructions.

In the second case the buyer buys an off-the-shelf model and adapts it to the desired use. In this case, the operating description of the equipment is key to acceptance. Will it perform the functions the buyer wants? Proposed use of the equipment must be fully disclosed to the bidders in the RFQ. In the vast majority of the cases, the seller will not bid or reply to the RFQ if the equipment will not perform the tasks desired by the buyer. If the seller sells the equipment and it fails to perform, there are issues of **failure of express purpose.** The equipment was not capable of performing the desired tasks. As a result, the seller faces liability for the equipment. It is essential that the potential buyer communicate the intended purpose or planned use of the equipment to the potential seller in the RFQ. Failing to do so, the seller can claim that the equipment was never designed for that purpose and the seller has no liability.

The third case is **intended use buying** where the buyer wants functions to be performed by the equipment and has the seller both design and build the equipment such that it is capable of performing functions.[9] Therefore, the speci-

---

9. In the design-and-build contract, care must be taken to ensure the adequacy of the design. In some cases, it may be a good idea to segment the contract into two parts: design and build. The adequacy of the design may be tested by competitively bidding the build portion of the contract. If the design is good, there should be no problem establishing adequate competition for the build portion of the contract. Final payment may be predicated on the bids coming in for the build portion of the contract. This is an area subject to negotiation.

fications are performance based. Does the equipment perform the functions desired in the time allotted or produce goods within the specified tolerances?

The supplier who bids on the design-and-build contract is saying the company has the capability in terms of engineering skills and manufacturing expertise to produce equipment that can perform or meet specifications. Again, the RFQ must carefully describe what is wanted. Failing to do so adequately or simply accepting what the supplier offers as good enough is insufficient and offers the supplier *carte blanche* in the order. Good communication is vital.

In some cases, the submission will exceed the requirements. Exceeding the requirement may be nice but may also cause the buyer to pay for something not needed. The well-defined RFQ will say what the requirements are for all responders. The key is coming as close to the need as possible at the best price.

In the evaluation process, there is no one best way. Systems can range from a simple checklist to point scoring each portion of the response and weighting each section to reflect the relative importance of each section. Naturally the technical capability of the equipment is going to carry the most weight, yet the business specifications must also be met. By having each portion of the quotation priced individually, it is possible to deal with the data in many ways.

Consider the following evaluation where a point scoring system was used, weighting the technical side by 70 percent and the business specifications by 30 percent. A point scoring system was used on a simple 1, 2, 3 scale, with 1 being *marginally meets specification*, 2 equating to *meets specification*, and 3 equating to *exceeds specification*. In addition to scaling, the RFQ was sufficiently detailed so as to allow a complete breakdown of where the total costs were located and their fraction of the total cost. To illustrate the evaluation process, consider the quotation shown in Exhibit 4-1 to design and build a specialized piece of equipment. Although the dollar amount is not large, the quotation will be analyzed to illustrate all the points to attend to before going into negotiation with the potential supplier. To separate the quotation from the text, all the pages of the quotation will be boxed.

Analyzing the RFQ

A view of the proposal requires looking at the technical as well as the business specifications presented in it. On the technical side, Dunkle wants a coil winding table capable of running two types of tubes. The factors of interest are cycle time and changeover time. Looking at output as a performance specification, fill tube production rate is 15 per minute or 900 per hour. Pigtail capillary tube rate is 360 per hour to 480 per hour. Changeover time is 15 minutes. Thus, changeover equates to 225 fill tubes or 90 to 120 pigtail capillary tubes, depending on what is being currently run. From these data, it should be relatively easy to devise the type of floor test that should be conducted. At the minimum, it should be 2 hours of production with one changeover included. This would allow a run to be made and a changeover and the second product set up by

(*text continues on page 118*)

Exhibit 4-1. Sample quotation to design and build a piece of equipment.

Hoskins Automated Controls Inc.
P.O. Box 407
Water Closet, Nebraska 67891
888/567-2345

March 16, 19x7

Mr. Walter Ferguson
Dunkel Industries Inc.
Bartle Road
Grandview, Missouri 64104

RE: Coil Winding Machine
Quote 01310

Dear Walter:

We are please to submit the following quotation for designing and building one (1) coil winding table per samples furnished to us by Dunkle Industries Inc. Please find enclosed terms and specifications for performing this work.

SCOPE OF THE PROJECT:
Hoskins Automated Controls Inc. will design a coil winding machine capable of running fill tubes and pigtale capillary tubes. Each tube will require a mandural change. Cycle time will be approximately 4 seconds per fill tube and 8 to 10 seconds for the pigtail capillary tube.

TERMS AND CONDITIONS:
We propose to furnish material and labor—complete in accordance with the following specifications for the sum of:

Ten thousand three hundred dollars ($10,300)

Terms of Payment
 • 30 percent on the acceptance of the proposal
 • Remainder net 15 days from completion
Minor changes or corrective work not affecting production shall not affect payment.

Interest of 1½ percent per month will be assessed on the unpaid balance of accounts over 30 days.

By issuing a purchase order to Hoskins Automated Controls Inc., for the work to be done, you are agreeing to all terms and conditions set forth in this quotation.

(continues)

Exhibit 4-1. *Continued*

All work will be completed in a professional manner according to standard practices. Any alteration or deviation from specifications involving extra cost will be executed only upon written orders and will become an extra charge over and above the estimate.

Orders canceled by the purchaser at anytime prior to the promised delivery date are subject to liquidated damages as follows: "accrued charges for engineering, material and handling, labor, project financing and reasonable compensation for the loss of business due to the cancellation. Such cancellation shall incur no liability on the part of the seller to the purchaser."

Prices quoted in our proposal will be firm for 90 days, FOB our facility, Water Closet, Nebraska. Prices are exclusive of all applicable state and federal taxes.

DELIVERY DATE:
Machine will be ready for run off in our shop 6 to 8 weeks from the date of the receipt of the purchase order. Every effort will be made to deliver as promised. However, delivery dates are estimates and not guarantees and are based upon conditions at the time of the quotation and subject to prior sales of capacity. The seller shall not be responsible for delays or nonperformance caused by strikes, fires, or any and all causes beyond our control.

WARRANTY:
Hoskins Automated Controls Inc. warrants the equipment to be free from defects in materials and workmanship under normal use and service for a period of one year after delivery, except for purchased parts, in which case the original manufacturer's warranty is automatically extended to our customers. The warranty shall not apply to and H.A.C. Inc. will not be responsible for any equipment or part which has been repaired or altered in any way that, in our judgment, affects its stability or its reliability or which has been subjected to misuse, negligence or accident.

CONTROLS:
The machine controls will be fabricated according to the latest J.I.C. (Joint Industry Conference) and NEC (National Electrical Contractors) standards. Full documentation of all wiring and programming will be provided.

Machine operation: Basic operation of the machine will be as follows:
• Operator loads tube in machine and hits foot switch.
• Winder starts winding.
• When winding cycle is complete, a light comes on alerting operator.
• Operator removes coil and installs a new tube to be wound.
• Cycle starts over.

MACHINE DESCRIPTION:

Basic machine concepts will be as follows:
- Changeable mandurals will be quick change, to require less than 15 minutes to change.
- Winder will have an adjustable torque, set to protect the operator.
- Controls will be capable of handling programs for future expansion.

Major machine components will include:
- Steel table painted any desired color—please specify color on purchase order
- Programmable steeper system
- 2-changeable mandurals
- Controls mounted in a NEMA 12 enclosure
- 2 sets of operator/maintenance manuals

CUSTOMER-SUPPLIED ITEMS:

Dunkle Industries will supply the following:
- coils for texting

DEMONSTRATION:

It is our standard policy to totally simulate system operation in our facility prior to shipment. We would expect Dunkle Industries to have representatives witness the simulated run on our shop floor and offer approval and acceptance of the simulated system on our floor.

INSTALLATION:

Actual installation of the machine will be the responsibility of Dunkle Industries. One of our technicians will be available to answer any questions you may have.

START-UP TRAINING:

Hoskins will provide informal operator training as part of this proposal. Our personnel will be present to instruct operators in operation of all controls and make any adjustments that are necessary. One (1) man-day of assistance is provided at no additional cost. If any additional time is required, our rates are:
- Monday through Friday 8:00 A.M. to 5: P.M. ....$45.00 per hour
- Saturday and overtime ....$67.50 per hour
- Sundays and holidays ....$90.00 per hour

Above rates do not include travel or living expenses

UTILITIES:

Dunkle Industries will be responsible for supplying the following utilities:
- 115 VAC, 1-phase of 15 amps

(continues)

Exhibit 4-1. *Continued*

OPERATOR SAFETY AND GUARDING:
Operator safety is a concern of all parties. All machinery that we manufacture is subject to the scrutiny of our personnel prior to shipment. All machines will be designed and manufactured to meet our interpretation of all applicable OSHA standards concerning safety and guarding.

Operation of the machine without proper operator protection devices is to be prohibited and enforced by Dunkle Industries. It is expected that Dunkle Industries will hold Hoskins AC harmless and indemnify Hoskins from any and all claims of injury due to the normal operation or misuse of the proposed machine.

We thank you for allowing us to respond to your Request for Quotation. We look forward to working with you on this project. If you have any questions, please feel free to call upon us.

Sincerely,

Merle Drenkpohl
Vice President for Sales

---

changing mandurals and running the second product. One aspect that bears consideration is the variability of the pigtail capillary tube. The cycle time has too much variation or variability in it.

The buyer is offered some additional standards in the area of the machine controls and the housing. In addition, the adequacy of the manuals and documentation of all wiring and programs can be evaluated in an objective manner. There is a parts description of major components.

Because on-site testing at the supplier's facility is stipulated, the design of the test should be at the discretion of the buyer. The test description is rather vague and needs to be clarified prior to acceptance of the offer. Certainly operation at the supplier's site does not constitute acceptance of the equipment. It is not going to be housed at the supplier's facility, and a test run should be made at the buyer's facility upon installation and training of operators. In addition, what is the basis of the proposed cycle time? Where do those data come from, and under what conditions have they been accumulated? Who is the operator, and how much skill does the person possess? These issues need to be cleared up prior to the order being signed.

Business Terms and Conditions

An initial payment at time of order placing is not uncommon. The 30 percent figure is slightly on the high side but typical of government contracts. The up-front payment does raise the effective cost of the machine since Dunkle will now commit to paying about $3,100 before it has anything and therefore loses the use of that money for 8 weeks. The payment of the remaining $7,200 is rather vague. Payment is to be made 15 days after completion, yet completion is never defined. Does it mean after completion of installation or acceptance of the machine? Nor is there any linkage of payment to performance. In addition, the term of payment's not being influenced by minor changes or corrective actions leaves Dunkle in a weak position. This term is unacceptable without a clearer definition.

The interest payment is onerous and should be deleted from the agreement. Terms should be net 30 days upon acceptance of the machine. All of the seller's terms and conditions are unacceptable to Dunkle because they give the supplier far more latitude than is customary. As for the issue of deviations from specifications, it is correct that the buyer pays for those, but it is also reasonable to provide an estimate of the extra costs before a change order is issued.

Note the liquidated damage clause in the quote as it applies to cancellation of the agreement. This clause would be considered dead on arrival in nearly all contracts. Its scope is far too broad and involves double counting. In addition, it absolves the seller from any accounting for the costs or documentation of such costs. The double counting is payment for engineering time, materials, labor, and overhead. The loss of business clause is absurd. The seller is being compensated for all costs incurred. The liquidated damages clause is really an attempt to add consequential damages that might have occurred had not cancellation taken place. The buyer has no recourse but to accept the damages without stipulated limitations. If the seller wants such a provision, then the buyer should demand the right to audit the charges, and a limitation should be placed on the value of liquidated damages relative to the due date of delivery of the machine. As this paragraph is written now, the liquidated damages could be $10,300 if the contract were canceled one minute after delivery of the order to the seller or one minute before delivery to the buyer. It is far too vague.

The quote is firm for 90 days, and this is in conformance with the UCC, yet there is another issue raised by the firm quote: Is the UCC even applicable in this case? This offer is for a combination of goods *and* services. What is the proportion of each in the contract? If the design portion of the agreement or the service segment exceeds 50 percent of the asking price, then the purchase is for a service, and the UCC is not applicable. This would allow the quote to be withdrawn any time prior to acceptance, and the 90 days is meaningless in terms of holding this quote firm.

A sticky issue is the delivery date. Only an estimate has been provided. This is a situation where the buyer can negotiate for liquidated damages in case of breach by the seller. Yet there has to be a date and period of cure for breach to occur. This paragraph is unacceptable; a delivery date would have to be provided. Included in this paragraph is a pseudo force majeure clause. It is not a true clause because of the wording of the clause. Strikes are not "acts of God," and "delays beyond our control" lacks definition. This would be a legal nightmare and represents a back door for the seller to breach.

The warranty is vague and leaves much for interpretation. Although the seller warrants the machine for one year, there are many vague or gray areas that need clarification. The warranty says nothing in terms of what actions shall be undertaken, by whom, where, and when. The transferability of warranty is something to be documented as to the willingness of the original manufacturer to allow transferability of that warranty. Are there limitations placed on the parts warranties that have special conditions or stipulations, or is Hoskins trying to evade the issue of supporting the equipment during the warranty period? If a failure occurs, what is the procedure or process for getting it resolved? Why does not Hoskins stand behind the equipment? Hoskins is quick to absolve itself of any responsibility for parts that have been altered or misused. It wishes to make the determination of misuse or alteration. It exonerates itself from faults in the original manufacturer's parts but refuses to back the machine up with a standard warranty. The clause is too vague and one-sided.

The demonstration clause is very vague. There are many definitions of the term *simulation*, and the fact the machine works at the seller's facility is no reason to accept it at that time and place. It should certainly be tested at the seller's site to show it works, but it should be tested at the buyer's site after installation and *before* acceptance and final payment are made. What takes place on the seller's floor is no guarantee of performance at the buyer's site. Payment is tied to performance.

The installation issue is clear as to responsibility for the installation but unclear as to the role of the supplier in the process. What will the representative do other than answer questions? Is this part of the start-up and training time or separate from it? What is the responsibility of the seller in the installation process? Is the technical representative providing advice or directing the installation? Who has liability for correct installation?

The start-up and training effort may not be adequate. This depends on the operation of the machine, the changeover procedure, and the skill of the operator. Much of this issue could be resolved in the supplier's site demonstration and the in-plant acceptance testing with the designated operator(s) participating in the supplier site test and the acceptance testing. It is one thing to have an experienced operator test the equipment and another to have the neophyte or untrained operator run the machine. This is a negotiation point.

Finally comes the term dealing with operator safety and guarding. This area is indeed one where the buyer must exercise caution. The seller has said, "All machines will be designed to meet *our interpretation* [italics added] of all applicable OSHA standards concerning operator safety and guarding." In the next paragraph, the seller wants indemnification from any injury claim. This is a situation where the seller decides what is correct, and if he is wrong, he is not responsible. Any buyer agreeing to the term on operator safety and indemnification would be placing his company at severe risk in case of an accident. The seller's interpretation of OSHA requirements should be backed up with a willingness to see that interpretation tested in the courts, and the seller should not be indemnified or held harmless if it can be proved that inadequate safety devices or insufficient guarding were present. The seller cannot have it both ways.

The Next Step

Notice that little was said about the price. Price analysis would be a consideration, and there are some ways to look at price. (See Chapter 10.) Yet there is a sufficient amount of information for the team to begin looking at the offer and developing a counteroffer. Many of the terms and conditions are totally unacceptable and need to be negotiated carefully with the seller. In addition, the issue of applicable law is important. Does the UCC apply or common law?

A cost breakout is the next step. If that is not readily available, the buyer faces a myriad of possible problems in getting the terms and conditions of the agreement to be mirror images of each other. Moving the offer along will take skill and patience and require negotiation with the supplier. There are elements that may be dispensed with quickly since their applicability covers a matter of weeks and others that may be around for years in the case of safety and guarding of the equipment.

A good portion of the example deals with the issues of purchasing law. There is no way to avoid these issues other than opening the checkbook to all types of legal liabilities. Given the litigious nature of our society, careful buyers are alert to the terms and conditions that bring about the assumption of risk on their part. Risk and rewards should be in balance. Failing to accomplish this balance, the buyer can be making an awful bargain for his company—one that may haunt it for years to come.

In the next chapter, on the negotiation process, this bid will be used as the case example for the process. Prior to the negotiation, the buyer returns to the seller for more information regarding the cost breakdown between goods and services. It would be in the best interest of both parties if the UCC were the controlling legal force for this contract as opposed to the common law. This is a matter of accounting on the part of the seller to show the design portion of the contract and the build segment. The build segment contains labor, but those costs are really product costs and can be counted as part of the product. This is also a good way for the buyer to gain additional information on the asking price of $10,300. The materials portion has been identified in the bid. If the design cost can be separated, the remainder would be labor and overhead plus profit. The buyer has taken the initial steps in analyzing the price.

Sourcing Checklist

1. Before sourcing can begin, do a complete analysis of where savings can be made in realistic dollar figures. Will the savings come from:

   ☐ Labor savings (reduced cycle time, setup times)?
   ☐ Energy savings (reduced energy consumption, alternate forms of energy)?
   ☐ Spare parts savings via longer service life, lower cost, improved lubrication?
   ☐ Scrap and rework reduction?
   ☐ Increased worker productivity?

2. How much capacity increase is needed
   now_____
   five years from now_____
   ten years from now?_____

3. Is the goal to purchase proven technology or something newer with less of a track record? _____

4. Where are the potential sources located: offshore or domestic? _____

5. If you are considering an international supplier:

   Is it represented domestically? _____

   How much do you know about the relationship between the parent and the representative? _____

   Does the supplier offer technical assistance in the form of custom design and service? _____

   Are spare parts stocked domestically? _____
   How complete is the inventory? _____

   Are major components such as drive systems or numeric controls in stock, or must they be custom made? _____

   When service is needed, what is the response time? _____

   Who will make the transporting and importing arrangements? _____

   Where does title change hands (FOB point)? _____

   Will cargo insurance be needed? _____

   Have terms of payment been negotiated and finalized? _____

   Is the supplier able to understand and comply with OSHA and EPA regulations?
   _____

   Have you visited with a current user of the equipment, and did you use a list of questions developed before the visit on key issues? _____

   How long has the supplier been in business? _____ What is the supplier's current financial viability? _____

   What is the supplier's backlog position? _____

   Are you looking at a current design, or is it about to be replaced? _____

   Does the supplier offer operator training classes? When? _____
   Where? _____ How much in time and training costs? _____

6. What do you know about the source? _____
7. Has this source ever been used before? _____ What is the supplier's track record for being on time, quality, service, and overall performance? _____ Were all the concerned parties satisfied? _____
8. Has anyone in your organization been to a trade show to make side-by-side comparisons? _____Is a trip report available? _____
9. What are the upgrade or retrofit capabilities of the proposed equipment? _____ Will the supplier offer improvements to the equipment free of charge or at a nominal charge? _____
10. Schedule a specific meeting of the buying team to evaluate all proposals. Provide each member with a scoring mechanism for each RFQ or supplier. Make the meeting time as productive as possible. That time is adding cost to the total cost of owning the equipment.

5

The Purchase Order

Perhaps the most important single document in the buying process, the purchase order is the official and legally binding document generated for the purchase of the capital equipment. It is possible to make mistakes of commission or omission (or both) on purchase orders, but this is the last place the buyer wants to have errors. They can be expensive to both parties to the contract. Accuracy in every segment of the purchase order is essential. Perhaps the greatest fault in putting together the purchase order is omission of key information in terms or conditions or using the descriptor of "as per attached supplier quote." This is poor buying from both a purchasing and legal perspective. By not being clear and complete, the buyer runs the risk of issuing a blank check to the supplier in the order. The offerer is master of the offer. There is no need to make the offerer master of the contract as well.

In addition to being a document, the purchase order involves a process that in some ways reflects the quality of the personnel in the company. Well-crafted purchase orders that clearly communicate the order as well as the terms and conditions of the offer, coupled with the procedures to be followed at stages of the purchase, reflect an ordered and structured organization that pays attention to the detail necessary to complete the order as well as a company realistic in its demands on its suppliers. The movement of the paperwork with the correct supporting documents, in the appropriate time frames, can facilitate a good purchase that keeps to schedule. A poor process that is frustrating to all can reflect poor organization and an unhealthy organization. A poor process and a poor order invite problems at the later stages of the purchase by sowing the seeds of confusion in the relationship between the buyer and the seller. The parallel would be a precise set of instructions for the assembly of any item. Clarity and precision stimulate the process; lack of clarity confuses the process.

The purchase order is also a legal document written to protect both the buyer and the seller in the transaction, and when properly executed under the Uniform Commercial Code (UCC), it can be of value to both. The value comes from an understanding of factors that are important to both buyer and seller.

The UCC is a great protector of both parties to the contract, allowing conflict to be removed from terms and conditions and still allowing the contract to move forward, based on the intent of the parties. The code also protects the parties from unfair surprises and unconscionable contracts or clauses that lead to the loss of legal remedy in the event of breach of contract.

Finally, the purchase order can be the road map and schedule for all the information to come together so the process moves along as smoothly as possible. This is not to say there will not be bumps and potholes in that path, but a well-written and -communicated purchase document can make the journey smoother.

Developing the Request for Quotation

Normally the process begins with the need determination and progresses through the development of the requests for proposal (RFP) or quotation (RFQ). The difference between the two is minor. Governmental units often use RFP since many of their purchases are for services. The RFQ is nominally associated with goods, but the terms have been used interchangeably.

Before discussing the purchase order, some consideration should be given to the RFQ and its wording as it relates to the potential purchase. It is being used as a document to solicit offers from suppliers to sell goods to the buyer. As such, it must be a bona-fide offer to sell, not an "almost offer." Since an offer is a legal act and a contract may result from the acceptance of that offer, it is important to stipulate certain terms in the RFQ. A viable and valid response to the RFQ will state, "We offer to sell you a _____." This response can be solicited by beginning the RFQ with the proper language, such as, "Please quote your most reasonable price in which you offer to sell us the following items." "Offer to sell" is the important term. Responding to it shows intent on the part of the supplier, and intent is an important consideration in commercial law. Since intent is difficult to prove in a court, absolutely explicit language is needed. Consider the following responses to an RFQ:

    1. "We offer to sell you one Hindi character typewriter at $1,200. This offer will be considered open for 30 days at the quoted price."
    2. "We have received your RFQ 12345, and the price on a Hindi character typewriter is $1,200."

Response 1 is an offer to sell. Response 2 is simply providing information. In the second case, the buyer places an order using the $1,200 price and is informed the price is now $1,400. There is no recourse since there was no offer made by the seller.

Responding to the RFQ

In terms of the response of the supplier, the proposal returned by the supplier, in which the item is clearly identified in terms of quantity, descriptions, catalog numbers, or other identifiers, will identify the subject matter of the RFQ. As important as intent is the proper and complete description of the subject matter or the item being offered. The essential details of the offer include the description, the quantity offered, and the price or a way to determine the price. In the case of buying capital equipment, the price should be included in some format. The format may spell out the way price will be computed, a not-to-exceed number, or a percentage.

Sometimes the price is not stated, and the phrase "Price in effect at time of delivery" is substituted. The lack of a firm price will not be sufficient to make the offer fail the test of a bona-fide offer. However, the offerer should provide some information on price, if for no other reason other than the hesitancy of buyers to accept *carte blanche* offers where the scope or depth of the buyer's liability is not known. Buyers like a firm, fixed-price contract with respect to price. Lacking that, the next best approach is a not-to-exceed value. Another approach could be price at last sale, adjusted by the appropriate producer price index (PPI) value at time of last sale. In this case, the seller pulls the last sale of this item and the date of delivery and then adjusts the price using monthly PPI data. The adjustment covers the inflation (or deflation) since the last sale. This may be satisfactory for both buyer and seller since both have access to PPI data via the Internet or from the Bureau of Labor Statistics.

One final note concerns the duration of the offer. The UCC does not provide a precise answer on how long it should be kept open. Subsection 2 of Section 1-204 of the UCC defines a reasonable time as depending "on the nature, purpose and circumstances of such action." Section 205 addresses the issue of duration of a valid offer, citing three months as the longest an offer can be considered firm. After three months, the firm offer lapses, regardless of what may be said on the response to the RFQ. The time issue is important from many perspectives. Sufficient time must be present to evaluate the proposals received from suppliers, and once supplier selection is made, time must be allowed to develop the purchase order.

Does this mean the supplier must keep the offer open for three months? No. The supplier, responding to the RFQ, may stipulate any time period for holding the offer open. Both parties recognize that the starting date for the open period is the date on the order. If the offerer elects to respond to the RFQ and stipulates the offer will be open for 10 days, then that is the period it is open. If the buyer deems that period to be unrealistic, the offer can be rejected or not accepted. The best way to resolve this issue is to stipulate the desired period that the offer remain open. Should the seller not follow the guidance in the RFQ, the buyer can deem the offer as not responsive and disqualify it as a valid response to the RFQ. Time is an important variable, and a buyer should not be panicked into a rapid response to a questionable deadline.

As a result, the buyer looks for a variety of elements in the response. In preparing the RFQ, the buyer is soliciting an offer from the seller. It is an invitation to do business with the buyer. The role of the RFQ is *not* to make any kind of offer to the supplier but to solicit an offer from the seller under the conditions specified in the RFQ. The RFQ has no legal status, yet there are legal positions that both parties must consider. To protect one's company and simultaneously contract is the responsibility of purchasing. In carrying out this responsibility, it is fundamental to ensure that the buyer has presented the information in a clear and unambiguous manner, using language and procedures that afford that legal protection. Overspecification in the RFQ removes doubts as to meaning and intent. If something is important, do not rely on the supplier's reading the reverse side of the RFQ. State the important considerations in the body of the RFQ, conspicuously displayed where they cannot be missed.

In looking at the responses to the RFQ, the first issue to consider is if the response is a firm offer to sell or an invitation to do business. The invitation has no legal standing and can also be dismissed as a nonresponsive reply to the RFQ.

In sending out the RFQ, the buyer may include the appropriate forms to be used in responding to the RFQ. The format of the forms is not important, except that the offeree (the buyer) wants to draw attention to some important points. There are a variety of reasons for this approach. One reason is to make comparison easier if, for example, pricing information appears on page 4 of the response form. A more salient reason is that of terms and conditions. Using the buyer's forms and thereby agreeing to the buyer's terms and conditions can be an advantage for the buyer, yet the law offers some leeway here. In preparing the RFQ, the buyer should not rely on the potential seller's reading the terms and conditions on the reverse side of the RFQ or on the offeree's forms for responding to the RFQ. If the response to the RFQ is made on the offeree's form, then the offer must be signed in two places. The first signature is making the offer to sell, and the second is a recognition that the offer is to be firm for the period specified by the offeree. The signature block or space is placed below the stipulation as to how long the offer will be kept open. Failure to secure the second signature on the offeree's response form makes the offer an ordinary offer[1] and revocable at the discretion of the offerer. The second signature is an indicator of understanding the duration of the offer as well as the intent to comply with that segment of the offer. This stipulation is a protection mecha-

---

1. An ordinary offer is one that does not contain some form of assurance that the offer will be kept open for a period of time. Lacking this assurance, the offerer, who is *master of the offer,* may revoke the order at any time before acceptance, if there is no consideration given the offerer to keep the offer open. A firm offer gives assurance that the offer will be kept open for some period of time. An ordinary offer lacks that assurance.

nism for the offerer. Again, if it is that important, incorporate it into the RFQ, displaying it in a conspicuous manner.

Is this a legal minutia? Obviously not. The desire is to obtain complete bids or responses to the RFQ. Incomplete responses are not valid offers and therefore cannot be counted on as enforceable in the case of acceptance and then what appears to be breach of contract. If a valid offer is not made in the beginning, there cannot be acceptance to an *almost* offer. The offerer tenders the *almost* offer to the offeree. The offeree accepts what he feels is an offer, only to find that the offerer now changes the offer. Why waste the time and effort of evaluation of the RFQ if it is not a valid offer or the offer will be later repudiated by the supplier for one reason or another? Assuming the responses have cleared the legal hurdles and are firm offers to sell, the next step is the preparation of the purchase order.

Preparing the Purchase Order

This is actually the preparation of a road map to the buying process. While a portion of the supplier's quotation covers the technical issues, the purchase order covers the business issues. The proposals contain the offers to sell, and in order to have a contract, there must be acceptance of that offer. This is one role of the purchase order. Acceptance *can* be made in blank with the requisition coming from the user stating, "Per attached quotation," but it should be avoided. It makes the offerer both master of the offer and master of the contract. Some proposals come with the acceptance form or space on the last page to allow for acceptance in blank. This is not the way to buy equipment or machinery. The purchase order must be written to meet the needs of the buyer. It should contain technical specifications of the product purchased by referencing the attached technical specifications. It must indicate a quantity to be purchased and specify the delivery date for the item. There may be an allowable delivery window established for delivery or a grace period. Therefore, the method of acceptance is repetition of the offer from the offerer. There is a direct relationship between the RFQ or RFP and what appears on the purchase order. A good RFQ is the groundwork to a good purchase order.

Other factors are important to consider in the purchase order:

• *Transportation of the equipment.* Where will title change hands? This is the FOB point, and risk follows the title. FOB the supplier's facility places the risks in the hands of the buyer during transit. This means reviewing the depth of liability of the carrier and being especially wary of carrier rules tariffs, used to limit the liability of the carrier in the event of loss or damage in transit.

• *Financing issues.* These issues may be stipulated in the acceptance indicating the amount of funds to be paid with acceptance of the offer and final payment or a schedule of payments and retainage (if any). Included in this section should be the standard terms of payment. If final payment is conditioned on performance, this should be clearly stated.

• *Information on quality issues.* Acceptance criteria and warranty provisions are delineated in the purchase order. Much of this information is a restatement of information provided in the RFQ and should not come as a surprise to the supplier. Remember that the purchase order is now an acceptance of the supplier's offer as generated by the RFQ. A change or alteration of terms or conditions by the buyer in the purchase order can be viewed as a counteroffer to the supplier, not acceptance of the supplier's offer.

• *Compliance with desired reporting on the part of the supplier.* Unless the purchase is viewed as a turnkey purchase, certain reporting requirements must be met. A schedule of progress on the equipment is essential. If progress payments are made to the supplier, those payments should be based on milestones of progress. In addition, time is of the essence, and a delivery date is specified along with the activities that must be accomplished to claim complete delivery of the equipment. If the relationship is to be kept at arm's length and the supplier promises the final product on a certain date, the agreement may call for **liquidated damages**[2] for late delivery. The seller must agree to the liquidated damages before they may be incorporated into the contract.

• *Provisions for testing.* Testing at both the seller's site and after installation should be clearly mentioned, as well as the responsibility of each party for the testing, installation, and any training needed of operators or maintenance personnel. In addition, the support offered by the seller in the installation is incorporated into the purchase order, as well as any training in programming as is normally needed with computer numerically controlled equipment.

• *Provisions for change orders.* These provisions should be clearly identified, as should the expected or anticipated schedule so that prior to initiating change orders, decisions can be made as to their value and cost. This is important since it is not wise to have to undo or redo work that has been done already because a machine has progressed to the point that change equates to reworking the assembly process. There should be a clear statement on charges for change orders. This is a difficult area since change orders often translate into prompt implementation to avoid rework costs. It has been evident that change orders do not get the thorough review and study they deserve. Many get implemented, and the savings generated in preliminary negotiations are given back to the supplier in the change orders. Now time is of the essence, and the supplier takes a degree of control over the cost of changing the original

---

2. If the supplier fails to deliver on the specified date, liquidated damages represent the per-day loss suffered by the buyer as a result of that late shipment. These damages must represent a real loss to the buyer, and not some form of penalty or punitive amount. Liquidated damages must be provable by the buyer as to losses occurring as a result of the late delivery.

contract. The normal procedure is to issue a change order, modify the original purchase order, and reflect those changes to the original agreement. Each change order should be numbered for identification and a notation or copy kept in the original purchase order file.

• *Cancellation clause.* This clause is necessary should unforeseen circumstances arise and make the purchase impossible. The cancellation clause does not come without potential costs. In order to assess the reasonableness of those costs, it is essential to ask for a schedule as to the fabrication of the equipment. In addition, the buyer retains the right to audit the cancellation charges presented by the supplier, including visiting the supplier's facility to verify progress up to the date of cancellation. The seller who receives notice of cancellation and has done little in the fabrication process has far fewer claims for cancellation costs than the seller who is in the last stages of assembly. Normally the seller has a number of options available at this stage. They include presenting the buyer with the cancellation charges or completing the equipment and selling it to someone else, if the design is not so unique as to render the equipment useless to all but the former purchaser.[3]

• *Any special terms and conditions as they relate to the specifics of the agreement.* There may be issues of spare parts, stocking arrangements, trade-in, extended warranty, and other provisions related to the RFQ or bid. If unique aspects are in the contract—such as a period of grace on the delivery date or incentives for the supplier for early delivery—make sure they are identified. Make sure that quality provisions such as process capability or machine performance are clearly spelled out. If quality is an important issue, make sure it is highlighted. In addition, consider Occupational Safety and Health Administration (OSHA) and Environmental Protection Agency (EPA) requirements carefully as they relate to the equipment.

All of these provisions go beyond the specifications for the equipment itself. They are necessary since the more clarity brought to the process by a good purchase order, the higher the likelihood is of getting what you want, when you want it, at a price agreeable to both parties. Problems arise in those areas when issues are left vague or obscure, either intentionally or by omission.

There must be the balance of the agreement where the contract is not viewed as so one-sided as to be unconscionable or contain unfair surprises. It should not be a contract of adhesion, committing one side to compliance while limiting or denying the applicable remedies available for noncompliance by the other. Onerous contracts do not find favor in the courts. Much of the language

---

3. If cancellation is an option, the buyer should investigate the backlog of the supplier. Cancellation of a contract with a supplier who has a large backlog may pose no problem to the supplier. It translates into one customer's getting the order filled earlier. This also illustrates the circular nature of the design process. The more custom elements in the design, the greater the potential is for significant cancellation costs if it is decided the company cannot use it.

of the agreement is legal and constitutes the expression of the rights and responsibilities of each of the parties to the agreement. Look at the purchase order as a tripart document. It (1) offers the description of what is being purchased, (2) offers the terms and conditions that the buyer places on all those who do business with the company, and (3) specifies the special terms and conditions that go along with that order.

Finally, the contract should contain a **merger clause** that specifies that this agreement represents the final writing of the contract. The parties to the contract agree that this agreement finalizes and incorporates all prior and current statements and communications. The merger clause thus provides final agreement between the parties as to the nature of the contract. Domestic contract law has been guided by the **Parol evidence rule,** which states that written contracts cannot be altered or amended by verbal testimony.[4] To allow the use of this rule of law to be applicable, the contract must be complete in its writing. Allowances and exceptions can be made with respect to this rule in allowing oral testimony in cases of mistakes or fraud in writing the contract.

The Flow of Paperwork

There is a physical flow of paperwork that must be considered. Initially, the approved requisition comes from the requisitioner with all the appropriate signatures indicating approval *and* concurrence with the data and calculations of the project sponsor or manager. Purchasing should log in the requisition and notify the requisitioner that the requisition has begun the transformation process and that process will take approximately *N* days to complete. In addition, purchasing tells the requisitioner how many meetings will be required, and the requisitioner will have a final reading of the purchase order prior to sending it to the supplier.

Because the purchase order is a legal document, purchasing is responsible for ensuring that all the appropriate legal terms are in it. Purchasing is responsible as well for directing the final purchase order to the legal department for review if it is deemed necessary.[5] Thus, the next step is a careful review of the requisition by purchasing and the development of any questions purchasing has about the requisition. Clarification and amplification are the goals in order to reach the language needed to convey exactly what is wanted from the supplier. The greater the amount of information conveyed in the purchase order, the less likely it is that the buyer will get something not wanted.

During the time the purchasing department is processing the requisition,

---

4. D. B. King and J. J. Ritterskamp, Jr., *Purchasing Manager's Desk Book of Purchasing Law,* 2nd Edition (Englewood Cliffs, N.J.: Prentice-Hall, 1993), p. 553.
5. This can be a sore point for several reasons. Initially, legal charges will be charged back to the local operation. Second, it is an ego issue. Local managers feel they are capable of solving their own problems. Pride cometh before a fall.

the requisitioner should not sit idly by and assume all is progressing well. Periodic follow-up is important. People are fallible creatures. Consider the case of the electric forklift truck requisitioned by the engineering department of a large company.

When the requisition arrived in the purchasing department, the purchasing manager decided that he would look around for a used truck with the same specifications, but he failed to communicate his plans to engineering. Two months later, the engineer, becoming concerned about his purchase, called the supplier specified on the requisition. The supplier had no knowledge of any order. Calling purchasing, the engineer found out about the substitute and the lack of success on the part of the purchasing agent in finding the appropriate substitute. Meanwhile, the price of the new forklift had risen, and the fiscal year had ended, so the funds allocated for the truck reverted out of the department. There was now no money for the truck. A supplemental capital appropriation was necessary, and the ill will between engineering and purchasing was amplified.

Communication is the solution. In this case, both parties had failed in their performance. Purchasing should have discussed the substitutability of the used truck and should have kept a wary eye on the calendar. Engineering should have followed up on the purchase more closely, since it was a rather routine purchase. Yet blame placing does not get the job done. The issue is frequent communication, and to facilitate that communication and act as a focal point for it, the project sponsor is a key player in the process.

As the purchase order nears completion, meeting with the supplier to discuss the requirements of the order and its terms and conditions can be a worthwhile effort. At this stage of the process, there are no real surprises. The RFQ response (offer) to be accepted is known to both buyer and seller. Recognize the legal position at this point. There is an offer on the table by the offerer (seller) in the form of response to the RFQ. That offer carries with it terms and conditions. The purchase order being crafted is a response to that offer. The issue is whether this response classifies itself as an acceptance of the seller's offer or a counteroffer to the seller. A portion of the answer lies in the wording of the RFQ. If the RFQ was clear and contained all the language to be repeated in the purchase order, it is likely that the act of restating or repeating the terms of the offer would be considered acceptance. If changes are made from the RFQ and incorporated into the purchase order, the offerer may feel the purchase order is a counteroffer and would be treated as such. Several options are open to the offerer. These include outright rejection of the offer or resorting to the Battle of the Forms.

The purpose of the meeting and discussion is to avoid rejection and the creation of a legal issue where none may have existed. Discussion before the fact may prove superior to discussions after the order has been prepared. The offer-counteroffer situation can cause delays in the process and escalate costs for both parties. Having resolved the issues, if any, with the supplier before acceptance of the seller's offer, the appropriate signature is needed. The buyer monitors the signature process since time can be consumed as a purchase order reposes in someone's in box, awaiting signature.

Once the purchase order is signed, the buyer may wish to fax a copy of the complete order to the supplier, with the original copy sent by mail, to give the supplier some additional time to check it over. Enclosed with the purchase order is an acknowledgment form. Technically, if the purchase order is an acceptance of the seller's offer, this form is not needed; the purchase order itself constitutes an acceptance. The UCC works for the buyer in this case if the seller sees the purchase order as a counteroffer. The seller has 10 days from receipt of the acceptance to respond to the counteroffer by rejecting the counteroffer completely or resubmitting a new offer. Remember that counteroffers make the offeree the offerer. It is an offer made to alter or change an offer directed to the person making the offer. If the buyer makes the counteroffer in the purchase order, the original offer of the offerer is a dead issue. The offeree (the seller) may accept the counteroffer, reject it, or counter the counteroffer.

Sometimes many offers with intent, properly delivered, and with subject matter coverage clearly expressed, are conveyed many times, with the role of offerer and offeree shifting during the course of the negotiations. In sending the acknowledgment form with the acceptance (purchase order) and requesting it be signed and returned to the buyer who initiated the acceptance, the offerer is responding that the acceptance was viewed as a true acceptance of the original offer and not a counteroffer. If the acknowledgment does not return for a period of 10 days beyond the anticipated date of arrival of the purchase order, it is reasonable to assume the order is moving forward and a true contract exists. The time period always noted in the UCC is 10 days, beginning upon receipt of the offer. In this case, the purchase order is acceptance of the supplier's offer, generated by the response to the RFQ. The purchase order is an acceptance of the offer. If so viewed by the offerer, the acknowledgment can be signed by the offerer, showing the acceptance to be a firm acceptance, not a counteroffer.

On average, allow two business weeks plus six calendar days for mailing back and forth. If any conditions have changed during the time period when paperwork was moving, a **change order** may be needed to reflect these changes. The use of the change order is determined by the changes themselves and the degree to which they materially alter the offer.

Following up on the acceptance is recommended. A brief telephone call can save hours of correspondence. If there are additions, corrections, or clarifications, make sure the buyer gets these areas identified in writing. The buyer may have to discuss them with the requisitioner or have the requisitioner as a participant in the negotiation with the supplier.

In order to avoid the possibility of prolonging the process, clear and complete communication in the RFQ and clarity of the purchase order are essential. Consistency between the two documents is important, even though the legal standing of the RFQ is nonexistent in comparison with the purchase order. Keeping the lines of communication open among all the parties is a fundamental aspect of the process. At the same time, the communication process tells the seller the process is moving and the offer is still alive and being considered or is in process of being accepted.

Special Provisions

The buyer must maintain a sense of balance in crafting the purchase order. An onerous agreement is not acceptable, yet there must be ample protection for each side. It is essential that both parties understand the purpose of the agreement and the protection afforded by it for each of them. Enforcement of violation of the agreement can be expensive and often results in a "no one wins except the lawyers" situation. Therefore, the buyer should consider both incentives and disincentives for the contract. The reasoning behind disincentives, such as penalties or liquidated damages, is easy to understand. These disincentives are the quantified and agreed-to damages resulting from breach of contract on the part of the seller. They represent the losses or damages suffered by the buyer when the seller fails to meet the agreed-on schedule. The sum of money agreed to is paid to liquidate the damages incurred as a result of the breach of contract.

Incentives

There can be incentives for the seller who is ahead of schedule. This is a more complex concept since it involves some flexibility on the part of the buyer. If the equipment was due on March 1, is there any benefit to having it arrive on February 15? That depends on the individual situation. If the buyer is ready to receive it, install it, test it, and put it into service *and* it fulfills the financial expectations as presented in the appropriation request, then moving it into service as quickly as possible generates revenue for the buyer's company. The airline buying the jumbo jet that will add significant sums to the revenue stream may be willing to pay an incentive fee to the supplier for early delivery. The builder of a power plant may be willing to pay incentives to the contractor constructing the plant to bring it on line early to allow power to be generated, assuming there is a waiting market for the energy.

The buyer may wish to look at incentives if the need is great or bringing the equipment into service offers some economic advantage. Yet both parties must be prepared to meet the obligations of the incentive portion of the contract.

Part of the multimillion dollar repaving contract for the main street in Appleton, Wisconsin, involved replacing water and sewer lines, and work was to begin in the fall. The contract, awarded to the low bidder, contained an incentive penalty clause stipulating a payment by the city of $1,000 per day for every day ahead of scheduled completion. The penalty side was a $1,000 per day penalty for being late. A 90-day limit was agreed to by both parties. The city did not take the clause very seriously, figuring there was little likelihood that any work would be done during the harsh winter. The contractor had other ideas. He dug his trenches and then covered them with a rooflike structure. Next, he installed portable heaters and continued to work during the winter. On the basis of his planning, he was able to complete the project 90 days ahead of schedule and was paid the $90,000 bonus. The city had to scramble to find the money. No one had anticipated the job would be completed ahead of schedule.

On the opposite side, make sure the supplier has the financial capability to pay the penalty or the liquidated damages. The clause does no good if it is not enforceable.

Disincentives

The use of penalty clauses in the contract or liquidated damages for compensation for breach must be approached with a great deal of care.

Two issues must be addressed. The first is the reasonableness of the damages relative to the provable losses. Unreasonable damages or damages sought as a penalty or punishment to the supplier will be voided under Section 2-718(1) of the UCC. There is no requirement of equity of liquidated damages. The seller who agrees to a liquidated damage fee of $1,000 per day to be paid the buyer for every day that delivery is late beyond the promised delivery date is not entitled to a bonus of $1,000 for every day he is early on the delivery.

The second issue is the size of the penalty. If the buyer is purchasing a $1 million piece of capital equipment, a $500 per day penalty for late delivery is a rather minuscule sum and will probably not do the job for which it is intended: keeping the supplier focused on the delivery date and satisfactory completion of the contract. What is the correct amount that keeps the focus yet is not considered excessive or unreasonable? This figure is going to vary from case to case, yet there are guidelines that may be used in setting the figure. Remember that the seller must agree to the penalty or liquidated damages. If this agreement on liquidated damages is not forthcoming, the option becomes arbitration or possibly litigation. An approach to determining the magnitude of liquidated damages considers these factors:

- Personnel time tied up waiting for the arrival of the equipment. Project engineers may be ineffectively used if the equipment is delayed.
- Costs associated with expediting the equipment such as premium transportation or overtime for certain employees.
- Lost revenues resulting from delayed arrival of the equipment. The inability to implement the equipment and produce the goods at lower costs may be grounds for damages representing lost income.
- Extra costs incurred keeping the existing equipment on line pending the arrival of the new equipment. This is sometimes included in standard terms on the reverse side of the purchase order.

Much of this information is available in the original financial justification of the equipment. It would not be excessively difficult to use that same information to assess the impact of the seller's breaching the contract. The better the documentation of this information, the more easily proven to the supplier that damages are really incurred if the equipment is late.

To convince the seller of the need for the clause, there should be a term that offers a period of grace in terms of delivery, with the understanding that the grace period is offered to cure the default on delivery. This is nothing more than codifying the "reasonable period to cure the contract" as required by the UCC.

The International Supplier

The discussion of putting together the purchase order assumes that the source of supply has been domestic. A generation ago, this would have been a valid assumption. Today this may not be the case. It is not uncommon to find the source to be in any one of a dozen foreign countries. Moving beyond the domestic shores raises a whole new set of issues.

Governing Laws

The role of the buyer is to ensure that the foreign supplier accepts American law in the form of the law of the buyer's state including the UCC (if applicable) as the laws governing the contract. Failing to gain that agreement, the buyer may have two options: The first is accepting the seller's position that the law of the seller's country will apply. This is not to be accepted without consultation with legal counsel expert in international trade law or comparative law. There may be vast differences between the laws of the seller's country and that of the buyer. The other is to have the contract governed by the Convention on International Sale of Goods (CISG). If both countries represented in the transaction have adopted the CISG, then if the agreement is silent as to which laws apply, the CISG will be applicable in the transaction. Thirty-eight countries have ratified the CISG, and these include the majority of the industrialized nations of the world. This option may be important in the transaction since often the buyer and the seller feel confident in dealing with domestic legal systems. The problem is that "domestic" means different things to each. The CISG is the middle ground so important in international trade. It is not required that the CISG be used, but its use is helpful if a dispute arises.

There are some major differences between the convention and the UCC, and they are listed in Exhibit 5-1. It is possible to avoid these differences by agreement to rely on the laws of the buyer's state in the dealing. This is done by so stating in the purchase order. If nothing is mentioned about legal systems, the CISG will be considered the appropriate legal mechanism.

Exhibit 5-1 by no means contains an exhaustive list. There are articles covering all aspects of the contract, and the alert buyer is going to craft the purchase order carefully to include precise statements to take full advantage of the convention. Care must be exercised to follow the shipment from the time of initial negotiation, when issues of laws, payment, transportation, delivery schedules, firm offers, acceptance, deviations from specifications, fundamental breach of contract, perfect tender, time allowances for curing a breach, responsibilities of the seller in the delivery process, documentation, and spares are discussed. It is only by walking through the process and careful documentation that a good purchase order can be generated. It is not meant to be onerous, simply careful, and one that removes some of the vague aspects of the convention or removes the applicability of the convention at all. This is not to say the convention is bad. It is different and represents a compromise between two legal systems in the interest of promoting international trade.[6]

Payment of the Foreign Supplier

Payment of the foreign supplier can be a complicated issue. With respect to the buyer, the ideal situation would be the same as the domestic case, where terms of payment are negotiated and the supplier waits 30 or more days to receive payment for the equipment. If the buyer is unable to secure an open line of

---

6. A copy of the terms in English is available on the Internet at http/www.jura.uni-freiburg.de/ ipr1/cisg/conv/convuk.htm (21 pages).

Exhibit 5-1. Comparing the CISG and the UCC.

Issues	UCC	CISG
Specifying Price on the P.O.	Not needed by the UCC, can have price in effect at time of delivery	Necessary and must appear, if not prevailing price at time of contract
Acceptance of Offer effective	When mailed to offerer	When received by offerer
Battle of the Forms	Conflicting terms dropped	Mirror image. Acceptance must comply exactly with the terms of the offer
Oral Contracts	Not enforceable over $500	Enforceable
Coverage	Goods, not services	Same as UCC
Termination of Offer	Section 2-205 silent, look to common law and counteroffer	Counteroffer terminates offer
Breach of Contract	Draws no distinction on type of breach	Describes a "fundamental breach" and gives buyer redress only when this happens
	No mention of foreseeing breach	Not a fundamental breach if not foreseen by party breaching
Contract Modification	No consideration required to modify	Same as UCC
Patent Infringement	Buyer protected by indemnification clauses	Protects buyer only if supplier knew about possible infringement suit
Time to "Cure" Breach	Reasonable period of time	Buyer gives precise time for curing a fundamental breach
Overruns	Silent, trade usage prevails	Prohibited from delivering and charging
Consequential Damages	Allows for recovery of consequential damages	Allows for recovery only if foreseen by seller

credit, the next best option might be, in the case of equipment, progress payments to the supplier. These are not unlike progress payments in the United States; both should be based on progress made by the supplier in the fabrication effort. The issue can be verification of this progress. After all, the supplier is not in the United States, and a visit to the supplier's facility to verify progress is costly. Handling the progress issue can be done via intermediate acceptance criteria.

Regardless of the method used for verification, the issue of currency differences remains. National pride aside, there is no world currency, and currencies will fluctuate against each other. Desiring the firm, fixed price, the buyer will attempt to make the purchase and the progress payments in U.S. dollars, placing the currency risk in the hands of the seller. Should the dollar strengthen against the foreign currency, the seller receives fewer of his own units of currency for each dollar, thereby lowering his price through a totally uncontrollable mechanism. The payment issue may have to be stipulated on the purchase order as to when payments are made and in what currency.

Assume the seller insists on being paid in his own currency. In this case, the buyer must purchase the foreign currency at the times the progress payments are due. Currency fluctuations could make the payments more or less expensive relative to the dollar. This is not the issue, however. The issue is how the buyer can handle the payment in foreign currency or the currency risk.

Two possible approaches may be used. In the first case, the buyer could convert the progress payment into the foreign currency and make the payments in the seller's currency.[7] This approach would ensure that the price paid for the equipment in the foreign currency would be equal to the trade rate at the time of currency exchange. This is a rather naive approach of escrowing the funds. The seller may insist on the intervention of a third party, such as a bank, if the buyer is unknown to the seller. Another option is purchasing currency futures. If the value of the foreign currency rose relative to the dollar (the dollar weakens), the value of the future rises, offsetting the drop in the dollar. If the dollar strengthens against the foreign currency, the future may be worthless, but that drop in value may be offset by the strengthening of the dollar.

Some of the procedural issues can be addressed by using a **letter of credit.** Assuming the supplier is to be paid at the end of the project and the buyer is unwilling to pay before the equipment has moved from the supplier's facility, a letter of credit is a possible answer. The buyer initiates the activity by purchasing an irrevocable letter of credit from the bank and stipulating what documentation must be shown before the letter can be honored. The buyer's bank then contacts its correspondent bank in the seller's country, notifying it that a letter of credit is in its possession payable to the seller upon presentation of

---

7. These are all banking transactions; no real currency changes hands. Currency being held would be invested in some interest-bearing account in the bank of the country where the purchase is being made.

certain documents to the correspondent bank for transmission to the buyer's bank.[8] The seller is then notified by the correspondent bank.

When the seller completes the equipment and packages it, the seller can present the documentation to the correspondent bank for payment. The documentation will include the order bill of lading, an invoice, and a sight draft or trade acceptance. These three documents are protection for both parties. The **order bill of lading,** presented by the carrier to the seller, is legal proof that the item is in the hands of the carrier and will not be given up by the carrier until it is presented by the buyer to the carrier.[9] Upon delivery of the items, the buyer presents the order bill of lading to the carrier as proof of ownership. The buyer has received the order bill of lading from his bank. The correspondent bank has sent the documentation to the buyer's bank, and the buyer's bank has presented the buyer with the sight draft or trade acceptance and the invoice from the seller. The buyer must now take up the draft—that is, pay the amount of the draft. This is the payment for the equipment. The buyer's bank transfers the funds to the correspondent bank, and the seller may collect from it (or the seller may have collected already with the correspondent bank paying the seller, less bank charges, and awaiting receipt from the buyer's bank). Upon honoring the draft, the buyer's bank releases the order bill of lading to the buyer. The buyer now has the order bill of lading to present to the carrier showing proof of ownership of the equipment.

Whose currency will be used in the transaction, and how will payment be made? These issues must be specified in the purchase order. Failure to include them is asking for problems in dealing with foreign suppliers. Although the use of intermediaries raises total costs, the value these people impart to the process is normally far in excess of their costs. In some cases, they are quick to invoice and slow to respond. The quality of agents varies widely, and their selection should be done carefully. There are several good sources for this area, but one favorite is the National Association of Purchasing Management (NAPM).[10] It is the professional association for the purchasing profession. Other sources can be transportation companies or freight forwarders.

8. In some cases this is not possible. It is wise to ask the supplier to provide the name of his bank, its address and appropriate numbers (telephone, fax), and a point of contact. Provide your bank with that information, and let the banks work out the arrangement.

9. This differs from a straight bill of lading in which the carrier is authorized to deliver the goods to the buyer without requiring the buyer to present proof of ownership, a copy of the bill of lading. In the order bill of lading, the carrier will turn over the goods to whoever presents the bill of lading. This allows the buyer to sell the goods while they are in transit. The resale of the goods would have to be accompanied by the passing of proof of ownership, the order bill of lading, to the new owner.

10. Call the NAPM Information Center at (800) 888–6276, ext. 3006; fax: (800) 329–6276; e-mail: K_Little@Enet.net.

Transporting the Equipment From Overseas

Purchasing equipment domestically may be complex, but that complexity pales in comparison to overseas purchases and shipment of the goods to the United States. Not only does the number of persons involved in the move rise geometrically, but the paperwork rises exponentially. Whereas in the United States, we have a limited number of places where title changes hands from seller to buyer or a third party, overseas buying may involve as many as 10 separate entities to accomplish getting the item to the buyer. The issue is also who is going to pay for what. The process is complicated by the fact that there must be export licenses, duties, clearances, time spent in possible storage awaiting an ocean carrier, unloading, passing through U.S. Customs, movement to the inland carrier, inland movement, and possible drayage from the railroad to the buyer's facility.

Overseas shipment may involve the following:

1. Moving the equipment from the seller's facility to inland transportation
2. Dockside storage
3. Moving the item to the ship
4. Loading the item and transporting it to the port of entry
5. Unloading it and possible dockside storage awaiting inland transportation
6. Transportation to inland transportation
7. Inland transportation to "near" destination
8. Drayage to final destination

All of these activities involve people and documentation of the shipment and risk of loss or damage in transit. Title retention and costs will range from **ex works** (EXW), whereby the buyer arranges and pays for all transportation and ancillary costs by taking title to the goods at the supplier's facility, to **delivered, duty paid, site designated** (DDP), whereby title passes at the buyer's facility and the seller is the responsible party for the transportation, duties, taxes, and other charges.

Transportation definitions are grouped into four categories—E, F, C, and D—in international commercial terms (INCOTERMS). The E term is a departure term standing for *Ex.* Group F contains shipment terms with the main carriage unpaid. Group C contains shipment terms with the main carriage paid, and Group D is an arrival term. For a detailed definition and classification, see Exhibit 5-2.[11]

Selection of the incorrect option for transportation can be a costly error on the part of the buyer. In most cases, the use of special agents, such as customs

(text continues on page 144)

11. A copy of these terms can be obtained from: ICC Publishing Company, 156 Fifth Avenue, New York, N.Y. 10010, or on the Internet by typing "Incoterms" in the search box.

Exhibit 5-2. International Commercial Terms (INCOTERMS), 1990.

Group	Term[a]	Buyer Does	Seller Does	Buyer Pays	Seller Pays	Buyer Documents	Seller Documents	Title Passes	Comments
E	Ex Works (EXW)	Everything	Nothing	All costs and taxes	Nothing	Everything	Certificate of Origin	Upon loading of goods	
F	Free Alongisde Ship (FAS)	Everything less delivery to dockside	Delivers goods alongside vessel	All costs after delivery	Shipping cost to port	Clears goods for export		Upon delivery by seller	
F	Free Carrier (FCA)	Everything after delivery	Delivers goods to carrier or freight forwarder	All costs after delivery	Shipping cost to carrier		Clears for export	Upon delivery by seller	Any mode of transport
F	Free on Board (FOB)	Everything after goods clear ship's rail	Delivers goods on ship	All costs after delivery	Shipping cost over the ship's rail		Clears for export	When goods go over ship's rail	Used for seas and inland waterways
C	Cost and Freight (CFR)	Everything at destination point and beyond	Contract for carriage paid by seller	All costs beyond destination point	Cost and freight to designated point		Clears for export	When goods pass the ship's rail at shipment	Seller pays main carriage, buyer has title and risk
C	Cost, Insurance and Freight (CIF)	Same as CFR	Same as CFR plus minimum coverage marine insurance	Same as CFR	Same as CFR		Clears for export	Same as CFR	Same as CFR
C	Carriage Paid to (CPT)	Same as CFR		All costs at and beyond destination	All costs to destination		Clears for export	When goods deliver to custody of carrier	Includes all forms of transport, including multimodal

C	Carriage and Insurance Paid to (CIP)	Same as CPT	Same as CPT plus seller buys cargo insurance	Same as CPT	For main carriage and insurance premium	Same as CPT	Same as CPT	Same as CPT	Any mode of transport, including multimodal
D	Delivered at Frontier (DAF)	Clears import customs	Delivers at frontier, but before customs border	All costs after delivery to frontier point	All costs to frontier delivery point		Clears for export	At frontier	Normally rail or motor freight
D	Delivered Ex Ship (DES)	Clears for import at destination	Delivers goods on ship at destination	Import duties and inbound costs	All costs on ship to destination uncleared for import	Clears for import	Clears for export	At destination but before import	Used for sea and inland waterway
D	Delivered Ex Quay (Duty Paid) (DEQ)	Responsible for inland transport only	Delivers goods to wharf, duty paid	All costs after title passes at destination	All costs, duties, and taxes to wharf at destination		Clears for export and import	At wharf or quay	Duty unpaid if buyer wishes to clear for import and pay duty
D	Delivered Duty Unpaid (DDU)	Responsible for customs and importation charges	Delivered to destination	All costs after title passes plus customs formalities	All costs up to delivery at destination, less importation costs	Clears for import	Clears for export	At named place in country of importation	Can modify by having seller pay other costs such as value-added tax (VAT)
D	Delivered Duty Paid (DDP)	No responsibility beyond normal receipt	Everything; bears all risks and costs	Nothing other than goods	Everything: transportation, insurance, export, import customs and duties		All documentation	At the buyer's receiving area or destination	Can exclude seller's obligations by noting, e.g., VAT Unpaid

Source: From descriptive pages of INCOTERMS 1990, Copyright ICC Publishing Company, New York, N.Y. 1997.
[a]Terms include destination, either named place, named place of destination, or port of destination or shipment.

specialists, freight forwarders, and import experts, is warranted. Clearing goods for export, purchasing marine insurance, and dealing with foreign customs and tax officials requires the knowledge of an expert on that country. Having a representative or agent present when the equipment is being off-loaded at dockside, transported to a warehouse awaiting arrival of the liner, transported to the liner, and loaded aboard, and having that individual expert in the paperwork needed to ensure timely clearance from the port is often well worth the dollars spent. The same may hold true for arrival at the port of entry. Supervising the unloading, clearing of U.S. Customs, and loading for inland transportation are not normal purchasing activities and are best handled by an agent. What the buyer seeks is an agent capable of doing much or all of these activities. Often freight forwarders have that capability. The point to consider is whether the freight forwarder has a terminal in the country where the equipment is being purchased. The physical presence in the country of origin is a definite plus in forwarder selection.

All the information about delivery must be in the purchase order. When the equipment is almost ready for delivery, it is advisable for the buyer to send a routing letter to the seller as a reminder of the transportation aspects of the order. This is done for two reasons. First, the period between the initial order and the time of shipment may be significant. Second, the buyer, depending on the terms of transportation, may have additional information to convey that was not available at the time of placing the order. For example, if the contract stipulated FOB (on ship), in which case the supplier delivers the equipment to the ship and clears the machine for export, the name of the liner may not have been known by the freight forwarder at the time the order was placed. However, knowing the name of the ship or the airline is important in the tracing process. Brokers, freight forwarders, and others can give information more rapidly if this information is available. If your cargo gets bumped due to lack of space, stay with the follow-up process until you get more information. *Take nothing for granted.* There are many reasons for delay, including the broker's being late with paperwork or customs' moving the item to a bonded warehouse or holding it for complete inspection. Any type of delay is normally costly.

Items Not to Be Forgotten

There are many details that should not be omitted from the purchase order that cover a wide range of miscellaneous items. They include manuals on the equipment. How many are needed, and in what language will they be printed? Were the manuals written in English, or are they English translations from a foreign language? There is a distinct difference between the two. What units of measure are used in the manuals? Practically the entire world except the United States uses the metric system. Foreign sources mean metric tools and gauges.

Who represents the supplier in this country: a sales office or a distributor? What is the relationship between the domestic representative and the supplier? One way to purchase the "foreign" machine in the United States is through the distributor. This places the transaction under the UCC and passes all aspects of dealing with a foreign source into someone else's hands. The buyer has the desired equipment and the support in terms of spare parts and warranty support all in the United States. If this is the case, the buyer is buying domestically, assuming the authorized dealer is taking title to the equipment before the buyer purchases it.

In some cases, the relationship will not be that strong, and the distributor simply carries spare parts domestically and supports the warranty. In that case, all dealings should include the distributor, and the buyer should carefully investigate to determine the true capability of the distributor to support the equipment. How much expertise does the distributor really possess? What happens if the distributor cannot perform the warranty repairs? If the technician must come from the country of origin, who pays for what? It is wise to ask all these questions in the negotiation or discussions with the supplier *and* include the responses as part of the purchase order.

Are spare parts in stock or is the distributor merely passing on paperwork to the original equipment manufacturer? While investigation of the source of support more correctly falls under the topic of source selection, we mention it here to remind the buyer to include pertinent information on the purchase order. This is part of the purpose of the merger clause. Identification of omitted terms is a very difficult process. If the seller plans to live up to the agreement and the equipment will be supported by a third party, then the seller will have no problem accepting the order with that information carefully spelled out. Should there be a problem accepting the order that defines the support arrangement, *caveat emptor* ("buyer beware"). It may be saying that the discussion of support was simply salesmanship and puffery.

It is far better to have a purchase order that overkills with respect to inclusion than one that suffers the sins of omission of key terms, conditions, and performance criteria. The desire on the part of the buyer is to prepare a fair and honest document that clearly spells out what each party will do in the contractual relationship. Finally, in any purchase order, *time is of the essence.* Make sure that term is included in all equipment purchase orders where late delivery is a source of cost and frustration.

Some Final Thoughts

There is no substitute for a well-written purchase order. If the material presented in this chapter seems excessive in terms of what should be in the purchase order, especially in the international purchase, it is not. There are many ways by which the buyer and his company can incur extra expenses in the buying process. A significant segment of these expenses can be avoided by using some common sense in putting the order together. For example, there are eight interstate carriers with "Best Way" or "Bestway" in their names. The buyer who specifies that the supplier is to ship "Best Way" is opening a proverbial Pandora's box.[12]

In the international arena, the wording of the purchase order is even more crucial. The same word may have a different meaning overseas, or there may not be a comparable word in the seller's language. Legal systems differ as well as trade practices. Time zones, monetary differences, systems of measurement, and manufacturing policies as they relate to lead time and spare parts all contribute to the likelihood of confusion between buyer and seller. Add to this the relative infrequency of the capital equipment purchase as compared to production materials, and the picture can become quite complex. In addition, there are all sorts of "agents" and "specialists" around who, for a fee, will guide the buyer through the intricacies of the buying process. Here is one area to rely on the seller in the case of transportation using the extreme of delivered duty paid to the site.

Review the purchase order with the requisitioner before it goes to the seller. Verify with accounting that the funds are still available in the budget for the capital item. Keep in contact with the project sponsor to show the costs of acquisition on the project. Review it with the seller to iron out the differences. Have a legal review if there are any issues that are not clear from that perspective. Perform these activities *before* the buyer and the requisitioner have to live with the results of the order. Many of these activities can be done in parallel with the activities of the project sponsor or the person who will be responsible for developing the requisition. Early involvement of purchasing can allow for some of these activities to take place when time is available. Treating the process of buying as totally sequential robs time from the buyer and may endanger effective buying by putting artificial time constraints on the buyer. Coordination and communication are paramount.

Purchase Order Checklist

☐ Have you clearly stated the requested delivery and acceptance dates in a separate clause in the order?
☐ If progress reports are required, have you specified dates or frequency of the reports? Who is to receive the reports? _____
☐ Have incentive or penalty clauses been considered? Are they acceptable to suppliers?
☐ Have provisions for trial runs and training of operators been addressed in the purchase order and clearly stated as part of the order?

12. Private correspondence between J. Johnson, U.S. Transportation Services, and Richard L. Pinkerton, July 24, 1996.

☐ Have standard change order clauses as well as a cancellation clause been included in the terms and conditions?

☐ Have quality assurance testing and validation procedures been accepted by the supplier and written so as to be included in the body of the purchase order?

☐ How many manuals will be needed, both operating and maintenance? Will they be written in English? Ask for a spare parts list.

☐ Have you specified the warranty terms?

☐ Who is going to perform service work, and what are the rates and charges? _____

_____

☐ Will spare parts be purchased as part of the machine order or on a separate order? Where will they be stocked? _____

☐ Check with the supplier on exactly how he wants his name and address to appear on the purchase order. (This will determine to whom and where the payment goes.)

☐ Who is going to perform the installation? _____

☐ Will a rigging company be needed? If so, how many days notice must you give?

_____

State the name of the rigging company on the purchase order, and instructions to notify of availability of the equipment for moving.

☐ Are you going to send the supplier any prints? If so, specify them in the purchase order.

☐ Are OSHA requirements stated?

☐ What color is required, if other than the supplier standard? _____

☐ Will test material be needed? How much, and where should it be shipped and when? _____

☐ If supplier personnel are coming on your property, are safety and indemnification clauses associated with those visits written?

☐ Will a confidentiality agreement be needed?

☐ Will the equipment be taxable according to state laws?

☐ What are the agreed-on terms of payment? _____

☐ State the machine output at both 100 percent and 80 percent of capacity in either units per minute or units per hour. _____

☐ Include a statement concerning packing for shipment to prevent in-transit damage.

☐ List any accessory items (e.g., feeders, robotics, computer controls, conveyers, tool changers) by brand names and manufacturer if made by others. Ask for the transfer of warranty of all non-OEM parts or components from the OEM to the buyer. _____

_____

_____

☐ Ask for the return of all prints, test material, and parts, if applicable.

☐ Reference discussion dates and understandings that took place and were accepted by both parties. Document where possible to include them in the final writing of the agreement.

6

Negotiating the Purchase

Of all the purchases made in the average company, buying capital equipment is probably the most susceptible to negotiation. This stems from the fact that the purchase is different from the buying of materials or maintenance, repair, and operating supplies (MRO), both of which are consumed relatively quickly. The capital equipment, in contrast, will be with the buyer for years. As Mark Antony said in Shakespeare's *Julius Caesar,* "The good men do is oft interred with their bones, the evil lives on." The modern version is, "Screw up the purchase, and they will remember for years." A buyer has to live with the purchase for years and is not likely to accept the seller's quote. There will be some negotiation on the purchase, normally in the area of **business specifications,** the terms and conditions of the agreement. The degree or depth of the negotiation will be determined by looking at the expectations of the buyer and the response of the seller. Are there significant differences between what the buyer is asking for in the request for quotation (RFQ) and the seller's response in the quote? Are there standard terms in the response that the buyer finds unacceptable? Will the buyer therefore reject the bid or counteroffer? Objecting to terms and conditions opens the door to negotiations of those elements.

Often there is disagreement between buyer and seller on the terms, with the seller trying to protect his or her position by altering the terms and conditions. From a practical perspective, it is a wise idea to reject the supplier's initial bid by making a counteroffer and offering to negotiate the areas of difference. This response takes the original offer off the table; thus there can be no mistake on the part of either party that the original offer has any legitimacy. Indeed, the original offer may very well be a counteroffer depending on the wording of the RFQ. It is accepted in most cases that the request for quotation (RFQ) or request for bid (RFB) is a request for the supplier to make an offer. It may be viewed as an invitation to do business by making an offer. The seller knows from experience that the offer will probably be met with a counteroffer, and negotiation between the parties will resolve the differences between them. This is the normal course of doing business.

Sometimes the buyer may specify a two-step process of bidding, followed by negotiation. The process and its definition are important. If the seller believes the selection will be made on the basis of the response to the RFQ with no further discussion, the bid may be different from one where negotiation will follow the arrival of the bids. In a two-step process, the seller will normally have some additional concessions to offer in the negotiation session. This process is different from negotiation to resolve differences. It differs in the fact that the buyer uses the bidding process to see who is interested in the business, get a sense of the competitive nature of the market, and then select the supplier or suppliers who are finalists for the order. This may seem somewhat elaborate as a process, but it accomplishes much by letting the suppliers know there is competition in the buying process. In addition, there is a qualification process or first hurdle for the supplier. A supplier who is not interested in the business simply bypasses the bid or bids high. The size of the bid indicates the extent of interest.

The buyer must consider the scope of the negotiation well prior to the purchase itself, so sufficient lead time must be allowed to explore all facets of the negotiation. Too tight a deadline places the buyer at a distinct disadvantage because the buyer may be pushed to make concessions that should not be made or could have been avoided if time was not important. Each element of the buying sequence should be allotted the proper amount of time for completion. Spending too long on the evaluation phase robs time from the negotiation phase, and all the efforts from analysis may be wasted if insufficient time is allowed for negotiation.[1] A common misconception is that the negotiations must be completed in one session. Rather, protracted negotiations can be a useful tool to allow both sides time to consider options and alternatives proposed by each other.[2] The buyer, of course, must heed the legal deadline posed by Section 2–205 of the Uniform Commercial Code (UCC) in setting up the equipment purchase schedule up to the point of contract formation.

There can be several levels of negotiation in the buying process. How the information goes out to the seller is extremely important. Are you soliciting an offer from the supplier without adding your own terms and conditions, or are you adding terms and conditions? In the latter case you are soliciting an offer under a set of conditions such that a response by the seller that does not mirror

---

1. A favorite negotiation ploy in Japan is to avoid serious negotiation with a foreign visitor right up to the day before that person returns home. The visitor is negotiating with the Japanese counterpart and the clock. Also recognize that when the Japanese say yes, the term is not one of agreement but an indication that your message has been heard. When they say, "No problem," there may be a serious one.

2. The deadline the buyer faces is the period of time that the price may be considered firm. The Uniform Commercial Code allows a firm, irrevocable price for three months. The seller may extend that period beyond the three months, but can revoke the offer anytime beyond the three months cited in the UCC. If revocation does not take place after the three-month period, the offer is still considered alive as long as the offerer keeps it alive. The offerer is free after the maximum three-month period to revoke or resubmit, regardless of how long the original offer was "firm" in the original bid or quote.

your terms and conditions could be seen as nonresponsive. Consider the RFQ or the bid going to the supplier with its terms and conditions specified in the bid package.[3] The seller responds to the RFQ or bid with an array of business specifications (terms and conditions) that may not be the mirror image of the buyer's specifications. The seller offers a firm price for 60 days instead of the desired 90 days. This can be an offer to sell but under different terms. The initial negotiation may have to be over the duration of the firm offer, and that may take place before any further negotiation on other issues begins. Failing to reach a satisfactory result may preclude any further discussion by the buyer.

Areas Open to Negotiation

Every element is open to some degree of negotiation. To be more specific, negotiation takes place when there are differences between the buyer and the seller as to the technical specifications of the equipment or the business specifications, although the vast majority of the negotiations will cover the business specifications. It is almost implicit that the equipment will have the technical capacity required. If the technical needs of the buyer cannot be met by the supplier, there is no reason to buy the equipment from that person. It is considered process incapable. There may be negotiations on the add-ons to the original requirement with respect to accessories or automated feeds, but the technical and service aspects of the purchase are often resolved in the source selection process.

The only time when negotiation is not needed is when the interests of the buyer and seller mesh as in gears: Everything the seller feels is important is viewed as unimportant by the buyer, and everything the buyer feels is important is viewed as minor or unimportant by the seller. When there is conflict, the gears do not mesh. Negotiation will contain some cooperation and conflict and an effort on the part of both parties to balance their risks and rewards. The end result should be each side's making concessions and both parties feeling they are in a better position than before the negotiation began. Another case where negotiations do not take place is in those instances when the buyer feels acceptance of the seller's terms and conditions is not placing the buyer at risk. These situations are rare. Buyers should read the terms and conditions carefully. What appears to be an innocuous statement may have serious implications, as in the case cited in Chapter 4 on the coil winding machine when the supplier attempted to indemnify himself on the Occupational Safety and Health Administration (OSHA) standards by requiring the acceptance of *his* interpretation of those standards and further requiring that he be held harm-

---

3. Normally, the RFQ form carries the statement, "This is not an order" or "This is not an offer," printed in a bold type in a conspicuous place on the form. It is a request for information or an invitation to present information that may result in business in the future.

less to any claim for injury due to normal operation or misuse of the proposed machinery. In this case, the buyer had two options: negotiate the term or ignore it when preparing the purchase order. In the latter case the buyer is sending a counteroffer to the seller and the purchase order is not an acceptance unless it stipulates acceptance of all the terms and conditions of the quotation. In all likelihood, negotiation would have to take place over the wording of "operator safety and guarding."

Negotiation takes place over a number of areas.

Delivery of the Equipment

When delivery will actually be made is often considered the most important element in the negotiation process. There are legal and lead time issues in this element. If the delivery is not made by the agreed or promised time, the seller has a right under the UCC to **cure** the contract[4] and make delivery in a reasonable period of time. The issue then becomes how many days or weeks delivery can be late before the buyer can truly claim breach of contract. If breach is claimed, what are the remedies available to the buyer, and how will they be exercised? How much "damage" has the buyer suffered from the late delivery? Can there be provisions in the agreement to liquidate the damages suffered by the buyer when delivery is late? This issue (as to the size of liquidated damages) must be carefully considered by the buyer for a number of reasons. If the equipment is stand-alone, the impact of its' being late may be minimal. If the equipment is a replacement for part of a production line or an integral part of a process, then the consequences of being late may be significant. This situation may be complicated by the fact a subcontractor may be late, particularly likely in the area of tooling development, where the supplier has little control over the subcontractor.

The range may be from inconvenience to shutting down a line. Monitoring the project is essential, and the addition of some slippage in schedule is a reasonable approach on the part of the buyer. The supplier no doubt is anxious to move the equipment to the buyer, but unforeseen delays may appear. In addition, the physical transportation of the equipment may add time to the process. The buyer must consider the entire delivery process and all the elements of lead time. The supplier has some control over the manufacturing lead time, and the buyer has some control over the administrative lead time in his own operation, but transit time may be out of the hands of both unless both buyer and seller cooperate in this area by careful carrier selection and rigging arrangements.

---

4. *Curing* or *making a contract whole* is the act of coming into compliance on the contract by performing according to the terms of the contract. It is the act of fulfilling the agreement. Having the right to cure is living up to the terms of the contract. The seller has a right to apply remedial actions to correct the problem prior to breaching the agreement.

The buyer should consider what steps are in the delivery process that the seller has little or no control over. If equipment is coming from overseas, the buyer should be aware of the source, the country of origin, and the transportation to be used. A seller wishing to minimize potential liquidated damages may argue for shipping the machine ex works (EXW) from the foreign location; that is, eliminating any seller risk associated with poor or untimely transportation and placing the transportation responsibility on the buyer. From the buyer's perspective, it would be wise to look at the supplier's backlog prior to negotiation of the delivery date. Is it possible to make that scheduled delivery date? Losses of time stemming from space allocations on board ship or aircraft can cause the cargo to be bumped and warehoused until space is available. Who is at fault?

Liquidated Damages

Agreement must be reached between the buyer and the seller as to the damages the buyer will suffer if receipt of the equipment is beyond the scheduled arrival time. Liquidated damages are the monies the buyer will receive from the seller to liquidate, or do away with, those damages and not seek to recover them in a court of law. They are not designed to be punitive on the supplier, but represent forgone profits for the buyer caused by the seller's not meeting commitments of schedule or performance. Liquidated damages must be agreed to by both parties. The initial question is whether they will be present in the first place and what they will be.

There are a number of ways to avoid these damages by both the seller and the buyer. One approach is strict adherence to a project schedule. Another approach is the use of intermediate acceptance criteria at stages of production to ensure that the equipment is meeting the required performance standards *before* completion of the manufacturing process.

This area is open to negotiation and emphasizes the concept of time as being of the essence. Even the mention of liquidated damages as a condition of the agreement should serve notice to the supplier that schedule is important.

Equipment Price

Price negotiation for capital equipment is a rather difficult area. Part of the reason lies in the lack of data or variations in the data. Not all capital equipment is alike; it is not a commodity like aluminum or copper. Each supplier may have different cost structures, and comparisons are difficult.

In preparing for the negotiation, obtain all of the financial data possible on the supplier: the annual report, the 10K, the 10Q, and information from private sources. Go into the Internet and get the 10-year history of the producer price index by seven-digit Standard Industrial Classification (SIC) code. What has been the pattern of price growth over the past decade? Ask customers of this supplier what they paid and when they purchased. Try to establish a base point, and then determine where a seller stands in the industry pricing structure. This approach is simplistic but does offer some idea of where the price should be relative to the offering price and should be the starting point for price negotiation.

Other approaches are more sophisticated and require a component-by-component breakdown and analysis of material costs plus labor skills and their costs. Sometimes this effort is justified. A 1 percent price reduction on a $500,000 item is $5,000. The experienced buyer knows that the amount of slack in the price increases as the price gets larger, and it is not uncommon to have 5 to 7 percent available to concede in price negotiation from the list or bid price to gain the order. There must be some way of inducing this lower price beyond simply asking for it. This translates to data gathering and analysis.

Acceptance Criteria

The quality control member on the buying team play the key role in the area of acceptance criteria. It is necessary to define these criteria and make them part of the bid. The potential suppliers are simply being told what the equipment is expected to do and produce. Lacking acceptance criteria, there are no standards by which to measure what is being purchased.

Acceptance criteria can be expressed in many ways. They may refer to specifications and tolerances, longevity of operation, or operating costs over a period of time if energy consumption is a major element in product cost such as in fiberglass insulation.

A closely related issue is when acceptance takes place. In some cases, the acceptance process takes months. During that time, title still remains with the seller. Technically, the buyer is not obligated to pay the seller the full price for nonaccepted equipment, which raises the issue of retention or retainage. In addition, the issue of express warranties is opened. Since title or ownership has not passed from one party to the other, the buyer should insist the warranty period does not begin until the title passes. Acceptance criteria is a complex issue and should be carefully considered when making up the RFQ, evaluating the supplier, and negotiating with suppliers. These criteria may finally determine if the equipment is actually purchased.

What happens if the equipment fails to meet the criteria? Does this stop the process? Indeed, failing to meet acceptance criteria that have been properly communicated to the supplier can be viewed as breach of contract by offering nonconforming goods. This raises the issue of **perfect tender**—that is, goods sent that are exactly what has been ordered by the buyer—of the equipment. They (acceptance criteria) also can become express warranties on the part of the seller since the seller says, "My equipment can and must meet them to be accepted." From a practical perspective, the buyer has two options:

1. Waive the acceptance criteria and move the process forward.
2. Hold the supplier to the criteria, allowing him more time to "cure" the breach of contract, which in all likelihood will delay the project.

Which one is accepted is a complex question in itself. Failure to meet the acceptance criteria may open the door to price negotiation. Instead of a perfect tender, we have a **substantial tender,** where the item substantially meets the criteria. Let's say a machine is supposed to produce 400 units per hour. It can produce 400 per hour, but the variation in the part specifications is too large. Slow the rate to 350 units per hour, and the variation falls into an acceptable range. It is important to qualify the acceptance criteria so there will be no confusion between perfect and substantial tenders.

Equipment Testing

Failing to test the equipment at the supplier's site is an invitation to problems. This provision should be part of the RFQ, with the buyer giving very little or nothing on this factor. This is a "buyer must win" item on the agenda. If the equipment cannot produce a good product or results at the factory, the process of shipping it will not improve it. In addition, failing to test at the factory may offer the supplier an excuse that transportation threw the calibration off; therefore, it was not the supplier's fault, and he cannot be held liable.

How many units produced or readings taken at the factory are subject to some negotiation, but the vast majority of suppliers will not object to this. It is better to catch problems before they become bigger and more complex. From the seller's side, it may be a small item, but it is important from the buyer's side. Almost all of these costs of testing will be borne by the buyer and should be added into the total equipment cost.

Transportation Costs and FOB Point

Skilled purchasing professionals know that the cost of transportation is always carried by the buyer. The cost is assumed directly, by paying for the transportation, or indirectly, by having the cost buried in the price. The issues are the carrier and the writing of the transportation contract.

In domestic cases, buyers may choose to make the terms FOB origin, freight collect. This allows the buyer to select the common or contract carrier or even have a private carrier. If the buyer is going to pay for the freight, directly or indirectly, then the chief concern is the issue of liability of the carrier and protection against damage or loss in transit. This is an area easily negotiated, with the supplier being a minor player.

The negotiation will take place with the carrier and the lawyer writing the agreement between the buyer and the carrier. The buyer wants ironclad protection of the equipment in transit and the avoidance of **carrier rules tariff** that limit liability of carrier. It is essential for a clause to be put into the purchase order covering this issue. The buyer does not want to incur the expense of additional insurance because he or she surrendered protection by signing the standard bill of lading and not reading the conditions on the back of the document.[5] This item can be disposed of quickly in the negotiation. The buyer should use this as a concession to the supplier since it entails more work for the buyer in carrier selection as well as the potential effort of filing a claim in case of an accident.

Shipping from foreign countries is infinitely more complex, and expert advice should be sought before negotiations with a foreign supplier on shipment.

The Warranty

There are two general categories of warranty: express and implied. In the case of **implied warranty,** the UCC is explicit about these three aspects:

1. Passing of clear title to the buyer
2. Fair or average quality of the goods
3. Fitness for a particular purpose

These are almost self-defining.

In the case of **express warranty,** the buyer and seller may negotiate the duration and coverage of the warranty plus the variables that affect it. A machine operated on a two-shift basis will suffer more wear and tear than the single-shift operation, for example. The nature of the production process may be such that one machine exhibits high utilization and one low use, as in the case of a job shop.

Maintenance is a significant factor in service life. There are vast differences between machines afforded preventive maintenance and those maintained on an as-needed basis. In addition to the warranty itself and its coverage, the buyer should have a clear position on performing emergency maintenance during the warranty period without voiding the warranty.

It is useful to discuss the scope of coverage of the warranty as well as the possibility of excluding the warranty and making a price concession for this service not being part of the offer.[6] If the warranty is not needed, there is little point in paying for it. Consider it at about 1.5 percent of the selling price of

---

5. Carrier liability for goods in transit was established in the English court of Lord Holt in 1703 in *Coggs v. Bernard.* Carriers have been trying to find ways around this liability ever since.
6. A common negotiation practice in the public utility industry is to negotiate the price of trucks without the warranty. Many energy companies possess large vehicle maintenance capabilities that often are better than those of the dealer from whom the purchase is being made. In addition, special needs dictate special specifications, such as strengthening frame components to carry a truck-mounted aerial work platform.

the equipment. Also look beyond the warranty to the time the buyer will be responsible for maintaining the equipment. The astute buyer looks at the issue of having the seller on the buyer's property while performing warranty work. This can be considered labor at the plant site, and the appropriate insurance and indemnification must be present in the agreement, holding the buyer harmless in the event of injury or accident in the repair or maintenance of the equipment.

The warranty begins when the buyer takes title to the equipment, not before. Having the equipment on the floor while it passes its acceptance testing may extend the warranty for weeks or months, depending on the acceptance period negotiated.

Maintenance Support for the Equipment

For foreign sources, is there a domestic source of spare parts and maintenance, or must this be negotiated up front in the purchase? Maintenance support can come in two forms: skill support and spare parts support. How readily available are the spare parts, and what do they cost? There is nothing so expensive as spare parts produced by the original equipment manufacturer (OEM). Go to your local auto parts store and buy an air cleaner for your automobile. Buy the top of the line, such as NAPA Gold, for $6.95. Now consider the price at the automobile dealership: $17.00. The dealer charges 2.4 times the price desired by the retailer. Are they different? Yes. The NAPA Gold has a red gasket, and the dealer unit has a black gasket. The gasket color is not an integral performance parameter. The key considerations of this negotiation are the availability of spare parts, their cost, and the delivery time. Does the supplier recommend a spares kit or provisioning (buying spares with the equipment)?

Does the industry practice include maintenance performed by the seller only, as in the case of copiers or poultry processing equipment? Is the equipment so exotic that it can only be maintained by a specialist in the field? These questions raise the issue of service contracts. Service contracts should begin at the completion of the normal warranty period. Buying the three-year service contract that begins immediately is paying one-third too much since many items carry a one-year warranty. The service contract seller will refer the buyer to the warranty in the first year. When maintenance is performed by the seller only, issues such as response time by the seller, availability of repair personnel, and hourly labor charges for personnel must be negotiated and, if applicable, made part of the purchase order or referenced in the order.

Related Services

What services go with the purchase in the form of training, manuals, videos, and technical support? A clear distinction must be made here as to what is technical support covering such items as installation, programming, and troubleshooting the equipment and maintenance. Technical support may not involve anything more than explaining a term, diagnosing a problem, or interpreting a statement in a manual. Normally this type of service is either free or available at a low cost to the buyer. It is a service provided to the customer from a marketing perspective. How extensive and available is it with the purchase?[7] How long does the support last, and what are the rates for support beyond the free period? The technical support aspects of the purchase are very important. Often simple instructions or advice can save the expense of a costly maintenance call.

Terms of Payment

The payment terms often depend on the nature of the purchase. If the equipment is custom made or the end product of a design-and-build contract, the normal trade practice may involve up to 30 percent of the value of the contract as the down payment. This allows the supplier to purchase the materials needed without having to finance the project. Payments should be made according to progress, not the calendar. Progress is measured by milestones in the project itself, and this should be negotiated between buyer and seller.

Another form of milestone completion is meeting acceptance criteria in the manufacturing or fabrication process. The buyer remembers that the cost of progress payments is the forgone opportunity to generate a return from that capital given to the supplier. Those forgone returns should be added to the price of the equipment to obtain the true cost of the item. In the issue of retention—the amount of money retained by the buyer to ensure compliance with specifications—there should be definite criteria for releasing the retention to the supplier. Here is an opportunity for the buyer to recoup some of the lost return from progress payments. The buyer should not be surprised if the seller tries to negotiate for the interest income on the retention, using the tactic that retention without interest is simply the seller's making an interest-free loan to the buyer. The seller may indicate that his/her company is not in the banking business. The buyer can counter with the argument that the higher the quality of the equipment and therefore the fewer problems associated with the equipment, the less likelihood for long-term retention. The discussion can be endless, but the retention and the interest issue can be significant. The interest issue can be a concession the buyer has available to give to the seller in exchange for some more important concession.

---

7. As an example, General Electric at Appliance Park, Kentucky, operates its customer service center on a 24-hour, 364-day basis. The customer may call in for information or order parts every day of the year except Christmas Day.

The Percentages of Labor to Material for the Equipment

Does the contract fall under the UCC or common law? Since the purchase is being made of an item of equipment, this may be a minor consideration, but it should not be overlooked. Which body of legislation will rule in the case of legal problems? If the purchase is made from an overseas supplier, is the Convention on International Sales of Goods (CISG) the appropriate body of law, or has the buyer decided on putting a clause in the agreement referring that issue to the state laws in which the buyer is domiciled? If the purchase is from overseas, it is prudent for the buyer to be familiar with the CISG and the major differences between it and the UCC.[8]

Force Majeure

It is not uncommon to attempt to lump a large number of items under the doctrine of **force majeure.** Although there are instances when the supplier may claim that it was "beyond his control," especially in the areas of getting materials, other events clearly do not fall into the purview of the mighty force. Strikes and work stoppages by employees are not natural acts or acts of God and therefore should not be included under the clause. The buyer is careful to require a detailed explanation of exactly what is to be included in that clause before the contract is signed. Too many reasons become a temptation to be late since there is no penalty or grounds for breach of contract if the cause is covered under this provision. A lenient buyer can lose leverage in this area. The lack of sanctions benefits the supplier and penalizes the buyer who must rely on expediting and constant persuasion as far as meeting schedule.

Equipment Specifications

Is the purchase for *intended use?* What are the limitations of intended use? What are *normal operating conditions?* There must be a clear definition of these terms lest the buyer find the express warranty to be of little value. Clarity in the negotiation stage will avoid problems at later stages of the purchase or during the warranty period.

Contract Cancellation

Often the issue of cancellation of the contract is viewed from the perspective of the buyer's being the party who cancels the contract and must rightfully pay for labor and materials consumed up to the point of cancellation. Suppliers may try to obtain additional cancellation costs relating to overhead expenses

---

8. D. B. King and J. J. Ritterskamp, Jr., *Purchasing Manager's Desk Book of Purchasing Law,* 2nd Edition (Englewood Cliffs, New Jersey: Prentice-Hall, 1993), pp. 620–622.

and profits. These are open to negotiation. Yet the seller may wish to indemnify himself against any liability to the buyer in case of this type of cancellation. Cancellation on the part of the seller in the form of apparent breach of contract or actual breach of contract can create problems for the buyer. This issue can be resolved through negotiation for liquidated damages or the requirement that the seller obtain a **performance bond** on the contract. The performance bond would reduce the risk of nonperformance by the seller and would compensate the buyer for the breach. Getting the performance bond and the price paid for it is a measure of the stability and reliability of the seller.

No insurance company is going to bond or guarantee performance from a seller where there is no reasonable likelihood of the insurance company's recovering its losses if the seller defaults. Although these bonds are used extensively in government, where the public entity is limited in source selection, its use should be considered in the private sector too. In addressing the potential loss incurred by the seller in the case of cancellation, several questions must be answered. Is the equipment unique or commercial off the shelf with minor or major modifications? Who performs the modifications? At what point does the value of the equipment begin to change from general to special? If the modifications are minor to commercial off-the-shelf equipment, the loss to the seller may be minimal. A market exists for the equipment, and it is simply a matter of finding another buyer. A smart buyer looks at the seller's backlog and can estimate the likelihood of possible buyers for the work-in-process equipment when it reaches finished-goods form. The astute buyer is careful not to obligate his company to a situation where the seller can reap significant profits from the resale of the equipment. While the UCC requires the seller to make a reasonable effort to sell the goods or return unused material, the buyer should retain the right to audit the charges and, if necessary, take delivery of the equipment.

Breach on the part of the seller is normally covered under liquidated damages, and the buyer would have to provide a period to cure the breach. If the breach is not cured, the buyer is entitled to **cover damages,** recovering the difference between the contract price and the price paid to replace the equipment. This is normally not complex for commodities, but with the lead time for equipment, the complexity in computing these damages is significantly increased.

Special Factors for the Buyer to Take Into Consideration

What does the supplier certify with respect to meeting safety standards? Worker safety is such a vital concern that all levels of government have intervened in the workplace to inspect and sanction employers that violate worker safety regulations. Therefore, in the negotiation and the contract following, there must be clarity of understanding as to compliance with safety issues, especially OSHA regulations. If there are safety-of-operation considerations, it is essential to have agreement on the interpretations of OSHA standards for worker safety and guarding as they relate to the equipment. The seller may feel that his interpretations are correct, but upon inspection by OSHA, the equipment is found deficient. Who then pays for the modifications to bring the equipment into compliance? If the equipment is purchased overseas, will it be modified to meet U.S. safety standards? Will it be modified in the United States by the seller's representative and then be shipped to the buyer, and will the seller stand behind those modifications? These issues must be negotiated *before* the sale is made. A simple approach is to make the standards part of the acceptance criteria. The same approach holds true for Environmental Protection Agency standards.

Copyright and Patent Issues

To what degree does the seller indemnify, hold harmless, and promise to defend the buyer from violations of copyright or patents? This clause in the agreement is fundamental. It must be present due to the nature of patent law, which provides for placing the damages on both the patent violator and those who purchased from the violator and benefited from the use of the goods. It is therefore possible to purchase a piece of equipment while not knowing or suspecting a patent violation exists and finding oneself a defendant in litigation as a beneficiary of that violation—and perhaps bearing the majority of the damages awarded the plaintiff. Patent law makes no distinction between willful violation and unknowing violation.

The issue is benefit to the violator and others who are innocent violators by accepting the word of the supplier that no patents have been violated. Therefore, there is no question of putting in the **indemnification clause,** which indemnifies, holds harmless, and promises to defend the buyer in cases of breach of patents or copyrights. This is a nonnegotiable element, but it is included in the discussion to ensure the buyer is made aware of its importance.

As an example, in California a supplier violated the patent of another company and was sued for damages. The violator had sold a significant amount of product to one customer, who was also named in the suit as a benefactor of the violation. The plaintiff won the case, and the damages were assessed at 20 percent to the patent violator and 80 percent to the customer who unknowingly had purchased goods containing the violated patent.[9] Patent law makes no distinctions on violations of patents and copyrights. It looks at benefits accruing to the violators.

Subcontracting

To what extent may the supplier assign the contract to others, and what permission and proof of payment of subcontractors is needed to ensure the buyer will

---

9. The names of the companies must remain confidential in this situation since the "winning" of the case was an "out of court" settlement.

not become a party to the subcontracting process? Although this is more common in construction projects, the buyer is prepared to negotiate this portion of the agreement with prime consideration going to two elements: approval of any assignment and the transferability of warranties of parts in the equipment where the supplier has purchased the parts from outside suppliers. It is essential to maintain control over the contract, and any assignment must have the buyer's approval, especially where it involves the presence of the contractors on the buyer's premises. In addition, purchased parts for the equipment will carry OEM warranties. These must be fully transferable to the buyer with identification of the suppliers, the duration of the warranty and its coverage, and the serial numbers and model numbers to allow tracking of the purchased parts. This information is important from two perspectives: It allows the buyer to go directly to the parts OEM for warranty relief in the case of failure, and it identifies the parts supplier. This identification may be very useful when the warranty expires, and spare parts need to be purchased. Going to the OEM of the equipment to purchase a spare part that this OEM is going to purchase from his OEM will add 15 to 20 percent on to the cost of the spare. It is "pass-through" pricing, and taking a markup for order processing can be a very lucrative process for the intermediary OEM.

Other Elements

The list of elements open to negotiation can be almost endless. What is important is the buyer's listing the negotiable elements and ranking them in order of importance. The list may be pared down later or handled by a term or condition, but omission is significantly more dangerous than making the list too long. The success in negotiation lies with the time, effort, and expertise expended in the planning process.

Preparing for Negotiations

After listing the elements over which negotiation will take place, the buying team decides on the appropriate values for each of the elements. Not only is there a desired position for the element but also a worst-case scenario. The variable of price is illustrated in Exhibit 6-1.

The **zone of price negotiation** is established on the basis of what the seller considers the minimum acceptable price and the desired maximum. The single points that mark the boundaries of the zone represent the desired price the buyer is willing to pay and the price that the buyer would like to achieve. Any price in that range is considered acceptable to the buyer. There must be overlap between the buyer's and the seller's positions to allow negotiation to take place. Absent that overlap, the seller's lowest acceptable price in Exhibit 6-1 lies above the buyer's highest affordable price. There is no room for discussion since both

Exhibit 6-1. Pricing relationship between buyer and seller.

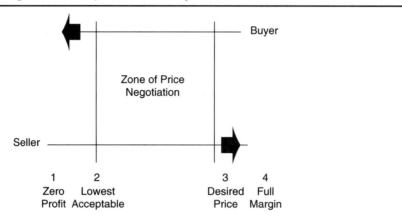

parties have reached the limits of their capability to make concessions, and there is no common ground between the two parties.

One of the functions of the buyer in the preparation phase is trying to determine where those points lie and how they may be effectively estimated.[10] If negotiation is going to take place, the buyer should consider the first offer by the supplier as an opening price, subject to counteroffers, and probably not the last price or best and final offer. The issue that must be made clear is that there will be negotiation with the supplier prior to the contract signing. Failing to make this clear to the supplier is changing the ground rules and may cause the supplier to withdraw the offer.

Setting Negotiation Targets

The process of target setting for the items on the agenda is crucial. Without targets, the whole negotiation process is meaningless and could be endless. Without knowing the points of conclusion, when is the negotiation complete? This is the definition of winning or losing, and absent these, the negotiation becomes a rather meaningless process.

In target setting, a wide array of tools is employed. They range from simply knowing the trade practices of the industry and a brief analysis of the supplier to complete cost and price analysis, studies of price movements, and the definition of rather exotic methods of keeping the supplier on schedule.[11]

10. For an approach to this see, R. Newman, *Supplier Price Analysis* (Westport, Conn.: Quorum Books, 1992).
11. One such situation arose in the purchase of pumps. The supplier was running behind schedule, and the customer needed the pumps for a job under construction. No amount of liquidated damages would have covered the potential loss facing the customer if the pumps failed to arrive

The value to the buyer of each item on the agenda differs. What are the high-value elements on the agenda? The low-value elements? Is schedule critical? Does the purchase integrate into the production of a new product? What is the impact of a delay in arrival of the equipment? Each case must be looked at on its own merits. There is no single answer to many of these questions because needs differ. In fact, the same machine being purchased by two buyers may have totally different priorities depending on the planned use of the equipment.

The key element is that gaining concessions from the seller is of little value if the worth of those concessions is not known or appreciated by the buyer. The tactics for buyers to use for gaining concessions are variable. In labor negotiations, the general approach is to fill the top of the agenda with relatively unimportant items and keep the important items at the bottom of the list. This usually results in easily reaching agreement on many issues and having the hard bargaining at the end of the negotiation process. Normally this is over the wage issue, where each side knows the limits of its position and often the limits of its opponent. Tactics may include marathon sessions stretching over long hours or even days. The negotiator with the staying power benefits the most.

A negotiating tactic can be to make a series of concessions to the seller and save the buyer's area of concern for the bottom of the agenda. The buyer then cites the concessions made to the seller and suggests that either some reciprocity be made by the seller or perhaps the negotiations should be concluded, with each party going its own way. At this point, the seller sees all the concessions won disappear—and the order too. Not willing to snatch defeat from the hands of victory, the seller concedes, and the buyer wins a key point. Another tactic is the recess. Taking a break or continuing the next day may allow time for regrouping and developing new options that move the negotiation off dead center.

Another approach is to try to determine the supplier's win items. What does the supplier want from the order? Is it possible to match concessions to win items? What is the source of this information? It may mean going back to the supplier's customers, the people visited when it was decided to deal with this supplier. This would be buyer-to-buyer conversation on the supplier and it would not be inappropriate to ask previous buyers of their experiences in dealing with the supplier.

Tactics cover a wide range, from presenting the offer to buy with an array of terms and conditions, thereby counteroffering to a bid or RFQ and stating that these are the terms under which the purchase will be made. This take-it-

---

on time. The customer purchased the services of an expediter who tracked the pumps and pulled them through the manufacturing process at the supplier's facility. The extra cost was minimal compared to the consequences of being late. The moral of the story is clear: Time is of the essence.

or-leave-it attitude may result in the supplier's accepting a counteroffer—or walking away from it.[12] It is not a recommended approach except when there is a lot of competition among the sellers and little product differentiation and the buyer has no specific loyalties. Another time that this approach can be useful is when business is very slow for the seller. Accepting a poor offer may be better than no offer at all. With sufficient competition, there are always suppliers who will sell the equipment.

The seller that occupies a unique market position with little competition can use the same tactic. The seller must exercise care if the buyer can rebuild existing equipment or retrofit equipment. Neither side should be so sure as to turn away the business with a disdaining attitude. These are extremes of the negotiating spectrum. The approach taken by the buyer should focus on listening to the supplier. Start the process by having the supplier review the offer and its terms and conditions. Upon completion of the review, the buyer begins to focus on the specifics of the offer. In order for the seller to be fully prepared for the negotiation, another approach is to send the seller an agenda of the negotiation, listing points for discussion. The seller could then prepare options or alternatives to the terms and conditions where the buyer has problems or concerns. The astute seller will prepare alternatives where possible in hopes of establishing some common ground, which may form the foundation for agreement to the disputed term or condition. As the buyer prepares options or targets for negotiation, the seller prepares the targets also. If overlap is achieved or the seller is prepared to concede the point, then the odds favor some sort of agreement.

The agenda is also the control device for the negotiation process. Prepared by the buyer to focus discussion on key points, it is essential for effective negotiation. Having the agenda identify the points of discussion, the process can move forward, covering each point in order. As each point is brought to closure, the negotiators move to the next issue. Sometimes closure is not possible, and the process gets bogged down. One acceptable procedure is to move the item to the bottom of the agenda. This approach allows movement to the next item, keeping the process from becoming bogged down. In addition, by the time the negotiators reach the final item, they have agreed on all the other points, and this single item is standing in the way of the agreement. Both sides may be willing to compromise if this is the only point of disagreement. Failure to agree or reach a satisfactory compromise on the final point can undo all the negotiations preceding that disagreement, and all the time and effort gone into carrying the negotiation to this point is of little or no value. There has been no agreement; both sides have lost. Remember that the concept of a contract is

---

12. Understand the use of the term *counteroffer*. If the buyer changes any of the terms or conditions of the original offer, it is a counteroffer. When the counteroffer is made, the supplier has three options: accept the counteroffer, reject it, or make a new offer. Once the counter is made, the original offer is a dead issue.

that both parties are better off with the contract than they would have been without it.

Eleven Important Negotiation Points

Following are the most important points relative to the negotiation process:

Be Prepared for Negotiation

The American Bar Association recommends that lawyers engaged in negotiation spend 80 percent of the total time planning and 20 percent of the time negotiating. Other entities will go as high as 90 percent on the planning time. No tactics or strategies can be a substitute for careful preparation for negotiation.

Be Prepared to Make Concessions

No negotiation ends with one side having all the concessions. The other side will break off the process before that happens. This is both a cultural issue and a legal issue. In the United States, the culture is fairness, equity, a level playing field, and other terms that allow for competitiveness but desire it in the context of gains for each side. Even the UCC contains terms such as "trust, good faith, and unconscionable," reflecting the moral integrity of the economic system. Giving in or making concessions is not losing but simply astute negotiation. The areas where concessions are made should be the relatively unimportant areas for the buyer. These are the "give-ups" in the process. Look to determine the important items to the supplier.

Be Prepared to Pay a Fair and Reasonable Price

Unless there is some extenuating circumstance, the supplier must make a fair profit to remain in business. Paying too low a price is often a clue to prices coming in the operating stage of the life cycle. In one instance, 96 percent of the list price for aircraft engines was traded for maintenance and support of those engines over a span of 25 years. The supplier will be making money on the spare parts. Trying to get a bargain on the purchase price may result in paying for that bargain later in the form of the spare parts.

Be Prepared to Conduct Serious Negotiation

The process is not a test of strength nor does a scoreboard come along as part of the process. It is not a personal experience, but the meeting of two persons or groups for the purpose of seeking a common ground and a contract. The purpose of the process is to reach an agreement acceptable to both parties. Both parties must be prepared and to some degree understand the position of the other side. Both parties want to reach agreement. Were this not the paramount objective, neither side would be present at the table. Both have something to gain by resolving issues.

Be Prepared to Be a Team Member

Negotiations on such complex entities such as capital equipment often require the skill and knowledge of technical experts, which equates to team negotiations. Using other team members is not a sign of weakness but simply good management. One person cannot cover all the possible bases, and bringing in the highly skilled technical people on your side keeps the playing field level. There is wisdom in using the team approach since it brings all the needed expertise to the negotiating table and conveys the message of the seriousness of both sides to reach an agreement.

Be Prepared to Listen to the Supplier

Listening, an essential negotiation skill, should take twice the time of talking. The seller's function is to convince the buyer to buy. A good strategy for the buyer is to ask the seller to review the offer in general and then retrace the offer looking at specific points on the agenda.

Be Prepared for Disagreement

When the gears do not mesh, there will be friction. This is negotiation; it is give and take. Do not personalize the disagreement. It is often the position of the seller's company to disagree with certain terms and conditions if they are felt to be onerous. The key issue is finding out the reason for the disagreement and seeing if there are ways to overcome the objections or compromises that can be reached. Can this part of the offer be reinvented in such a way as to minimize the objections? Where can actions of the buyer overcome the seller's objections? Can joint interpretation of government regulations be obtained as they relate to safety requirements so one side does not feel at the mercy of the other in this area?

Be Prepared to Notice When Emotions Are Taking Over

When this begins, the process starts to unravel. What may have been an amicable session now turns difficult as concessions gained become measured by some scale other than the contract itself. Individuals begin to look at how concessions will be seen in their companies and how their personal status in the organization will be viewed as a result of the agreement. The rule becomes,

"No contract is better than a bad contract." This is the time to recess or regroup in the process before emotions take over and the process becomes contaminated.

Be Prepared for Multiple Sessions

There is no reason to complete the negotiation in one session. Multiple sessions allow each side to examine offers and counteroffers and analyze positions in the light of new information conveyed in the previous session. There should be no rush to closure if it appears that multiple sessions are necessary. Sometimes a break in the process allows both sides time to reassess and reevaluate. This underscores the need for sufficient lead time for the process.

Be Prepared to Negotiate, Not Haggle, Threaten, or Coerce

A good negotiation benefits both sides. A poor one wastes everyone's time and money.

Be Prepared for Innovative Approaches Toward Problem Solving

In some instances, the simple act of telling the supplier why the product is unacceptable or what has to be done to make it acceptable can turn a failure into a successful negotiation.

A utility was trying to buy a bulldozer to move coal around in the storage yard. When the primary source changed the specification of one of its models by reducing the weight, the utility dismissed the model as unacceptable. Why was weight important? The weight of the bulldozer aided in compacting the coal, thereby reducing the chances of spontaneous combustion in the coal pile. Satisfactory in all respects but weight, the redesigned bulldozer fell short. The supplier, not wanting to lose the sale, recommended the next bulldozer in the product line that gave the user the needed weight and increased capacity. Both buyer and seller had gone from a product to a function or functions. The functions were moving coal and compacting coal. The buyer purchased on the basis of intended use.

Predicting the Outcome

There are three indicators as to how the negotiation will end and, indeed, if it is even worth the time negotiating:

1. *The size of the seller's company relative to the size of the buyer's company.* Small buyers often do not do well in negotiations against larger companies. What may be a large order for the buyer can be a small order to the seller, and along follows an unwillingness to make concessions to the small buyer. Consider the relative importance of the order to both parties in developing the negotiation strategy.

2. *The nature of the industry.* In certain industries, negotiations are a futile exercise. The terms and conditions of the offers are standardized by trade practices or are institutionalized by virtue of the economic structure of the industry, such as in the case of steel or bearings. Competition is absent or quite limited. Where concessions may not be present from the OEM, dealers or wholesalers may be willing to make concessions to gain the business. Consider changing the negotiation partner when looking at spare parts. The dealer may be more flexible than the OEM, especially if the spare parts business is small for the OEM and big for the distributor.

3. *Situations where the seller has established uniqueness via patent or process and does not have to make concessions to any buyer.* Negotiation in this environment is difficult, if not impossible. Moving into a buying position where patents are involved can do little but ensure the seller's price being met. In these situations, avoid frustration and do not attempt to negotiate price; rather, employ the possible leverage of the order. Do not become frustrated when there is no give in the seller's position.

Knowing the individual situation, the buyer gauges the effectiveness of the negotiation process, and the rule is simple: *Negotiate if there is an economic advantage to be gained.* The one exception would be the case where the seller's terms and conditions are so onerous that failure to negotiate would create huge potential liabilities for the buyer's company.

Some Closing Thoughts

With the passage of the UCC and its subsequent ratification by all the states except Louisiana, the legal profession recognized the impossibility of a uniform sales act: that the terms and conditions of the buyer and the seller are not mirror images. Unless the buyer accepts the seller's offer in blank, accepting all the terms and conditions of the seller, there will be some negotiation. The purpose is to obtain a meeting of the minds, clarify the information presented, perhaps modify the efforts of each party, and divide the risk and rewards. Negotiation should be viewed as an opportunity granted each side to come together, face to face, to offer, counteroffer, and reach acceptable terms and conditions. It is a chance to strengthen the agreement, an opportunity to gain understanding of the position of the other side and find out the relative importance of each negotiable element, and a learning experience and a training opportunity. It is also a place to save money. Lacking negotiation, the buyer is accepting the seller's offer. Given the basic principle of self-interest, this may be a poor choice. The seller acts in his own best interest, as does the buyer. Concessions are made because the value of those concessions is less than the value of gaining the contract through agreement.

Negotiation should not be viewed as a test of strength between buyer and seller but as an opportunity to add clarity to the buying process, opening up new options to consider and reaching a rewarding conclusion for both parties. There will be gains and losses for both parties, yet a good negotiation results in both parties being better off than they were prior to the start of the process. It is a win-win situation.

Checklist for Negotiations

- ☐ Have you considered a penalty or incentive clause for performance?
- ☐ Are transportation arrangements clearly defined?
- ☐ Have acceptance criteria been defined?
- ☐ Is the warranty acceptable?
- ☐ Have maintenance issues been negotiated?
- ☐ Are the payment terms acceptable?
- ☐ Has the completion date been clearly defined?
- ☐ Is a performance bond needed?
- ☐ Have you prepared an agenda to send to the supplier two weeks before the negotiations?
- ☐ Have you identified where you want to be at the end of the negotiation with respect to each point on the agenda?

7

Leasing Capital Equipment

Long a popular form of having the use of capital equipment, leasing, which offers several alternatives to the conventional purchase of capital equipment, can cover a short period of months to the service life of the equipment. Illustrating its popularity are data provided by the Equipment Leasing Association, shown in Exhibit 7-1. This exhibit shows the percentage value of leases as a percentage of investment in equipment during the period 1987 to 1997. During this period, leasing amounted to an average of 31 percent per year. The percentages in the exhibit show the proportion of overall equipment investment accounted for by leases.

The predominant fields in which equipment is leased are transportation and computers. In transportation, the major portions are accounted for by aircraft, railroad, and trucks and trailers—all big-ticket items in terms of capital expenditures. Thus, leasing may provide the opportunity for the lessee to obtain the use of the equipment without the capital expenditure or the down payment.

The second largest type of equipment leased is computers. Estimated at amounting to over $26 billion in 1996, the reasons for leasing are extensive and varied. For example, the rapid technological advances in computers can render the equipment obsolete almost overnight. Investing in a product that will be obsolete in three years does not make good sense; renting that same product and upgrading at the end of three years does make sense.

The spectrum of items leased is wide. It covers everything from copiers to computers, railroad cars to airplanes, medical equipment to manufacturing equipment—and actually anything else the lessee wants to "rent" from the lessor. It is a highly competitive industry and relatively nonregulated; lessors take a different perspective from the traditional source of credit: banks. Not concerned with compensating balances and being highly entrepreneurial in their approaches, professional lessors are interested in putting the package together as opposed to lending money.[1] In some cases, leasing does not require

1. For an interesting overview of the industry see J. Marshall, "Is There a New Lease on Leasing," *U.S. Banker* 106, no. 2 (February 1996): 36–39.

Exhibit 7-1. Domestic equipment leasing, as percentage of equipment purchases.

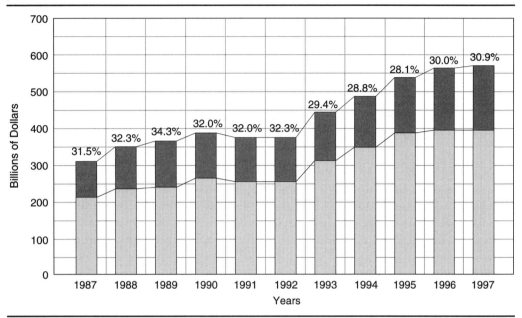

the lease to be shown on the balance sheet, thus not affecting the profits-to-fixed-asset ratio.

Industry composition, involving over 2,000 lessors, can be divided into four major groups:

1. *Large, independent leasing companies.* These are the major players in the industry. They are independent of parent companies and normally specialists in certain types of leases and types of equipment.

2. *Captive leasing companies.* These companies, such as General Electric and IBM, are owned by the parent companies and represent the financing arm of the parent. There are many such companies, and they offer the advantage of bundling services on the equipment. When maintenance of the equipment is best performed by the original equipment manufacturer (OEM), the captive lessor can offer the total package in the lease. This amounts to a turnkey operation for the customer and frees the customer of any problems relating to the equipment.

3. *Banks.* Banks have started to become active players in leasing, with about a 25 percent share of the industry. They can be active lessors or participants with the leasing companies in leverage leasing, or they can buy the paper of the leasing companies. In a **leveraged lease,** the lessor does not provide 100 percent financing and takes on others as partners, who can take either an equity or a debt position. The lessee should be aware of the source of financing

of the purchase since it will affect the payments on the lease. From the bank's perspective, it is a wise investment, since the lessor receives the monthly payment on the lease and as owner of the equipment, it may depreciate it and thereby shelter the income from taxes. Cash-rich institutions can take either equity or debt positions in the leveraged lease or themselves engage in the leasing process.

4. *Smaller independent leasing companies.* These companies, which specialize in dealing with smaller customers, may be truly independent or can offer themselves as supplier leasing services to aid the supplier. They become the leasing arm of the supplier but are not viewed as captive companies. Rather, they are a service extension of the supplier and are often the home of niche lessors. They provide the appearance of a seamless operation, with the supplier being able to provide a wider scope of service, including the equipment and its financing. Sometimes this is called **middle market credit.** The smaller companies are often candidates for leasing due to growth or short cash positions. This does not classify them as riskier but indicates a separate set of needs.

Why Lease?

Leasing may have a number of benefits.

Avoiding Cash Outlay

Leasing an item does not require any cash outlay or down payment. The asset does not go on the books of the company leasing the equipment, thereby preserving the prelease financial position. By not having to show the debt level on a fixed asset, the company maintains its creditworthiness. This does not mean the lease is not accounted for in the financial statements of the company. The lessee is required to footnote the extent of the lease obligation. The added value of the lease becomes the preservation of bank lines of credit by not requiring compensating balances in the banks.

This issue of "off the books" should not be overstated. The lease is a liability. It is an obligation to pay, and it is a contract. Although leases were attractive in the early days of leasing (i.e., not having to incur long-term debt to finance equipment purchases as well as improving the profit-to-fixed-asset ratio) they still were a liability and had to be treated as such in the reporting process. Thus, a careful analyst of financial statements will catch the presence of the leases, even if they do not have to be reported as long-term liabilities.

Tailoring the Use of the Equipment to the Leasing Process

This is especially true when considering a limited-life project, a limited use or seasonal use of the item, limited production runs, or anticipated limited use.

Large sums of capital, especially in capital-intensive industries, are not tied up in projects where the equipment may not be needed. The project costing is aided by the leasing process since the equipment may be needed for just that project; the leasing cost can be assigned to the project and costed against that project only. This avoids the allocation process and arbitrary allocations of cost and use to projects.

Rapidly Moving Technology

Changing technology results in the use of the **operating lease** for the equipment. In an operating lease, the lease life is less than 75 percent of the service life of the equipment. When the lease is completed, the lessee can (1) renew the lease for the same equipment, (2) upgrade the equipment with a new lease, or (3) walk away from the lease.

The risk lies with the lessor, who may have to remarket the equipment, which may be difficult or even impossible in the case of custom-built equipment. Therefore, the lessee who wants customization should be prepared to pay for it in the form of higher lease payments. The residual value of the used, customized equipment may be very low or nil.

The lessee must have a very clear picture of what customization is to be done and how it will affect the equipment's future value in the used market. That information can normally be obtained from the supplier doing the customization. Is the customization really enhancement to improve performance of the equipment or modification for a highly specialized use? There is a wide difference between the two. The lessee has no obligation beyond the length of the lease and is spared the effort of disposal of equipment whereby the lessee may have little or no experience in remarketing it.

Tax Considerations

Tax considerations are many and complex in the leasing field, depending on the type of lease. In the simplest form, the **operating lease,** the expenses associated with lease payments are viewed as a current business expense and are written off as such. The lessee normally assumes the responsibility of maintenance of the equipment, and the logistical support of the equipment is usually between the lessee and the equipment manufacturer. If the lease payments exclude all costs associated with the use of the equipment such as insurance, maintenance, and taxes, the lease is called a **net lease.** This type of lease provision is common with **capital leases.**

Specific Projects

Leasing is especially useful when dealing with a specific project. When the project is completed and there is no further use for the equipment, the lease is over. Often construction companies lease heavy equipment or specialized equipment covering the period of projected use or construction. This uncomplicates the costing of the project by charging the lease payments off to the project as opposed to making accounting allocations as to costs.

Supplier Selection

Supplier selection is the lessee's decision in most cases. It is the lessee who negotiates the contract or purchase with the supplier and sets up the acceptance criteria and all ancillary activities with respect to the equipment. The lessor enters the process in paying the supplier and holding title to the equipment.

Used Equipment

A buyer interested in leasing used equipment may find leasing to be a viable option as opposed to purchase of new equipment. For the buyer, the equipment may carry a lower lease payment than new equipment, and for certain projects it may be more cost-effective than purchasing used or new equipment. An example is in the word processing field where the 386 computers can be used as effectively as the 486 or Pentium hardware. If the input rate is a manual 70 words per minute, what is the need for a calculation capability of thousands of computations per second?

Flexibility

Flexibility may be important in the case of a company with a seasonal cash flow. Each lease is somewhat tailored to the needs of the lessee and the lessor. An aggressive lessor, dealing with a company that is strongly seasonal in terms of cash flow, can structure the lease payments to fit the lessee's financial position. While rates may be fixed to avoid interest rate market fluctuations, payments may be structured to meet the realities of the lessee's cash flow. Seasonal businesses still need the equipment, and leasing may be the correct option.

Influences on the Leasing Process

Leasing has maintained a solid segment of the capital equipment business, yet the rate of growth of the lease has not surpassed the rate of growth of the purchase of the equipment. If leasing is so wonderful, why has it not displaced the purchase of capital equipment in this country?

Many factors influence the leasing process—not only the actual costs of the lease, but perceptions, responsibilities, and risks. Some of them may be quantified, and others are subjective. Much is based on the perception of the lessor, as well as how the lessee perceives himself in the marketplace.

Collateral

Leasing is viewed as renting the equipment, and it has a connotation of non-permanency of the business or the inability to purchase the equipment. The unwillingness of an organization to purchase equipment and lease it instead reduces the owned assets of the organization and can place limitations on the availability of credit to it. The lack of "equipment assets" to act as collateral places a lending institution in the position of asking, "What is backing the company?" One company, a service organization, took many years to develop a creditworthy relationship with its bank, mainly because it leased much of its equipment. The collateral was the past performance of the company, not machines or equipment, whereas banks favor tangible assets in lieu of past performance. Mortgage bonds have the highest priority on the assets of the borrowing company. Collateral is sometimes very important to the buying process.

Connotation

There is a psychological conflict with the American dream of ownership of real plant and equipment. Anything else is simply corporate sharecropping. Leasing may portray an image of lack of resources on the part of the lessee. The connotation may be that the company cannot afford to buy it but can only rent it. This may be a totally incorrect picture. The issue with capital equipment is its use as opposed to ownership. Idle capital equipment owned by the company can be as expensive as leased capital equipment sitting idle. In many cases, the motivation to make better use of the leased equipment may be stronger since the lease represents the outflow of dollars readily identified with that piece of equipment. The issue here is the cost-effectiveness of each of the options and which does a better job of improving profitability or productivity of the lessee.

Tax Benefits

That the owner of the equipment is entitled to the tax benefits is a given. It is often the case in a lease that the lessee is offered the opportunity, at the termination of the lease, to buy the equipment at **fair market value,** defined as the price a rational, well-informed, independent buyer, acting in his/her own interests, is willing to pay for the property. This is known as a **fair market value lease** or sometimes a **tax lease.** It also provides for renewal of the lease at the fair market value of the equipment. As owner of the equipment, the lessor is entitled to the tax benefits of ownership. In this case, the lessor has several options available to make the lease more attractive, including passing on some of the benefits to the lessee in the form of lower payments. The tax benefits provide a buffer for the lessee to use in lease negotiations.

Cost of the Lease

Allied to the tax issue is whether the cost of the lease is going to exceed the purchase price. The lessor is in business to make a profit, and that profit is a function of the price charged for being the lessor and the potential profit that may be made by changes in the residual value of the equipment leased. Known as **residual upside**—either the appreciation of the equipment during the lease or a slower depreciation during that period—the value of the equipment may be significantly greater than anticipated by either party when the lease was structured. When the lease ends and the lessee is faced with paying fair market value for the equipment, the lessee may find it to be very expensive, especially when the lease payments are added to the present fair market value.

The reverse is also true. The bottom can drop out of the market, leaving the lessor in the position of having to re-lease or sell the equipment at a lower price than anticipated. This is risk. These are events that may happen in the future, and there is no way to predict their occurrence, except by careful market analysis or analogy of similar equipment. To stay in business, the lessor must factor in those subjective estimates in developing the lease.

Other Parties to the Relationship

There are other parties involved in the leasing process; it is not a clear one-on-one relationship. If capital equipment is involved, especially high-technology equipment, the maintenance issue comes into the picture. The lessor is the owner of the equipment and has the right to approve any third-party maintenance agreements. This is often an advantage to the **captive lessor.** Because the manufacturer or dealer also has the capability to finance or lease the equipment, the maintenance issue can be handled by the dealer or the authorized provider performing the maintenance, normally under a separate agreement. This provides the captive lessor with something of an advantage on complex equipment and, depending on the market conditions, can be a contributing factor to residual upside. One party that will always be involved in the lease is the Internal Revenue Service (IRS). The provisions of the lease determine the way the IRS looks at the tax implications.

Down Payments

The lessee requires 100 percent financing on the purchase of the equipment. Anything less than 100 percent can make a bad lease look good by reducing the amount financed by the equivalent of a down payment. (In leasing automobiles, it is a common practice to offer a bargain lease payment but require a **capital reduction payment** upon signing the lease. Regardless of the terminology used, it is still a reduction of the lease value and makes a bad lease look good. Caveat emptor or caveat lessee.) This is one reason that negotiation is necessary with many or all leases. The example of the computer numerically controlled socket machine illustrates the point. A portion of the cost of the machine was in tooling for specific customer products. No lessor is going to ignore the fact the tooling has little or no value in the marketplace. The lessor will finance a piece of equipment with its factory or manufacturer-provided accessories 100 percent, but do not look beyond that for anything special or customized. If the lessor does pay for the enhancements in the lease, consider the fact that the lessee is going to pay for those enhancements somewhere in the lease.

This type of situation runs parallel to the valuation of used cars. All those items that were accessories when purchased new are standard equipment when sold as a used car. If the lessor sees little or no market for the accessories or alterations to the basic equipment, the lease will reflect that perception. The lessor owns the equipment, and at the termination of the lease, the value of the equipment is the fair market value. Accessories and any degree of customization will affect the lease payments.

The Components of the Lease

What is included in the lease payment? Obviously the payments include principal and interest payments going to the lessor, yet are there other charges included? In one case, the lease payment indicated that the payment included the equipment, labor, shipping, and tax. The lessee was not only paying the tax but being charged interest on it. The lessee was *financing* the shipping cost over the term of the lease.

The astute lessee looks for a **net lease,** where all costs used in connection with the lease, such as taxes, maintenance, and insurance, are paid directly by the lessee. On the matter of insurance, the lessee's normal business insurance should be sufficient to cover the leased property. This is also a point of negotiation. Avoid duplication of coverage.

Issues of warranty and acceptance criteria should be resolved before leasing the equipment. If these issues are not resolved and clarified to the satisfaction of all parties concerned, the lease may be a most unpleasant experience and a costly lesson on asking questions before signing.

This is not an area where the lessee makes assumptions. Thus, the request for quotation (RFQ) for the lease should be carefully developed and formulated to provide the potential lessee with the clearest possible picture of the costs, support, and responsibilities of all parties. This does not equate to the lowest cost of the lease, but clear knowledge of costs allows for comparison shopping where possible and an understanding of the flexibility of the lessor in the process. The objective is to root out hidden costs or bundled portions of the offer that raise the cost of the lease and amount to very expensive financing schemes.

Murky Issues

There are murky issues that come up in the leasing situation. Perhaps the best illustration is in leasing copying equipment. The common practice is to lease the lower-capability machine and run the hell out of it. The repair person becomes almost a part of the office staff. At the end of the lease, what has been fair wear and tear on the machine if it was intentionally leased knowing it was not capable of standing the overuse? In practice, the cost of the lease will reflect this phenomenon, with the lessor probably charging a fixed rate plus a per copy charge. The lessor is self-protecting against the risk of taking back a worthless machine at the end of the lease. If the customer wishes to run the copier into the ground, there is the charge per page to cover that overuse. It is the same issue that arises in the case of warranties where the warranty is valid under normal operating conditions. What is the definition of *normal?* From the lessor's perspective, excessive use will lower the residual value of the equipment and raise the cost to the lessee.

Another murky issue is the maintenance aspect of leasing. Who will perform the maintenance, and when? The lessor has the right to expect the equipment to be maintained in a fair and proper manner as suggested by the manufacturer. The lessor may also want written documentation that the maintenance and repairs have been performed by the person who is maintaining the equipment. If the lessee is going to maintain the equipment, where will lessee personnel receive the training to perform that maintenance? Can the lessor require periodic inspections by a third party to see that maintenance is being done by the lessee? Does the lease include preventive maintenance, or failure maintenance, or both? What is the time duration between a service request and the arrival of service personal? Does it affect the lease payment?

There are no clear answers to these questions, but they do have to be considered in developing the RFQ.

Add to this another issue of spare parts for the equipment. Where are they stocked? What impact, if any, does this have on the lease? Is this strictly an issue between the manufacturer and the lessee, or does the lessor become involved as the owner of the equipment? Does the lessee want the lessor involved in that issue, or is there a charge for passing through the spare parts or delivering them to the lessee? The Robinson-Patman Act is very specific on the issue of tie-in contracts where the owner is required to use the supplies of the manufacturer on the equipment: It forbids these types of arrangements. It does not forbid the *recommendation* of using only XYZ Company supplies on XYZ machine, yet the lessor may have a vested interest in having the lessee use only factory parts. A well-maintained machine with a complete paper trail on that maintenance can command a premium in the remarketing of the machine. This issue must be resolved at the time when the lease is crafted.

Information

The potential lessee may not know where to turn to get an objective opinion. The lessor is providing the information and has the ulterior motive of getting the leasing business. So where does the potential lessee turn for information? Sources of data on leasing are numerous. A good first step is building on the knowledge provided in this chapter, which is by no means all inclusive. A glossary of terms, commonly used in the leasing field, appears at the end of this chapter. Leasing is a precise field with specific terms having very distinct meanings and implications. The inability to speak the language is a serious handicap. Any analyst looking at the leasing option should know the terminology of the field.

It is important to know who the lessors are in the field and what their credentials are. They or the lessor of choice is the owner of the equipment the company is leasing. Their financial stability, market knowledge, and the array of products and services offered are key issues by which the lessor is evaluated. Indicators include:

- Years in business
- Experience in the lessee's industry
- Reputation of the lessor among customers
- Products and services offered
  - Types of leases
  - Variations on lease payments
  - Response with the written proposal (canned or thoughtful?)
  - Perceived value as potential lessee
- The lease agreement itself
  - Understandable
  - Comprehensive
  - Flexible
- How well the lessor works with suppliers (e.g., training the lessee's staff in maintenance and operation, supporting the lessee with problem areas)

The same general principles apply to selecting the sources of raw materials or equipment or maintenance, repair, and operating supplies (MRO) as do to the selection of the lessor. Quality of the lease at a fair price by the equipment owner (the lessor) is an essential characteristic of a good leasing source. The products may change, but a good source is a good source, and a poor one is a liability.

Termination Clause

Since most leases will contain a **"hell or high water" clause** that stipulates the lessee will continue to pay for the lease regardless of changes in circumstances and these changes are not the basis for lease termination, it is a worthwhile idea to consider a termination clause in the agreement. This has financial consequences, and there may be a termination fee that the lessor wants for this privilege. One such clause may stipulate:

> The lessee reserves the right to terminate the lease and have the described property removed from the company premises no longer than 30 days after lease termination. In consideration for the privilege, the lessee agrees to pay the lessor an amount equal to n percent of the remaining value of the lease. Lease termination before the passage of 25 percent of the duration of the lease will not be allowed.

This, of course, is only a sample; the true conditions and financial arrangements must be developed through negotiation between lessee and lessor. There must be some form of consideration present for the lessor. Termination not agreed to by both parties can be viewed as breach of contract and the consideration provided amounts to the equivalent of liquidated damages for the lessor.

Acceptance of the Equipment

Incoming equipment is normally shipped from the supplier to the lessee. The lessee is not the owner of the equipment but nevertheless has a strong interest in the equipment's arriving in good condition. Depending on the type of lease used, the cost of transportation could be carried by any of three parties: the seller, the lessor, or the lessee. The transportation portion of the agreement should be carefully spelled out due to the ownership-in-transit issue.

Should the equipment be damaged in transit, who will pay for the return shipment of the equipment? From the lessee's perspective, it is an issue between the buyer and the seller, and the lessee's responsibility does not commence until the **certificate of acceptance** or **certificate of delivery and acceptance** has been signed and returned to the lessor. Using an **equipment certificate of acceptance form,** the lessee is authorizing the lessor to pay for the equipment. Failing the acceptability test, it is an issue between buyer and seller. The lessee should have a clause in the leasing agreement providing for a **rent holiday** until the necessary repairs or damages have been corrected at no expense to the lessee, either for repairs or transportation back to the manufacturer or distributor. It is a small item but one that can be bothersome.

Types of Leases

The number of possible leases can be infinite if unique clauses define a different type of lease. For the sake of illustration, there are four basic types of leases used in equipment leasing in the economy today:

1. Standard finance lease or the capital lease
2. Operating lease or true lease
3. Fixed purchase option lease
4. Convert-i-lease

According to R. H. Chamides in his article in *Business Credit,* the latter two are classified as true leases for income tax classification and operating leases for financial accounting purposes.[2] These distinctions are important. Consider first the tax implications. A **finance lease** (also called a **capital lease**) is a specific classification of lease and exists when *any* of the following four tests are met:

1. At the end of the lease, the lessee takes title to the property.
2. At the end of the lease, the lessee can purchase the property for a **bargain price.**
3. The lease term is at least 75 percent of the economic life of the equipment.
4. The present value of the minimum lease payments is equal to 90 percent or more of the cost or fair market value of the leased property, less the related investment tax credits retained by the lessor.

A capital lease or finance lease is actually a deferred purchase of the equipment, and the lease concept is a financing mechanism. Therefore, the IRS views this as nontax lease and it must be considered an asset to be capitalized on the lessee's balance sheet. The deductibles for the lessee become the depreciation on the equipment plus the interest payments on the lease. This type of arrangement can also be viewed as a **conditional sales contract.** There are several parties involved in this case, legal issues of ownership, federal income tax issues, the lessor and lessee. If any of the four conditions occurs, the lease is a capital lease. Since a conditional sales contract allows for title to pass at the end of the payment period, the first condition is met, and it is a conditional sales contract.

The normal finance lease requires a 10 percent down payment and repayments over a five-year period. Title to the equipment lies with the lessor, but

2. R. H. Chamides, "Leasing Provides Alternatives Means to Expand Capital," *Business Credit* 96, no. 2 (February 1994): 37–38.

the lessee maintains the right to depreciate the equipment using accelerated depreciation. Couple the interest write-off and rapid depreciation, and the finance lease has created a tax shelter for the company well beyond the 10 percent down payment. The negative is the down payment that removes capital from the company's after-tax profits if internal financing were the source of funds.

If the company borrowed from a bank, the negative would be the interest paid and the compensating balances that might be required to ensure the bank's exposure to minimum risk. Dollar-for-dollar financing or even 90 percent financing for anything other than real property is not likely. It is not uncommon that the bank will require up to 25 percent of the value of the lease as a down payment and compensating balances. Even with these "limitations," there are valid reasons for the capital lease due to the tax shelter created and the rapid depreciation allowed.

As to the **bargain purchase option,** this clause in the agreement allows the lessee to purchase the equipment at substantially below the fair market value of the equipment when the option can be exercised. Sometimes this is called the $1 price and is a token payment for the passing of title. With respect to the other two ways of classifying a capital lease, the duration of the lease is an indicator of the actual desire to lease the equipment or make it a deferred purchase. The present value test looks at the lease payments and if the discounted lease payments are 90 percent or greater than the present cost of the equipment. A worthwhile net present value would have to be positive to make the investment attractive. The 90 percent threshold is used to distinguish between a financing scheme and a true lease. As a financing scheme, no lessor is going to have the present value of future payments less than the original investment. Having the present value of future payments less than the original cost is a sure path to bankruptcy. The key element here is the discounting rate. The lessor may discount at a lower rate than the lessee. The lessor is interested in the **spread,** the difference between funding costs and the rate of return on the lease.

If none of the conditions exists, then a true lease is present. A true lease, with an **operating lease** as an example, must meet all the inverse conditions of the finance lease:

- The lease term must be less than 75 percent of the estimated economic life of the equipment.
- No bargain price is offered at the end of the lease.
- Title will not automatically pass from the lessor to the lessee at the end of the lease.
- The present value of lease payments is less than 90 percent of the equipment's fair market value at the time of the lease.

Thus, the operating lease would normally be considered to have the following characteristics:

- The lease term is short, nominally between one and five years.
- The lessee is allowed to purchase the equipment at the end of the lease for the fair market value of the equipment.
- The lessor can re-lease the equipment to the same lessee, remove the equipment and find a new lessee, or sell the equipment to the lessee or anyone else.
- The 90 percent rule is not violated because of the short lease. The shorter the lease, the greater the residual value of the equipment.

The operating lease allows the lessee to deduct the lease payments as an operating expense from the income statement. Although the lease is not on the balance sheet, it is a financial obligation and will be footnoted on the income statement by the auditor to call attention to it. An operating lease is a true lease or rental of the property.

The **fixed purchase option** is an addendum to the operating lease where both parties agree on a fair price at the completion of the lease. This process takes place in the inception of the lease and establishes the price at lease completion. There are other variations that may apply, such as stipulating the fair market value at the end of the lease, determined by the marketplace or a percentage of the original purchase price, whichever is less. A typical provision would be fair market value or 30 percent of the purchase price, whichever is less.

This is an option that the lessee may exercise or refuse to exercise depending on the residual value of the equipment at the end of the lease. It is an effective clause for both the lessee and lessor because it defines the risks to each party. Negotiated at contract inception, it removes the issue of residual upside or downside from the leasing situation. From the lessor's perspective, the actual percentage of the original cost acceptable to the lessor will depend on experience in the equipment field and the lease charges. In some cases, the leasing costs allow the lessor to sell the equipment to the lessee at the end of any year in the lease, providing the lease duration is specified at inception. Exhibit 7-2 sets out the figures for a company that will lease an item of equip-

Exhibit 7-2. Comparison of options on leasing a $10,000 item and fixed price purchase option.

Lease Length (months)	Monthly Payment	Total Payments	Spread[a]	Purchase Price	Total Outlay
24	$456	$10,944	$1,944	$1,000	$11,944
36	326	11,736	2,736	1,000	12,736
48	264	12,672	3,672	1,000	13,672
60	226	13,560	4,560	1,000	14,560

[a]Calculated as total payments plus purchase price minus original cost.

ment costing $10,000 for periods of two, three, four, or five years. At lease end, the lessee can buy the equipment for 10 percent of original cost.

From the lessor's perspective, it is a win situation. The lessor recovers the initial outlay and makes a fraction over 9 percent on his money if the lessee exercises the purchase at the end of the lease option. For the lessee, the early purchase option is attractive since the fair market value of the equipment is highest at the end of 24 months compared with the other options. The example could be expanded to consider the time value of money by discounting the monthly payments as well as the purchase price and bringing all the data up to present value. Discounting would give a more accurate picture.

The fourth type is the **convert-i-lease.** This type of arrangement allows the lessee to convert from a true lease to a financial lease prior to the true lease termination date for an amount equal to approximately 50 percent of the original cost of the equipment. Thus, the lessee has an operating lease for a portion of the lease, enjoying the benefits of the true lease, and then converting it to a financial lease and avoiding the cash outlay to exercise the purchase option at the end of the lease. The key issue in the conversion process is when that conversion takes place. Prior to entering into such an arrangement, the lessee should determine when the halfway point in the equipment cost is reached. This can be a tricky computation. The equipment is being leased on a true lease to the lessee, who has no way of knowing how the lessor is paying for the equipment. That issue is not the lessee's concern. Toward the end of the lease, the purchase option is provided. The lessee, to ensure the purchase option is viable under the terms of the financial lease, should:

- Determine the fair market value of the equipment.
- Accept the convert-i-lease as an option that may be accepted or rejected.
- Determine the interest rate for the loan on the part of the lessee for buying the equipment.[3]
- Determine the amount of depreciation available if the lease is converted.
- Determine any other tax benefits left in the original equipment.

On the face of it, the convert-i-lease appears to offer benefits of evening or leveling the cash outlay of the lessee and picking up the best of the true lease and the capital lease. It would do this by allowing for operating lease payments for half of the equipment life and then, in lieu of exercising the purchase option, allow the lessee to lease it on a capital lease. The issue becomes how much the lessee is really paying for the equipment. If the lessor has financed the purchase, much of the lessee's early lease payments to the lessor go toward interest payments on the lessor's loan. From a practical perspective, if the offer sounds too good to be true, it probably is not true. Look for the hidden ele-

---

3. The term *loan* is used here because the financial lease is really a financing mechanism.

ments, and always concentrate on fair market value as the bellwether in the purchase segment of the lease.

The key issue is what other benefits the lessee (the customer) wants from the lease other than the use of the equipment. These benefits could include tax considerations, a healthier looking balance sheet, or the ability to use the equipment for only short periods. The following questions must be answered to draw the distinction between the types of leases:

- How long a lease period?
- Operating expense or depreciation?
- Bargain price or fair market value at the end of the lease?
- Size of the lease payments relative to the original cost?
- Options at the end of the lease?

None of the types of leases represents insurmountable obstacles to either the lessor or the lessee. There is no "one size fits all" solution to the leasing issue. An operating lease can easily be turned into a capital lease, and vice-versa. There are parameters that must be met, but the aggressive lessor can show how adjustment of the parameters can meet the needs of the customer. The answer lies in the customer's knowing what he/she wants from the lease and the rationale for each type of lease. Armed with that knowledge, the lessee is able to communicate with the lessor and evaluate the lease proposal.

The Request for Proposal (RFP) for the lease becomes the information-gathering device. A good RFP forms the basis for a good lease analysis; a poorly prepared one serves only to add confusion to the leasing process. If the buyer does not know what he/she wants, the seller will sell him/her what makes the seller the most profit. Knowing what is wanted is communicated to potential lessors with the RFP for the lease.

Putting Together the Leasing RFP

The RFP for the lease must address many areas. It is not simply a "What's it going to cost me?" letter to the supplier, especially if multiple RFPs are sent out.[4] The RFP should delineate the general purpose of the proposal as well as advise potential responders that no action on behalf of the company should be undertaken prior to receipt of written acceptance of the proposal. This precludes the lessor from making any commitments where the lessee would be deemed responsible for the commitments. In addition, the general guidelines

---

4. For two excellent books in the field of leasing, see R. M. Contino, *Handbook of Equipment Leasing—A Deal Maker's Guide,* 2d ed. (New York: AMACOM, 1996), and R. M. Contino, *Negotiating Business Equipment Leases—Insider Strategies for Getting the Best Deal* (New York: McGraw-Hill, 1995).

should provide that any verbal representations made by the respondents shall be incorporated into the formal agreement between parties. This is written in the RFP to place potential lessors on notice that sales promotional promises may have to be honored.

Procedural Considerations

The next segment of the proposal deals with procedural considerations.

The RFP defines a responsible response to it: the reply in writing, by a specific date, addressing all the subject matter issues raised in the proposal. Failure to address specific issues becomes the basis for rejecting the proposal. Of course, the drafter of the RFP must be reasonable as to what is being asked. Proposals take time and expertise to draft and submit. Although the potential lessee reserves the right to rescind or cancel the RFP at no cost or obligation or amend it, there is a sunk cost aspect in the preparation process.

A postcard or fax form can be enclosed asking recipients of the RFP if they plan to respond to it. Its purpose is to let the potential lessee know the expected volume of responses and therefore the time that should be allotted to this phase of the analysis.

That the information submitted by respondents is confidential is ensured. So are information obtained from the originator of the RFP that is contained in the RFP and any information released to third parties from the RFP.

Administrative tasks and supporting documentation are covered:

- The required number of copies of the proposal.

- The need for the signature of a company officer on the proposal to make it a binding offer.

- How long the offer remains open.

- Financial information on the lessor in the form of financial statements going back a specified number of years, bank references, and pertinent legal issues facing the lessor.

- The person who will be the point of contact for questions and his or her telephone number, fax number, e-mail address, and location.

- That any additional information will be made available to all bidders.

- Details on the award process. Is the award to be made on the basis of bid evaluation or bid and negotiation with selected bidders? The award process or procedure is extremely important to the lessor. If bidding is just to get in the door, the lessor should know this from a time and cost perspective. A multistage process is more costly than a single-stage process and requires a more strategic approach. Giving away all the concessions in the bid process leaves nothing to be given away at the negotiating table, and failure to convey the message on how the process is to be conducted could be considered an act of bad faith by the respondents.

• Whose forms will be used for the contract itself. This is extremely important since the lessee's purchase order contains terms and conditions that the lessee considers to be important. This is no less true for the lessor, but a review of the terms and conditions of the lessor *before* contract award may require modification of final terms and conditions.

Equipment List

Once the procedural considerations have been delineated, the next major issue is the equipment list—the description of the equipment to be leased in such detail that the responder can fully analyze the proposal. This includes pertinent drawings, specification sheets, conditions of warranty, and issues dealing with hazardous materials that may be part of the purchase. It basically is the same information included in the capital equipment purchase order.

It is also useful to indicate in the RFP as to the anticipated use of the equipment. Will it be used on a single-shift basis, multiple shifts, or overtime? How many work turns will be allocated for maintenance? What is the anticipated downtime per 24-hour day? This information can provide some indication as to the issue of fair wear and tear on the equipment. It is certainly different to run a machine 8 hours per day compared to 24 hours per day. Try to give some substance to "normal operating conditions" and point out any abnormal conditions such as heat or humidity that might affect machine performance.

In addition, it would carefully spell out the following items:

• The issue of packaging, crating, or rigging.

• The disclaimer of the lessee as it relates to damage in transit and the cost of returning defective equipment.

• The certificate of acceptance and when the lease begins.

• The site at which the equipment will be located.

• The role of the lessor in disposing of displaced equipment by sale to the lessor or consignment to the lessor for remarketing or resale.

• All the costs of the equipment with an appropriate range above and below the stated price. This is basic to the RFP. The potential lessor must know exactly what is wanted and what its price range should be, along with other costs the lessee wants included in the lease and excluded from the lease. This would probably be specified by delineating exactly what would be leased and paid for by the lessee. The lessee would probably reimburse the lessor for transportation, installation, and testing after acceptance of the equipment. The issue of tooling, accessories, and manufacturer's upgrades should be specified in the RFP. Some upgrades add to the residual value, while others limit the use of the equipment. Does the lessee want to pay for this separately or "finance" it in the sense of having it be part of the lease? This is a question to be resolved on a case-by-case basis, but be aware of it when putting together the RFP.

• Handling the issue of maintenance on the equipment as to the documentation required by the lessor on the performance of maintenance, the use of third-party maintenance, as well as the maintenance downtime allowed before the lease payments are affected. Is the nature of the equipment such that only the manufacturer is equipped to handle the maintenance, or can the lessee handle it? Who will train the lessee's personnel, and is that training included or excluded from the cost of the equipment? Can it be unbundled from the equipment cost, making the lease as close to a net lease as possible?

• Access to the equipment for periodic inspection by the lessor or the period of notification needed before access is granted.

• The issue of confidentiality of use of the equipment.

• Issues concerning the approval process for any modifications made to the equipment by the lessee. Are they allowed and, if so, what type? What is the impact on the residual value of the equipment? Customized equipment may be difficult to resell, and the lessor must approve the modification processes and have some leeway in being able to step up the lease if the residual value of the equipment is altered by customization.[5] The issue of customization must be carefully defined by both parties as to expanding capability or limiting capability.

• The duration of the lease period and the options open to the lessee at the end of the lease, along with associated costs and benefits and the method of determining fair market value.

• The desired method of limiting risk on the part of the lessee and the ways that the lessor can aid in limiting the risk for both parties.

• Independent appraisal within 90 days of the end of the lease by a mutually agreed upon independent party as to the fair market value of the equipment.

• Estimated delivery date of the equipment after signing of the lease.

Financial Aspects

The RFP next begins to look at some of the financial aspects of the lease:

• The type of lease required.

• The payment of the equipment supplier by the lessor and the beginning of the warranty on the equipment.

---

5. This does not mean that customization always reduces the residual value of the equipment. In many cases upgrading may enhance the value of the equipment. For example, Swiss Air

- The end-of-term options.
- Early termination notification and penalties.
- Insurance of the equipment and necessary documentation.
- Renewal notification.
- Upgrading procedure and notification.
- Size of payments and payment options, such as arrears or advance and payment periods. This is important from a cash flow basis. Quarterly payments allow for the use of the budgeted cash for three months.
- Capped fair market value.
- Definition of default.
- Casualty value schedule on the equipment.
- Single source of financing preference if desired. This is the case in which the lessee does not want or prefers (depending on the wording) third parties brought into the transaction. Is a leveraged lease allowed or permitted, and if it is permitted, what information is required before third-party debt or equity participation is allowed? If leveraged leasing is allowed, what is the maximum interest rate the lessee will accept on the debt portion of the leverage lease? By specifying the maximum interest rate, the lessee is not allowing an excessively high lease rate to appear on the proposal. The lessee may specify that its sources of capital may be the ones to provide the debt portion of any leveraged lease. If this occurs, the relationship is between the lessor and the financial institution. The lessee benefits from the relationship but is not part of the transaction.

Why is this last point important? Consider the fact that these financial arrangements often involve millions of dollars over medium ranges of time. A quarter-point difference in interest rates over the term of the lease can amount to a significant sum of money. In addition, the existence of third parties in the relationship can open the proverbial Pandora's box in the event of default on the part of the lessee or changes in the leasing agreement. In the leveraged lease, the third parties often have a significant financial stake in the equipment and will do their best to protect and ensure an adequate return on their investment. In addition, if the financial interest is in the form of debt participation, the debt holders have a mortgage type of claim on the equipment, which raises issues of access to the equipment, removal of equipment, and legal repossession.

Finally, the RFP should stipulate no liability for costs or fees to the lessee to execute the lease other than its own legal fees and expenses. The lessor cannot pass on administrative or legal fees incurred by the lessor in the cre-

---

routinely in its orders for Boeing 747's specifies hundreds of upgrades on the aircraft. The aircraft is more valuable after these changes.

ation of the lease. Those costs are overhead costs to the lessor and part of the normal costs of business. In addition, there will be full disclosure of any broker-age arrangement on the part of the lessor regarding that lease.

This information provides guidelines for a formal proposal from the lessor. Not all of it may be needed. If the lessor is known to the lessee or there exists a master lease with the lessor, much of this information is already known. If the lease is relatively small in size, the depth of detail may not be necessary or is not practical from an analytical perspective. The cost of analysis may outweigh the value of that analysis.

Once the lease is signed, it is a legal obligation on the part of both parties, and activities and actions begin to take place that are irreversible or at least costly to stop. It is far better to determine the pitfalls before the lease is signed than after. Even being careful in the RFP process is no guarantee. Leasing goes well beyond simply renting.

Analyzing the Responses

A good RFP has gone out, and the responses have returned to the buyer. It is now time to analyze the lessor's proposals. What have the respondents said in the proposal? To illustrate the "how to do it," consider the following informa-tion. The cost of the equipment to be leased or purchased is $1 million with a 20-year service life and an estimated residual value of $50,000 at the end of the 20 years. The current borrowing rate from a bank requires 10 percent down payment, 10 percent compensating balances, and an interest rate of 10 percent. The company's desired return on investment (ROI) is 15 percent. The company has specified a net lease arrangement so that any payments for the lease ex-clude taxes, insurance, and maintenance. The federal income tax rate of the company is 36 percent of earnings before income tax.

One approach to the leasing situation is to set up the options open to the company:

• Purchase the equipment using internal funds and charge the company a cost of capital equal to the desired ROI and compute that total cost.

• Purchase the equipment under a finance or capital lease from the bank, making the down payment and keeping the compensating balances in the bank and financing the purchase as long-term debt. The bank or financial institution is not going to provide 100 percent financing for the equipment, even if it holds title to the equipment. The down payment and compensating balances offset the risk associated with the declining value of the equipment. From the bank's position, the capital lease is a financing mechanism or deferred purchase, and its income is derived from the interest on the debt plus interest on the compensating balances.

• Securing an operating lease for the equipment for a selected period (say, five years) and using the residual value as the straight-line depreciated value of the equipment after that five years have the options of releasing the equipment, buying the equipment at the fair market value, or releasing the equipment back to the lessor. The lessor, by providing 100 percent financing, has title to the equipment and the right to depreciate a portion of it over the term of the lease. (Check on MARCS—1986 tax depreciation rules for both cases.)

By setting up the three cases, the buyer is able to look at the leasing issue from a cost-benefit perspective and settle on the best option from a strictly quantitative perspective. How far from the ideal have the respondents deviated? What type of return are they seeking? What is a fair profit for them, and what is the true cost of each option? All of these issues must be considered before turning to the qualitative aspects of the offer. Once that issue has been determined, what are the qualitative dimensions that must be evaluated? What is the nonfinancial impact of pulling $1 million from the current liquid assets of the company, remembering that these are net, after-tax profits. What will it do to the financial statements in terms of future analysis?

The process presents the clearest possible picture as far as leasing is concerned, recognizing there will always be murky areas and areas of disagreement on the part of the lessor and lessee. These must be handled by negotiation prior to signing the lease. If the lessor is making an excessive profit in the eyes of the lessee, then a looser definition of fair wear and tear may be in order. The lessee who is not informed of the options is in no position to bargain with the lessor.

The Lessee's Checklist: The Important Qualitative Issues

Although there is a wide variety of issues of a qualitative nature and it would be impossible to capture all of them, consider the following factors in evaluating the proposals, and well before the lease is signed.

Provisions for the Start of the Lease

When the lease begins must be put in writing. There should also be a delivery date specified, with the supplier providing any support stipulated in the purchase order from the lessor. The legality of the lease is based on acceptance of the equipment, so no lessee should accept a start of the lease until the equipment is installed and operating, having passed the acceptance testing phase and sending the certificate to the lessor. Upon the lessor's receipt of the certificate, the lease begins. The lessor is responsible for all costs up to receipt of the certificate of acceptance as it relates to the equipment. Normally the lessor, upon receipt of the acceptance certificate, will pay the supplier to secure full title to the equipment.

Provisions for Unloading and Installation

This cost is borne by the lessor but should also be a vital concern of the lessor. The lessor is the owner of the equipment and would probably be the filer of any claims against the carrier for damage during transit.

Provisions for Setup and Acceptance Testing

The installation, setup, and acceptance testing are usually done with the supplier present. Often the supplier will support these activities, and in the cases of high technology, the supplier may be the installer.

Provisions for Return

Failure of the machine or equipment to perform properly may be reason to return the equipment to the original equipment manufacturer. Provisions must be made in the agreement for this contingency, including any disassembly, crating or packing, and carrier selection. Since the equipment was not acceptable, these costs will not be borne by the lessee. This is an issue for the supplier and lessor to discuss. Often the supplier finds it much less expensive to send people to the site of the equipment to resolve the problem at the user's site as opposed to shipping the equipment back.

Warranty Claims

Determine how warranty claims are filed and whether there are any expenses to the lessee. In this situation, it is essential to have the clear and concise spelling out of any disclaimers from the lessor as to the issue of warranty and maintenance. It is even more important if the net lease is used. If the agreement calls for a full service lease, then recourse provisions must be included in the agreement if the lessor fails to maintain the equipment properly.

Several options are available with no rental payment during the repair period. Failure to repair in a reasonable period of time would be grounds for suit to cancel the lease. Get a clear definition of *reasonable*. If the equipment does not work and there is no way to fix it, the lease may be viewed as unconscionable.[6] This raises a tricky area resulting from the specification of the equipment

6. P. M. Perry, "How to Avoid Pitfalls in Equipment Leasing," *Area Development* (May 1995).

in the beginning of the whole leasing process. It may be necessary to include performance specifications in the leasing agreement, much in the same manner they appear in the purchase order. The lessor is a financial party to the lease and does not depend on his expertise in your application to ensure the performance of the equipment. Failing to be clear as to intended use may place the lessee at a distinct disadvantage if it becomes necessary to cancel or amend the lease. Although the implied warranty of suitability of purpose has held for the sale of goods, the leasing may be another matter and may not enjoy the protection of the Uniform Commercial Code.

Time Allowances for Warranty or Maintenance Calls

What is considered reasonable in terms of coming to the site for repair work? This also raises the issue of allowable downtime before lease payments stop. A close consideration is the inventory position of the supplier as it relates to spare parts. Knowing what is wrong is useful, but not having the spare parts to accomplish the repair is frustrating to all parties.

Spare Parts and Stocking Programs

The issue of spare parts should be incorporated into the leasing agreement directly or indirectly. Where are the spares? Who stocks them? What is the proximity of the spares to the site? What is a reasonable period to get the spares to the site where they are needed? All of these issues should be discussed before signing the lease.

Access Granted to the Lessor for Inspections

The lessor still owns the equipment and therefore retains the right to inspect that equipment periodically. The inspection schedule should be agreed on before the lease is signed as to frequency of visit and any issues relating to the possible proprietary nature of products being produced on the leased equipment. It is common to secure areas where new products are being produced or tested. The inspection issue can easily be clarified between the parties.

Fair-Wear-and-Tear Provisions

Be wary of any provision that states the equipment is to be returned in its original state. This is impossible and occurs only when the equipment is never used. Nevertheless, this is a tricky issue and an area to apply leverage to the lessor. What is the expectation of the lessor with respect to the condition of the equipment at the end of the lease? This is one of the advantages of leasing from an experienced lessor who understands that use takes its toll. If this proves to be a difficult area with the lessor, a third party-appraiser should determine if the use was excessive and beyond reasonable wear and tear. Expert third-party opinions can be helpful in resolving potential problems in leasing.

Loss Valuation and Insurance

The lessee has the equipment on his property during the term of the lease and thus has the responsibility to exercise reasonable care and security over the equipment. Insurance should cover the equipment against the normal hazards of fire and theft.

Consider the location of the equipment. Will moving it to a new location void the insurance? Again, this is a cost that the lessor should bear, but often the lessee carries that expense as part of the lease. Is it part of the lease or a separate entity?

Early Termination Provisions and Costs

Carefully spelling out the conditions under which termination takes place, other than lessee bankruptcy, can avoid confusion and ill will later. Termination cannot be for the convenience of either party. Thoughtful consideration of a fair termination settlement before the agreement is signed is good planning.

Payment in Advance or Arrears

The vast bulk of lease payments are made in arrears. This does not mean they are late or in default of the lease, but are often made at the end of the month and are technically late. Industry practice allows for this situation, and it is therefore not uncommon to read industry statistics showing better than 93 percent of the lessees are 30 days in arrears. In some cases, however, the lessor may want advance payment. This amounts to a small fraction of the leases and may hinge on the creditworthiness of the lessee.

Secondary Losses or Consequential Losses as a Result of Poor Workmanship

The UCC allows for a limited warranty on the part of the seller, wherein the seller will repair or replace defective parts or components and bring the equipment back to its intended state as new equipment. Limited warranties disclaim any responsibility for loss of materials or other costs arising from the failure of the equipment to perform properly. These are consequential damages stemming from equipment failure. Although it may be difficult or impossible to collect these damages, they may be avoided by proper acceptance testing before signing the certificate of acceptance.

OEM Support in Training or Programming

What will be the level of OEM support in training operating personnel, maintenance personnel, and programmers in the case of computer numerically controlled equipment? These are issues to be resolved before signing the lease, and these provisions should be included in the RFP when seeking information in or referenced in the purchase order and in or referenced in the lease to ensure compliance.

Options at Lease End

This is especially important when the lease has an option to purchase. This is one area where leasing can come apart and the operating lease becomes the capital lease. Consider fair market value and the use of a disinterested third party to determine that value. A used equipment appraiser, paid equally by the lessor and lessee, could be a source of an arm's-length estimate. Be sure the equipment appraiser is a certified used equipment appraiser, and recognize there are six separate values for used equipment. (See Chapter 8 on buying previously owned equipment for some interesting differences among the values.) This approach avoids the problem of estimating value. Should the lessee terminate the lease and refuse the purchase option, the lessor has an independent assessment of the value of the equipment.

Basis for Renewal, Duration, and Other Options With Associated Costs

Should the buyer elect to extend the lease or exercise some other option, such as conversion, what costs are going to be incurred by the lessee? Can the lease be terminated with a purchase at any time during the lease period or only at the end or at mutually agreed upon times?

Taxes to Be Paid by Lessee

In the net lease, the tax issue is clear, with the lessee often paying the taxes. The level of taxes and basis should be clarified as well as the position of the taxing authority as to rates, time of assessment, and general nature of the taxing philosophy of the entity. For example, with assessments done annually, a person can purchase an item of equipment on the day after assessment, have one full year before it appears on the tax rolls, and then six to ten more months before the tax bill comes. Buying the equipment one day before the assessment equates to paying the taxes the year following the purchase at a higher rate since the depreciation has not taken place as in the first case.

Indemnification of Taxes by the Lessor

This also includes the tax situation down the road. Taxing entities can change positions as to rates and assessment. Not having that provision carefully delineated in the agreement opens the door to increased payments further into the lease. This is simply protection for the lessee and provides for future protection.

Impact of Financing on the Lessee

Depending on the type of lease and how the lessor pays for the equipment, 100 percent or leveraged, there may be third, fourth, or fifth parties behind the scenes who are lending the lessor the capital to make the purchase. They have a financial interest in the equipment. The lessee must have protection and indemnification for the lessee from actions on the part of the equity or debt holders in the leveraged lease. The indemnification serves as the shield for the lessee if troubles occur between the lessor and these parties.

Shipping the Equipment to the Lessor at the End of the Lease

When this is the situation, it is a good idea to spell out in the agreement when the lease is over and how the disposition of the equipment is to be handled. Stipulate that the lessor has costs associated with all aspects of the return of the equipment, including teardown, crating or packaging, rigging, and transportation to any site selected by the lessor at the lessor's cost. The lessor has the right to inspect the equipment at the end of the lease and is encouraged to do so prior to teardown and preparation for transportation.

These are all issues that can affect the cost of the lease for the lessee. Many of the items could also occur when making a purchase, but the failure of legal title to pass to the buyer upon acceptance of the equipment places a third party in the relationship. The third party is present primarily for financing purposes, and the concerns of the third party, the lessor, are often not in concert with the lessee with respect to support of the equipment, its maintenance, and its operation. Yet the lessee does not have title to the equipment under either of the main types of leases discussed. This means the lessor must be in the middle as the owner of the equipment. Does this help the lessee by having someone who is possibly a more frequent buyer than the lessee putting some pressure on the supplier, or does it mean the lessor is interested only in the monthly payments and leaves the lessee to fight his own battles with equipment problems? Some attempt to answer these types of questions should be made before signing on the dotted line. The lessor is in business to lease equipment. There is little or no money in servicing that equipment, and servicing is not a leasing function. The lessee should ask if the lessor will stand behind the lessee—and how far away he will stand.

Communication is vital in the field of leasing. It is important the lessee understand some of the basic terminology used.[7]

Glossary of Leasing Terms

acceleration clause   A provision of a lease that allows the lessor, upon default by the lessee, to require all payments due in the future to be made immediately.

advanced lease payment   Lease payments made at the beginning of a lease, for instance, lease payments due on the first of the month. This is contrasted with *arrears lease payment.*

arrears lease payment   A payment made at the end of a lease term, such as at the end of a month.

balloon payment   A large payment made at the end of a lease. Use of a balloon payment in a lease will have the effect of reducing the periodic payment during the lease term.

bargain purchase option   A provision in a lease giving the lessee the right to purchase the leased property for a price less than its anticipated fair market value. This term is most often used in connection with classifying a lease for accounting purposes. Similar to a purchase option.

broker   An intermediary between the lessee and lessor who arranges a leasing transaction and is usually paid some fee by the leasing company for its services.

capital lease   A specific classification of a lease for accounting purposes. The classification of the lease will determine how the lease is to be accounted for. A lease is accounted for by the lessee as a capital lease if it meets one of the following criteria: (1) at the end of the lease, the lessee owns the property being leased; (2) at the end of the lease, the lessee can purchase the property for a bargain purchase option; (3) the lease term exceeds 75 percent of the estimated economic life of the leased property; (4) the present value of all lease payments is equal to 90 percent or more of the cost of the leased property.

capped fair market value   A provision in the lease allowing the lessee to purchase the leased property for its fair market value but without exceeding a certain amount. The advantage of the cap is that the lessee will know the maximum payment required to purchase the leased property.

captive lessor   A leasing company that has been set up by the manufacturer

7. This glossary of leasing terms comes from several sources. We thank the Equipment Leasing Association for generous permission to reproduce the terms in the glossary.

or dealer of equipment to finance the sale or lease of its own products to customers.

certificate of acceptance   A written verification by the lessee of receiving the property to be leased. Most leases begin after the date stated on the certificate of acceptance.

conditional sales contract   An agreement for the purchase of an asset in which the lessee is treated as the owner of the asset for federal income tax purposes but does not become the legal owner of the asset until all the conditions of the agreement have been satisfied.

coterminous   Two or more leases that end at the same time.

cross corporate guaranty   A guarantee by one corporation to pay the lease obligations of another corporation.

default   A lessee does not comply with the terms of the lease. After a default, the lessor generally can exercise all of its rights under the lease to repossess the property and seek money damages.

direct finance lease   A nonleveraged lease by a lessor (not a manufacturer or dealer) in which the lease meets the definitional criteria of a capital lease plus certain other additional criteria. Same as a capital lease except this accounting classification applies only to a lessor.

discount rate   The interest rate used to bring a series of future payments or earnings into today's dollars.

dollar buyout   An option at the end of the lease to buy the leased property for $1.

early termination   The return of the equipment to the lessor from the lessee prior to the end of the lease as stipulated in the original lease or subsequent modifications. This action may require a financial penalty to be levied on the lessee.

economic life of leased property   The estimated time the leased property can be used with normal repairs and maintenance.

end-of-term options   Options upon expiration of the lease that may include renewal of the lease, purchase of the equipment, or return of the equipment to the lessor.

fair market value   The price a willing buyer will pay a willing seller for leased property on an "as is, where is" basis with both under no compulsion to buy or sell. In reality, this is a vague term, often creating a question between a lessor and lessee regarding what the fair market value is. Stated another way, what will an informed buyer, acting in his own best interests and independent of both the lessor and lessee, pay for the leased property at the end of a lease?

fair market value purchase option   A lease term that gives the lessee the ability to purchase the leased property at its fair market value at the end of a lease. Similar to a purchase option.

FAS 13   The statement of Financial Accounting Standards No. 13 entitled "Accounting for Leases." Sets forth standards for how parties to a leasing transaction should account for such transaction.

FASB Financial Accounting Standards Board—the group that dictates the general accounting policy and theory that is to be followed by both internal accountants and external auditors.

FAZ-BEE Another name for FASB.

financial statements Accounting statements that provide specific information about a company's financial position. They include the profit and loss statement (also known as the income statement), the balance sheet, and the statement of cash flows. Financial statements can generally be audited by an outside CPA firm or be unaudited and thus prepared by the company.

financing statement A document specified under the Uniform Commercial Code that puts the world on notice that a security interest has been filed against the person on the form listed as the debtor. See also *UCC financing statement*.

full payout lease A lease in which the lessor recovers through lease payments the full costs incurred in the lease plus an acceptable rate of return, without reliance on the leased equipment's future residual value.

guideline lease A lease written under criteria established by the Internal Revenue Service to determine the availability of tax benefits to the lessor.

hell or high water clause A provision in a lease agreement that indicates the lessee is required to pay the lease payment for the entire term of the lease. Problems encountered by the lessee with the leased property are not valid reasons for not making lease payments.

interim rent Rent paid for an interim period of time. Many leases begin at the start of a period such as the first of the month. If leased property is received and a certificate of acceptance is signed prior to that date, often there is an interim period between the acceptance and the start of the first lease rental. During this interim term, the interim rent is paid. The interim rent is generally calculated as a percentage of the standard monthly rent prorated over the number of days in the month the lessee has use of the leased property.

investment-grade credit Generally refers to a lessee of high credit standing. Technically, an investment-grade credit is a company rated highly by one of many recognized credit agencies such as Standard & Poor's.

lease A contract giving the lessee the right to use the leased property for a period of time.

lease line A line of credit similar to a bank line of credit that allows the lessee to add leased property under the same terms and conditions without negotiating new agreements.

lease rate The interest rate charged on the lease.

lease rate factor A percentage that when multiplied by the cost provides a periodic rental. It is a helpful number when used by either a salesperson or the lessee. In the event the cost of the leased property is not exactly known or may change, having the lease rate factor allows a quick recalculation of a lease payment when that number becomes known.

lease term　The fixed term of the lease. See also *term*.

lessee　The user of leased property under the lease.

lessor　Depending on the type of lease, either the owner of the leased property or the owner of a security interest in the leased property.

letter of credit　A specific arrangement between a lessee and one of its banks. The bank agrees that in the event of a defined event, the lessor can look to the bank instead of the lessee to make payment. This is similar to a security deposit in that it is one way for a lessor to ensure that it will be paid under a lease.

leveraged lease　A leasing situation whereby the equity position of the lessor is significantly less than 100 percent of the value of the equipment leased. The lessor has third parties, often in the form of trusts that put up the remaining capital to purchase the equipment leased. Under this arrangement, equity partners have a nonrecourse arrangement with the lessor. They must look to the lessee for payment of the lease or the equipment itself in the case of lessee default. The lessor is not responsible for the third-party investment in the case of default. A third party can also take a debt position in the leveraged lease and can therefore have a mortgage claim on the property of the lessor.

master lease　The primary document between the lessor and lessee containing all the general terms and conditions for leasing. Individual leases can be relatively short and incorporate the master lease by reference. It is a convenient administrative document so that once agreed, legal terms and conditions never need to be negotiated again.

middle market credit　A lessee without an investment-grade credit rating but generally with sales greater than $50 million annually.

municipal lease　Same as a capital lease except that the lessee is a public entity. Although the product and features are identical, the legal documentation is different because of the unique status of public entities.

net lease　Any lease in which all costs in connection with the use of the leased property are paid by the lessee and are not part of the periodic lease payments. For instance, maintenance, insurance, and taxes are paid directly by the lessee. Capital leases are generally net leases.

operating lease　An accounting classification for a lease that does not meet the criteria for a capital lease. With an operating lease, the lessor is generally taking a risk that at the end of the term, the lessee can either purchase the leased property or renew the lease, or the leasing company can remarket the leased property for its residual value.

payment in advance　Periodic payments made at the beginning of each period in the lease, in effect paying in advance for the use of the equipment.

payment in arrears　Periodic payments due at the end of each period, such as the month. The lessee has used the equipment and pays for that use at the end of the period.

personal guaranty   The guarantee of someone to be individually responsible for the obligations under the lease. Generally for Subchapter S companies and small businesses, a leasing company may ask for a personal guaranty as a way to ensure that the lease payments will be made.

present value   The discounting of future payments or revenues using a specific interest or discount rate. The value of future payments is expressed in today's dollars. Use of the discounting process removes the time value of money.

progress payment loan   Milestone payments made by the lessor and required by the vendor until all equipment, customization, training, installation, and conversion have been provided by the vendor. This product is generally used with larger transactions that require milestone payments over a short time (between 3 and 18 months). This is normally found in the data processing area where the purchase of the equipment by the lessor and its leasing to the lessee are accomplished over a significant period of time as contrasted to a piece of equipment that is purchased, shipped, installed, and accepted.

purchase option   Option to purchase leased property at the end of the lease term.

refundable security deposit   An amount paid by a lessee to provide extra protection to the lessor to ensure that the lessee will pay its obligations under the lease.

remarketing   The process of selling or re-leasing leased property that has been returned to the lessor at the end of the term or as a result of a default in lease.

remarketing fee   A fee paid for selling or re-leasing leased property.

rent holiday   A period of time during which a lessee is not required to pay rent.

residual value   The value of leased property at the end of the lease term.

sale-leaseback   A transaction that involves the sale of property by the lessee to the lessor and a lease of the property back to the lessee.

security interest   An interest in property that is acquired for the purpose of securing the payment of a lease obligation. A security interest allows the holder of the security interest to obtain the property in the event of default and gives the holder additional rights in the event of bankruptcy.

spread   The difference between funding costs and the rate of return to the lessor on a lease.

step-down lease   A variant of the step rental lease whereby lease payments decrease over the term of the lease.

step rental lease   A lease where the rent may change during the term of the lease. The change is known at lease inception and is agreed by both the lessor and the lessee. Often a step rent lease allows the lessee to pay less initially and more later in the term.

step-up lease   Similar to a step rental lease and a step-down lease except that the lease payment is increased during the term of the lease.

stipulated loss value   A term in a lease requiring the lessee to pay the value of the leased property in the event there has been some type of damage or destruction to the leased property.

term   The length of time for leasing equipment or software, generally 12, 24, 36, 48, or 60 months.

UCC financing statement   A document filed with the county (and sometimes the secretary of state) to provide public notice of a security interest in personal property.

vendor   An entity that provides leased property to customers.

vendor leasing   A working relationship between a leasing company and a vendor to provide leasing to the vendor's customers. In some sense, the leasing company is working as an extension of the vendor, providing credit checking, billing and collecting documentation, and customer service. The leasing company generally is accepting the credit risk.

8

Buying Previously Owned Equipment

Nearly every time a piece of new equipment is purchased, a buying and selling opportunity is created because the displaced equipment must go somewhere. Unless it rusts or crumbles, is scrapped, or feeds the furnaces of the minimill, it provides some potential user with the chance to buy the equipment to fulfill a particular need immediately and often at a lower price than new equipment. The buyer looking at previously owned equipment must consider an array of positive and negative factors that may influence the purchase and an array of costs associated with previously owned equipment that may be absent from new equipment. Yet there are factors that make previously owned equipment very attractive beyond its lower price. This equipment may save 30 to 70 percent when comparing the costs with that of new equipment.

Issues in Purchasing

Consider previously owned equipment on a case-by-case basis. Each buying opportunity is unique, and there are few all-encompassing decision rules in this area. While appearing simplistic at first, there are four major issues.

Is It Absolutely Necessary to Have New Equipment?

In many cases, new equipment is the only possible solution. If the previously owned supply is inadequate or the cost of previously owned equipment is substantially the same as new equipment, the buyer has few options. If the objective of the buyer is to incorporate the newest technology, previously

We wish to thank Sam Freedenberg of the Machinery Dealers National Association for his help in developing this chapter. His suggestion of the term *previously owned* as opposed to *used* casts the view of the purchase in a totally different light.

owned equipment is not a viable option. If there is not some overriding requirement for new equipment and the buyer is willing to look at all the options available, previously owned equipment can offer an attractive option. Simply because the equipment has been used by someone else, it cannot be stereotyped as shoddy merchandise. It may have many, many years of performance left in it. Previously owned equipment may offer the buyer a bargain in terms of price, availability, and performance. Previously owned equipment represents an opportunity worthy of exploration.

The first issue is not letting the mind-set of the second-hand, previously owned, or used item undermine the viability of the option. This is equipment, not clothing or automobiles or any personal use item. The image of the company is not going to be affected by having some previously owned equipment as part of the total capital equipment pool. The perception of the term *used* must be overcome. This is sometimes difficult since it often evokes an image issue. This is not to say that used is better than new, but the informed buyer who knows what to look for can often purchase the used equipment at significant savings in both time and money. In turn, the seller can realize a significant return on the original investment by having a desirable item of equipment to sell. Desirability in this situation is nothing more than a machine in good operating condition, with its history documented with respect to repairs and replacements, plus any appropriate spare parts that are available. The fact that someone else has used the equipment for some period of time may not be of any consequence. Adjustments, repairs, modifications, and customization may actually add to the original value of the equipment. The distinction between the dollar value of the equipment in the marketplace and value to the user must be understood and appreciated. Although accountants may depreciate the used equipment over a shorter period of time, its relative worth or value to the organization may have no relationship to a depreciation schedule. At the end of its **accounting life,** the equipment may have many years of productive operating life left in it. The issue to analyze is the contribution that piece of equipment can make to the company, not who owned it before purchase.

What Types of Information Does One Look for in the Purchasing Process?

Four issues come into play here: (1) not buying from the original equipment manufacturer (OEM), (2) the validity of descriptions and inspections, (3) warranty issues, and (4) the real value of the equipment.

Not Buying From the OEM

Although the equipment may not be purchased from the OEM, this is not saying that the buyer is buying blind. Any seller can warrant the goods sold. In fact, the Uniform Commercial Code (UCC) adequately covers the issue of implied warranty. The issue becomes the source itself and the real value of the warranty. Supplier reliability is as much an issue in buying in the used equipment market as in the new market. To avoid confusion, we turn to terminology used to define used equipment.

If the equipment is defined by the seller to be **rebuilt** capital equipment, by definition this equipment has been torn down, with worn parts or service life parts replaced, cleaned, reassembled, and painted. It has been brought back as close to new as reasonably possible. Is the machine **repaired?** Repairing implies that all badly worn parts are replaced, the machine is cleaned and painted, and it is put back in reasonable operating condition.

Where the repair or reconditioning takes place is an important issue. It may be far different to have the work accomplished by the OEM than some other repair facility. Are the replaced parts genuine replacement parts or clones of the original parts, possibly lacking the physical specifications of the original parts? If the internal parts are not up to original specifications and reliability, who will warrant the equipment, and how valid is that warranty? In other cases, the dealers who repair or rebuild equipment are maintenance specialists and could do a better job than the factory. It all depends on the quality of the source and the value of the business as perceived by that source. The real agenda may be the financial capability of the source to back the sale in terms of warranty.

Descriptions and Inspections of Used Equipment

There is a significant difference between reading a description and looking at a picture of an item versus actually looking at the item. Photography and graphics are capable of making any object appear in any desired condition. The brochure view of the hotel room can make the broom closet appear to be a spacious chamber by focusing the camera at the proper angle. The written description can also convey the intended image without being dishonest in the presentation of the product or misrepresenting it. This is accomplished by the use of value words, which often have multiple meanings or are subject to individual interpretation. In addition, the law allows for some puffery, or exaggeration of the quality of the product where individual interpretation is necessary.

The seller cannot make a performance claim that is impossible or fraudulent, such as the Yugo's being capable of sustained speeds of 150 miles per hour. A statement of that nature is an outright lie and constitutes an attempt to deceive. However, it is permissible to use words such as *very clean, runs well,* and *in good condition* and not be misrepresenting the equipment. These are perception terms that vary from person to person. This all equates to reading about the equipment and considering the written descriptions to be representations of goods available for sale. *There is no substitute for going to see the equipment.* Failure to see the equipment, at the very least, translates to buying a picture and a promise.

The key is the inspection process for used equipment. This means visiting the site of the equipment with at least two or three people who are capable of assessing the appropriateness and value of the equipment to your company. Each person on the team will see the equipment from a different perspective, and it is those combined perspectives that make a wise and educated decision possible. There are few differences in the inspection process between used and new equipment. We look for the same features or factors and evaluate with just as much care—and perhaps more due to the lesser support or warranty afforded by the previously owned equipment.

The inspection team should have a maintenance person on it because this person will be responsible for keeping the machine running and should be able to estimate the key parameters of doing the job. Representation of the quality function is important. If the machine is in such a condition that meeting the quality requirements is impossible or accomplished only after significant expense, the purchase may have an **effective cost** beyond all reasonable levels.[1] Catching the potential quality problem before the purchase is made is best. In addition, if extensive expenditures must be made to ensure the quality of output with the used equipment, the **total cost** of the equipment could easily approach the cost of new equipment. Often the third person should be the lead operator or a floor person having experience on that type of machine, if possible. The operator views the machine from the perspective of using the machine daily.

Quality used equipment dealers welcome these inspections. They are an integral part of the buying process, and the buyer should begin to gather information needed in making the decision, such as offering price, documentation available on the equipment, spare parts that come as part of the offer, reasons for the sale, if brokered, warranty, terms, and any proposals made by the dealer.

The visit is especially important if the equipment is going to be purchased at an auction. Practically all auctions offer the equipment "as is, where is," and the buyer is responsible for all repairs to bring it into operating condition. Disclaimers are made to even the implied warranty. The only legal protection is if the equipment cannot perform the function for which it was sold, even after reasonable repair and maintenance. The buyer then has some recourse, but normally the auctioneer will not take the item in such bad condition because it poses a possible legal liability. The issue then becomes, Whom do you as the buyer go after? If the purchase was made as a result of liquidation, then what you got is what you got. See before you buy. In addition, auctioneers go to great lengths to stress they are special agents of the principal, empowered only to conduct a sale of the goods offered.

---

1. If the cost per unit of output rises due to an increase in the defective rate or extensive re-working is necessary, the cost of good units rises. The good output must carry its own costs but the added burden of defective units. The effective cost of each good unit increases.

Duration and Validity of the Warranty

Previously owned equipment may carry warranties from the seller. Any warranty offered will be a limited liability warranty, as in the case of new equipment, limiting liability to repair or replacement necessary during some finite period of time. All sellers of goods will go to great lengths to protect themselves against consequential damages or losses incurred by the buyer as a result or consequence of using the machine. This could include wasted material, damaged or broken tooling, or lost labor time. The only remedy offered in law for the buyer is the failure of the equipment to perform "its essential purpose." Relief can be granted for that reason under Section 2–719 of the UCC.

The significant difference between previously owned and new is the duration of the warranty. Used equipment may be covered for only a fraction of the original warranty period. The duration of coverage normally will be of sufficient time to uncover **infant mortality failures** or **burn-in** problems encountered in the early stages of operation. The buyer should seek a warranty that is expressed in operating hours, not calendar time. A calendar time warranty may expire before the machine has been used sufficiently to discover any problems associated with it. This is a point of negotiation between buyer and seller and depends on many issues, including proximity to the buyer, the use of third parties for repair work, and the seller's capability.

Allied with the duration issue are the questions of who is providing the warranty and to what extent the warranty is capable of being supported. Is the seller going to perform the warranty work, or is that to be contracted to a third party? Is the third party an independent contractor or an agent of the seller or a subcontractor of the seller? Is the seller responsible for the actions of the third party, or must a separate contract be drawn up?

Since the equipment will be at the buyer's site, any warranty work will require the provider of the service to visit the buyer's site. This visitation raises all types of issues including, but not limited to the following:

• *Insurance certificate of the warranty maintenance provider.* Has the provider adequate insurance, and what is the extent of the coverage? Anyone doing any type of work at the buyer's facility must be covered by the appropriate types of insurance.

• *Access to the plant site.* How will access be gained? What identification will be needed and accepted? A simple way is to fax the provider a copy of the work order or work request, which will serve as proof of need to be at the facility.

• *Liability for warranty work provided by the third party.* Who will bear any liability for warranty work not properly performed, and what is the limit of the liability? Obviously the provider of the effort is liable to his principal since the seller who subcontracts the maintenance work has an agency relationship or at least a contractual relationship with the provider. This clarifies the seller-provider relationship, but what is the recourse of the buyer who receives sub-standard warranty coverage by the third party?

• *Time between failure and arrival of third-party maintenance provider (waiting time).* Has the agreement specified a maximum period of time the buyer must wait to get the warranty work done? This is downtime for the machine owner, and having a machine down waiting for warranty repair work can be more expensive than not having the warranty at all.

• *Quality of the maintenance effort.* Perhaps the most difficult area to handle is the quality of the warranty work performed. Even the simplest repair job has a number of options open to it. Good repair work will often involve small steps, such as fastener or filter replacement, gasket changing, lubrication, adjustment, and clean-up as part of the process. These are low-cost steps and often take little or no more time than the job itself, yet performing these tasks or making these replacements gives the job a cosmetic appearance that helps to define quality. The expectation is that the warranty work is going to bring the machine back to its level of performance. The secondary activities add a dimension of appearance to the job. Quality of the service effort is quite difficult to quantify, yet its absence is easily recognized. Perception plays an important role.

• *Coverage of the maintenance.* What does the warranty cover? Are certain components covered for a longer period of time than others? Not all items fail or need replacement at the same time, or, put another way, dynamic components are subject to faster failure rates. (See Chapter 9.)

• *Work that may be done on the machine that will not void or invalidate the warranty.* Failure and breakdowns are normally unpredictable. If a failure occurs and some form of action is necessary, what is the latitude afforded the machine owner in making some type of repair that will not void the warranty? Events such as a broken pipe or seal causing a leak or a defective electrical component causing a safety problem or broken teeth on a gear that threatens to do catastrophic damage may call for immediate action on the part of the machine operator or a maintenance person. These actions should not void the warranty; however, it is a good idea to have a clause in the purchase order that places the seller on notice that the owner of the equipment can perform certain repair or maintenance activities in case of emergency or any act deemed necessary for plant safety. By way of example, a computer seller placed a sticker on the back of a desktop indicating that opening the case housing the computer would void the warranty. This was nonsense and simply an attempt to secure more business by installing any additional internal features in the machine. It is best to have these terms spelled out before the purchase, especially if the equipment uses any hazardous materials or contains material that is considered hazardous by the Environmental Protection Agency.

If these issues are not settled prior to the purchase of the used equipment, maintenance activities in support of the warranty may be delayed or may not be performed at all. The provider of the warranty will surely have terms and conditions of that warranty clearly spelled out. This is all part of the purchasing process. Care must be exercised to understand the terms and conditions as they apply to the purchase before the purchase is finalized. Violate those terms and conditions, and the entire warranty may be invalid.

The warranty itself is only as good as the person making the sale. If the supplier cannot back up the warranty with good repair or maintenance service, the warranty is worthless. This should be viewed as a negotiation point. If the buyer realizes the weakness of the warranty, why pay for it in the price? Why not simply buy the used equipment without a warranty and get the reduction in price or limit the warranty? Many large utilities purchase vehicles without the warranty since their repair and maintenance capability is often far better than the dealer from whom they buy the vehicles. Without the warranty, the OEM may be a better source than the auto or truck dealer.

In the case of used equipment purchased from a used equipment dealer, the buyer carefully evaluates the scope of the dealer's operation. What services does the dealer normally provide? What is the dealer's capability to support the equipment and provide service beyond the sale? Like any good sourcing program, the buyer looks at all facets of the source's capabilities. The buyer who sacrifices service for price or does not ensure an adequate supply of spare parts for the used machine is not doing the job and may be sacrificing short-term savings for long-term costs.

There is another term that must be considered in the purchase of used capital equipment: **as is, where is.** Normally associated with auctions, it basically conveys the message, "What you see is what you get." Equipment purchased under these conditions bears no warranty except the passage of clear title to the goods. The performance is not warranted or guaranteed, and upon buying, the purchaser has the responsibility for the movement of the equipment from the purchase site in a specified period of time. A time allowance of nominally 24 hours is allowed before the seller has the right to charge rent for storing the equipment. Purchasing equipment under these conditions or in as is, where is condition places the entire burden of transportation, support, and suitability of the equipment on the buyer.

It is possible to obtain equipment that is inexpensive and good, but it takes time. It is possible to get good equipment quickly, but it can be costly. Inexpensive equipment can be obtained quickly, but quality is questionable. The buyer can have two variables but not all three. Take your choice on the two desired. This is the anatomy of the capital equipment buying decision.

Real Value of the Used Equipment

This is one of the most complex issues in the decision to purchase used equipment. Its complexity evolves from the numerous reasons that used capital equipment is available on the market:

- The machine has been displaced by a new machine.
- The current owner is liquidating assets.
- The current owner is bankrupt, and the equipment is being sold to satisfy creditors, or the equipment is repossessed by creditors and being sold.
- The product line requiring that machine is being dropped, and there is no further use for the machine, making it excess to the seller's needs.
- The seller has used the machine for a planned period and is replacing it per a predefined schedule.[2]

Each of these situations generates a different price for the capital equipment. Superimpose the use of different channels of distribution for the selling of used equipment—ranging from the auction to direct sale to used equipment dealers to tax sales—and the picture can become quite complex. Each party to the transaction except the buyer has expectations of profit. Each type of sale creates an expectation in the mind of the buyer relative to the price being paid. The need to sell the equipment on a timely basis will be present in the forced liquidation case but not in the case of excess equipment.

The final complicating factor is the relative strength of the two markets: the buyer's market and the seller's market. Basic economics, guided by the relationship of supply to demand, dictate prices. Increase the supply, and the price drops. Raise the demand significantly while holding supply constant, and price increases.

The cause or reason for the sale creates the price or value expectation in the mind of the seller. Consider the following three cases individually as the potential buyer and reflect on the reason for the sale and therefore the urgency of that sale, the expected or needed price from the sale, and the flexibility or latitude in negotiating a final price or a final package for the equipment.

Case 8-1

The company has acquired a new piece of equipment and displaces an old piece of fully depreciated equipment. From a financial perspective, the equipment has been "paid for" by depreciation. It may

---

2. This may be the case with computers that are in place for three years and then replaced with state-of-the-art machines.

have some residual value, and as long as it does not cost the company money to have it moved or disposed of, there may be little urgency for its sale. It may be taking up some space and represent an inconvenience, but the pressure to sell is absent. The company in this position may take its time in the selling process. It may select a selling channel that offers a reasonable opportunity to get a fair price with an absolute minimum of liability for any type of warranty. The seller has a variety of channels to review. It may advertise locally for a direct sale, recognizing the implied warranty under the UCC, but selling as is, where is.

It may wish to have the supplier of the new machine take the old one as a trade-in on the new machine, thereby moving the used equipment into the hands of the OEM, who may have better access to potential customers for the used equipment.[3] This may be a possibility where the lead time is extensive for new equipment and potential customers need the equipment quickly and desire a quality piece of equipment. The OEM may be willing to accept a trade-in and recondition the machine if there is a buyer waiting. The OEM has many options available with the trade-in. It can be rebuilt and used as a loaner pending the arrival of the new equipment. It may be leased by the OEM after reconditioning.

The seller also has other options. He can make the machine available to other departments or divisions of the company by declaring the equipment surplus to the present needs and keeping the whole transaction simple. The other options include selling to a used equipment dealer or putting the machine up for auction. If there is no time pressure and the monetary factors are not critical to the company, the timing element is in the seller's favor. The seller may establish a base or floor price for the equipment, verify the accuracy of the asking price by having a professional appraisal done on the equipment, and wait until the timing is favorable. Lacking the pressure or urgency to sell, the seller can hold the line on the price.

Case 8-II

The owner is liquidating assets. This type of liquidation is not forced, nor is it the result of any adverse action against the seller. The asset

---

3. This can be an advantage to the OEM in taking used equipment in as trade-ins, rebuilding it, and then selling it in the used equipment market. The disadvantage is that the dealer may be competing with himself. Yet many dealers perceive the existence of several markets—new equipment buyers, used equipment buyers and lessors—with very little overlap. They choose to segment the markets themselves.

liquidation can be taking place for a variety of reasons: The machine is obsolete; the product line produced on that equipment is no longer being produced; the company is going out of business. The reasons are endless and really not germane. What is important are issues of depreciation, urgency of need for the funds, and market size. Much like Case 8-I, the seller has a number of viable options, providing time is not of the essence.

Case 8-III

The seller is being forced to sell due to bankruptcy, or the mortgage holder on the equipment must repossess due to failure to pay for the equipment. This situation introduces many new dimensions into the selling process and places a burden on the seller to act quickly in the disposal of the equipment. Since time is important, the issue of price compromises rapidly appears. Urgency of need in fulfilling obligations to creditors makes price concessions very likely. The seller in need of liquidity must offer some inducements. For the buyer in this case, the warranty issue is probably a moot point. If the seller is not going to be in business, there is little hope the seller will make good on the warranty or even offer one. It is the fast, inexpensive situation. The favorable nature of the market may have little impact when time is very important and there is a strong need to raise cash.

What Price Will Be Paid for the Used Equipment as a Percentage of the New Equipment Price?

To place percentages on used equipment as fractions of the cost of new equipment is all but impossible. What is possible is benchmarking with the new equipment cost and features and attempting to make valid comparisons of proposed costs of used equipment. There are some very general rules that say the cost of repaired will be 50 percent of new and rebuilt will be 70 percent the cost of new equipment, but these should not be taken to be hard and fast. The price is a function of the marketplace, the supply, the demand, the product itself, and the willingness to pay for the value received.

The employment of used equipment also offers a competitive price advantage. The fixed-cost segment of the price is reduced, and either the profit margin widens or price can be reduced. The burden per operating hour is less, offering a degree of pricing flexibility that can manifest itself in many ways.

Consider the recent case of the company bidding on the construction and operation of a power station in the Philippines.

All bidders but one specified new turbines as the generation medium. That other company proposed previously owned turbines. The market price between new and previously owned was sizable, and the price differential—approximately $20 million—led to his selection as the low bidder. Having won the bid, the company purchased previously owned turbines, had them fully inspected, and insured their continued operation with Lloyds of London.

The company built the facility with used turbines. Nine months after the project was on-line, one of the turbines failed, but the insurance covered the loss in revenue and the repair cost.

If a cost advantage is needed, previously owned capital equipment may offer the buyer an opportunity that might not exist if new equipment is employed.

Pricing is a complex issue, and each case must be considered on its own merits. There are subjective approaches to determining the value of the equipment by using a ranking or rating approach of features of the used equipment versus the new and assigning point values to features. Used equipment dealers, of course, are no different from anyone else in that they must make a profit to stay in business. The price is going to be less than new, but do not expect the equipment for free.

If there is a real concern over the price, the use of a third party is reasonable. Hire a professional appraiser. The Association of Machinery and Equipment Appraisers (AMEA) is a not-for-profit association that accredits and certifies appraisers of equipment and machinery. Over a decade old, the association monitors its member appraisers and continuously ensures they meet the standards established by the Appraisal Foundation. The purpose of the appraiser is to introduce objectivity into the transaction. The seller wants to make a profit, the buyer wants to save money, and the appraiser makes the same dollars regardless of the final price. The appraiser represents himself.

If there is an impasse in reaching the final price, a possible solution is an appraiser as the disinterested expert with that cost borne equally by buyer and seller or simply by the buyer as a measure of value of the purchase. If price is going to be an issue, remove it as a variable by using the professional appraiser. There are, however, different views of price.

Pricing is a complex issue, and each case must be considered on its own merits. There are subjective approaches to determining the value of the equipment by using a ranking or rating approach of features of the used equipment versus the new and assigning point values to features. While this may appear subjective, such an approach provides the buyer with an estimate of the relative value of features that the new equipment possesses—relative to older models. If the new features or improvements are needed or exhibit greater value, the choice is obvious: Buy the new equipment. In some instances, the new features are more costly than they are worth, or their use is so sporadic that their purchase makes no economic sense. The fundamental question becomes, "How much more am I getting purchasing the new equipment versus the previously owned equipment?"

Recognize the used equipment dealer is no different from anyone else in that they must make a profit to stay in business. The price is going to be less than new, but do not expect it for free. This raises the question: What is a fair price for the previously owned equipment? There are always two prices. The seller has a price communicated by the offer, and the buyer has a price based on perception of the value of the equipment. In fact, there may be a range of prices for each, with the seller having a "floor" or minimum price and a desired price, and the buyer having a "ceiling" price and a desired price. For example, the seller wants to sell a piece of equipment for $50,000, but is willing to take $40,000 for it. The buyer will pay up to $42,000 for it, but would like to pay $35,000 for it. There is an overlap between the buyer's high price and the seller's low price, and a deal is possible between the two parties. What happens if there is no overlap? The seller's lowest acceptable price is $45,000. The difference between the two (seller's low and buyer's high) is $3,000. Two events can occur. First, there is no deal or even price negotiation. There cannot be a meeting of the minds unless one or both of the parties make significant price concessions. Making those concessions weakens the basic underpinning of the negotiation itself, the real value of the equipment. If the seller makes the concession of moving the lowest acceptable price to $40,000, the buyer could question the accuracy of that value. Why could it not be $35,000 or $30,000? A significant price concession can alter perceptions of value and may not bring about the desired result.

If there is a real concern over the price, the use of a third party is reasonable and is the second option. Hire a professional appraiser. Bring a disinterested party into the pricing situation—someone who has the expertise to add objectivity to the process and who has no interest in the end result. The appraiser perceives no benefit from the sale. The payment for services rendered is a flat fee and the appraiser or his company has no financial interest in the equipment. Where does the buyer find the information necessary to find and select an appraiser? The Association of Machinery and Equipment Appraisers (AMEA) is a not-for-profit association that accredits and certifies appraisers of equipment and machinery, and represents a source of information on appraisers. The purpose of the appraiser is the introduction of objectivity into the transaction. The seller wants to make a profit, the buyer wants to save money, and the appraiser makes the same dollars, regardless of the final price. Anyone representing both the seller and offering an expert opinion on value should be viewed as suspect. Objectivity and loyalty to one's employer are often mutually exclusive.

One of the important considerations in using the appraiser is an understanding of terms and conditions under which the appraisal is made. Sales of previously owned equipment takes place under different conditions, and those conditions influence the price. Selling under forced liquidation is different from an orderly liquidation. It is therefore equally important that the appraiser convey the reasons for the sale or define the conditions under which the seller is offering the equipment for sale. Is it the normal course of business of the seller, as in the case of used equipment dealers? Is it an orderly liquidation where a company is replacing existing equipment and wishes to dispose of the displaced equipment? Is it bankruptcy, where a third or fourth party is forcing the seller to liquidate assets? Each case is different, and those differences are reflected in the appraisal. The AMEA has developed six important definitions of "value." They include:

1. Fair market value
2. Market value—in place
3. Forced liquidation value
4. Orderly liquidation value
5. New replacement cost value
6. Desktop opinion

Without going into the details of each definition, it is easy to see there are going to be differences in value depending on the conditions under which the equipment is sold and how the appraisal was made (either in person or working only from descriptive material and the physical location of the equipment). In addition, awareness of relevant facts at the date of disposal is also important.

Forced liquidation carries the burden of appraisal with an eye toward rapid disposal, and raises issues of the adequacy of interested buyers in the equipment. This is one reason for the auction as a method of disposal (with the forced liquidation disposal being different from the orderly disposal). In the case of the orderly disposal, the seller normally has sufficient time to advertise and structure the sale. The pressure to "raise cash" or liquidate assets is not present.

Thus, the buyer seeking the expert opinion should:

1. Ascertain the conditions under which the appraisal was made or will be made.
2. Determine how the appraisal was conducted. A desktop appraisal does not actually require seeing the equipment and is just as its name implies—an opinion—based on information or data, not observation.
3. Determine when the appraisal was made. Time is an important factor.

4. Determine the definition of value being used by the appraiser. Which definition is being used if the appraiser says the equipment is valued at $25,000. Where is it located? What is its condition? What data was viewed in addition to the equipment itself? Were maintenance records available for review?

5. Is the appraiser truly an independent participant to the potential transaction, and does the appraiser maintain an "arm's length" relationship with respect to the transaction?

6. What are the qualifications of the appraiser? Being an appraiser may or may not qualify the person to pass on an expert opinion. Specialization is important.

7. What references can the appraiser provide? Appraisal is a service, and all services are difficult to evaluate. Make some calls before hiring an appraiser, and determine "customer satisfaction" with the appraiser.

8. Does the appraisal report provide estimates of other costs associated with packing and moving the equipment? How complete is the appraisal? Are there guidelines provided to guage the relative value of the equipment as a percentage of new? What relative measures are provided?

9. Is the cost of the appraisal fair and reasonable? What is the cost of the appraisal relative to the asking price of the equipment? If the relationship is reasonable, then the appraisal may be worth the money. An appraisal that costs too little can be worth just what it costs.

10. Finally, why is the appraiser being used? Is there an impasse between buyer and seller, with the appraiser being the final point of agreement as in the case of arbitration? Is the appraiser the outside expert to verify value, or is the appraiser the person who helps the seller determine value in an objective manner, removing many of the subjective aspects of valuation?

Understand conditions, reasons, and motives that influence the setting of price before paying that price. Auctions and other previously owned equipment sources may limit the leverage of the buyer after the purchase has taken place. "As is, where is" has definite legal meaning.

Terminology is important, as is knowing the conditions under which the appraisal was performed. When receiving an appraisal, the astute buyer questions the type of appraisal offered. Type reflects conditions.

Are There Advantages to Buying or Leasing Used Equipment?

Used equipment, purchased or leased, equates to getting older technology. This means that someone in the organization must make the decision as to the level of technology needed and the applicability of trading lesser technology for lower cost and better and faster availability. Fundamental to these issues is the application for the used equipment. Is the latest technology needed? A company may not be ready for that new technology if its addition places strains on all the other equipment or the new one sits idle much of the time waiting for the older models to catch up to the new ones. The issue is one of balance in the manufacturing process.

What will be the utilization of the technology in the present application: 100 percent, 75 percent, or 50 percent of the time? What features are needed versus desired? Are they critical to the operation? Do they involve tolerances, safety of operation, or quantifiable dimensions on which a decision can be based? The whole issue of new versus used must be carefully defined for each situation.

There may be a limited scope or time of use of the equipment. New equipment is expected to have a relatively long service life, for anywhere from 5 to 20 years. It involves the normal calculations of return on investment (ROI) and decisions on depreciation, maintenance, and other areas. The used machine may not have that duration of life. It may be a project-oriented purpose for which there is limited need, and when the project is completed, the need goes away. The options then become leasing versus new versus used equipment. It may be that the older or used equipment is less complex and easier to learn on. Pilots do not learn how to fly on F-18s; they begin with trainers that are usually older and easier to fly, and if they are lost many millions of dollars will not crash into the ground. Again, the decision becomes a cost per situation. If limited service life is needed, used equipment and less than state-of-the-art equipment will be viable alternatives.

Previously owned equipment often is an option for training employees. Training of new employees on the use of the equipment should be a transitioning experience. Start off with the simple and move to the complex. The simple solution can be the used equipment. Crashing a 12-station machine and devastating $25,000 in perishable tooling in learning how to use the machine is not a cost-effective approach. Learning the basics, employees are able to move to the more complex. Previously owned equipment fills that gap.

New equipment may not be needed or wanted. Buying in excess of needs and growing into the use is applicable to children's clothing but not equipment in many cases. Each feature of the new equipment comes at a price and adds cost to the purchase price. There are numerous examples of buying the latest technology and never using it. When PCs are used solely as word processors, 99 percent of the technology remains unused. The scope of the secretarial job is such that the power of the personal computer is never used.

New equipment may be too expensive, subject to rapid depreciation in value such that previously owned equipment is almost as good as new and not that old. The higher the technology, the greater the likelihood is that the value of the equipment will fall rapidly. Capital equipment is not purchased for resale purposes, but there is the reality of depreciation of value. Does the company wait until the rapid depreciation has taken place and buy as previously owned equipment or buy as new? The same situation holds true for the manufacturer. Some companies let the competition be innovators and come out with new features. By the next year, the follower has incorporated those innovations, and the buyer has only to wait for a short period to capture both aspects of new equipment and innovations.

The relative utilization of the technology may be such that used equipment will be sufficient and its utilization rate will be higher than new equipment, thus lowering the cost per unit. Expensive medical equipment in many hospitals today contains technology that moves so rapidly that current equipment will become outdated in one or two years. Yet that outdated equipment is new to the smaller hospital or group of hospitals that individually or collectively could not afford the new equipment. The used equipment offers an opportunity that new equipment never presented because it was financially out of reach for the prospective buyer.

Technology must be viewed as a relative entity. Older technology can still perform its function and in some cases can do a better job than newer technology in some applications. The M1 rifle carried through most of World War II by U.S. troops is a far better weapon than the more modern M16 at ranges of 500 to 1,000 yards. As in the case of the rifle, used equipment has a place in the technology pattern of the industry, and what is technologically obsolete to one user is sufficient or satisfactory to another. Sometimes the need cannot be satisfied by the newer technology when the older technology is totally capable of meeting that requirement. Modern jet fighters were found inferior in Vietnam for missions calling for aircraft to remain on station for long periods of time. C-47s from World War II were put back into service and renamed "Puff the Magic Dragon," carrying Vulcan (Gatling) guns and vast quantities of ammunition. Their slower flight speed made them ideal for the missions. In some cases the available technology exceeds the needed technology.

Another issue is the question of balance in the manufacturing operation. If the replaced equipment is going to operate at speeds beyond the capability of the remainder of the production line, is an imbalance going to be created? Will the imbalance cause the machine to be used at far less than 100 percent of operating capacity? What must be determined is the fit of the equipment into the existing configuration. In some cases, used or lesser technology equipment is a better overall fit with the company's manufacturing operation. There is little point in having high-technology equipment available but idle.

The distinction between new and used can also become blurred, and variations can crop up between those two definitions. If *new* is defined as never having been owned or used by any other entity and *used* does imply ownership and use, then consider some of the intermediate classifications. How is last year's model classified? It is unsold equipment and therefore new but does not have the features of the newer model. It may have depreciated in value simply because it has been displaced by more advanced technology. Consider the modular designed computer that may be selectively upgraded as the technology moves forward and the user needs expanded capability. Only part of it is used, and the "used" part is often not the technological driver. What of the case of the bare-bones model, purchased new and then upgraded and used for a period of time, only to be sold at a higher price than the original purchase? Where does it fall in the definition? These elements show the need to focus attention not on the definitional issues but on the use of the equipment and the appropriateness of the technology for that use.

The Time Factor

Perhaps the most compelling reason for the purchase of used equipment is lead time. Used equipment does not possess the long lead time normally associated with new equipment. This does not mean there is no lead time with used equipment, but the duration of that period is considerably smaller. If equipment is needed now, used equipment is a viable option for the buyer. Of course, there are still the issues of testing, transportation, installation, and acceptance criteria that have to be considered in the same manner as in the case of the new equipment.

Sourcing Previously Owned Equipment

The element of lead time present in the purchase of used equipment, and normally not present in the new equipment market, is the search time for sources of supply. Much of this time can be reduced by effective use of the Internet. There are literally hundreds of dealers in used equipment, many of them on the Internet with home pages. Simply select the engine of choice, type in "used equipment," and press the Search button.

Ensuring the Quality of the Source

The key issue in buying previously owned equipment is the quality of the source. Like every other purchasing decision, sourcing is a fundamental element. A quality source of supply for previously owned equipment can resolve many of the issues raised in this chapter. In this area, the buyer should look beyond the dealer and investigate the role of the professional association in that industry. In the metalworking industry, the Machinery Dealers National Association (MDNA), established as a nonprofit trade association in 1941, represents over 500 member companies. One of the cornerstones of MDNA is the code of ethics that members agree to abide by, and they renew that pledge annually:

MDNA Code of Ethics

MDNA members proudly display their emblem. This emblem identifies dealers who concur with MDNA's high standards of business practice. It is a symbol of integrity and reliability. It also recognizes dealers who have a wide range of technical expertise and data to help customers improve their productivity

The Code of Ethics underwriting this emblem provides that each MDNA member will:

1. Carry out the spirit and letter of all agreements and contracts in which he engages.
2. Respond to inquiries, advertise and offer machinery and equipment as accurately as he is able as per:
   a. Name of manufacturer
   b. Serial number
   c. Condition
   d. Specifications
   e. Adherence to standard industry terms and definitions
3. Honor every option a prospective buyer is offered.
4. Advise prospective customers of conditions and circumstances of sale when offering customer-owned machinery and equipment through a brokerage arrangement.
5. Accept within 30 days from shipment any machinery and equipment with return privilege, freight prepaid, for refund of the purchase price if proven mechanically unsatisfactory, or repair at the dealer's option.

Reprinted with permission of the Machinery Dealers National Association.

There are several interesting aspects of the code of ethics, including disclosure of information, expressions of intent to be bound to options provided, fairness in dealings, and advising the prospective buyer as to the reason for the sale. The code of ethics mirrors many of the provisions of the UCC that address the issues of ethics. Supplier integrity is an essential ingredient in the transaction, and the trade association stands with its membership in maintaining the integrity of each and every transaction.

Finding the Sources

Who are the used equipment sources, where are they, and how is communication established with them?

A rapid scan of the Internet reveals hundreds of used equipment dealers nationally. Call one, and ask for a particular machine. If the supplier does not have it, he may be able to locate it for you. It is a potential sale, and based on the volume of information available to anyone, the lead will not be ignored.

Finding sources of used equipment in the age of computers is child's play. An opening scan of the Internet under the search words "used equipment locator" brought forth over 61,000 replies. It would be impossible to search all of the listings, yet they are present on the Internet and offer a wide array of options in finding the needed equipment. The Internet user has the capability of communicating directly with suppliers who have the wanted equipment, posting the needs to a bulletin board and waiting for responses, exploring dealerships, or looking at the possibility of auctions as a source. It also allows the buyer to explore at an arm's-length distance from the supplier.

One of the most complete sources of information is the *Surplus Record.* Published monthly and updated daily, this 700-page index of available capital equipment provides potential buyers with the names and brief descriptions of tens of thousands of pieces of capital equipment as well as more than 800 dealers nationwide. *Surplus Record* is not affiliated with any entity that buys or sells equipment or machinery. Exhibit 8-1 shows a copy of *Surplus Record's* home page.

Another outstanding source is MIS, *Locator* of Used Machinery, Equipment & Plant Services. It is the largest directory of metalworking equipment available worldwide. It may be found on the Internet by searching for "MIS Locator."

Although this is an industry-specific publication, it is typical of what one finds in the search process. The field is so extensive that specialized directories appear to fill specific industry needs in buying used equipment, from medical equipment to marine equipment.

The *Surplus Record* and *Locator* act as gateways to large numbers of possible suppliers of used equipment. The buyer's process of source selection and the criteria used must be as rigorous as any other selection process.

Equipment Auction

Another option for the buyer is the equipment auction. Auctions are true examples of the impact of supply and demand. Beyond the economic model, they are places where bargains may be obtained, but the risk is such that only experienced buyers should attend.

The auctioneer is a special agent of the seller, hired for the purpose of organizing, promoting, and holding the auction. Normally the auctioneer receives a percentage of the sale proceeds and for this sum will schedule the auction and promote it to the widest possible audience of interested and potential customers. The auctioneer will have the equipment at the designated site for some period to allow customers to inspect prior to the auction.

The auctioneer sets a careful and stringent set of rules concerning the auc-

Exhibit 8-1. *Surplus Record* home page.

the SURPLUS RECORD

Machinery & Equipment Directory tm

Since 1924 Surplus Record has provided industry with its source for locating available machinery & equipment. Please contact the "dealers" directly for information and pricing pertaining to their individual listings. If you wish to sort & download large categories (i.e., motors) for a specific item(s), a **TELNET connection** may be more efficient for your search. *Surplus Record is not affiliated directly or indirectly in any manner or means with any association, corporation or individual buying and/or selling machinery and equipment.*

● Browse the Machinery & Equipment Database
(index of available machinery & equipment, everything from Air Compressors to Woodworking Machinery)

● Browse the Electric & Power Database
(index of available boilers, circuit breakers, generators, controls, motors, switches, transformers and turbines)

Best viewed with:  or

E-mail: *surplus@surplusrecord.com*

Return to the Surplus Record Machinery & Equipment Directory Home Page

Source: Copyright 1997 Surplus Record Machinery & Equipment Directory. All rights reserved. http://www.surplusrecord.com. Tel: 312-372-9077. Reprinted with permission of *Surplus Record.*

tion. Mainly these rules refer to issues of payment, yet a significant segment of the rules are warranty disclaimers. The auctioneer is simply a facilitator of the selling process, and it would be difficult to see where any express warranty would be created by the actions of the auctioneer. To avoid surprises, the potential buyer should take the opportunity to inspect before bidding.

An auction is a *caveat emptor* situation. The cost of the lower price may be in the quality of the product offered: What you see is what you get. In the case of auctions, the auctioneer totally disclaims any warranty responsibility, either implied or express. Disclaimers will not remove the responsibility of passing clear title or notifying the buyer of a lien or mortgage on the property and saying the sale and therefore the passing of clear title is accomplished only when the encumbrance is cleared.

Retrofitting Equipment: Another Option

Consider rebuilding existing equipment to return it to nearly its original state when purchased new or adding newer technology in the form of retrofitting. The retrofit process is one of modernization, adding or replacing certain components in such a way as to retain the function performed by the original equipment but upgrading the performance by adding newer controls or subsystems that are compatible with the existing equipment.

Another option is rebuilding or reconditioning the equipment. This is based on the concept that not all parts wear out at the same time. Service life exists for literally a hundred years on some parts that are not exposed to stress, wear, tear, or any element that would reduce their serviceability. The reconditioning can be done by the owning company or by machinery and equipment dealers with the expertise and equipment to do this work.

Machines that are decades old are still in use. The issues as to whether to rebuild or purchase a new or used machine are much more technology oriented. Returning to the use of the personal computer, there are still many places where the 386 or 486 may be used with reasonable productivity rather than replacing them with machines whose true capabilities will never be tested.

In the light of the technology issue, the question of which option to select should not rule out the rebuild alternative. There are a number of issues that favor the rebuild or recondition option:

- Lower cost associated with rebuilding than replacing
- No extensive training of machine operators
- Spare parts on hand
- Shorter lead time as compared with purchasing a new model
- Gain of output on the new model or new features only marginal
- Clear indication that the capacity of the rebuild will not create a bottleneck in the operations
- Plant maintenance personnel who are capable of rebuilding
- Testing and inspection technology capable of identifying parts or components reaching the end of service life or technological problems
- Making do for a short period of time pending major equipment replacement

The issue becomes what the criteria are for rebuilding versus replacing. There are a number of criteria that may be used.

- *Cost comparisons.* What is the cost to rebuild as compared to getting the new or used machine? The cost measure should not be viewed by itself. In almost all cases, it will show the rebuild as the less expensive option. Along with the costs, however, must go some performance measures to show the outcome of the rebuild compared with the new machine. These measures can be operating hours of new versus rebuilt. Determine what kind of service life can be expected from the rebuild, and then relate that back to costs.

• *Total cost of ownership* of the rebuilt versus the new, including maintenance costs, spares costs, and training.

• *Development of the appropriate decision rules* on the repair versus replace option such that when the cost of rebuild exceeds a certain percentage of the new equipment, the replacement will take precedence over the rebuild.

• *Development of a decision rule with respect to accumulated costs* for the rebuild candidate that when the investment in the machine, including original price, maintenance, spares, and any other costs, reaches 250 percent of the original cost, it is no longer a candidate for rebuild. This approach must be tempered with the expected benefits coming from the rebuild.

• *The approach of using a cutoff point for investing in the existing equipment* must be carefully examined. The paradigm at work here is that of residual value. One approach is that the book value of the equipment is zero at the anticipated end of its service life. It will be worth nothing at that point, and perhaps the company will have to pay the scrap dealer to haul it away. Thus, the process of rebuilding is investing in the equipment to keep it running. As long as the total cost of running it and keeping it running are below the cost of replacing it, then reinvesting in the old machine makes good sense. The orientation is toward the manufacturing process and the role of the equipment in that process, not some accounting notation to recoup a fraction of the price paid years into the future. The second approach could be intentionally upgrading the equipment over the first five years of its service life as a quasi investment. As an example of the application of this strategy, consider the case of Premium Allied Tool of Owensboro, Kentucky. Its strategy, formulated by Jim Hines, CEO, has been to purchase U.S. Baird four-slide machines and upgrade and improve them over a five-year period of ownership. The improvements not only add value to Premium's products, but make the machines more marketable at the end of the defined period of ownership. After five years of use, the company has a waiting market for the equipment at a price well above the market replacement value. It has a standing order for six new machines every year. That strategy is the other end of the spectrum with a definite focus on getting the best out of the machines and having them all but presold at the end of the five-year period. This strategy is one of investment to receive a return on that investment in the form of the price premium. However, it is impossible to have it both ways. The approach must be consistent and realistic. No one is going to pay a premium price for a piece of equipment that has had all of its service life consumed. Conversely, upgrading only to receive a higher selling price five years into the future makes little sense unless the benefits of use are there during the holding period. Some assets appreciate, and others depreciate. Knowing what direction the value goes is the first step.

Issues to Consider

In the case of the rebuilding option or reconditioning, one prime issue is the person or organization that performs the work. If it is the OEM, which possesses the parts and expertise, then the OEM may be competing with itself by being both a producer and maintainer of the equipment. It has long been known that spare parts or replacement parts often carry high mark-ups and are a never-ending source of profits for suppliers. Before the decision is finalized, have a solid cost estimate associated with rebuilding.

The advantage of this source is the technical expertise to repair and restore the equipment to an almost-new state. This is the factory rebuild or reconstruct. Although there is a legal definition of these terms, any repair or replacement activity is driven by economics. There must be an upper limit as to what can be spent in rebuilding the equipment. This means decisions are made as to what to replace. Some cases are clear and uncomplicated; others may present some difficult decisions, especially if the part or component is marginal. What were the hours of operation? When did it fail last? What has been its maintenance profile? Can the profile be documented? A simple document of a machine log can add value to the decision process and allow the buyer to make a valid comparison.

Finally, the question becomes, What do I get for my rebuild money? What is the service life of the rebuilt equipment relative to both new and used? Obviously, the service life of the rebuild may be less than the new, but so is its cost. If the cost of the rebuilt equipment is 50 percent of the cost of the new, then if its service life is greater than half the life of the new, rebuilding is a viable option. What is the anticipated service life of the used equipment relative to the rebuilt or the new? This may be the difficult question to answer, but one that must be considered if valid comparisons are to be made. Used equipment may not have to be someone else's used equipment. It can be your own. It comes with far fewer unknowns than used equipment from a dealer or an auction.

On the negative side is the issue of supporting a rebuilt piece of equipment or a used piece. The OEM will produce spare parts for only so long, and once they are no longer actively produced, they become very expensive to purchase, *if* they can be found at all. The lack of spares or difficulty in obtaining them can easily dissuade the buyer from both used equipment and the rebuild option. Like any other equipment purchase evaluation, look at the total cost of the option plus the projected support costs over the service life of the equipment. That value is the total cost of ownership.

Is it possible to compare used equipment and new equipment on a rational basis? Answering this question is the test of the comparison. It may involve creative approaches such as using the index number approach or relative measures using the new equipment as the benchmark and allocating points for such aspects as service life, spare parts, ease of maintenance, and costs. The system does not have to be perfect. A measuring system of this nature is measuring on a relative basis, not absolutes. A point scoring method may add up the points for each alternative. The highest point total will probably be the new equipment. Divide the cost by the number of points for each alternative (new, used, or rebuilt) and see the cost per point. The lowest cost per point indicates the best option. The points can be weighted to reflect relative importance of the feature under consideration. This is not a foolproof method, but it allows some objectivity to be used in a rather subjective arena. The precision of the methodology is not the issue; consistency of application is the issue. Whatever the weights are or the criteria selected for inclusion, they are applied to all the alternatives. Each option is graded and a decision is made.

Documentation: The Key Element

Accurate records of maintenance, replacement of parts, or components plus documentation of reasons for failures (if known) can provide a wealth of information on the equipment and show the prospective buyer the true value being received in the sale. All of this information can accompany the equipment or can be made available prior to the sale if the seller has it and wishes to provide it. The astute buyer should ask for this information before engaging in serious negotiations with the seller. If the sale of surplus equipment or the disposal of displaced equipment is not the main line of business of the seller, the seller should nevertheless provide the important information:

- A history of the maintenance of the equipment, including repair and replacement of worn parts
- Spare parts that are on hand at the seller's site
- Tooling to go with the equipment
- Specific information on that machine with respect to any unique aspects of operation or modifications made to the equipment
- Manuals for the machine

Much of the information is captured with a computerized maintenance management system (CMMS). Buying the equipment from a company with good CMMS documentation may relieve some of the anxiety associated with purchasing something that has been used before. (Chapter 11 contains fundamental information on CMMS.)

If the seller of the equipment is in that business, then expect to pay a higher price for the equipment. As a reseller, the dealer may be a pure used equipment dealer or a new equipment dealer who sells used equipment. There is a difference between the two, yet there are common factors also. Both are in business to make a profit. Both may be capable of performing maintenance to varying degrees on the equipment. Both may have a wider selection of equipment, beyond the typical one or two from the disposer. The amount of documentation from each may vary from none to extensive, depending on what is available when they purchased or received the machine. Do not look for tooling when buying from these sources. They are in the used equipment business, and the resale to the new buyer is their line of business.

Like any other business transaction, it is essential to know:

- What you want
- What you are willing to pay for it
- Whom you can buy it from
- What they have to offer
- What you can realistically expect for your money

Previously owned equipment offers an option and an opportunity. The option is balanced against new equipment and evaluated against the need. The opportunity is to save 30 to 70 percent of the price of the new equipment and weeks or months of waiting. It may not be the selected option, but it should be evaluated and considered as a reasonable alternative. Many of us make our largest single personal investment in an item that may be second, third, fourth, or even fifth hand: our homes.

Checklist for Buying Previously Owned Equipment

- ☐ What is the cost of new versus used equipment?
- ☐ What features do I get with the new equipment that are not present on the old?
- ☐ Can the old be retrofitted to get these new features?
- ☐ What is the time savings of old versus new?
- ☐ How many dealers have the desired used equipment?
- ☐ What is the support capability of the used dealer?
- ☐ What does the warranty say?
- ☐ Can the warranty claims be supported?
- ☐ Who will perform the actual warranty work?
- ☐ How accountable is the warranty provider?
- ☐ In rebuilding, whose parts go into the equipment?
- ☐ What sort of warranty is available on the rebuild?
- ☐ Who will perform the rebuild?
- ☐ What is the cost of rebuilding relative to the new cost, and what is the company decision rule on the cutoff point?
- ☐ What is the cost of used relative to new or rebuild?
- ☐ What is the rebuild lead time?
- ☐ What is the present value of the current equipment as it stands on the floor?
- ☐ What is the service life of the rebuild relative to the new?
- ☐ Who is going to do the rebuild?
- ☐ What sort of warranty comes with the rebuild, if done outside my own operation?
- ☐ Are spares still available for the rebuild and the used equipment?

- ☐ Are the spares still produced by the OEM, or are they somewhere in the channel of distribution?
- ☐ Where are they exactly, and what do they cost?
- ☐ Is it possible to bring all the options back to valid comparisons considering such factors as initial costs, support costs, and different service lives to allow side-by-side comparisons?

9

Spare Parts and Maintenance Support of the Equipment

The purchase of the equipment is only part of the process. It does not tell the entire cost story from a total cost perspective. No one is so naive to think the purchase of the automobile is the end of the cost stream associated with that automobile. It is just the beginning of an array of small costs that may appear relatively insignificant when compared to the price of the vehicle, but when accumulated, tell the complete story of ownership.

The options selected for stocking spare parts, ordering spares, and knowing which spares go into the machine can have a profound impact on costs. A single policy may be insufficient. The stocking level for spares is often dependent on value, use, service life, and the organization's maintenance practices. Selecting the correct maintenance program can return large savings by avoiding downtime in the future and extending the service life of the equipment. Does equipment have a finite service life? Probably yes. How long is it? No one really knows. Its duration depends on the treatment it receives along the way coupled with its serviceability or usefulness to the organization. There are valves in place today that are 70 years old and impossible to replace. And if they are working, why replace them? The Castanea Company in Baltimore had a milling machine over 70 years old still in operation. It is not uncommon to find equipment from World War II still functioning well. Automobile engines have lasted hundreds of thousands of miles. Vacuum cleaner motors can last 10, 20, or 50 years if properly maintained. To place a single value on the life of the equipment is to assume it is all treated in the same manner—indeed, a foolish assumption.

Maintaining the equipment to extend its service life is but one option. A company may consider a high maintenance profile for its equipment and still view it as having a finite life in the plant. One approach is to maintain a high level of maintenance and sell it after some period of time, well short of its service life. Commanding a premium price on the used equipment market, its value to the potential buyer may be better or higher than that of a new piece of equipment. The perspective is that all the bugs have been worked out of the equipment and the item is in the bottom of the traditional bathtub curve.

Extending service life and avoiding failure maintenance and downtime come at a cost. This is the cost traditionally associated with the maintenance activity. The goal is to achieve a balance between the costs of maintaining and the costs of downtime. This balance is often tilted due to the costs of spare parts.[1]

There are many paths to profit. One of the most easily trod is the spare parts business. A legal license to steal, it is a snare for the uninitiated and a chance for the supplier to reap all kinds of profits that were not available on the sale of the original equipment. It can be so lucrative that the supplier could literally give the product away if guaranteed the spare parts and maintenance business for some period of time. This was illustrated by the deal put together by the Engine Division of General Electric and Saudi Air whereby GE would discount the engines if Saudi Air would sign a 25-year spare parts and maintenance contract with GE. The discount was 96 percent off list price for the engines. This is an extreme, yet examples abound of 200, 300, and 500 percent markups on prices for replacement parts. One does not have to venture much beyond auto dealerships to see cost-value relationship in action. Not limited to this arena, spares are often the bread and butter of many equipment manufacturers. The ends to which the manufacturer will go to protect that business boggles the mind. Try to install a new headlight in your automobile. No standard screwdriver will fit. A special star-shaped head is needed, so replacing the $10 lamp becomes a $50 project. One salesman admitted a willingness to "give the machine to the customer" to get the spare parts business.

What, then, are the buyers to do? Canny buyers know these costs are coming, think ahead, and plan to avoid them or minimize their impact. Yet minimizing their effect can be tricky, especially when dealing with capital equipment. The difficulty comes with the issue of downtime of the equipment. The buyer does not want to save a dollar on a spare part and have it fail, causing the machine to be down for a day and incurring a cost of hundreds of dollars. That is false economy. Thus, it is a matter of selecting the correct option by looking at those areas that afford the greatest potential savings and being willing to invest the proverbial buck when it is needed. As an example of this concept, consider the case of the automatic dishwasher.

---

1. Often cited is the example of the Chevrolet automobile. Purchasing all its parts as spare parts through the normal channels of distribution can cost twice the manufacturer's suggest retail price. Either the spares are overpriced or labor is extremely efficient.

Every dishwasher has a sump pump, which is a critical component of the machine. In the case of one popular model, the pump was permanently attached to the electric motor in the dishwasher. Housed inside the pump was a valve controlling the backflow of water from the tub of the dishwasher. Encasing the valve was a gasket. The gasket was subject to wear as it opened to discharge the soiled water and closed to prevent water from flowing back onto the dishes. When the gasket wore out, the seal between the valve and the inside of the pump was lost, and repairs had to be initiated to replace this 25 cent gasket. This translated to a new gasket, a new sump pump, and a new motor. It was designed in such a way that a 25 cent item required about $150 in replacement parts, excluding the labor. It was obvious the designer was looking at the pump from a perspective totally different from that of a maintenance person. From the design perspective, it made sense: Cost could be reduced if the assembly could be purchased as one unit. From a maintenance perspective, it was a disaster for the customer as well as a waste of monies because of having to throw away useful parts due to poor design.[2] It is essential to look at equipment from both perspectives, design and maintenance.

Another approach is upgrading the quality when repairs are made. Nothing says that replacement is same for same. Consider the case of a pump on a machine. It may have a cast-iron housing and nitrile seals. When replacement takes place, a bronze housing and Viton rubber seals could be used, doubling the life expectancy at a modest increase in cost. It is a worthwhile practice to query the supplier about upgrading parts when replacement takes place. The impact may be extending the service life, reducing downtime, and decreasing maintenance frequency and costs.

Consider the company whose machines were equipped with proximity sensors. Maintenance was replacing the sensors on two machines at the rate of six units per month at a material replacement cost of $18,000 per year. Looking into the problem, it was determined that the sensors were being shorted out by the coolant in them after some period of operation. Waterproof and more advanced sensors were tried and proved to be successful. The annual failure

---

2. The problem was eventually resolved with a redesign of the sump pump. Molded in two side pieces with a cork gasket between them, it was now possible to open the pump, replace the valve and its gasket, and close the pump, all without having to remove the motor. It could be accomplished in less than 30 minutes, and the only replacement parts were the valve and the gasket, the least expensive parts involved.

rate declined from 72 to 6. Although the cost was twice as much as the cheaper sensors, the improved models were very cost-effective.

Ignoring the issue of maintainability of equipment at the time of purchase is inviting problems further down the road of ownership. Someone is going to have to maintain the equipment, and not considering this aspect of the total cost of ownership is naive. Maintainability is a combination of factors, including ease of maintenance itself, access to areas that require maintenance, universality of spare parts, and time required to perform the maintenance. The ability to maintain the automobile or its *maintainability* is not positive if the engine must be removed to change the oil filter or asbestos gloves must be worn because the oil filter is so close to the manifold. If the time required to gain access to the area being maintained is high relative to the actual maintenance time, maintainability is considered low. If major assemblies or subassemblies are inaccessible and require removal prior to performing the maintenance, maintainability is low. If the equipment is designed in such a manner that work areas are cramped or special tools are required to access parts or assemblies, maintainability is low. The Maytag Corporation prides itself on high product reliability. Yet if repairs must be undertaken, key components are easily accessed. Accessibility reduces the overall maintenance time—and the time actually spent is maintenance time, not make-ready time.

Maintenance and spare parts are connected. They depend on each other and benefit from each other. They can be directly related, with more maintenance requiring spare parts, and they can be inversely related, with spares being a substitute for maintenance and vice versa. The relationship can be complex, and there are few decision rules that hold for all equipment. Thus, the buyer, focusing on total cost, develops a set of options based on the buying situation. Again it is a team effort with multiple players. Maintenance is a prime player since that function determines what and how much is going to be sufficient. Stores is a key player because it maintains the spare parts stock levels. Purchasing, knowing where the spares are outside the plant, is on the team. Finance watches the investment in inventory, lest the company configure itself like a stocking distributor with itself as the best and only customer.

Spare Parts

Consider first spare parts and the question of their logistics, prices, and stocking levels. There is an old adage that says, "If I knew what it really would cost, I probably would never have bought it." The problem is that the spares are needed. They keep the expensive (half trillion dollars) equipment running. Yet that number fails to tell the real story. How much is spent on spare parts, periodic or routine replacement of parts, or simply spares purchased to have on hand may never be known. Those costs often are buried in different budgets and never really identified. Yet the numbers are significant, and their importance should not be lost on readers. They may represent the biggest single source of savings available to a company. It is a basic truism that the average piece of equipment will consume twice its original cost in spare parts over its service life. Components wear out, parts fail, or parts are simply replaced before failure on a periodic basis.

The selling of spare parts can be a significant revenue stream for the supplier. Once the machine is purchased, the spare parts supply can be a captive market, offering the buyer few or no options as to source, price, or delivery. Uniqueness is often established by the supplier to maintain that hold on the market, and the lengths to which the supplier will go stagger the imagination. The issue is not what is going to fail (that is predictable to a large degree) but "when it will fail." The argument against spare parts stocking has been the same since day one: "What if we don't need it over the service life of the machine?" The answer is, "Then you have spent money to protect yourself against an event that has never taken place but could have." It is called insurance. The counterargument is, "What if we had needed it, and it was not around?" The discussion goes on, citing real costs, hypothetical costs, and downtime issues with extensive effort to measure the unmeasurable. This type of exercise is often futile and counterproductive. Issues of this type will hardly ever be resolved. It is better to focus on the issues that can be measured and resolved.

Buyer Options

One option is the timing of the spare parts stocking decision. Buying at the time of the initial purchase may be a conservative approach, yet buying after the failure has occurred can be expensive if downtime is considered. The argument for stocking at the time of purchasing the equipment is sound. Producing an extra gear for the machine may incur only marginal labor and material costs when the machine is in production. Setting up for that single gear on a non-scheduled basis may be very costly. It may also be argued that the role of the seller is to support the equipment by having the spare parts available at his site or somewhere in the channel of distribution. The argument is endless, but the team investigates the individual situation before the purchase is made. There are two issues here:

1. *Investigating the spare parts situation as part of the buying process.* This includes the logistics of the system with emphasis on the location of the parts and the cost of spares. Location may be at the supplier's plant, the stocking distributor, or a machine owner's site. It is common practice for hospitals to use each other as emergency sources of supply, lending the needing institution what is required and being reimbursed with either goods or payment later. The same approach can be used in industry. It is another reason for installed site visits prior to purchasing. One of the issues to raise on the visit is the user's spare parts policy, program, and experiences.

2. *Trying to develop plans for a reasonable balance between not having the spare part and being down and carrying the spare part.* A segment of this cost can be determined up front as to the suggested spares stocking program. What is the spares policy? How is it specified? Can the buyer count on having 5 to 10 percent of the value of the equipment available for spares purchases when the equipment is purchased?

To visualize the relationship, consider Exhibit 9-1 and the balance between not having the spares and its associated costs versus having to dispose of the spares since they were not needed.

Exhibit 9-1. Balancing spares costs and downtime.

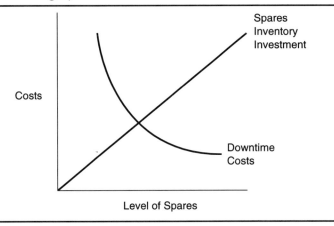

A number of fundamental considerations emerge concerning spare parts. What spares are going to be needed? All parts of the equipment do not fail. In fact, some parts never wear out or even deteriorate. Others are subject to periodic replacement, regardless of condition, and some are replaced only when they fail. What fits into what category, and where is this information obtained? Initially, what is the buyer interested in with respect to spare parts?

To determine the parts subject to failure under normal operating conditions, look first at **dynamic components**—parts that rub surfaces or are connected to moving parts. Movement results in friction, and friction causes wear. Look at parts that must be lubricated to reduced wear or friction, plus parts that sustain unusual physical extremes of heat or pressure, such as stampings, moldings, formings, and extrusions. These forces all have an impact on the part or component. Consider the environment in which the part operates. The radiator sustaining fluid temperature of over 400 degrees is a good example.

The source of information on what is exposed to what comes from the supplier. It can come as a recommended spare parts list. These are the parts subject to failure or periodic replacement. Keeping the spare parts in stock ensures their availability when needed. On the face of it, it is only logical. But then look below the surface. The costs can be very high if one buys on faith. Promises of validity of the data should be backed by hard data gathered from in-house testing and feedback from users. Data should include **failure curves,** examples of the ability to turn historical data into probability distributions. Failure curves reflect the historical performance of a part or component. Buying the spare parts kit without seeing the failure curves or failure data in some form is totally trusting the supplier to have your best interests at heart. It is a gigantic leap of faith.

If the supplier does not believe in probability theory, the next best item of data would be the raw failure data. Exhibit 9-2 contains failure data on valves, which can be used to develop the failure curve in Exhibit 9-3. Maintenance should be able to formulate a policy on the maintenance of the equipment from the failure curve data. For example, at least 63 percent of the valves fail before reaching 1,000 hours of operation. The greatest likelihood of failure is in the 800- to 1,000-hour range. If the equipment is operating on a single shift, this means that downtime can be expected every five to six months of operation. If a valve survives to 1,600 hours of operation, there is a very small chance it will survive to 2,000 hours. The raw data make it possible to gather some basic statistics about the valves. This includes the average life of a valve and its dispersion. The average life is 1,020 operating hours, and the dispersion, as measured by the standard deviation, is 590 hours. This figure is not very useful in predicting failures due to its size relative to the mean. The dispersion is too large.

Exhibit 9-2. Failure data on valves.

Hours of Operation	Number of Failures	Cumulative Failures	Cumulative Proportion
200	3	3	0.03
400	7	10	0.10
600	16	26	0.26
800	20	46	0.46
1,000	17	63	0.63
1,200	14	77	0.77
1,400	8	85	0.85
1,600	7	92	0.92
1,800	5	97	0.97
2,000	3	100	1.00

Other useful data should include mean time between failure (MTBF) data on key components or mean time between removal (MTBR) data. Data must be varied to reflect field experience as well as laboratory conditions. It is often the case that companies simulate failures to determine service life by placing loads on the component to determine its MTBF. (Waiting until it fails can be a long process.) Using the MTBF and its standard deviation allows for a probabi-

Exhibit 9-3. Failure curve for valves.

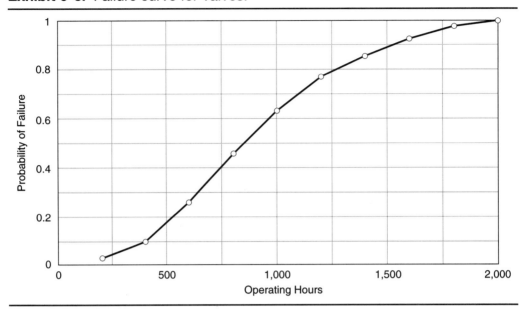

listic estimate of the total life of the component. Since the value is a mean, the standard deviation about that mean, assuming a normal distribution, will provide the likelihood of the part's failing at the MTBF at 50 percent as well as a 97.5 percent probability of failure at the MTBF + $2\sigma_{\text{MTBF}}$. This would represent the maximum expected life on a statistical basis. Knowing the service life of parts allows for maintenance planning and scheduling, as well as stock planning for the logistical support of the equipment.

Still, several important questions remain. What, for example, has the supplier done in the design stage to ensure equipment reliability? Reliability is concerned with the ability of the equipment to operate for a specified period of time without failure. Does the equipment have other reliability analysis data available? Quality without reliability is a hollow concept. Having the machine operate is not sufficient; it must operate for some time period free of problems. Along with the spares come the appropriate data and feedback information on the equipment with respect to the service life of the spare parts. Without this information plus the recommendations of the supplier on changeovers, it is impossible to formulate a maintenance policy that balances the cost of maintenance and downtime. Therefore, as a segment of the purchasing process, consider the information that must be collected to formulate the maintenance and logistical policies to support the equipment.

What has the supplier done to ensure safety of operation of the equipment, and how does that relate to reliability? A safety system with poor reliability is worthless. Consider the case of the cherry picker, or aerial workstation (the extended arm vehicle with the bucket at the end commonly used by public utilities in line work). Along the boom is a paint strip. The color of the strip changes to red when the boom is extended to a length that may cause a shift in the center of gravity and cause the vehicle to tip over, even with the stabilizers properly positioned on the ground. This is a safety of operation feature, yet it depends on the observation of the cab operator. That is insufficient, so a trip switch is installed, causing the arm or boom to stop by cutting off power to the motor and ensuring the bucket will not go beyond a certain point. The reliability of that switch must be high. It is the last safety feature for an individual 50 to 100 feet in the air. As a result, a manufacturer of this vehicle will pay a 50 percent premium for that switch because it has a backup system built in to ensure safety of operation. As in the case of the sensors, extra money spent wisely can pay big dividends. In the case of the telescoping lift, safety of operation is a significant marketing tool.

Spare Parts Stocking Level

Beyond the issues of reliability and quality are the concerns over stocking policy, a pragmatic issue that should be addressed by the team members early in the purchasing process and well before the purchase is finalized. The first step is the classification of spare parts into three groups:

1. *Consumables*—items that are consumed or used by the equipment such as lubricants. They are of moderate cost in most cases and readily available. Watch out for those that should be low cost but are not.

2. *Spares that are not capable of being repaired.* They are throwaways in the spare parts field—for example, V belts, filters, worn gears, and gauges.

3. *Spare parts capable of being reconditioned, repaired, or remanufactured*—for example, post hole diggers on utility trucks, transmissions, and telephones. They have value even in a nonoperating condition and may be used as a replacement after fixing or as a trade in for a new one.

Thus, the initial determination is the mix. Coming up with a number or value for the spare parts expenditure by category can significantly influence the content of the purchase order and can be a strong negotiating point when dealing with the supplier.

What spares will be carried, and how many? Numerous options exist for determining these values. They include cost balancing, which attempts to balance the cost of carrying the inventory with the downtime cost associated with needing the spare and not having it. Another approach is planned or preventive maintenance, which discards parts that still have some service life in them. The idea is to replace the part in anticipation of its failure.

The majority of the information needed is vested with the supplier, the producer, or the original equipment manufacturer (OEM) of the spare part.

Faith and trust play an extensive role in these determinations. Part of the answer comes back to the supplier selection process. Industry is resplendent with stories of price gouging on spare parts, including a utility selling another utility a $100 spare part for $22,000 because it needed that part in an emergency. It is important to formulate the spares strategy early in the process and ask for the right information.

One option is initial provisioning of spare parts, which specifies the stock level of spare parts to be purchased when the equipment is ordered. The spares are an integral part of the order and allow for continuing operation of the equipment after replacement of the part. The objective is to minimize downtime due to stock-out or lack of part availability. The extreme form is the modular, or "black box," approach, where an assembly containing the defective part is removed and the assembly is sent back to determine where the defect is or simply discarded.

There are a number of criteria that can be used for determining the spare part purchase:

• A dollar figure based on the value of the order, such as initial purchase plus 25 percent provisioning. This would be an order for the equipment plus 25 percent of the value of the equipment in spare parts. The mix would be determined jointly by the buyer and seller.

• A spares level based on the ability to rebuild or recondition the spare part. In the case of aircraft engines, a 20 to 30 percent maintenance float is common. This means 20 to 30 percent additional units to provide engines while some are being overhauled or rebuilt.

• A spares kit provided by the OEM to ensure the availability of spares when maintenance takes place. This approach is often used when the OEM maintains the equipment, based on complexity or special tools needed to maintain the equipment. There is some danger in this approach from the buyer's perspective because not all the parts in the kit may be needed. The electronics field is another example. A resistor fails, and the buyer must purchase the whole board with little or no value for the old or replaced board.

• A spare parts level based on a company formula or historical data that provide for a spares level of a certain percentage of the value of the equipment, nominally 5 to 10 percent.

A different tack can be stratification of spares into mutually exclusive groups, with a stocking policy established for each category:

• *Periodic replacement items.* These are spare parts that will be consumed over some period of time because failing to replace them can do severe damage to the equipment. This includes belts, gaskets, springs, and filters. No one doing periodic maintenance would not replace these items as a normal part of the maintenance process. These are consumable maintenance items.

• *Major overhaul or shelf life items.* Replacement of these items is clock based or output based due to wear and tear, limited life, or simply running out of the material contained in the part, as in the case of toner, fluids, blades, or hoses.

• *Parts used in or on the equipment.* These are parts associated with the use of the equipment as it relates to specific applications or products being produced on the equipment—for example, tooling, jigs, and fixtures. Tooling spares are specific in many cases and represent insurance to keep production going if the tooling breaks or wears out. Determination of how much to carry is done by having an estimate of the functioning life of the tooling. How many units can be produced before the tooling must be replaced? In injection molding, it is measured in shot life. In making ammunition casings, it is thousands of rounds for the center fire bunter. A good maintenance operation will keep track of this information to ensure the production of quality output on the machine.

An important consideration is the issue of unique inventory. When stocking spares, the company makes a commitment to stock items that may have very limited application or be off the shelf. This is especially true in the case of the machine custom-built for an organization. One of the reasons that spares can be such a lucrative business is due to unique design. It is an intentional effort on the part of the manufacturer to get the business now and keep a monopoly position on the spare parts. The role of the team can be to avoid getting trapped in the position of having to buy spare parts from one source. This is the part that value engineering plays in the decision. It is a difficult position because a reason for the new equipment may be to replace older technology.

The Issue of Timing

The question is often asked, "why buy spares now, especially if the equipment is under warranty?" The warranty does have a finite life. If the spare part is a standard bearing, available from a local distributor, then carrying the stock makes no sense. If it is custom made, purchase at the time of machine manufacture can go a long way toward reducing the future cost of that custom-made replacement. If it is impossible to avoid the custom-mades, then at least try to minimize their impact. Even if the spare is readily available from the distributor, it is worthwhile to have the distributor maintain a number of pieces specifically for your company.

What is the lead time for purchasing the spare parts? How must the part be shipped? What priority does the OEM give to spare parts? How much does downtime cost per hour? Industry abounds with horror stories of spending $500 to charter an airplane to fly in a $5 gauge that was not stocked to save money on spare parts. The problem in the stocking level is the "meat cleaver" approach to inventory management that many companies take. Inventories are reduced by 10 percent via edict, and the target is far too broad. Add to this the generally miserable job done in the management of maintenance, repair, and operating (MRO) items, and the problem is compounded. Adding to the confusion may be the paucity of data on the equipment with respect to the service life of the parts or components. The result is repair it when it fails and buy the parts needed to effect the repair. Both of these policies keep the parts producer and the repair service in business and often highly profitable. The cost of spare parts, maintenance, and energy often far outstrips the original cost of the equipment; the statement that a machine consumes twice its original cost in spare parts is true—in many cases because the issue of spare parts at order time was either missed or neglected in the purchase decision. The parts are not that expensive, except when they are needed to avoid $300 or $500 per hour charges for downtime on a machine.

The situation becomes more critical if the part must be manufactured for the customer. If this happens, be prepared to pay staggering costs, including setup charges, premium pay for workers, high material waste, and premium transportation. Some companies have even required premiums to be paid to move the spare up in the manufacturing queue. These types of situations can be avoided or minimized in these ways:

- Careful maintenance planning
- Investigation of critical parts before machine purchase, looking for the unique aspects of the part or the tools
- Value engineering for substitute parts that may be stop-gap or short-term quick fixes
- Asking other users about their experience with certain parts
- Knowing the capability of local machine shops

Other relevant considerations on the spare parts stocking situation include:

- What is the shelf life of the spare part?
- Does it have some time limitation before it becomes useless?
- What is the warranty for spare parts?
- Do spare parts carry some degree of protection if they are defective?
- Is there an incentive afforded or made available to the buyer to stock spares at the time of machine purchase versus buying when needed?
- How long is the discount period?

This last question is especially important. The discount period should be at least one year since the machine is covered under warranty for one year from date of acceptance.[3] If the differential is significant, then the differential can be considered the savings to pay for the cost of possession for some period of time. For example, a 30 percent discount on spare parts would allow the buyer to buy the spares and carry them as inventory for one year before the nondiscounted spare costs would equal the discounted spare costs plus inventory carrying costs. Looking at the data in this manner allows the team to determine the indifference point in the decision. At the end of one year, the accumulated costs of discounted spares plus inventory carrying costs equal the current spares price. At one year in this example, the buyer would be indifferent between buying a year ago and storing versus buying now. This example assumes no rise in price for the spares. The issue becomes one of when the savings are going to be eaten up by inventory-carrying costs.

Other issues include the source of the spares: domestic or foreign. If the source of the equipment is foreign, are there domestic stocking distributors that can support the equipment? If not, the issue can become critical for the buyer as lead time expands and the physical movement of the goods becomes complex. Issues such as customs, tracing and tracking, payment, and installation become part of the equation. In addition, how much leverage does the distributor have with the OEM? If the number of domestic installations is relatively small in this country, the distributor may carry limited stocks of spares and may simply be a relay point for the orders. Does the distributor do more than stock parts? Does the distributor customize the equipment, aid in the installation, train people in maintenance, and support the equipment by performing contract maintenance on the machine? In general, what is the role of the distributor in the total purchase and support of the equipment? A wide range of services provided by the distributor may compensate for time and distance between the buyer and the OEM. Sufficient domestic demand for the equipment may induce the OEM to have an active support structure in markets considered foreign. The appearance of the spares channel and the value it provides must be considered, especially when dealing in overseas purchases.

What is the true cost of the spares? What is the markup on the spare parts? Is there any reasonable way to obtain the information? For common industrial parts, simple quotes may be used to determine the costs. Consider the example of the company using a standard bearing selling for $1.20 on the open market but charging $4.75 for that same bearing. This does not mean the team investigates every nut, bolt, or screw, but getting some ballpark sense for the parts markup is valuable.

---

3. This issue will be raised again in several places. Ownership begins on acceptance of the equipment, *not* its arrival at the plant. The warranty should begin at acceptance. Up to acceptance, it is still the property and responsibility of the supplier.

What about the use of substitutes or non-OEM parts? Will they compromise performance or quality of output? Is there such a difference between the OEM part and the non-OEM part that substitution is impossible? In some instances, the parts are protected by patents, or the limited number of sources producing that part makes substitution impossible. In these cases, the single nature of the part may have to be accepted, regardless of how economically distasteful it may be. There may be other opportunities for replacement that do not compromise performance, output, or quality of the end product. This situation warrants specific investigation by the engineering members of the team. Remember that the machine is being purchased for its service life, and many dollars will be spent on spare parts. Are the spare parts truly unique? The extra effort required for checking the spare parts as to their origin can be of significant benefit. Most parts cribs have a cabinet or drawer dedicated to storage of spare parts for a particular machine. The packaging indicates it is a Timkin bearing or a Fafnir bearing, yet it carries an original equipment manufacturer (OEM) part number. A simple change to the record-keeping system will reflect the true OEM and probably significantly reduce the price. Carry this example to all the other high-cost components of the machine and the savings will be significant.

The whole issue of spare parts stocking, moving, and using is a complex component of the buying process. It should not be overlooked or anything assumed about the process. The availability of spares at reasonable prices from supportive sources is essential to the total buying process. High-cost spares, excessive waiting time, and lesser-quality spare parts can often sour the sweetness of a good equipment purchase. The initial buy is only part of the process. Continuity of operation is essential, and a portion of that continuity is based on having the spare parts available when they are needed.

Maintaining the Equipment

The ideal machine would never fail, would run with zero maintenance using permanently lubricated systems, and would give warning if it was about to fail. This is the material from which legends and children's stories are crafted.

The maintenance process is a vital component of ensuring the machine lasts its service life. Improper, incomplete, or inadequate maintenance is probably the major cause of catastrophic failure of equipment. Machines are normally built to withstand the rigors of their environment. A ladle incapable of carrying molten steel in a mill is of no value. Presses unable to absorb the shock of tons of pressure being placed on sheet steel would have little place in the factory. Machines can be the product of the finest technology and still be damaged by insufficient lubrication. In certain cases the results can be tragic. The failure to replace an O ring on the base of a contamination detector in the hydraulic line of an airplane caused the aircraft to lose fluid over the ocean.

The plane landed with just barely enough to bring down the landing gear. Another 10 minutes, and a tragedy would have occurred. An approach to machine maintenance that is becoming increasingly popular is looking at it as a Material Requirements Planning application, except that M = maintenance. This equates to analyzing the maintenance requirements using levels or echelons and attempting to standardize the process of having adequate levels of spare parts available for that level of maintenance. The first step is to subdivide the maintenance activity into echelons or tiers. Consider structuring the maintenance activities into five levels:

1. Periodic minor adjustments, lubrication, and minor repair
2. Periodic major repair by maintenance personnel
3. Periodic major repair by maintenance personnel supported by the OEM on site
4. Ship back to the OEM for repair work
5. Unscheduled failure maintenance

Each level has associated with it a spare parts level. It is the bill of materials used in the maintenance of that piece of equipment at that level of maintenance. In the first two cases, major and minor adjustments, the spares stocking level can be determined by the nature or depth of effort and the frequency of performance. At the third level, the cost of stocking may be so extensive that it may be cheaper to have the OEM support the spare parts, even considering the costs normally associated with that type of decision, such as supplier profits on the spares and shipping expense. The fourth level is an admission that the expertise is not present to perform the type of maintenance required. This is not a failing on the part of the equipment owner. No one repairs their own copiers. The fifth level is the difficult one that plagues equipment owners. It is the failure maintenance that is random or unpredictable and the unknowns compound. A variant of this is found in public utilities where a major teardown or planned outage of equipment will consume spare parts, yet what spares will be needed is unknown until the equipment is removed from service and torn down. Lack of knowledge coupled with lead time often extends outages for weeks or months. Since the utility must provide power, there must be standby capacity or agreements in place to purchase the power from other utilities during planned outages. It is the curse of having to produce the product all the time. The downtime issue can be significant.

A company that organizes the maintenance activity in this fashion is able to look at the spares issues from a different perspective. Spares and maintenance cannot be separated because they are interdependent. While not getting a 100 percent picture of what is needed, the echelon approach will allow the company to define the point where it cannot or will not carry spare parts and at least try to project the needs over some period to support a planned maintenance program. Although catastrophic failures cannot be predicted with 100 percent accuracy, their occurrence can be minimized by good preventive maintenance. Preventive maintenance equates to planning, and planning means logistical support of that plan or spares in place at the plant site or on order from the supplier and due in when the maintenance activity needs them.

The way around the spares issue means:

• *Understanding they will be needed.* This is often a difficult concept to present. The machine is new and shiny and looks as if it will last forever. The last concern is about adding to the stock of inventory in the form of spares that appear will never be needed. There are no perpetual motion machines.

• *Understanding they will be used.* Spare parts consumption can be equal to or greater than the original cost of the machine over the service life of the equipment. Initial cost is but a fraction of total cost of the machine.

• *Planning for their effective use.* The decision must be made to engage in preventive maintenance on the equipment or simply wait until failure occurs. This is a management decision and should be made on the basis of cost minimization.

• *Not being upset when some are not used.* No one can predict the future. The lack of failure of a part or component in the machine that is carried as a spare is often a random event. It has long been known that companies can carry spare parts that are never needed. If machine designers knew when the parts were going to fail, they would have them replaced a minute or a unit before they failed. Failure is a function of a wide range of factors. It is not uncommon in Europe to see taxicabs with over 200,000 miles on the engines. The person who maintains the automobile with periodic lubrication and careful driving can expect an 8- to 12-year service life from the vehicle. It is a trade-off: Carry the parts and potentially never use them, or do not carry them and need them. A balance must be achieved.[4]

Keeping Detailed Records

There is no substitute for complete documentation on capital equipment. There are numerous purposes for the documentation, and keeping complete records should not be viewed as simply a clerical inconvenience. Records of maintenance activities indicate part consumption by machine, labor hours expended on the machine, and routine versus nonroutine maintenance and allow for the accumulation of maintenance costs. All of these elements of information play an important role in the economics of machine replacement on the micro- and macrolevel. Excessive consumption or failure of a particular part may be an indicator of a more serious problem. The consumption pattern may show a

---

4. The echelon issue is a relatively simple way of looking at the maintenance issue from both a parts and a people perspective.

design flaw. Part failures add information to the mortality curve for that component and may change the failure curve entirely.

Accumulation of maintenance costs, operating hours, or units produced can provide indicators as to machine replacement. At what point should the machine be replaced? What does maintenance cost equaling twice the original cost translate into operating hours or units produced? How much does maintenance cost add to product cost when costed over the output? Finally, at the disposal stage, the availability of complete records is a benefit for the potential buyer. The complete documentation of that equipment gives the prospective buyer an overview of the depth and degree to which that equipment was maintained by its original owner and goes a long way in making the sale.

How to Document the Equipment

There are a number of ways to document, and the vast majority are computerized. Under the overall heading of computerized maintenance management systems (CMMS), there are almost 200 such systems captured in Thomas Publishing's *CMMS Directory and Comparison Guide*.[5] The guide is a one-stop shopping source for descriptions of the systems. It is well worth the price of the book or, better, the CD-ROM version that allows users to create the specifications and issue the request for proposal. Menu driven, it is an absolute must for the first cut in system selection. It also provides the overview of what systems are available, how extensive the installations are, the depth of technical support in each supplier, and descriptions that allow potential buyers the chance to evaluate their requirements versus the available products. In addition, many of the systems are designed for Windows 95 or are compatible with Office 97.

The initial issue is selecting the most effective system for each application. Effectiveness encompasses a vast array of factors:

• *The span of coverage of equipment or vehicles.* In some instances, the vehicles make up a significant portion of the investment in capital equipment. In addition, what is the depth of breakdown of the equipment? Much like a product tree, equipment can be represented as a product tree, and the issue of how far the end item is dissected is important. If the system does not go deep enough in the product structure, then assemblies can be discarded when a subassembly replacement may be the solution to the problem. The information entered into the model's database, in both quantity and format, is important. This also raises the issue of ease of data entry. Making the data entry a difficult task may defeat the purpose of the system by introducing errors. How flexible is the system? Is

---

5. To order, call (212) 629-1114 or (800) 647-1908 or fax (212) 629-1159. The cost is $95 plus shipping and handling. It is well worth the expenditure.

it modular in the sense that additional modules or subroutines can be linked into the system, thus expanding it without starting from ground zero?

• *The number of equipment records that may be tracked.* How many pieces of equipment will be covered by the system? How many records will be generated to provide the desired coverage, and what gets classified as a candidate for coverage? What information is generated from each record, and what can be put in to improve the system? Does the system allow for the transfer of data or information into a software suite or purchasing software to allow consolidation of information and integration for ordering purposes? Tracking equipment is but one consideration. The ability to transfer that information so that parts may be ordered is equally important. It would be an MRP type of roll-up of requirements.

• *The ease of use of the system.* This is often related to the user. A program that is easy to use in accounting may be difficult in the maintenance shop. Is it user friendly, and what must be the comprehension level to understand the system? Is there a good system overview provided to illustrate the portions or segments of the system and how they interact? How easy is it to add instructions to the work orders detailing procedures for inspections? Does the system generate a schedule for routine maintenance activities and projected maintenance needs? The system must serve two purposes: allow for maintenance planning for routine activities and preserve historical data for analysis purposes. It must be capable of looking both forward and backward in a manner comprehensible to the user.

• *The type of information provided and the way the information integrates into the system.* This is essential. For example, work orders generate demands for spare parts. This has an impact on stock levels and should cause activities in the tool crib or stockroom. There must also be an adjustment to the stock records. The completed work orders should update the equipment history, accumulate the costs, and prepare reports on the maintenance activities in total or as they relate to an individual machine or vehicle. Just as one activity becomes the initiator for many others, the information should follow the same path.

From the perspective of planning for maintenance, the system should be capable of scheduling maintenance activities by date or meter number for periodic maintenance and, employing the same philosophy of MRP, contain a bill of materials for each routine maintenance type of activity. These data could then be used to project the maintenance, repair, and operating (MRO) items required to support the preventive maintenance program as well as costing out the program in terms of material dollars needed. Extending the application to the labor side, a flat-rate manual of labor times by machines, by level of maintenance activity, could also be interactive with the work orders. By using the customary clock in, clock out on the job, the work order data could validate the flat-rate manual data and show variances. Analysis of the variances could lead to revision of the definition of routine maintenance or the expansion of the preventive maintenance program for the equipment. This application could be expanded for planning purposes to project the number of maintenance hours by skill craft needed to support the plant operation on a routine basis. Emphasis is placed on the word *routine* since catastrophic failure or firefighting maintenance is predicted by simulation. Knowing the consumption of maintenance hours for routine activities and the total number of hours available would indicate the maintenance capacity to handle the unexpected.

Excessive maintenance costs on a machine may be an indicator of poor machine quality or the need for the OEM to take a look at the machine. There is no way to measure except by comparison to a standard. If the quality of the machine is good, the routine or normal maintenance is properly performed, and there is no misuse of the equipment, it should not experience excessive downtime or failures.[6] If excessive maintenance is required, many of the possible causes of that maintenance have been eliminated and there may be deeper problems, yet without accurate records, how can this be documented? A good CMMS can provide the information.

Like any other system, the desire for better information and more complete integration can be insatiable. Along with the desire goes cost. The more costly system provides more information to the user, and therefore a balance must be struck between the benefits derived from the system and its costs in terms of price of the system, training, upgrade capability, integrative capability, and the type of operating system on which the CMMS is based. In some cases the needs are simple and can be best served by a simple system that is low in cost and easy to use. In other cases, the complexity of the equipment, the number of machines, and the size of the operation dictate a significantly more sophisticated system. The issue is again proper selection. Buying the low end on the price scale and expecting it to perform as the high-priced CMMS is unrealistic. Going in on the high end of the price scale and using only a small fraction of the output is a waste of money. The balance is essential. How is it achieved? This is the reason for buying the CD-ROM from Thomas Publishing. Using its exclusive application wizards, the potential buyer is able to define the "must have" elements of the user's system. What is really necessary, and what is nice to have from the user's perspective?

---

6. As a practical matter, excessive failures of the same module or component should trigger negotiations on trade-in or warranty replacement of that component or module. Be sure that downtime is broken into categories that explain the problem. What is the time spent on diagnosis of the problem as opposed to wrench time? Some employees can use the system to create goof-off time.

System Requirements

Each system will provide something different for the user, and not unlike any other purchase, the more you pay, the more you get. Here are the necessary components:

- *Equipment definition.* This includes the equipment hierarchy to a number of levels along with warranty information and machine parts cross-references.
- *Work order tasks.* What is the definition of the task, and what activities are involved in performing it?
- *Work order generation.* A system should easily create and issue work orders for all types of work including preventive maintenance and failure maintenance on the basis of the appropriate measure of need, such as meter values, time, or urgency.
- *Work order scheduling.* A system should maintain the jobs and generate schedules based on personnel available, skill levels, equipment priority, and available parts.
- *Inventory management.* A system should maintain parts information on inventory locations, quantity on order and reserve, use patterns, and ordering. The system should also generate requisitions and purchase orders and have Electronic Data Interchange (EDI) capability.
- *Reports generator.* A system should be capable of producing detailed reports on schedules, job costing, histories of equipment maintenance, inventory transactions, and ordering information as well as being able to graph data for presentations.
- *Employee data.* The system should store and retrieve information on individual skill level, labor rates, availability, and training.

This is rather a minimum of desired data that coupled with ease of use makes a good CMMS program. Exhibit 9-4 contains a capsulated overview of what is available.

Bill Swanton, senior consultant with Advanced Manufacturing Research, Inc., of Boston, describes the evolution of the CMMS from its first generation in the 1960s as custom-designed, in-house systems to today's fourth generation, including the natural evolution from mainframe to minicomputers and mid-range computers.[7] There are inexpensive systems, midpriced systems, and expensive systems. There are also a number of niche players in the market with systems designed to fill a specific need, coming at a low initial software cost and allowing new users the opportunity to reap the benefits of CMMS at a reasonable cost. The ability to gain the benefits of reduced MRO inventories,

7. B. Swanton, "Should You Buy Your Maintenance Management from your ERP Vendor?" *Report on Manufacturing* (Advanced Manufacturing Research) (February 1997): 5.

Exhibit 9-4. CMMS product information.

Company	Product	Platform	Database	Typical Cost	Installed Base
Bonner & Moore	*Compass 7*	Windows NT	Oracle, SQL Server, Sybase in beta	$360,000	200
Champs Software	*Champs CMMS*	IBM Mainframe, AS/400, VAX, Alpha, HP9000	Oracle, Sybase	$550,000	400
Datastream	*MP2 4.6 Maintain IT Pro Maintain IT*	NT compatible	SQL server, MS access	$ 75,000 $ 6,000 $189	24,000 total units sold
Datastream SQL Systems	*R5 CAMMS*	HP-UX, RS/ 6000, DEC, Sun, NT servers	Oracle	$450,000	600
EDS	*EMPRV*	UNIX and Windows NT: HP, DEC, Intel, IBM	Oracle, Sybase, SQL server	$1–1.5 million	400
Fluor Daniel	*Tabware*	Windows NT, HP-UX, DEC, Alpha, Sun, RS/6000	Oracle and Sybase (a native version for each), SQL server	$500,000	40
Indus	*Passport 5.0*	HP-UX, Alpha, RS/6000, ES/ 9000	Oracle, DB2	$1–5 million	60+
JB Systems	*Mainsaver*	IBM AS/400, PS/2 VAX, DEC 5000, HP9000, Pentium machines	Oracle, Sybase, SQL Server, Informix, SQL, Anywhere	$ 35,000	3,500 units installed
Marcam	*Avantis XA Avantis Pro*	AS/400, HP 9000, RS 6000, Intel, or Alpha NT	DB2, Oracle, SQL server	$ 80,000	800 300

(continues)

Exhibit 9-4. *Continued*

Company	Product	Platform	Database	Typical Cost	Installed Base
PSDI	Maximo 3.0	Intel servers, UNIX servers	Oracle, Sybase	$400,000	3,000
	Maximo Workgroup	Intel servers, UNIX servers	Oracle Workgroup,	$ 75,000	
	Maximo ADvantage		Centura SQL server, Access	$ 5,000	1,000
Revere	Immpower	HP, IBM, DEC, Sun	Oracle, Sybase, Informix	$800,000	65
TSW	Enterprise MPAC	UNIX, Windows NT	Oracle	$500,000	800

Source: T. Grace, "A Tactical Look at CMMS Vendors," *Report on Manufacturing* (Advanced Manufacturing Research) (February 1997): 19. Reprinted with permission of Advanced Manufacturing Research Inc.

better maintenance planning, and reduced downtime is a function of the relative independence of the maintenance function. Maintenance is either planned or takes place when failures occur. In the former case, it is not totally dependent on the level of output but may be related to it. Failure is a random event and can or cannot be output driven. From the perspective of total cost of ownership, the value of the computerized system lies in the accumulation of relevant cost data.

The system used is a company decision and beyond the scope of this chapter; however, the potential user should consider the benefits that accrue from computerization, aside from the maintenance function itself. Analysis of purchase orders may show that a significant portion of the orders going to suppliers represents purchases for MRO items. These are either consumables or repair parts. The issue of repair parts can be handled by the CMMS system in preparing the requisition or the purchase order or in some cases using EDI. This will reduce the workload of the purchasing department in a typically unproductive area: MRO. The next step, already available, is the linking of the needs to an outside supplier or to another fully integrated MRO supplier, which may be running the toolroom or MRO stocking point. While this is tangential to the equipment issue, it does offer opportunities to save money in the overall scheme. Secondary benefits should not be ignored, especially in an environment where reductions in the labor force are common. Computerizing the nonproductive tasks allows the company to deploy its human resources in a more productive manner.

CMMS Systems

There are almost 200 CMMS systems, and it would be impossible to review them all, but we will consider five systems, representing segments of the price spectrum: Mpulse, MaintainIT Pro, MP2 4.6, Maximo, and Mainsaver.[8]

MPulse

For smaller users, MPulse offers a fairly wide range of capability. It performs many of the needed tasks at a reasonable cost level in the $1,000 range. Using the Windows operating system, it is an easy-to-use system. It is one of the niche players that are important components of the marketplace. Single-user systems definitely have a place in the market, and a low-cost, user-friendly system can be as big an advantage to a farmer as to the airline and its need to integrate its maintenance activities. Small niche players prove the adage that one size does not fit all. Providing work order generation, creation of preventive maintenance schedules, inventory records, costing of repairs, vendor data, and vehicle records with up to 10 user-developed fields for product structure data, this lower-priced option has a definite place in the CMMS field for the smaller company or on a department-by-department basis. One unique aspect of MPulse is the option to purchase a sample of the system for under $20. It is a full working copy of the system and will handle up to 10 pieces of equipment.

Exhibits 9-5 and 9-6 show two screens from the MPulse system.

Maximo

Considered the market leader in the CMMS development field, the developer of this system, PSDI (Project Software and Development Inc.), a 30-year-old company, has established an enviable track record. Being the first large CMMS supplier with a client-server architecture, the company has placed emphasis on the product area. Recently having signed an agreement with United Parcel Service (UPS) for a $1.5 million facilities maintenance contract, Maximo's integration capabilities will allow UPS managers to view and track work in their areas of responsibility, as well as reducing downtime, controlling maintenance expense, reducing spare parts inventories, and improving overall efficiency in a variety of areas, including purchasing and maintenance.

Maximo is definitely for the sophisticated user; it has been installed at

---

8. MPulse Computerized Maintenance Management System is distributed exclusively by SPEC-TECH, L.L.C. Reach them at mpulse@spectech.com on the Internet or at (800) 944-1796. MaintainIt Pro is the registered trademark of Datastream Systems Inc of Greenville, South Carolina, and may be reached at (800) 995-6775 or on the Internet as Datastream.com. Maximo ADvantage is the registered trademark of Project Software and Development. It may be reached at (714) 955-3516 or at PSDI.com on the Internet. Mainsaver is the product of JB Systems of Woodland Hills, California, and may be reached at (800) 275-5277.

Exhibit 9-5. MPulse work order and scheduling menu.

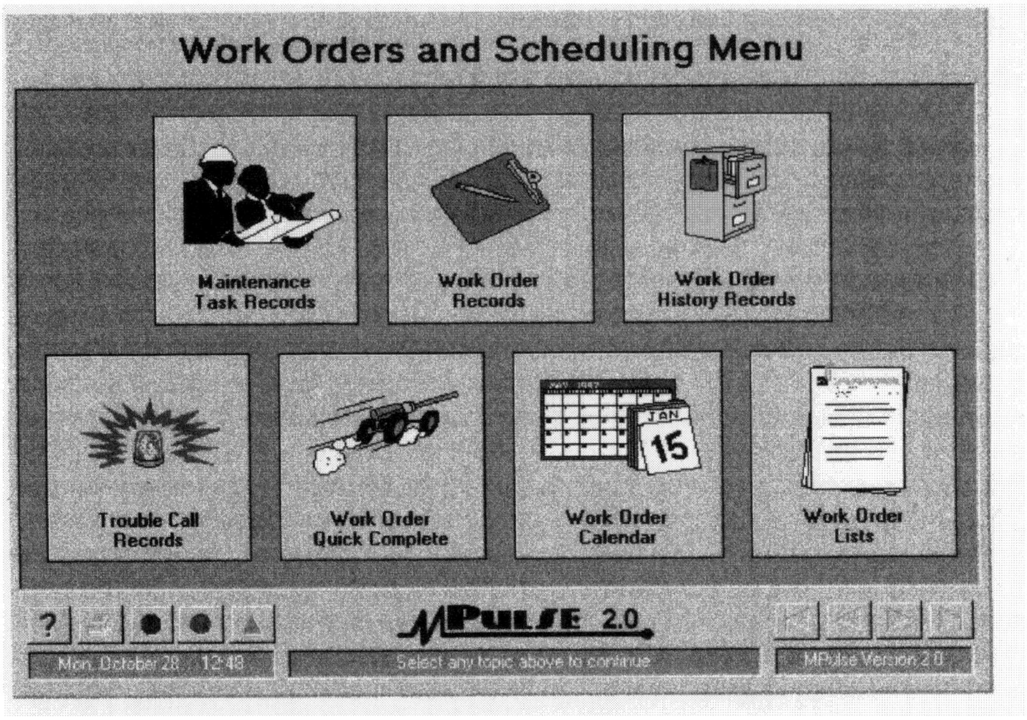

Iveco Ford Truck Ltd., Sunstrand, FR Aviation, and Master Lock Company. It is a well-established product from a visionary company.[9] The smaller-end version, Maximo ADvantage, can suit smaller users at a fraction of the cost of its big brother. Fleet applications for state and local governments are possible customers for the smaller version, where cost tracking and standardization of maintenance procedures and scope of maintenance activities can create problems.[10] Advances by the Oracle Corporation in the introduction of the Oracle8 network server, which is 10 times faster and stores 100 times more data than its Oracle7 server, will have an impact on the capabilities of this CMMS system.

---

9. An ancillary benefit is that this information may play an important role in determining the value of the equipment in the case of a buyout of the company. The assets will be plant and equipment, and their value is important.

10. The problem is normally the scope of activities performed. Since many governmental units use their own personnel and facilities to perform maintenance, there are budgetary transfers to pay for the work. If the scope of work is not clearly defined by the user, the maintenance provider will add on all sorts of extras to the job, and the user will be billed for them. The excuse is either, "It was torn down already, so why not do it?" or, "It doesn't involve paying anybody," or, "We all work for the same city." Without CMMS, standardization of activity is difficult, and cost tracking is complicated.

Exhibit 9-6. MPulse preventive maintenance menu.

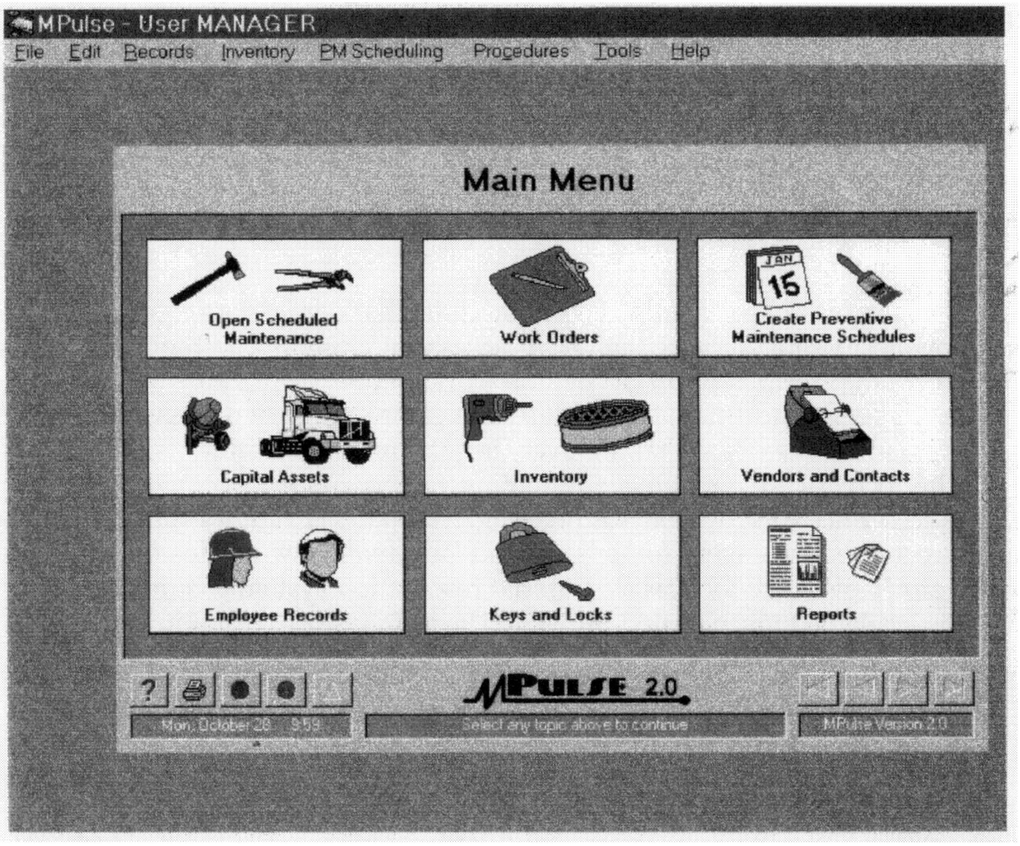

MaintainIT Pro and MP 2 4.6

Market leadership is always challenged, and as markets become segmented, new leaders emerge. Datastream in the midsized market is such a leader. Accepted by midsized companies due to its flexibility and cost, MP2 features the electronic link to Grainger Supply for the seamless supply of maintenance parts and consumables. With sales in excess of 24,000 systems, it offers a range of products at costs commensurate with the applications, ranging from the $189 MaintainIT to the $75,000 MP 2. Still at the top of the Datastream price line, MP 2 4.6 offers a great deal without significant capital investment. Appealing to the interim user or the smaller company, it is a system that offers much for a reasonable price. Naturally, it contains more in the form of reports and greater depth in product structure and has been widely accepted. One satisfied user of Datastream commented, "It has a lot of capability which can be used and integrated as the user becomes more experienced."

Mainsaver

Offered by JB Systems Inc., this system has been available since 1983. Consisting of three basic modules, available as a complete system or separately, Mainsaver comprises the:

M Module: Maintenance work management
I Module: Inventory Control
P Module: Purchasing

In the maintenance work management module, work orders are created as well as allowing maintenance personnel to access the system, see the work order list, ascertain priorities, and start or stop work on line. Gone is the paper aspect of work orders. In addition, in the multishift environment, it is possible to leave information for the person taking over the job on the next shift.

The focus of Mainsaver is eliminating paperwork and providing instant access to service information via imaging. The parts inventory module maintains cost-effective levels for spares and automatically creates requisitions when stock levels are too low. A material reservation system ensures sufficient stock is available for scheduled projects. The purchase order module generates purchase orders for both stocked and nonstocked parts, tracks open orders, and lists past-due orders. Historical data on equipment, maintenance, parts consumption, and supplier performance are available, as well as cost data on the maintenance costs of each piece of equipment on the system.

This is a complete system that moves the user into the electronic age and may require extra training. Recognizing this need, JB Systems Inc. has developed a series of training efforts with customers spanning 45 weeks beyond the sale of the software, consisting of 14 days of installation and training at specified intervals over the first year. In addition, there is a 2-day annual users' conference to share ideas and applications plus unlimited telephone support. Costing in the $35,000 range, this system should be considered by medium to larger companies, especially when multishift operations are essential due to short customer lead times.

Limits on space preclude discussion of other systems, but interested readers should use the Internet to search under "CMMS" or purchase the *CMMS Guide* from Thomas Publishing Company and use the unique search capability provided on the CD-ROM as the initial step.

Maintenance Resource Allocation

Often the issue arises as to the real cost of maintenance. Is it a variable cost, or nothing more than a fixed cost? Rather than addressing accounting issues, a more realistic approach is to address the utilization of maintenance resources in the total cost of ownership calculation. How frequently will maintenance actions be needed? To get an answer, divide maintenance activities into two broad groups and then subdivide one of the groups into three smaller segments. Maintenance is performed on equipment or in the plant for nonequipment entities. The latter group ranges from changing a light bulb to rewiring the plant. Maintenance on equipment can fall into three categories: preventive maintenance, repair of reparable parts, and failure maintenance. The tracking system should be designed to capture all types of maintenance, even though only a portion of it is predictable. The other data can be used to estimate other maintenance costs. The CMMS system is an invaluable tool for the company if used properly for capturing labor information. It is possible to track all types of maintenance, determine the availability of skill crafts, and ascertain where maintenance bottlenecks exist. The failure to have an electrician may cause downtime on an expensive machine. Conversely, there may be an oversupply of high-priced skills in the plant where the need for a greaser or oiler could solve some delays or reduce the maintenance burden.

Another option is the assignment of certain maintenance persons to do nothing but preventive maintenance for a portion of the day or work on certain machines only. Maintenance specialization has long been a method of maximizing productivity in auto repair shops. Specialization reduces job time and increases efficiency. Maintenance personnel become service specialists. Specialization is one of the pillars of standardization.

This phase of the life cycle can be expensive but also informative. Good maintenance scheduling and good cost tracking make the next capital investment decision that much easier.

Who Does the Work?

Who is going to maintain the equipment is a key issue and a significant cost driver. During the first year, the warranty normally covers some of these aspects, but beyond the first year it opens some interesting questions as to maintenance. These questions should be answered before the equipment is purchased because options or alternatives incur costs.

Capital investments drive operating expenses. One, two, or three years from now, costs are going to arise as a result of the decision to purchase that equipment. A proactive approach is essential. People are not trained instantaneously. Spare parts may have to be manufactured. Waiting until the first failure occurs is not the time to discuss the issues. Plan for it. Do not respond to it. Maintenance issues include the following:

- *What is the existing maintenance capability at the plant?* What is the level of proficiency of the maintenance workforce? Are there levels of proficiency by skill trade?

• *Does the company have the ability to maintain the equipment?* Or will additional people be needed? If additional skills are needed, is it better to hire those skills on a permanent basis or contract for their use?

• *Where will the maintenance training take place?* How long will it take? How costly will it be? Who will conduct the training? Is it part of the purchase order, or on a separate contract? What does it consist of, and what will be the end result?

• *Are there economic advantages to giving up the warranty* and maintaining the equipment from the first day of ownership? Public utilities and municipalities often negotiate for a lower price on fleet vehicles by giving up the warranty coverage. They have such large fleets to maintain that new ones represent no added demands to the maintenance system. In addition, they believe their personnel do a better job than the selling dealer. They also customize the vehicles and tend to "overmaintain" the vehicles to get a longer operating life. Standardization is a key ingredient to avoid excessive investment in tools and maintenance equipment.

• *Are there echelons of maintenance on the equipment?* Categories might be operator-performed maintenance (oiling, greasing, and minor adjustments), periodic maintenance based on time or hours of operation, teardowns, and major maintenance.

• *Are there individual indicators kept on each machine,* such as hours of maintenance per 100 hours of operation? Are there ratios or data available from the OEM that provide insights into the percentage of time the machine will be down for planned maintenance?

• *Does the equipment contain specialized items,* such as fault detectors or special measuring gauges? Who is responsible for that equipment? Have all warranties been transferred when the machine was purchased? If the OEM installed the gauges or detectors, is the OEM prepared to maintain them? Where must the maintenance take place? Can the supplier of the "specialty" items disclaim responsibility if any maintenance was performed by nonauthorized personnel? This area should not be overlooked in buying or maintaining capital equipment. The buyer may find the cost of replacing these gauges to be very expensive.

Developing the Preventive Maintenance Schedule

Much of the information on suggested schedules to repair or replace parts or components either on a time or meter reading basis should come from the OEM. The CMMS system should have a scheduling module that allows for generation of the schedule, but the initial input is by the owner of the equipment using data from some or all of the other sources.

Remember that hint we made previously about visiting at least two installations of the equipment and taking the maintenance person with you on the trip? This is why the visits are important. Talk to a user. The user has no vested interest in your business and can probably give you good insights into the maintenance issues, especially when two maintenance people talk to each other. The questions should address these areas:

- What fails most often?
- How long is the teardown time?
- What are the problem areas?
- Are special tools needed?
- Is there one part or component that is the real "heartburn" of the machine?
- How much adjusting is needed to bring the machine back on line?
- How good are the fault indicators or warning systems?
- What is the amount of time spent reaching the problem in relationship to the corrective time? If the teardown time to repair time is excessive, it is often more economical to perform an array of maintenance activities while the machine is torn down and areas accessible.

Costing Issues in Maintenance

Many of the costing issues in maintenance are discussed in Chapter 11, but we mention some basic elements here. One of the fundamental issues is in-house versus outsourcing the maintenance. In some cases it is a no-brainer, as in the case of copiers. No one maintains their own copiers unless there are so many that it is economical to do so. However, with many organizations, it is possible to have several options available, as shown in Exhibit 9-7.

There are other issues too. For example, are there standard costs that can be developed per maintenance hour? Does the OEM provide data on how long it should take to perform the maintenance on the machine (preventive maintenance)?

Repair or replace decisions arise when the cost has reached the point that repairing or maintaining has become so expensive that replacement is a viable option. This issue must be looked at from two perspectives: the accumulated costs of repair versus replacement cost and how much additional use will be gained from the item if it is repaired again. Is the service life constant or variable? Is there a significant difference between a new unit and an overhauled unit?

If contract maintenance is used due to the specialized nature of the equipment, who will be the contractor? The following factors should be considered in this make-or-buy decision:

- Cost of the third-party maintenance efforts
- What is in the contract on typical provisions, such as hours and days of the week

Exhibit 9-7. Maintenance source options.

Maintenance Capability	Costs Incurred	Benefits Obtained	Comments
OEM	Higher cost of labor, parts costs often carry significant markup, may not be local, downtime can be extensive, availability of parts can be problem, diagnosis may take time	Most highly trained to perform maintenance, has tools to perform the job, may take least time to perform if parts are available, may be low total cost, carries some implicit warranty	Lowest risk due to the highest skilled people doing the job, strong technical support, should have the OEM technical resources totally behind the machine, OEM's reputation important
Distributor	May have the expertise if highly experienced with that line or model, more diagnostic time, portal-to-portal charges, extras, spare parts availability, captive market case, spares are a part of the job	Local or regional, may wish good relations with customer, knowledgeable about the machine, issue of complex repairs (Can they handle them?), local or regional support versus national	Perhaps lesser cost and less expertise if the range of products supported is large, spare parts will be available
Third party	Who is the third-party, contractor to OEM or renegade repair, costs may be lower but expertise may also be less, takes more time and may not stock or carry parts needed, warranty issue on repairs	May be less costly and more responsive since it may be the core business, has tools needed and may make money on a time and overhead type of call and charge material or parts at cost	If a contractor to OEM, agency relationship, OEM backing the third party, some warranty and recourse, *caveat emptor*—cheaper, but a risk unless well known to buyer
Owner	Tools, training, and gaining the expertise; no warranty, no guarantee; time may be extensive	People available on site, labor cost is often viewed as sunk cost or overhead; parts may be cheaper	Depends on the quality of maintenance staff and how well they know the machine; could be very risky

- Response time
- Access to the plant
- Warranty of repairs
- How charged
—time and overhead only
—parts at cost and verified with invoices
—service call basis with a flat rate
—portal to portal
—overtime and premium time
—emergency situations

If you select outside maintenance or it is the only viable alternative, plan on building it into the budget. It is contracting for a service, and expect some guarantees from the service provider that the service is acceptable. It can be an expensive process if the problem of what is wrong can be determined only after the machine is taken apart. Separate the issue of diagnostic efforts from repair efforts. This can be writing a blank check to the supplier of the service. It is a complex issue and part of the initial decision process. Keep it up front of the analysis in capital equipment decision making.

If it is to be your own employees doing the maintenance, make sure the issues of training, manuals, videos, and retraining are discussed in the negotiations. If there are attachments to the equipment, find out from the supplier or the manufacturer of the attachments the correct procedures for their removal. Improper removal can cause the warranty to be voided. Warranties must be transferred from the supplier to the buyer for warranted parts. Keep them on file. They should be read before removing the part under warranty.

If you plan on using the distributor to support the maintenance activity, have representatives there at the installation of the equipment. Build that bridge early in the process.

A Final Thought

Maintenance and spare parts are not issues to be taken lightly. No machine was ever built to last forever. Failures and breakdowns will occur. If the machine is used only 10 percent of the time, it may not present a problem, and much of what has been discussed can be ignored, but if it is a critical machine in the production sequence or a bottleneck in the operation, downtime becomes critical. How much should be spent preventing failures is a difficult question to answer. What is prevention worth? Each company must answer that and make the resource allocation accordingly. Most of the cost over the life cycle will be in this part of it. Admit it will happen, and plan for it.

Checklist for Spare Parts and Maintenance Support

☐ Have you asked for a recommended spare parts list from the supplier?

☐ Did you ascertain the spare parts stocking policy of people who are operating the same machine?

☐ Is this a custom-designed or off-the-shelf machine or a hybrid?

☐ If there are add-ons, who made them, and what do their warranties say?

☐ Is there a shelf life for any spare parts or supplies for maintenance?

☐ Have you specified that the warranty begins at acceptance, not arrival?

☐ Will the supplier offer a discount on spare parts you are going to carry the first year?

☐ Have you identified stocking distributors in your area for spare parts and materials for maintenance?

☐ Have you reviewed the warranty for coverage of parts beyond the first year?

☐ Is maintenance training provided? If not, what is the cost of that training?

☐ Have you seen the maintenance manuals before issuing the purchase order?

☐ Is an electronic defect monitor available as either an option or as standard equipment? (These are fault detectors that tell what the most likely problem is and how to correct it.)

☐ What is the supplier's policy on warranty work during weekends or holidays or beyond the workday?

☐ Is contract maintenance available, and at what cost?

☐ Can the supplier provide the information to load into a CMMS program?

☐ Will the supplier identify the key components in the machine and the supplier of each?

10

Pricing of Capital Equipment

The most complex issue with respect to purchasing capital equipment is pricing. The difficulty in pricing is a result of the interaction of the buyer, the seller, the marketplace, and the economy as a whole. Some of these forces that shape the price fall under the control of the buyer, some are influenced by the buyer, and a large segment are totally beyond the control of the buyer. They are elements the buyer must simply live with in the buying process.

The picture is not significantly different from the seller's perspective. Although the seller has a solid picture of the measurable areas of price, the labor and materials that go into the equipment, the overhead, selling expenses, and profits are allocated values, and concessions may have to be made to sell the equipment to the buyer. Competition is a powerful influence in the pricing decision, especially if the buyer is price oriented and has a reasonable number of alternatives.

In order to appreciate fully the impact of competition, it is important to divide the equipment into three broad categories:

1. *A line of equipment such as screw machines or punch presses.* Selection is made on features and options after quotes are received. They are commercial off-the-shelf, and a significant degree of competition exists to allow for a varied choice among alternatives.

2. *Standard machines that need some customization that goes beyond the supplier's expertise,* such as adding a robotic pick-and-place or some quality assurance monitoring electronics. The basis for selection is still function but also adaptability. The selection base narrows to some degree, and because there is a lack of significant competition, the price is somewhat more inflexible.

3. *The complete custom-built machine for a specific application.* This normally accompanies the development of a new product line. The selection process is on the technical expertise of the manufacturer. Components of price may now

include research and development funds as well as substantial up-front monies to get the project moving. This category must be most closely monitored since there are no other commercial applications for the equipment, and the likelihood of cost overruns is much higher than in the other categories. There are also issues of rights to data and patents on technology developed during the R&D efforts.

Periods in the economic history of the country have shown sellers' markets where the scarcity of materials raised the price to the buyer *above* the manufacturer's suggested price.

Demand and supply intersect, and the result is price. Raise the supply, holding the demand constant, and the price falls. Raise the demand, and hold the supply constant, and the price rises. These are elements that lie beyond the control or influence of the average buyer, yet keeping tuned to the size of demand and supply and the resulting price can be helpful in determining when to buy. Options include buying when demand is low or the market is slow or sluggish, buying before the supplier typically raises prices or seeking out suppliers who have excess capacity and would be willing to negotiate better prices. A good measurement of size of demand is the backlog of the supplier. Heavy backlogs equate to many orders on the supplier's books and probably not much flexibility in pricing. Large backlogs also equate to long lead times for delivery.

Moving to micro considerations, there may be factors that influence the price, even before the purchase is made. There may be additions to product costs that the seller may have to bear even before getting the order. If the cost of responding to a request for quotation (RFQ) is expensive, this cost must be recouped somewhere in the price of the item. Was the request for quotation a serious one or a shopping expedition? Due to the cost of responding, the seller may be in a position where only the serious bids or requests can be answered. These are cost elements that add to the final price. Somewhere these overhead types of costs must be covered or recaptured. The only place is in the price of the equipment. Factors such as lead times, market conditions, and costs of responding to bids or request for quotations (RFQs) are all considered as qualitative indicators to the degree of flexibility in the supplier's pricing process.[1]

Buying capital equipment may be so risk laden for the buyer that price considerations may be bypassed or not considered. The seller has all the information and may have other advantages that are impossible to overcome. These include patents, licensing agreements, and exclusive channel arrangements where the buyer must go to one domestic source, even if that source is not the original equipment manufacturer (OEM). In no other area is the buyer so ex-

---

1. In the field of major power plant construction, the bid preparation may cost more than $400,000. This cost is incurred simply to make the bidder's presence and interest known. It is not a guarantee of the business. This figure was supplied by one of the major power plant engineering companies in the country.

posed or at the mercy of the supplier from a price perspective. The degree of control available to the buyer is limited by the size of the market. The fewer the number of sources available to the buyer, the more time required to produce the capital equipment, and the degree to which the purchaser wants the equipment customized to meet specific sets of needs all place constraints on the buyer. Normally, the larger the dollar value of the purchase, the less control the buyer has over the price. There may be some negotiating room in the price, but the advantage lies with the seller, especially if the time factor is crucial. This is particularly true in the third category. The seller, and in this case the quasi designer, holds all the cost information. The only thing the buyer can do is attempt to assess the reasonableness of the price, given the information the supplier will provide. In this case the buyer should ask for some cost estimates and the level of effort going into various stages of the equipment development. The buyer must ascertain if 20 percent of the cost going into R&D is reasonable or excessive.

There can be no meaningful attempt to look at the price of each piece of capital equipment and determine if the price is fair and reasonable. The pricing decision is made by the supplier after looking at costs and competition, capacity and backlog, sales, and spare parts. There is no universal pricing algorithm. Each situation must be investigated on its own merits, yet if the pricing horizon is so clouded and if the deck is so stacked against the buyer, what options are available other than rolling over and playing dead?

There are a number of possibilities explored in this chapter, yet they all come down to two terms: analyzing the purchase and benchmarking the purchase. Analysis of the purchase looks at the equipment under consideration, the uses of that equipment, and the offer made by the supplier. Properly performed analysis attempts to isolate costs and functions, computing what is being paid to have the machine capable of performing certain functions and assessing if those functions are really needed. It is the prepurchase value analysis on the equipment. This does not mean that the options will be excluded, but what is being paid for those options will be pondered. How is the price of the options related to the features themselves?[2]

Benchmarking is done with respect to price movements. When do prices traditionally rise in the market? Is there a pattern of increases? Benchmarking occurs with respect to the size of price increases over time or inflation or deflation. Benchmarking takes place with respect to features found on the equipment. Is everything that is purchased really needed? Does the deluxe model suit the needs, or does the standard meet the requirement? This chapter will focus on some tools and techniques that allow for valid comparisons to make the pricing analysis more science than art.

---

2. To illustrate this concept in a simple example, go to an appliance store and inspect the washing machines starting with the lowest-priced model. As you move up the price line, notice what additional features are available and the cost of each feature or function performed.

The process by which initial prices are determined is one of soliciting quotations from qualified suppliers. The quotation is just that: the price that will be paid by anyone wanting to purchase the item. In some instances, the quote is the final price since there may not be any other options in terms of sourcing or the specifications are unique, so the equipment is custom made to meet specific customer needs. Where competition is present, the use of competitive bids is strongly suggested. The bids will probably not be exactly comparable due to equipment differences, but the buyer is afforded the opportunity to make some basic comparisons. Bids should include not only the bid price but lead times as well. A low price can quickly fade as a competitive advantage if the supplier presents an unrealistic lead time for delivery. It is also essential that the bids be as close to identical as possible with respect to performance criteria. A Gould pump is not an Ingersoll Rand pump is not a Dresser pump. Different manufacturers produce different products, all of which may be quite capable of producing the same end result or performing the same functions. From the pricing perspective, the idea is to begin getting a range of prices on the equipment where possible and an idea of what the buyer's money buys.

The last statement as to what is being purchased is important. Unless the equipment is being built exactly to the user's specifications or needs, it is possible to purchase features or functional capability that are not needed and will never be used. Somewhere the cost of that unneeded capability must be borne, and usually it is in the price of the item. The buyer is paying for some feature or attribute that will never be used or does not add any value to the function being performed. The buyer is buying too many functions or features in the product. This is one reason that the decision process for buying capital equipment should not be viewed as a set of sequential steps but as a continuous feedback loop. When the bids come in and are being evaluated, it is as much an engineering function to look at what has been proposed by the suppliers as it is a purchasing function to look at the business side of the offer. The astute engineer can easily identify features that may be considered excess to his/her needs. This recognition may raise the question of why the buyer should buy them. One person cannot have all the expertise needed for an outstanding decision; the team approach is necessary. While in theory the practice of using the team is excellent, the engineer on the project may become a one-man show. The engineer claims there is insufficient time to explain everything to the team members. Thus, he or she goes off and makes decisions without coordination. Consider the case of the company buying a custom tube bender.

The supplier specialized in custom tube benders and had a track record with the buying company. The requirement called for a machine that would put a 180-degree arc on stainless steel tubing with a 20,000 pounds per square inch (psi) rating. The highest pressure the supplier had worked on was 6,000 psi in phosphor bronze. By not recognizing the capability of the supplier, a purchasing responsibility, the engineer had endangered the project. The machine was built, and it did perform. Now the supplier had experience with 20,000 psi pressures.

Somewhere between the engineer and the supplier, it was decided to add a $40,000 electronic gauge to the machine for process capability analysis studies. Six months after the machine was in use, the gauging malfunctioned. The maintenance department took the unit off the machine and returned it to its manufacturer. The machine was still under warranty from the supplier. The gauge manufacturer claimed the warranty had been violated by "improper removal causing the destruction of certain electronic components." The manufacturer wanted $6,000 to inspect the gauge and then would provide a repair cost estimate. Purchasing went to engineering to ascertain the next step. What did engineering want done? It was then that the buyer, a project team member, learned the machine had demonstrated good repeatability and the gauging equipment was no longer needed. The buyer was also informed that no money was left in the project budget. The gauge manufacturer was asked to return the malfunctioning gauge. The buyer also learned the gauge had not really been necessary. A quality assurance technician could have taken the necessary readings to measure repeatability of the equipment at about 5 percent of the cost of the gauge.

The buyer was looking at the commercial side of the transaction while the engineer was looking at the performance or technical side of the offer. Both views are valid and important, and they often interact, especially where price is concerned. Price is the sum of costs, and costs are charged for features or functions performed by the equipment.

Gaining price concessions in the capital equipment area can be very difficult since many of the trump cards remain in the seller's hand. The seller should know the price structure of the product, the lead time, the backlog in the plant, as well as some estimates of future volume and future costs. The buyer may feel relatively insecure with the perception that little usable information is available. This is not truly the case. There are several data sources that may be useful to the buyer in terms of getting a fair price. The usefulness of the data depends on the ability of the buyer to be aware of the capital equipment needs as soon as possible or have the greatest amount of lead time possible in order to have the appropriate information when it is needed.

Are there opportunities for price negotiation with capital equipment? Yes. Suppliers do not have infinite backlogs to work against. Suppliers also realize that pricing is more an art form than a science, and the offering price in a competitive bidding situation is often the starting point for negotiation. The motives of the seller in lowering the price may be varied and include:

- A desire to have the company as a customer (the prestige issue).

- The ability to integrate this order into others in production, adding on to the production run and eliminating or reducing setup costs or being able to allocate the setup costs over a larger base.

- The ability to get price concessions on materials through quantity discounts from the supplier's suppliers.

- A high marginal contribution to profit if all of the fixed costs are covered and only variable costs are present, producing above the break-even point.[3] At a certain level of output, using the concept of break-even, all fixed costs have been covered or absorbed by the production up to the break-even point. Beyond the break-even point, additional orders carry only the variable costs of labor, material, and some overhead, and the incremental profits on these orders or sales are significant. Timing is a key consideration in the placing of the order.

- The possibility of follow-on business or spare parts business that would make up for forgone profits on this order. A supplier may make significant price concessions to get the equipment in the door. Once inside, the true cost of ownership is determined when replacement parts or repairs are needed.

- The possibility that business is so bad that a supplier would be willing to accept a reduced profit margin or no profit margin just to sustain the business. This can be measured in the macrosense by looking at the growth in the volume of capital equipment sales and leases and using the producer's price index (PPI) to discount or deinflate the dollar value for sales. If inflation has been growing at a faster rate than sales, then real or constant dollar sales are actually down, and price growth is inflation driven. The physical output may be the same. To determine the nature of the market, one must look at both sales and inflation. Both are important market indicators.

The reasons are numerous and the seller's motives varied, yet price concessions are possible and can be negotiated, especially when the seller is a quality product producer but is trying to sell too much product to the buyer. Typical price negotiating techniques will go only so far, and there is a need for firm data to back the buyer's position on prices.

Another unique aspect of the purchasing of capital equipment is the pricing system itself. Most goods and services purchased are bought under fixed-price arrangements stemming from quotes or bids. In the normal process of

---

3. The analog in this case is the automobile dealer that has one more car to sell to reach the quota set by the manufacturer. Upon reaching the quota, the retailer gets a 3 percent rebate on *all* automobiles sold. That final car may go for cost to reach that sales level.

purchasing the equipment, the buyer desires a firm, fixed price on the equipment. This is one technique to minimize price risk—the likelihood that the price of the equipment will exceed the original cost figure on the purchase order. It ensures that the price to be paid is known and the budget for the purchase is not exceeded. Exceeding the budget requires that the additional money be found somewhere else. What are the chances that the purchase will come in exactly as stipulated in the cost estimates or budget? The chances are rather small due to all the possible factors that can create unfavorable variances from the original purchase order price or from the estimates.

There are numerous sources of variations. Some may be anticipated and therefore covered by designated contingency planning dollars; some are random events that just happen and are therefore unpredictable. Nevertheless, they still occur and must be considered. There are rules of thumb that tell us to set aside a percentage of the overall purchase price to cover contingencies. If the dollars are not used, they can be reallocated, but they are still available if needed.

The Complicating Factor of Lead Time

Producers of capital equipment do not normally inventory the end item. The costs would be astronomical, and the risk of obsolescence would far exceed the potential benefits of having the goods in stock. For the most part, capital equipment is a build-to-order product, exhibiting significant lead times from the placement of the order to the receipt of the equipment. Orders taken today may have delivery dates well into the future. On smaller pieces of equipment, a supplier may be able to compress the lead time by having one or two pieces of equipment available or taking advantage of an order cancellation by some other customer. This lead time element sometimes makes the used equipment option attractive.

One pricing mechanism favored by buyers is the firm, fixed price. The supplier agrees to sell the equipment for a fixed price as per the quotation, offer, or bid solicited by the buyer. Yet what lies behind that firm, fixed price is another matter. No seller is going to commit to a price without some degree of protection against uncontrollable price increases in the future. Take the example of Ericcson in Sweden, a company long known for building quality central office equipment for telephone companies. A 400,000-station item of switching equipment may have a three- to four-year lead time. No one is going to quote a price based on today's labor and material costs for delivery three or four years from now. If the offering price is fixed, there must be some allowances for cost growth in the pricing process. Consider Boeing Corporation with its multibillion dollar backlog of aircraft orders. Were they truly fixed-price contracts? Yes and no. They may be fixed price in the sense that the price will not increase from the initial order, but what went into setting that price surely accounted for increased labor costs, material costs, process improvements, and engineering change costs. If many of the orders come from foreign countries, there must be protection against currency fluctuations, especially given the long lead times. They are probably quoted as "price in effect at time of delivery." There must be the realization that the process of building the equipment takes time, and as that time progresses, especially crossing a fiscal year or anniversary date of a labor agreement, costs may escalate. The costs associated with that time are numerous and include:

- Potential increases in labor costs associated with fabrication
- Potential increases in material costs
- The forgone use of capital if the supplier insists on progress payments
- The costs of doing without the new equipment while waiting for it to arrive

In the case of the firm, fixed price, the supplier has factored these future cost increases into the quoted price. The question becomes how much has been factored into the price. It is possible for the equipment manufacturer to be quite precise in these projections. The supplier would then be adamant about giving any price concessions during negotiations. If there are price concessions offered, then it is an indicator of a generous add-on to cover both time and negotiation contingencies and a perceived lack of competition for the order.

There are several ways to measure these additions to equipment cost. Starting with the macroapproach, the price of capital equipment is no different in its behavior from the vast majority of products in the economy. Over the past four decades, there has been a continuous rise in prices. Inflation is present in all sectors of the economy and is a noncontrollable element. All that can be done is to measure the inflation properly. Using the correct yardstick allows the buyer to predict the future behavior of prices and get a reasonable estimate of what the price could be when the order is placed or the equipment delivered. Note the distinction between the last two terms. Term 1 was "when the order was placed" and term 2 was "when the equipment was delivered." These are the ends of the capital equipment price spectrum with respect to the equipment itself.[4]

While the buyer prefers the firm, fixed price for future delivery, it presents more problems from an analysis perspective than its hated counterpart: price in effect at time of delivery. Ask the majority of buyers, and see which is preferred. Agreeing to the uncertainties of an unknown future price creates a twinge of anxiety with the buyer. It is offering an open-ended agreement, a

---

4. Like the tip of the iceberg, the cost of the equipment itself may be a fraction of the total cost incurred.

signed blank check, or agreeing to pay the supplier all the supplier wants. In either case, the buyer sees himself at a disadvantage. Unless there have been extensive value engineering efforts, source analysis, and financial study of the purchase, the price quoted by the supplier is often taken as a given. The philosophy becomes one of saying that some information is better than none, and none is represented by "price in effect at time of delivery."

The buyer should not consider the situation hopeless. The buyer is not totally dependent on the price quoted by the supplier. There are macro- and micromeasures that the buyer can use to reduce the level of pricing uncertainty often associated with capital equipment. Starting with the macroapproach, the buyer should consult the PPI for capital equipment. Getting the PPI off the Internet is a simple process. See Appendix C for detailed instructions on how to obtain the information as well as setting up a spreadsheet to monitor the equipment. The PPI for this capital equipment is shown in Exhibit 10-1 along with its **chained values.** Chaining is a simple statistical process that allows an index value to be compared on a year-by-year basis. Normally, indexes have a base year, and every measurement of that index is against the base year. By chaining the values, it is possible to show the growth from year to year. It is simply the most current year value divided by the previous year's value with the result multiplied by 100.

Exhibit 10-1. Producer's price index for capital equipment, 1986–1996.

Year	PPI Value	Chain Value
1986	109.7	
1987	111.7	101.18
1988	114.3	102.32
1989	118.8	103.93
1990	122.9	103.45
1991	126.7	103.09
1992	129.1	101.89
1993	131.4	101.78
1994	134.1	102.05
1995	136.7	101.93
1996	138.4	101.24

The base year for this PPI series is set in 1982 at 100. By 1992, a decade later, the index stood at 129.1. This means the machine costing $100,000 in 1982 would sell for $129,100 a decade later. Using the PPI for longer-range projections of prices on capital equipment is not suggested. It is highly unlikely that the same machine would be available a decade later. Technology marches on. Therefore, the use of the PPI should be limited to shorter-range forecasting, probably not exceeding three years. Yet a view of the annual index values for the PPI does reveal some interesting information.

Notice that the rate of growth in prices has slowed considerably from the early part of the decade. Although the data presented here are annual data, monthly figures are also available over the 11-year period, giving the analyst a potential time series of 132 observations. Therefore, a forecast of 1 year or even 2 into the future is not difficult. The starting point for any type of analysis and projection can be seen in Exhibit 10-2.

Exhibit 10-2. Projection of capital equipment price.

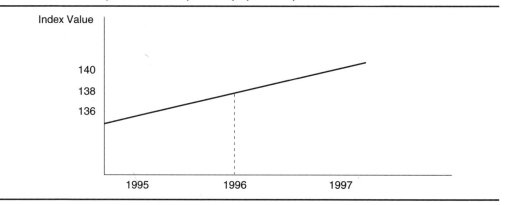

Going beyond 1996 requires a projection, and depending on the value of that projection, an estimate is possible for the next year. This estimate has value only if the comparison is between like items of equipment. Therefore, if the estimate is for a 1.5 percent increase in price, the comparison must be made with the same item. Thus buying model A of the machine for $100,000 in 1996, the buyer could expect to pay $101,500 for the *same* machine in 1997. Assuming the price quoted is $105,000, the question becomes what is so different between the two models as to justify the additional $3,500 in cost. Now we begin to bring the concept of **value analysis** into the pricing picture. What features are in the 1997 model that do not exist in the 1996 model? In some instances, there are upgrades in performance and quality that can justify the higher price in the eyes of the seller, but the buyer must be able to see these differences and want or need them. Increases in performance that are perceived to add little or no value for the buyer are not valid excuses for price increases. This simple example is nothing more than a basic application of value analysis to the pricing of capital equipment.

The purchase of a piece of capital equipment by a company is a process of exchanging value between the buyer and the seller. Money, a store of value in the economy, is traded for the equipment. Selling is the art of persuading the customer that the value received from buying the equipment will exceed the value of the money or that the machine is capable of creating value by transforming material from one form into another. We purchase equipment because it performs basic functions of cutting, bending, shaping, assembling, or forming. The function performed by the machine should be definable in two words: a verb and a noun. The function of the lawn mower is to *cut grass*. The washing machine *launders clothes*. Basic functions that need to be performed are the basis of the desire to buy. Yet it is possible to go well beyond the basic functions and provide an array of secondary functions that the equipment is capable of performing that enhance or enrich the basic functions—for example, a lawn mower with a grass catcher, an electronic ignition, a fuel gauge, and a frame sufficiently large to allow the operator to sit on the mower. All of these secondary functions satisfy the user and make the equipment more convenient, yet they do not go beyond the basic function in many cases. However, they add cost to the equipment. The issue the buyer must consider is the added cost versus the additional functions received versus the need for those functions. If the additional $3,500 worth of features illustrated in the newer model will not be used or represents marginal improvements, then it is not worth $3,500 to the buyer. Incremental increases in price over the preceding year's price that are not material and/or labor caused can be viewed as questionable. The issue is paying for something that is not needed or that has a service life far in excess of the anticipated service life needed.[5] No need equates to no value to the buyer. Yet the buyer must have the benchmark against which to measure. This equates to getting the information on anticipated purchases as quickly as possible to allow time to set up the measuring scheme with the PPI.

Making Use of the Data

Having the data is one thing; making use of them is another. The simplest application would be a projection of the expected price that would be paid if the equipment was to be purchased sometime in the future. This involves making the current price the benchmark and looking at the rate of growth of the PPI and extending that information into the future. It is simplistic, but it may be useful in isolating causes for the price increase in the future. Price increases occur for a variety of reasons. There are legitimate reasons reflecting cost increases and questionable reasons such as margin enrichment. The value-adding portions of the product include direct labor and direct materials plus some overhead in the R&D and engineering areas and may be considered bona-fide reasons for the increases. The buyer is loathe to pay for increases in supplier profits or to cover inefficiencies in the supplier's operation.

The buyer can bring the analysis down to a more specific level by increasing the number of digits in the Standard Industrial Classification (SIC) code.

---

5. A simple example is the Blaupunkt stereo system for automobiles. A superior stereo-CD system that delivers high-wattage performance with multiple speakers, it will still be operating long after the car has become fodder for the minimill.

Using SIC code 3541 brings the buyer into the category of machine tools. This is still a rather broad range, and the buyer may wish to delve deeper into the code by expanding the number of digits, thereby tracing down specific types of machine tools. As an example, consider the case of buying a horizontal numerically controlled turning machine. This product category is represented by SIC 3541519.[6]

Asking the Bureau of Labor Statistics for the pertinent data through the Internet, we obtain the data shown in Exhibit 10-3. Although the PPI for capital equipment was used as a broad-based indicator, the greater amount of depth into what is actually being purchased allows the buyer to look more closely at the individual piece of equipment. Although over 120,000 series are tracked by the Bureau of Labor Statistics under the PPI alone, not every product is monitored. Here is a case where the buyer must recognize limitations on the data available and perhaps use other sources, such as other customers of the supplier to provide price information. The salient point is not simply accepting the offer as the final price. Buying capital equipment is similar to buying an automobile. As long as competition is present, there will be pressures for price concessions.

Exhibit 10-3. PPI data for horizontal numerically controlled turning machine.

Year	Period	Value
1995	March	111.1
	June	114.4
	September	119.3
	December	120.1
1996	March	120.4
	June	123.6
	September	125.1
	December	126.8

Although the data cover only eight quarters, they may be extended to monthly data and backward 10 years to 1986. The trend is obvious with rising index values and the larger increases coming in the summer months. Although the general SIC code gives broad-based information, the closer the analyst can go to the actual machine being purchased, the better cost overview can be established for the pricing segment of the purchase. Buying that machine in 1997 will probably result in paying a higher price in September than in January. Using the PPI for the capital expenditure budget or the proposal preparation is also a good use of the data. This approach can illustrate the impact of timing in the buying decision. The PPI for the item is nothing more than a measure of inflation or deflation of the price over time. It is quite simple to illustrate the

6. Getting the information on SIC codes is addressed in Appendix C. The procedure is quite simple on the Internet and easily learned.

cost impact of waiting for the decision. It is also a useful tool in negotiating the price in effect at the time of delivery with a maximum value. For example, consider the purchase of the machine from a price perspective.

A machine is ordered for delivery in June 1998, and the supplier quotes a price in effect at time of delivery as part of the order. The buyer inquires as to the current price. The hypothetical current price of $50,000 is quoted with the index at 126.8. Projecting the index forward to June 1998 would give a value of 129.2 based on the size of the June-to-June change from the preceding year.[7] Having established this value, the buyer would expect to pay $50,000 (129.2/126) or $51,000 for the machine. The additional $1,000 would be the anticipated inflation in the industry over the next six months. Since that figure is based on a June 1998 projection for the index, the price should be established not at $51,000 but *not to exceed $51,000.* The inflation factor provides the upper limit in a range of $50,000 to $51,000.

While this is a simplistic way of arriving at the upper price level, it does remove some of the uncertainty from the pricing aspect in effect at time of delivery. It may also be used to assess the realism of prices quoted for future deliveries on a firm fixed basis. The company that "quotes" the firm price of $52,000 for June 1997 delivery is certainly protecting itself from inflationary pressures. The clever buyer considers the PPI when looking at current price and adjusting for anticipated inflationary impact on price. The buyer can also use the PPI to determine the best time to place the order to secure the best price. If the PPI is used for this purpose, make sure there is a long history (10 years) of data on which the decision is based. Prices are influenced by many factors beyond the control of the supplier.

Cost-Raising Elements

In many instances the price of the equipment itself is a fraction of the total cost of procurement.[8] There are numerous elements that can add to the costs be-

---

7. The method of projection can range from simply projecting past data to statistical analysis using the last 24, 36, or 120 months of data. The purpose is to arrive at some mutually acceptable ceiling for the price.
8. It is important to draw the distinction between cost of procurement and cost of ownership. Total ownership or life cycle costing of the equipment is distinct from total cost of procurement since procurement is a segment of the life cycle. Total cost of ownership is covered in Chapter 11.

yond the machine cost itself. The key areas to consider that affect the price of the equipment are listed below:

• *Cost of modifications or customization of the equipment—the accessories or add-ons to the basic model.* The starting point is often the **plain vanilla model,** with the basic functions provided for in the equipment. Moving away from the basics and beginning the customization process escalates the cost of the machine.[9] The added features may be necessary or nice-to-have accessories that provide convenience in one form or another and satisfy the user. These must be evaluated or costed on a case-by-case basis. Do they add value to the output, reduce cost, save time, improve performance, or reduce maintenance? There are no single answers to these analyses. Realize there is also a markup or profit on the accessories on the equipment, especially if these can be added to the equipment *after* manufacturing has taken place. These additions to the basic model can be installed somewhere else in the channel of distribution, by perhaps the factory-authorized dealer or representative. These accessories are therefore negotiable with respect to price and should be viewed as such. Accepting the full price for the additions in the channel is giving money to the element in the channel that performs the service.

• *The costs of buying overseas.* If the purchase is made in the domestic market, the sources of deviation are somewhat less than buying overseas. Later in the chapter, some consideration will be given to the sources of deviation encountered when buying overseas.

• *The costs of changes.* Regardless of where the purchase is made, the process is complicated when the buyer deviates from the original specifications by wanting more features or upgrading parts or components of the equipment. This is the controllable element of the pricing structure from the perspective that once the design is agreed upon, it should be frozen.[10] Agreement on design, performance criteria, and acceptance criteria allows for the development of a firm or reasonably firm price. The cost of any changes made between the time of order placement and delivery or completion of fabrication at the supplier's facility should be negotiable. The process of purchasing capital equipment affords the buyer numerous opportunities to boost the seller's profit margin. One of those opportunities arises when the change order process begins.

Change orders are modifications to the original agreement because there

9. A differentiation must be set up between customization where the customer sets the specifications and the addition of supplier-provided options. In the latter case, the supplier is still providing the machine built to *his* specifications, not the customer's. These are features or additions to the equipment, much like automobile options.
10. There are several schools of thought in the case of the frozen design. One school feels the restriction of the design changes or engineering change proposals is essential to get the machine at a reasonable price. Another school maintains that building in flexibility allows for incorporation of the newest technology. There is no correct answer. The best that can be achieved is a balance between technology needs and costs.

will be a design alteration or an addition to or a modification of some piece of equipment or part going on the machine. Perhaps a larger motor is desired, or a larger pump, or different bearings or seals. Change orders add to cost in two ways. They add to the price paid for the end item since they are normally upgrades to the existing design, and the buyer loses the potential to negotiate the price of the changes, allowing the supplier to recapture some or all of the profits that may have been lost in the original price negotiation.

In one company, the original negotiation had succeeded in reducing the price paid for pumps by some 10 percent, only to give back that 10 percent and more when it was decided to upgrade the pumps. The decision was made rapidly, and there was no time to negotiate. If time had been taken to stop the fabrication process, the end item would have been delayed and the delivery window missed. Improper planning benefited the seller, who happily replaced the original pumps at discounted prices with the upgrades at standard prices.

Somewhere the design is frozen, and we live with the results of freezing the process. The alternative is continuously incorporating the newest technology and living with a significant price differential from the original price.

• *The cost of spare parts.* The issue at the time of purchase is always an economic one when it comes to looking at spare parts. Is it cheaper to buy a quantity of spares with the initial purchase or wait until the spares are needed? This is not a simple question to answer. Involved in the decision is the compounding element of the warranty, whereby the seller stands behind the product with respect to parts and labor and warrants acceptable performance for some period of time or operation. From a warranty perspective, the buyer is protected for the duration of the warranty against the possible need for spare parts. In the case of maintenance, the warranty may specify that the dealer or seller of the equipment must be the person to perform warranty work; anyone else working on the equipment during the warranty period other than authorized persons will void the warranty. Investing in spares would then be a waste of money. Some companies avoid the cost of carrying the spare parts in inventory by extending the warranty. In terms of how much to pay for the warranty extension, recognize this is a risk situation. The seller may never be called upon to service the equipment during the warranty period. Thus, any monies received for extending the warranty can be pure profit. If the warranty were not on the equipment, the cost would probably be 2 percent to 3 percent less. Thus, the extended warranty may be limited to 2 to 3 percent above the equipment price. The warranty would cover replacement of defective parts and associated labor. Another approach is not carrying spares at all. The spares, if needed, will still cost the buying company, but only when they are used. There is an array of other options open to the buyer. Options include having the spare parts on consignment from the seller, to be paid for as they are used. This ensures availability of the spares, but does not tie up the capital in the spare parts. There is also dealer stocking of the spare parts and a guarantee by the dealer as to availability. This approach reduces the lead time since the spare part inventory is on hand at the dealer, in the case of a stocking distributor, or at the OEM. The spares stocking process can be selective with only certain spares carried in the inventory or, perhaps, only one spare part of each type with replacement of the spare when it is used. Each option has its associated costs and benefits, and the buyer should investigate to determine the most cost effective approach for his or her company.

There is no simple answer to the spares question, yet it is well established that spare parts often carry impressive profit margins. The buyer should determine the cost of the spares at the time of equipment purchase, even if the purchase does not go through. This is done to establish the baseline price for the spares in the future. The extra or hidden costs would be the carrying costs for the spare parts as they are waiting to be used. Even allowing for a 3 percent per month inventory carrying cost, the average company could carry the spares for three years if it were able to leverage the price on the spares in the initial purchase. Spare parts markups often are 100 to 500 percent over cost. Getting the spares at or near cost would allow the buyer to carry the spares for a significant period, and the three-year figure is not unreasonable.

• *The costs associated with testing the equipment at the supplier's site to see that it meets acceptance criteria.*

• *The cost of rigging, shipping, and setup in its final site.*

• *The costs incurred with making progress payments to the supplier,* especially in the case of custom-built equipment. An adder to the price is the forgone use of money when progress payments must be made to the supplier. Regardless of what the pattern of payments may be, payment to the supplier before the machine is installed and producing product means the buyer has funds tied up in a nonproducing asset. The use of that money is gone, and the buyer should add the forgone returns on those funds to the price of the equipment. The appropriate rate for computation would be the expected rate the buyer normally gets with investments.

Dealing Realistically With Price in Effect

"Price in effect" pricing is difficult to deal with but not a hopeless situation. It requires a rational methodology for analysis of the pricing structure, keen negotiation skills, and the ability to remove some of the uncertainty traditionally associated with this pricing scheme. As in any other comparative pricing system, it requires a baseline or benchmark from which to compute the expected deviations and, in effect, forecast the future price. The purpose is not establishing the future price but developing a rational or reasonable projected price to allow for negotiation with the supplier on that price. The analysis includes these elements:

- Determination of the current price
- Determination of the elements in the price that are subject to growth— normally labor and material and perhaps fuels
- Determination of the fraction of total cost encompassed by the growth elements
- Determination of the growth of these elements over the period from order placement to scheduled delivery[11]

Consider the following example:

A company has decided to purchase an item of equipment with an eight-month lead time. The order is placed on October 1 with a delivery date of June 1. The machine is custom made and sells for $100,000. The material portion of the machine is estimated to be 30 percent of the price and the labor 10 percent of price, with fuels at 3 percent of price. The major material cost drivers in the machine are stainless steel, an electric motor, a fluid motor and pump, and limit switches with the respective percentages at 50, 20, 10, and 10 for the four respective material inputs, with the remaining 10 percent as miscellaneous.

The company is located in Alabama and is considered medium sized. The fuel used is natural gas. The buyer has been quoted price in effect at time of delivery and will attempt to define an upper limit as to a reasonable price to pay for the machine.

Analysis: On the basis of the data provided, the initial analysis shows that material constitutes $30,000, labor $10,000, and fuels $3,000. Now the issue becomes one of looking at each of the material components, with $15,000 in stainless steel, $3,000 in electric motors, $3,000 for fluid motors and pumps, and

---

11. The receipt of the order and its acceptance constitutes the formation of a contract between buyer and seller, all other stipulations on contracting being met. The seller who produces to order normally will begin the purchasing process for materials associated with that order, and these materials are the financial responsibility of the buyer since they are traceable to the order.

$3,000 in limit switches.[12] It is now necessary to extract the appropriate PPI values for the commodities and the wage rate index and the natural gas index to project the labor, materials, and fuel portion of the price. Since the other elements of price, such as overhead, selling costs, and operating income, are often a percentage of the measurables (direct labor and materials), it is assumed these percentage allocations will stay the same and escalate as price increases on the measurables. The spreadsheet is depicted in Exhibit 10-4.

This is a typical "should cost" analysis that goes beyond simply using the PPI to project end item price, but attempts to look at what goes into the machine in terms of material and labor and then project these values to the delivery date. This would set up the maximum price the buyer is willing to pay. A spreadsheet approach would be used, and the buyer would get the appropriate data from the Internet on the PPI data for the major components of the equipment.[13]

The spreadsheet contains three segments. The first breaks out the materials cost into the five components that make up the $30,000 figure. Material is 30 percent of the machine cost of $100,000. Sector #2 looks at the Producer Price Index for each cost component, and shows the values for the period March 1994 to December 1996. A projection is made for the planned buying date, March 1997. Sector #2 reveals that stainless steel, fluid pumps, and limit switches have steadily risen in price over the three-year period, while electric motors have been stable.

In Sector #3, the buyer attempts to project the March 1997 price of the material portion of the machine by taking the current price of the major cost components and adjusting those prices for growth in their respective categories. If the estimate is made in December 1996 for stainless steel, the base would be 125.00 and with a projection on 129. The price growth of stainless steel would be $129 \div 125$, or 1.032. This would mean the March 1997 price would be 3.2 percent higher than the December 1996 price. Applying that growth factor, stainless steel in the machine should cost $15,480 as opposed to $15,000. The cost growth is applied to each identifiable material component. The reason for undertaking this type of analysis is to develop reasonable limits for material cost growth. The data show that each major cost element in the machine grows at a different rate, and, therefore, one rate of growth could easily distort the true cost growth of the material. After the computations are complete, it is easy to return to the answer and see the overall, weighted average growth has been

12. This is a totally hypothetical machine. Its purpose is to show price benchmarking taken down to the component level. For a complete discussion of this approach, see *Escalation and Producer Price Indices: A Guide for Contracting Parties,* U.S. Department of Labor, Bureau of Labor Statistics, Report 807, September 1991. (http://stats.bls.gov80/ppiesc.html-Internet address)
13. This approach of analyzing the major equipment by components or major assemblies is underway in several large companies. The concern is limiting cost growth and attempting to determine the segment or portion of that growth attributable to materials. The day of "all the traffic will bear" pricing may be over in this field.

Exhibit 10-4. Component price analysis.

Sector #1

Material Portion of Equipment

	Description	
	Cost	$100,000
Material Portion of Machine	30.00%	SIC Code	3623
Labor Portion	10.00%		
Fuel	2.00%		

Materials Used

Stainless Steel	$15,000
Electric Motors	$6,000
Fluid Motors	$3,000
Limit Switches	$3,000
Misc.	$3,000

Sector #2

Producer Price Index by Component

Date of Index	PPI Value Stainless Steel	PPI Value Electric Motors	PPI Value Limit Switches	PPI Value Fluid Pumps
Component				
3/1/94	114.60	100.30	138.00	114.40
6/1/94	114.60	103.70	138.00	114.40

(continues)

Exhibit 10-4. *Continued*

9/1/94	114.60	100.80	138.10	114.40
12/1/94	113.30	100.90	141.10	114.40
3/1/95	116.60	101.80	142.80	119.30
6/1/95	121.90	102.80	142.80	120.20
9/1/95	119.80	102.60	142.80	
12/1/95	127.00	102.70	145.80	data not
3/1/96	127.00	102.70	145.80	available
6/1/96	127.00	100.30	145.80	
9/1/96	125.50	99.90	145.80	
12/1/96	125.00	99.90	151.80	
3/1/97—Projected	128.0 to 129.0	100.00	151.80	126.00

Sector # 3

Should Cost Segment Component	% of Material Cost	Base Index	Projected Index	Projected/Base	Cost Projected
Stainless Steel	50.00%	125.00	129.00	103.20%	$15,480
Electric Motors	20.00%	99.90	100.00	100.10%	$6,006
Limit Switches	10.00%	145.80	151.80	104.12%	$3,123
Fluid Pumps	10.00%	120.20	126.00	104.83%	$3,145
Misc.	10.00%	—			$3,000
Projected Material Cost					$30,754

2.5 percent. This number is obtained by dividing the projected material cost of $30,754 by $30,000, and obtaining 1.0251. Multiply that number by 100 to get 102.51 or a 2.51 percent increase in cost. This approach not only looks at each cost component, but its proportion of the total material cost.

This is a hypothetical example. The depth to which the buyer may analyze will vary with the material composition of the product. Picking the two or three cost drivers in the equipment might account for the vast majority of the material costs. Normally 80 percent of the material costs are incurred by 20 percent of the parts. Since this is a cost estimate, 100 percent accuracy is not expected. What is desired is an upper boundary that represents the most realistic and reasonable cost growth that can be expected. This is the counter to the blank check mentality engendered by "price in effect at time of delivery."

Added Cost From Overseas

When the decision is made to purchase from a supplier overseas, the pricing issue really begins to take on a life of its own. Complexities begin to abound quickly since we leave the safe harbor of a single legal system, a single monetary system, a single language system, a single culture, and a uniform measuring system and enter the global arena where pounds refers to money, not weight; where *inch* may be a meaningless word, and where green money can have one value today and another one tomorrow. Here the costs that must be added to the price of the equipment may skyrocket.

In some instances, the supplier may make the process simpler by having a domestic representative who stocks spare parts, follows the order, and assists in the process from both a technical and logistical basis. The contract may be with the domestic company acting as a general agent for the foreign supplier, which somewhat reduces, but does not eliminate, the legal complexities of dealing with two or more legal systems. Or the supplier may be a domestic company having a facility in a foreign country for the purpose of fabricating the machine. The foreign presence is seamless to the buyer.

In exploring the overseas true price, the worst-case scenario will be used of the domestic buyer's purchasing the machine from a foreign company located in Europe or Asia.[14] In order for a fair comparison to be made, consider the factors that must be paid for in the foreign purchase compared to the domestic acquisition. These factors are summarized in Exhibit 10-5.

The National Tooling and Machining Association suggests the conversion of these factors into a **true cost** worksheet. One is shown in Exhibit 10-6. The purpose of the comparison is not to discourage the use of foreign sources of

---

14. It is of little consequence which country is used, except to illustrate the issues of measuring, shipping, communicating, and using third, fourth, or even fifth parties to accomplish the purchase.

Exhibit 10-5. True cost comparisons of foreign vs. domestic sources.

Cost Factor to Consider	Domestic Source	Foreign Source
Currency	Single currency	Subject to fluctuations
Payment and associated payment paperwork	Simple process	May be complex and expensive
Measurement	English system	Metric system
Shipment	Simple	Multiple modes involved
Customs duties	N.A.	Adds to costs
Use of agents	Not necessary	Necessary
Communications	English	≅ English
Manuals	In English	?
Lead times	?	In-country delays possible
Features to bring into conformance with U.S. standards	No problem	Possible extra costs and delays
Spare parts	Domestic availability	Possible domestic availability
Insurance costs	Depend on FOB	Must include CIF or IF
Fails acceptance tests	Domestic retrofitting or rectification	Expensive process as to where and how
Testing and inspection	Could be done at destination	Must be done at source
Verification for progress payments	On site domestically	On-site foreign or independent foreign agent
Travel to supplier	Reasonable	Expensive in time and money

Source: Many of the costs cited in this table have come from *Contracting for Machining and Tooling: The Hidden Costs of Sourcing Abroad,* published by the National Tooling and Machining Association, September 1987. Excerpts are reprinted with permission.

supply but to avoid the problem of making incomplete or inaccurate comparisons between the domestic and foreign sources. Indeed, this type of comparison may have to be made between foreign sources since the rules of law governing exports vary widely among countries.

Adding up the numbers, the benchmark estimates show an added 17 to 69 percent that must be added to the foreign quoted purchase price to make the necessary adjustments to compare costs accurately. These are benchmarks, and individual cases may vary significantly, but they do represent a starting point for true cost comparisons. These data do not include the added costs that may be incurred by having to maintain two sets of tools or unique spare parts for that machine alone or the possible downtime experienced when buying

Exhibit 10-6. True cost worksheet.

Hidden Costs	U.S. Supplier	Benchmark Estimates of Added Foreign Costs (% of U.S. Quoted Price)	Foreign Supplier
Freight and packaging costs		Freight, packaging, insurance, and financing costs combined will add	
Insurance costs			
Financing costs		4–12% combined	
Travel and communications		3–8%	
Custom duties	None	4–6%	
Exchange rate risk	None	1–3%	
Added features to bring into line with U.S. standards	None	5–36%	
Paperwork problems		2–4%	
Total hidden costs (%) × Quoted purchase price = Adjusted total cost			

spares from an overseas operation. The buyer must also be aware of the extras that may accompany the transportation of the equipment from source to destination: the use of outside agents, dockside storage, in-country inspection, transportation from the supplier to the port of embarkation, transportation from the port of entry to your location and trial runs on the equipment, and domestic support upon installation as well as possible trips to the supplier during the fabrication stage to verify the passing of acceptance criteria. All of these elements cost money and must be added to the cost of the equipment, even though they are not part of the equipment itself. This is the only way to level the playing field in the comparison process.

Just as the focus on domestic purchases should be on total cost of ownership, with initial purchase cost as one segment of the cost picture, a foreign purchase should include all the costs to bring the equipment to the same state of operational readiness in the plant as from the domestic source. The transportation issue is very important. If air freight is specified or is the mode, determine what it will cost. This is determined by distance, weight, and space occupied, or number of cubic feet (cubes). Often there are strict limitations based upon the size of the cargo, based upon the cargo carrying space available on the aircraft. Air freight is the most rapid way to move equipment, and it can reduce concealed damages. It is also very, very expensive as the weight increases.

What It Translates To

To say there is one price for the capital equipment item is to cite one price for the automobile or the airline ticket or the overcoat. There are literally hundreds of prices that can be charged depending on the terms and conditions of the sale, the willingness of the customer to pay a specific price, the desired delivery date, the deviations from standard or off the shelf, and a hundred other possible factors.

The buyer must first draw the line between the equipment purchased and all other costs. This is the base price of the equipment. Then add on the customization or special features that make the equipment unique. Now come the additional nonequipment costs that must be paid for but are not part of the equipment itself: the rigging, shipping, testing, installing, adjustments, training, initial spares stocking, tooling, and maintenance support. Every aspect of cost should have a dollar figure placed with it. What part of the total cost do these other elements constitute? Does the equipment segment of the total price of the equipment represent 50 percent, 60 percent, or 75 percent of the total cost of the purchase? The smaller the percentage, the more the equipment is going to have to carry the other costs. It is the equipment that generates the revenue, but it also bears all the other costs.

All of these other costs must be absorbed by the equipment over its service life or, more accurately, its operating time. Since the current approach is to look at capital equipment from a cost per hour basis, then all of these costs must be one part of the equation. The nonmachine costs must be paid for somewhere and rather than disguise or slough them off, it would be better to include them in the computations from an accounting perspective. They are present however they are to be paid for. Thus, the cost tracking of the overall cost of the equipment is but one important step in determining the burden to place on the machine for product pricing purposes. If the final computation shows the burden to be $100 per operating hour, this will give a different price to the product produced on that machine than if the burden was reduced to $75 per hour by reallocation of the costs.

The capability of the buyer to analyze the price to see if it is honest is limited but not impossible. It must be a cooperative effort and must make use of as much relevant outside data as available. It should be oriented toward getting what the buyer needs in the form of data to perform the analysis. While it is difficult to get exact numbers, it is possible to set the upper limits or ceiling for the equipment cost using index numbers. It is possible through the budgeting process for individual companies to establish guidelines as to the allowable percentage above the equipment price to cover other nonequipment expenses and avoid spending $100,000 on a $50,000 piece of equipment.

The most important consideration comes in knowing what the buying organization really wants with respect to the equipment. If it is the plain vanilla piece of equipment, then that is the equipment to purchase. If it is the fully loaded model with all the customization, then that is the correct model to purchase. A buyer who is not sure of what is wanted will always pay too much. The buyer who never knows what he or she wants can never know if the organization has received any real value from the purchase.

A buyer who never fully determines what is needed has made the seller's job simple. All the salesperson must do is convince the buyer that the product is the best of the unknowns. This is a simple task since there are no comparisons or standards or yardsticks to measure.

Checklist for Pricing Capital Equipment

- ☐ How has the pricing process begun?
    - ☐ single quoted solicited
    - ☐ competitive bids
- ☐ If there are multiple bids, how extensive are the deviations:
    - ☐ between the bid specifications?
    - ☐ between the responses?
    - ☐ and have bidders been contacted to determine the reason why?
- ☐ Is it possible to establish a baseline or benchmark on the specifications so that deviations can be measured from the benchmark?
- ☐ What proportion of the deviations are:
    - ☐ Needed?
    - ☐ Nice to have?
- ☐ Are the basic requirements or specifications comparable?
- ☐ Is there one bid that can be used as the baseline for comparison purposes?
- ☐ Who are the other users of the machine?
    - ☐ Have they been contacted?
    - ☐ Are there lesser-volume items that could be made on the machine?
    - ☐ What are the tooling costs?
- ☐ Has information been obtained on what was purchased, and when and for how much from these customers?
- ☐ What was their experience on promised delivery and actual delivery?

11

Total Cost of Ownership

No book in this area would be complete without addressing the issue of total cost of ownership of the equipment. Sometimes called **life cycle costing,** this approach involves looking well beyond the initial cost to estimate the total cost incurred over the life of the equipment. The emphasis is placed on the long term, as opposed to looking at the initial costs associated with the purchase. This means that a higher initial cost may represent the best long-term value. The cost of ownership must also consider output from the equipment. Without the measure of productivity, even total cost of ownership comparisons are lacking. Equipment is dynamic. A piece of capital equipment produces units of output. If the output of machine A is 5 percent greater than machine B, then the allowable total cost of machine A can be up to 5 percent greater than B and still be a better investment. Productivity is the key issue.

There may have to be analyses of second-generation productivity. For example, helicopter engines traditionally go in for overhaul after a number of flying hours. Do overhauled engines give the same service life as the new engine? If the overhauled unit gives 60 percent of the lifetime performance of the new engine, then the maximum that should be paid for the overhaul is 60 percent of the cost of the new engine. At what point does it make sense to retire the equipment because the incremental operating cost per unit is beginning to increase above the cost of the same item produced on a new piece of equipment?

Multiple machines may be capable of producing the same product or performing the same function. Yet the cost of machine A in terms of fixed and variable costs may differ significantly from that of machine B. The difference is such that total costs at different volumes show it is economical to shift from one machine to another as volume increases. The process of comparing these options leads to the development of a **crossover chart,** shown in Exhibit 11-1. In the chart, the shifting slope of the total cost function is such that at various volumes of output, it is better to employ one machine rather than the other. As volume increases, the choice becomes more obvious. The favored machine is the one with a higher fixed cost and lower variable cost.

As output increases, the fixed costs are allocated over an increasing base,

Exhibit 11-1. Crossover chart.

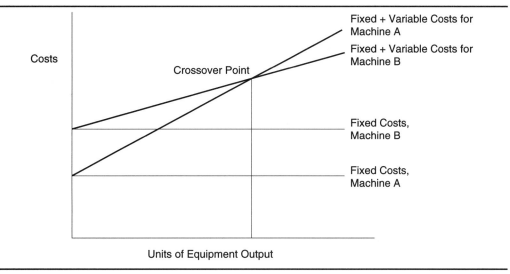

Costs

Crossover Point

Fixed + Variable Costs for Machine A

Fixed + Variable Costs for Machine B

Fixed Costs, Machine B

Fixed Costs, Machine A

Units of Equipment Output

and the lower variable cost per unit slows the rate of growth of total cost. Thus, the unit cost growth increases at a decreasing rate. If only the initial cost were considered in the decision, the higher fixed-cost equipment might never be a serious candidate. This is the key issue in total cost of ownership and the weakness in much of the financial analysis. Looking only at the initial cost, as is done in many buying and construction situations, the decision maker ignores the reality of any operating piece of equipment: Parts wear out, tolerances are exceeded by friction, the elements degrade finishes, and metal fatigue takes its toll. Equipment must be maintained if it is to survive.

Any organization that does not realize that capital expenditures are prime drivers of operating budgets should not be in business. It is ignoring reality and will eventually pay the price for it. Even if the costs of maintaining the equipment come from other budgets in the organization, ignoring the driving impact of capital projects is myopic. At some point, the piper must be paid. This can lead to the selection of the option of fixing it for now and catching it later. The need for maintenance does not go away, and what might be a small problem today becomes a large one tomorrow. Duct tape and bailing wire go only so far. As far as the variable costs are concerned, these represent direct cash outlays on the part of the company. Any improvements that reduce the variable costs may quickly pay for the additional expenditure at the time of equipment purchase.

The equipment must be viewed over its total life, even if the funding for spare parts and maintenance comes from other budgets in the organization. Looking only at initial cost is tantamount to worrying only about the visible ice in the iceberg. The captain of the *Titanic* made that error in 1912. Low initial costs can be deceptive. Low initial costs also can be purposeful on the part of the supplier to entice the buyer and then have a captive customer for spare parts and supplies. Initial costs are simply one segment of the cost structure and do not reflect the investment in the equipment over the life span. This is a rather simplistic approach, but it does open the discussion of total cost of owning and operating the equipment. The subject goes under several labels, including life cycle costing, total cost of possession, and total cost of ownership. Regardless of the label, the focus is on *all costs associated with the equipment,* from determination of the need to transfer of title in the disposal phase.

The Components of Total Costs

Labor Productivity

Consider labor productivity. How many units will be processed per time period? Let us say that the automotive assembly line capable of assembling 60 cars per hour is modified so that output is raised to 63 per hour—a 5 percent increase in output—without any increase in labor costs. Material costs are constant, but the labor portion of the variable cost has declined by 5 percent. This increase in productivity reduces the labor cost immediately. (Do not be shocked if labor wants a share in those gains when the collective bargaining agreement comes up for negotiation.) Therefore, it is not just the capability of the equipment to produce but also the rate of production. This rate is obviously linked to demand for the product or service, and therefore the decision must be viewed in terms of that demand. If it is low, then the more expensive machine may not be justified due to the higher cost per unit generated by that machine. Higher demand causes us to rethink the decision in the light of lower unit costs. The issue is that a single number with respect to cost is almost meaningless unless there is only one option available for the decision. Introduce more than one alternative, and there are now choices to be evaluated.

Energy Consumption

Energy consumption can be a significant segment of operating costs; indeed, such items as electric motors will consume many times their initial cost in power over the service life of the equipment. Power consumption data should be available from the manufacturer of the equipment, and turning that into a dollar figure is a simple task. The data in Exhibit 11-2 show the relationship among three key variables—energy consumption, maintenance costs, and initial investment—when looking at four types of equipment: a lighting system, an electric motor, an oil-fired furnace, and an automobile.

Exhibit 11-2. Total lifetime costs.

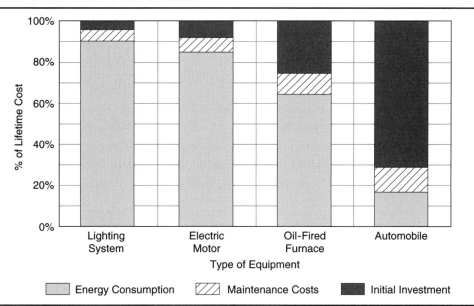

The Human Element

Factored into the total cost of ownership is the human element:

- Who will operate the equipment, and how will the selection of the operator be made? (In the union environment, it will probably be bid, most likely on seniority.)
- What will it cost to train the operator?
- How long will training take?
- Where will the training take place?
- How will training be evaluated?
- What role will the supplier play in the training effort?
- What does the supplier have available to aid in the training process?
- Are there videotapes illustrating the machine's operation?
- What proportion of the initial cost has been allocated to the training effort of the machine operator(s)?
- When is the operator fully qualified on the machine?
- What is the material spoilage or waste factor that has been added into the total cost for this phase of bringing the machine on line and into full operation?

A **white elephant** is a machine ready to be used but lacking the skilled personnel to operate it or the demand to make its use economical. There are numerous white elephants in industry today. Many are computers that never attain their computational capability for the lack of trained personnel who can utilize them fully.

Machine Design

The machine design issue is a factor. Returning to the basics, the productivity of the equipment will be influenced by an array of factors:

• *Accessibility for maintenance and repair.* How easily can repairs, adjustments, or maintenance be performed? Is the portion of the equipment subject to maintenance activities easily accessible? What proportion of the time will be spent on reaching the problem versus resolving the problem? The classic example is the automobile. In an effort to reduce weight and increase miles per gallon of gasoline while also adding creature comforts, the area beneath the hood has become a maze of wires, belts, and parts. It is far beyond the capability of the average person to effect any type of repair and is a guarantee of future business for the dealer in maintenance and repair. At $60 per hour and up for labor, accessibility becomes an expensive issue.

• *Design with respect to energy consumption.* Is the equipment energy efficient—and efficient compared to what? What is the energy consumption rate of the equipment? Does its use take place during peak consumption times, or does it operate off peak? How much does energy consumption add per operating hour? One company wanting to avoid finding itself in a peak demand rate category caused by a power surge had a maintenance person come into the plant one hour before the start of the day shift and put four 100 horsepower electric drive air compressors on line in 15-minute intervals.

• *Emissions from fossil fuel burning.* Does the operation of the equipment create emissions that may lead to clean air problems and call for additional investment in particle scrubbers (environmental investments that have no return on investment beyond the social one)? Equipment that reduces costs in one area but creates costs in others may not be the bargain it appears to be. The view must be toward total cost. What will be the total cost of the installation of the new equipment, and has the design of that equipment created secondary costs that are now not present in the operation?

• *Scrap generated in the manufacturing process.* How much **scrap**—the planned residue from an operation—will be created by the new equipment? Scrap reduction can become a cost-reducing element of total cost of production. The new equipment may be capable of more precision and therefore reduce the scrap or deliver it in such a manner that it may have higher secondary market value. At the Remington Arms facility in Illion, New York, walnut gun stocks are turned and finished. The raw stock, called a *flitch,* weighs 5 pounds.

The turned stock weighs 2.5 pounds. The 50 percent loss wood is used as fuel to heat a segment of the plant.

Scrap can take many forms. Consider other uses of energy conservation during the winter—for example, running the cooling water from the electric drive air compressor into the heating system. In one case this flow reduced heating cost by 50 percent. Another situation is a college campus that was dotted with lovely fountains. The water for the fountains came from the air-conditioning system, and cooling by aeration reduced cooling costs by 30 percent during the summer.

The Maintenance Program

The maintenance program is an element in computing any total cost of ownership. What type of maintenance will be undertaken? Undertaking preventive maintenance can go a long way in eliminating catastrophic failures. Preventive maintenance also equates to periodic downtime, the cost of maintenance, and money spent for spare parts, as well as possibly discarding parts prior to the end of their service life. There must be a balance achieved.

How does one determine the route to follow? The answer lies in simulation of the failure of key components or the use of supplier-provided failure curves. Once having simulated or determined the failure rates, a policy of replacement is established using decision rules such as these:

• When the probability of failure reaches 50 percent [this equates to a finite number of hours of operation or units of output], replace the unit.

• When a unit fails, replace it and all other units having a probability of failure over 50 percent. [This is the case where accessibility is an important issue and if the machine is torn down for maintenance, there is no reason not to make it an extensive process. What is the teardown cost?]

• Repair only what fails. [This is the light bulb example, where accessibility is easy and repair is effected rapidly. Why keep records and also throw away a unit that still has some service life in it?]

What is the percentage of spares that are repair parts that cannot be repaired themselves as opposed to spares that are replacement items capable of being repaired? At what level must the spare repair take place? Can that work be done in-house or must the spare parts be returned to the original equipment manufacturer (OEM) for repair? What are the associated costs of repair versus replace? What *is* repair? Is repair of the spare part simply replacement of one or two key components such as a metal rod in a small pump that turns when a current passes through it, or does it consist of reworking, as in the case of a mold or rewinding a generator? Does the entire part become scrap, or only a portion of it? This is worthy of investigation in the early part of the decision process. Is the design going to create a demand for parts or services later in the life cycle? Is the buyer going to become entrapped in the unique design such that there are no sources of spare parts or tools and the buyer must keep returning to the OEM for support? A lack of understanding of the implications of uniqueness is the gateway to dependency. Companies have been known to sell below cost just to get the equipment in the door.

Maintenance encompasses both labor and material and will take place in the future. Economists maintain that these costs have to be discounted to bring them back to the present time for side-by-side comparisons of options. Yet both variables of labor and materials are subject to inflationary pressures. The repair work costing $25 today will cost $35 three or four years from now (unless there has been a marked change in the economy). Therefore, the idea of discounting to compute the present value will be offset by the increasing costs of the parts and labor into the future. Assuming the discount rate and inflation to be equal, it then becomes a matter of summing future maintenance costs at today's prices over the life of the equipment. The difficult part is evaluating costs as the machine comes to the end of its service life. Here one must rely on failure frequency curves or analysis. Certain parts will never fail; they are the static parts. Dynamic components or static parts coming in contact with dynamic components are subject to wear. As the frequency of failure of dynamic components increases, there is a cutoff point where replacement is advantageous to repair.

Supplier responsibility for life cycle costing can come in many forms. This includes the designing of the equipment to make it maintenance free or reducing the accessibility problem. There are ways to bring about this result in the design phase:

• *Permanent lubrication of units.* By design, components can be permanently sealed with lubricant and thus reduce the need for lubrication. Another option is in the initial design where lubrication can be performed at one central location on the equipment.

• *High-reliability components or redundant systems.* These systems can be designed into the equipment to reduce or eliminate catastrophic failures. Although redundancy costs money, its presence can be quite cost-effective. Another option is to use electronic fault detectors that will shut down the equipment to prevent a major crash. Simple systems also exist, such as magnetized screens in cooling systems to screen out metallic particles that may contaminate the coolant.

• *Periodic replacement.* This may avoid any form of more serious or detailed maintenance by protecting expensive components. The air cleaner on automobiles filters air going into the carburetor, thereby protecting it and its performance from small particles that would seriously degrade its performance.

• *Simple maintenance,* such as checking fluid levels, filters, or gaskets and having them readily accessible for replacement.

• *Data.* The supplier can provide data to the customer in terms of mean time to failure, failure curves, scheduled replacement in terms of hours of operation, as well as indicators of the need to repair or replace.

• *Warning systems.* In the design phase, attention should be paid to the issue of feedback systems that warn the operator to attend to potential maintenance actions. The simplest example is the copier that tells the operator of the need for fluid or when the machine is jammed and where the problem is located. Suppliers can also provide training data on videotapes detailing repair procedures and indicating the repairs that must be undertaken and how. These are fail-safe systems that are the essential feedback loops on the equipment. They are as important as the equipment itself.

Royal Caribbean Cruise Lines found this out the hard way. The lube oil pump on one of its ships, *Sovereign of the Seas,* failed on one of its four main diesel engines. The engine seized up in 4.5 minutes. This reduced the ship's speed from 19 knots to 15 knots per hour, resulting in the elimination of one port of call—and refunds of $100 per stateroom. Continuing to operate in this fashion for four weeks, the 2,246-passenger liner made four 7-day cruises. The refunds alone amounted to $450,000 plus the goodwill lost in a highly competitive market.

Periodically checking the checker is not a bad idea.

An ongoing supplier responsibility is the maintenance bulletin or periodic updates on maintenance issues to advise owners of changes in procedures or possible problems that may be occurring with the equipment after it has been in operation at the customer's site for some period of time. It is nothing more than a warning system for potential problems or problems that have occurred with other users. If the frequency is sufficient, the supplier has a moral responsibility to alert the customers. In addition, customers should report problems back to suppliers.

Inventory Stocking Levels Associated With Spare Parts

Who has the spares responsibility? Do we stock ourselves or do we let the supplier stock and employ premium transportation? Obviously, the physical characteristics have a great deal to do with that decision, yet there are trade-offs to consider on the site issue.

Addressing the issues related to spare parts, the buyer is faced with a number of cost issues as they relate to the spare parts stocking level. How many sources are available for the spares? Many sources create the competitive environment that lowers costs. Many sources assure availability that reduces or eliminates downtime. Many sources ensure a willingness on the part of suppliers to make such concessions as supplier stocking and consignment purchasing possible. Many sources can reduce the lead time for spares acquisition. Thus, the competitiveness of the spare parts business is an influencing force on both stock levels of spares and their costs.

When are the spares acquired? At the time of machine purchase or when failure occurs or replacement is necessary? Acquisition at time of purchase may be more cost-effective, but the inventory costs money to carry and there is a possibility that the spare parts may outlast the machine on which they fit by not wearing out.

Where is the inventory located? Is it necessary to have the spare parts on site, or can the financial commitment be made to the spares supplier and a spares stocking program initiated? This could give greater flexibility to the customer by reducing the likelihood of buying spares that are not needed. This is accomplished by carefully monitoring the spare parts consumption patterns and incorporating the results into the composition of any spare parts kit. Albeit this is difficult to determine with new equipment, but the alert supplier can offer inducements to the buyer in the form of refunds on spares not used to aid in "selling the right spares" when the machine is purchased.

Agreeing on Yardsticks

Although total cost of ownership is a superior method of making cost comparisons, it is not without its problems. Many of the issues, however, are a result of the orientation of the individual making the decisions. Accountants think in accounting terms; engineers view the issues from a technical or operational perspective. Problems arise when these perspectives come into conflict with each other. If positions on issues harden, the evaluation of the total cost of ownership becomes very complex. Each side may be talking in its own language and not viewing the cost in its totality. This is not to say there is one correct answer to each problem or question, but simply that there must be agreement on the measuring tools used. Each team member agrees to apply the same yardsticks in his or her own area of expertise. If this is not agreed to in the beginning of the process, measuring becomes an exercise in futility and a frustration to all concerned. There are two key issues here:

1. *Accounting life vs. service life.* For tax purposes, assets have a **defined life,** the period of time over which they can be depreciated, and theoretically monies are set aside for their replacement. Since this is a set-aside, depreciation is subtracted from gross profits, thereby relieving the business from taxation on monies that will be used for replacement of assets at the appropriate time. The issue is: What is the appropriate time? Going beyond the depreciation schedule, the equipment may still have years of acceptable service in it. That its replacement has been paid for may have absolutely nothing to do with its performance. The argument for accelerated depreciation is an accounting issue in many cases. There are reasonable arguments for the acceleration with high-technology equipment, but there must be some meeting of the minds on the issue of how long it really lasts or when it will be replaced. What is the service life of the equipment?

2. *Residual value.* Prediction of the value of a piece of equipment a decade or a generation into the future is educated guessing. Anyone can point to any number of items carrying large price tags that have had their value disappear in the marketplace. Other items appreciate in value as time proves them to be good values in both the past and the future. Government regulations have converted "trash into treasures" and the march of technology comes out with products that last longer but are priced at 10 times the value of the system.[1]

A simple rule could be to set the residual value at zero. This approach has several advantages. If the philosophy of the company is that the residual value is zero, there is no reason not to modify the equipment or customize it to meet the company needs and increase productivity or reduce product costs. The customized machine will have no economic value at the end of its lifetime. Why not capture the benefits of modifications? In addition, the customization can add value to the equipment. The tax treatment of the sales or disposal of the equipment is an accounting issue and should not be confused with the technical capability of the equipment. In addition, that which may happen in a decade should not be the rationale to sacrifice productivity gains now.

Standardization

If there is one lesson to be learned that has been missed by the vast number of companies in this country, it has to be the classic words of Henry Ford: "Any color you want, as long as it's black." A profound message was sent with that simple sentence. Failure to standardize has cost billions of dollars to companies in every conceivable cost area. Lack of standardization means more inventories

---

1. Consider the stainless steel exhaust system for automobiles. It will last the life of the car, but if it needs replacement, be prepared to spend $1,800 on its stainless replacement. This is about 10 times as much as the conventional metal exhaust system.

of parts, more tools, more training, more time spent maintaining, and therefore more total costs. This does not mean that every unit is the exact clone of its predecessor; what it does mean is the proper classification of the function to be performed by the equipment.

One midwestern city had 108 different makes and models of cars and trucks in its vehicle fleet. Each purchase was done independently, and there was little effort to look beyond the purchase price. Cheapest was best. There was no appreciation for the ancillary costs that would follow in terms of parts, tools, and maintenance productivity.

It is obvious that there had to be more than one type of truck, but the automobiles could have been standardized into two categories: public safety, such as police cars and fire department vehicles, and non-public-safety, which would encompass all others. In the area of trucks, the range went from the light panel truck to the dump trucks to the cherry pickers. Standardization is somewhat more difficult here, but could there be standardization on the frame of the vehicle, with the starting component being the cab and the flatbed? Panel and light pickup trucks could all come from the same assembler.

Standardization can wear many faces. A simple matrix approach listing the desired characteristics on the vertical scale and the models on the horizontal, with checks in the cells, can help identify candidates for standardization. Consider the expense if the average consumer were to purchase the right vehicle for the job. The sedan would be needed to go to work. The minivan is essential to take the children to their activities. The pickup truck is needed for the trips to the hardware store or lumber yard. The station wagon is essential for vacations. Yet the seats come out of the minivan, and it opens from the rear. It is designed to perform many functions. Its popularity is proof that versatility is a component of standardization. The panel truck might be replaced by the minivan.

It may not be possible to carry standardization to its extreme, yet there are opportunities that are continuously missed by claims of a "special need" that can be satisfied by only one particular brand of equipment. This is an area where life cycle costing can play a significant role in looking at the cost of the standard versus the outlier over the life cycle of the item. Having a standard, the "special" is evaluated on the basis of the *incremental* cost associated with that special. What will the special cost over and above the standard, and therefore what are the costs of the special capability needed? The requisitioner of that special must consider all the costs normally associated with going beyond the standard:

- Spare parts carried in stock
- Special tools needed
- Maintenance training needed
- Average maintenance cost per year
- Training time or contract maintenance cost
- Downtime awaiting contract maintenance and maintenance action
- Difference in initial cost
- Energy consumption

Proliferation outside the standard raises the overall costs. If the incremental costs clearly outweigh the benefits, then the special need is questionable, and other options should be explored, such as outsourcing or leasing.

There is no simple answer to this issue. The request for the nonstandard item may be totally legitimate or may be based on a variety of motives. Past experience with the nonstandard is present, and learning on the new machine or system will require extra effort. Requirements may differ between units or elements of the organization, and the standard is not designed to perform that function.

Rather than dwelling on reasons *against* standardization, how does one make it work? The first approach is to look at possible areas of standardization. What equipment can be standardized? The answer here will probably be support equipment rather than production or line equipment. Once the possible opportunities have been defined, the next step is getting the users involved. It is amazing how equipment purchases involving the users seem to work better. The process is as much psychological as anything else. The user is part of the evaluation and selection and becomes a stakeholder in the process. The user sees the trade-offs that must be made. The user is part of the process, not simply the recipient of the end result.

It will be the user who will generate that requisition, so user involvement and approval or agreement are essential. This translates to a committee. As onerous as the term sounds, getting together to discuss the issues and define the parameters is essential. The objective is standardization, but if the user has a specific need that the standard cannot satisfy and the special is needed, all the buyer wants is some estimate of the incremental or additional costs generated by the special. It is simple cost-benefit analysis.

At this juncture, one might be tempted to take the requisitioner's position of, "It's *my* money; buy what *I* want." Yet the cost goes far beyond the initial purchase price since the outlier will have to be maintained, repaired, and supported over its service life, and the accounting system may not be capable of tracking that one single item or the maintenance budget is a lump sum in the organization. If this is the case, a computerized maintenance management system (CMMS) is really needed. The objective is not to be punitive or limit options, but simply to point out the costs of nonstandardization in the organization.

Once standardization becomes part of the organizational culture, it will not encounter the barriers now present. Standardization is not conformity for the sake of conformity but the elimination of waste or costs associated with marginal or questionable value.

Standardization typically has been overlooked as one of the cost savings methodologies for a variety of reasons, including these:

• A lack of understanding that standardization is not designed to limit choice but to define the function to be performed and select the best piece of equipment to perform that function. It is not buying the cheapest, and, in fact, the initial cost can be much higher than alternatives. It may mean buying the more expensive to achieve the versatility needed.

• The connotation of limiting freedom of choice, an affront to the requisitioner. This person's needs are being subjugated and replaced by the appropriate standard, and he or she is out of the decision process. Personal involvement is a strong force, and this is why total cost of ownership must be the criterion. Adding the special costs money.

• A focus or orientation on the single purchase, not the impact of this purchase as it relates to all the other similar types of equipment in the organization. The equipment purchase is just one part of the entire process.

Standardization does not work because people do not want it to work. They do not wish a limitation on their freedom of choice, nor do they consider the totality of costs. Many of the experiences in standardization have come from either the military or the bureaucracy of various governmental units, and the good of standardization is often submerged in the inefficiency of these institutions. Standardization encompasses a degree of conformity that people basically dislike and fight, even in passive ways.

It is a management responsibility to fight this war over and over again. The lack of understanding of the impact of standardization is frightening. Where it has been understood, the results are amazing.

Southwest Airlines is a model of standardization. The airline has shown a profit in 103 of its 104 quarters of operation and is still considered the lowest-priced carrier in domestic service. Uniformity of aircraft, operations, procedures, and policies has made it a profit leader in the industry. Using the same model of aircraft, it gets maximum use from each airplane, minimizes turnaround time, and has won the triple crown, awarded to the airline with the best on-time departure record, the highest on-time arrival rate, and the shortest waiting time for luggage, for five straight years.[2]

Setting the Scene

There are no simple answers to the collection and proper application of the tools of total cost of ownership. Using a life cycle costing approach is complex; it requires effort, knowledge, and good data collection skills. It requires as well good decision rules for maintenance, repair, and replacement and may be expensive since "good" parts may be discarded before the end of the service life. The solution to this problem is creativity or common sense.

East Kentucky Power replaces post hole digger vehicles every 10 years. The post hole digging equipment is removed from the vehicle, sent to an outside source for rebuilding, and then placed on a new chassis. The expected life of the digger itself is 20 years. By separating the chassis from the functional component of the vehicle, a good digger is not discarded before the end of its service life.

There may be some corporate infighting to resolve issues of service life versus accounting life and residual values. They certainly require forethought and careful planning. It is a given that a visionary horizon of years is needed with the emphasis on the entire life cycle, not just the initial purchase. It must be supported by records and their ongoing analysis. The computer using a good CMMS system offers that opportunity.

Figuring Out Total Costs

One approach to development is to select the efforts of someone else by purchasing a life cycle cost model from a known developer and using it. This can be a rather inexpensive process. Some of the models available are shown in Exhibit 11-3. (This is not a complete survey of the market, but just a capsule view.) Analysts interested in using a modeling approach should attend a seminar on the subject of life cycle costing or at least get a demonstration of what goes into the proposed model. Reference the Internet by using the term "life cycle cost."

2. The airline uses the Boeing 737 in several configurations and sizes, but all are 737s.

Exhibit 11-3. Life cycle cost analysis tools.

Model Name	Source	Major Use	Price
Building Life Cycle Cost (BLLC)	Energy Information Services P.O. Box 381 St. Johnsbury, Vt. 05819-0381 (802) 748-5184	Buildings and building systems—long-term model, has three major subprograms	No cost, downloadable
Life Cycle Cost in Design (LCCID)	Blast Support Office 1206 West Green St. 140 M.E. Building Urbana, Ill. 61801 (800) UI-BLAST	Ranks design alternatives for new and existing buildings, standard	$100
LIFE	Elite Software P.O. Drawer 1194 Bryan, Texas 77806 (409) 846-2340	Basic economic analysis using present worth method of life cycle cost analysis; breaks project into phases and looks at all costs	No cost given
Right-$	Wright Associates 394 Lowell Street Lexington, Mass. 02173	Heating and cooling equipment analysis program	$329
Life-Cycle 2.0	Carmel Software Corp. 27060 Cedar Rd. Beachwood, Ohio 44122 (800) 339-6030	Life cycle cost analysis for private-sector building investments	$195
LC2M Life Cycle Cost Analysis	MC^2 Engineering Software 8107 S.W. 72d Ave. Miami, Fla. 33143 (305) 665-0100	Computes total life cycle owning costs over the life of equipment	$115, license
Engineering Economic Analysis	Carrier Corp. P.O. Box 4808 Carrier Parkway Syracuse, N.Y. 13221 (315) 433-4247	Life cycle of HVAC systems	$95 (annual renewal fee of $20)

Source: Geoexchange Information Center. This is but one source of the hundreds that exist. The issue becomes one of screening the inventory as opposed to creating one with well-known and easily programmed spreadsheets, available in most organizations.

The problem with commercially available models is the spectrum of coverage. Commercial models have a broad range capability and therefore may miss part of the individual needs and requirements or include parts of the model that are not appropriate or applicable to the given situation.

The review process should provide ideas as to what is available and how well it may fit the individual situation. It may also provide information on what data are considered essential for costing. Before buying commercial, review the model to see if it contains the cost elements that are really drivers in your situation and if the data gathering process to provide input into the model will be beyond the capability of the organization.

In many of the available models, the data requirements are extensive, and the model operates with the data provided. If the data are no good, do not expect the model to cleanse them or make them good. The advantage of using the commercially available model is its availability and cost relative to the development of an in-house model for life cycle costing.

The development of the internal life cycle cost model is an iterative process. It is best considered in stages and begins with the process of identifying the cost elements of each activity in each of the stages. Some costs are estimates, and some are based on experience from similar purchases. Some are budgeted costs, as in the case of travel expenses for visiting other users of the equipment. While the standard argument may be, "You are working here and being paid, regardless of what you are doing," the determination of life cycle costs requires an activity-based costing approach. In order for the numbers to have some meaning, it may be necessary to group or categorize items purchased into different categories—for example, by dollar value, duration of the depreciation period, or service life. This differentiation is needed so similar items are compared. Spending $20,000 in support costs for a $1 million machine may be totally justified; spending that same amount on a $20,000 machine is excessive. Identifying these costs forces the buyer to look beyond the equipment cost and recognize the need for additional funds to be available to cover these necessary expenses. Failure to cover them in the first stage may give rise to second-stage costs that could have been avoided.

The first step is the agreement of what shall be included in each of the stages. This is one function of the team.

The three stages of the life cycle of the equipment are:

• *Stage I—Acquisition.* This includes all activities and costs associated with purchasing the equipment. It begins with the need determination by the user through all parts of the buying process, and ends with the acceptance of the equipment and placement into operation in its operating environment.

• *Stage II—Maintenance.* This includes all activities and costs associated with maintaining the equipment while in operation or available for operation. Included in this stage are all forms of maintenance activities on the equipment, retrofitting, modifications, or upgrading the equipment.

• *Stage III—Disposal.* This includes all activities associated with the decommissioning of the equipment, including any refurbishing, cleaning, preparation for shipment, preparation for "mothballing" or storage, preservation, or packaging. This stage also includes any costs associated with equipment disposal such as advertising, auction commissions, or transportation, as well as disposal of hazardous waste associated with the equipment (such as PCBs in the case of transformers).

Stage I

Following are the costs associated with Stage I:

- The basic item of equipment (the base price from the manufacturer without any options)
- The options as ordered—installed at either the OEM or the distributor level
- The transportation and installation of the equipment
- Testing at the supplier's site (includes material, travel, and analysis of test results)
- Visits to installed sites
- Spare parts purchased at time of delivery of equipment
- Making ready the equipment site
- Testing or meeting acceptance criteria prior to payment for equipment
- Progress payments made to the supplier prior to receipt of the equipment[3]
- Training operators, documentation, and programming that may be associated with the equipment
- Import duties, use of special agents, currency losses or gains, and fees associated with overseas purchases
- Additional tools for maintenance of the equipment (metric versus English measurements)
- Paperwork and documentation associated with all phases of this stage, from requisition to acceptance, in both hours and dollars
- Bringing the equipment into compliance with U.S. requirements for health, safety, and environmental requirements, such as emission control[4]

3. This cost is often excluded from the calculation of total costs. It is the earnings forgone by having to make progress payments to the supplier, prior to having the equipment producing goods. Capital is tied up and making no return on investment. This figure represents that which could have been made had the funds not been sent as progress payments to the supplier. It is an opportunity cost concept.

4. This is listed as a separate category because of its importance. The compliance issue should be addressed very early in the equipment selection process. Bringing a piece of equipment into compliance can be frustrating and expensive. In addition, environmental expenditures bring no tangible return on investment. Environmental regulations have a tendency to proliferate and

By far, Stage I contains the majority of costs and the most diverse sets of costs. Some are pure expenses, and some must be depreciated over the life of the equipment. By the time all are accumulated, the buyer has a complete picture of the costs and is ready to articulate the following ratios:

- *Equipment cost to total cost.* What percentage of the total cost is made up of the equipment versus the cost of buying the equipment? Remember that it is the equipment that is going to generate revenue, and this figure provides some idea as to how much of a burden the machine is really going to carry.
- *Expense items to total cost.* What proportion of the total cost is made up of costs that are simply expenses and would be incurred if the work was done and for some reason the equipment was not purchased?
- *Support costs to machine costs.* What fraction of the machine costs (base plus accessories) is being spent for tools, spares stocking, and expendable supplies?

In the initial calculation, these are indicators. Eventually they may become guidelines for planning the expenditure for capital equipment. Recognize the need for flexibility in thinking. For example, domestic spare availability is different from foreign spares availability.

The issues faced in Stage I of the life cycle cost approach include these:

- *How much of total cost is really equipment?* Upgrading on the equipment may not add that much more to the total cost of the stage and may save money in the next stage by reducing the outlay for spares or maintenance by having longer maintenance intervals or lower energy consumption. In addition, upgrading during the initial production of the equipment may be far less expensive than upgrading at some later stage in the machine's life. Adding features later may not be possible or practical. ·
- *Do expenditures in the early stages of the buying process improve that process or add little to it?* Consider the expenditures for site visits of the installed equipment. This money is probably the best investment made outside the equipment itself. It allows the potential buyer to see the equipment in operation, discuss the equipment with a user, and get first-hand information about the operation, maintenance, and reliability of the equipment. Actually seeing the equipment in operation may trigger the light to be turned on in the mind of the observers. This is money well spent. Although it is impossible to quantify the return on investment (ROI) associated with this information gathering, the information garnered from these visits has great value. Other investments relative to the

---

become impossible to meet realistically. There is no point in starting out with an environmental problem with the equipment. It will not get better, only worse, since the people who draft the legislation are often uninformed as to the nature of the equipment, the process, and the problems.

equipment can have significant returns also. Adding a CMMS can have significant value in determining overall maintenance costs.

• *Has the company adopted guidelines for nonequipment expenditures relating to the purchases of equipment* for such areas as site visits and testing and in-process inspection and acceptance? A rule of thumb could be the addition of 10 percent to the purchase price to cover contingencies related to the purchase. Are the proportions or the percentages reasonable by class or type of expenditure? Do not look for equality of expenditure percentages. Lower-cost items may run at 10 to 25 percent for nonequipment costs of total costs. At the upper end of the equipment cost scale, the figure may drop to 15 percent or less. The buying organization should budget a floor percentage for nonequipment expenses. This is not a cost overrun on the equipment but the extra expenses incurred in the buying process. This percentage should vary by the size of the equipment expenditure, with the percentage being inversely related to the equipment cost. A $25,000 purchase could need $5,000 worth of extra costs; a $1 million purchase might need $50,000 in extra expenses.

Estimating and Tracking Costs

A first step is to summarize the cost associated with the purchase of the piece of equipment. A simple system will suffice initially, with a brief project description. These are the costs associated with Stage I. Exhibit 11-4 shows a sample cost sheet. The cost tracking allows the buyer to track estimates to the actual and compute the variance associated with each of the estimates. The value of this approach is that costs are not hidden and the true cost of this stage is established or estimated *before* the project is undertaken.

The buyer can use the Comments section to reference other documents, such as bids for other services that may be included in the overall transaction. The sources of the information include the quotes, the purchase orders, and allied documents.

Analyzing Stage I Cost Data

Analysis of Stage I data now shows the key ratios to be:

Equipment to total cost:	$24,800/$38,470 = 64.5% (without options)
	$31,000/$38,470 = 80.5% (with options)
Options to base price:	$6,200/$24,800 = 25%
Expense to total cost:	$7,700/$46,070 = 16.7% (this ratio includes items 4, 5, 8, 10, and 13)[5]

5. What is included in this category is open to endless debate. It should include all costs that are "sunk" in the sense they are nonrecoverable and are for such items as travel, training, and time consumed on a project that did not work out.

Exhibit 11-4. Cost summary for Stage I.

Project No.: _____   Project Mgr.: _____

Project Description: _____

_____
_____
_____
_____

Cost Factor	Estimated Cost	Actual Cost	Variance	Comments
1. Basic equipment cost	$24,800			12 weeks lead time
2. Options	$6,200			Installed by domestic representative
3. Transportation and installation	$1,200			See RFQ 12223 for details. Check on in-transit insurance
4. Testing at supplier's site	1. Travel, $1,400 2. materials, $300 3. 1-day evaluation, $200 Total, $1,900			1-day trip for 3 people (QA, Mfg. Eng., and Operator)
5. Site visits	$1,800			Mfg., QA, and Maint. to two sites
6. Cost of spares	$1,600 recommended spares list			Review after site visits
7. Make-ready costs	$760 for labor (15 std. hours) $210 for materials			220-volt outlets, 80 p.s.i. air
8. Acceptance criteria testing	$1,200 if passes, 2,400 for second test.			Materials, labor, supervision, and analysis
9. Progress payments	N.A. Terms net 30 days			Depend on acceptance tests
10. Personnel costs	$1,500 (estimated)			Operator training, trial runs, and videos
11. Foreign purchase costs	None. U.S. representative handles as part of price			
12. Additional tools/ costs to meet U.S. standards	None. Foreign producer builds to U.S. requirements			Verify and include in warranty

(continues)

Exhibit 11-4. *Continued*

Cost Factor	Estimated Cost	Actual Cost	Variance	Comments
13. Paperwork costs	Estimated at $2,500			Based on time estimates provided by key personnel
14. Other factors (specify)				
_____				
_____				
_____				
_____				
_____				
15. Miscellaneous				
16. Total	$38,470–$46,070			Approved AR 56-223

The values for the numerators of the ratios may be varied depending upon what costs are included and what is excluded. The integrity of the ratios and their value is enhanced by including all the costs associated with the purchase, even if these costs are in different budgets. A common way of masking the true cost of the equipment and the process of buying it is hiding costs in other budgets. This subterfuge is sometimes used to make a poor investment look good from a financial perspective.

A look at the results shows 80 percent of the total cost going into the machine, its options, transportation, make-ready, and installation. The maximum downside risk is less than $8,700 on the project, with the worst case being cancellation of the order just before shipping.

Stage II: Costing

Stage II of the life cycle is more complex since it involves the maintenance of the equipment and all the unpredictability with respect to failures and spare parts costs. In addition, certain operating expenses and depreciation must be charged against the equipment to develop a cost per hour or overhead rate to charge on the machine time. This computation is complicated by the issue of anticipated use of the machine over an annual period. An additional factor is the distinct possibility that more than one machine is capable of producing the same product. If this is the case, then it is possible to produce the product on machine A and make a per-unit profit on the output. The same product can be made on machine B and lose money on each unit, all depending on the burden that each carries.[6] These issues can be addressed by the accountants.

The problem facing the buyer in Stage II is the division between routine and/or preventive maintenance and failure maintenance. In theory, if the former is properly performed and monitored, the chances for the latter decline significantly. There are even cases where a good preventive maintenance program has literally done away with catastrophic failures. The planning of such an effort should be accomplished in the procurement stage or Stage I. This is part of the benefit of the visits to installations of the equipment: selection of key components that are of high quality and carry good warranties from the manufacturers.[7] Allowing that predicting failure is accomplished by estimating or simulation, the planned maintenance activity can be developed and costed, if the seller provides information on suggested maintenance procedures, failure curves, and MTBR or MTBF data. (MTBR is the mean time between removal, or the average time that may pass before the part or component should be replaced. It is the average suggested or recommended interval between changes of that part. Consider the air filter as the example. It gets dirty but still operates, albeit less effectively. MTBF is the mean time between failure, or the duration or life of the part. Consider the sparkplug. Having reached its failure point, it fails to perform the function.) Visits to installed sites provide information not only on failures but on the idiosyncrasies of the equipment itself. It is not sufficient to sit in a conference room and discuss these issues. If permitted by your host, go out on the shop floor and talk with the operator. This is one reason that the site visit team makeup is so important. The purpose is to gather all the information possible from the best sources. Sometimes there are minor elements that are annoyances rather than problems, but knowing them before the fact is helpful. Using a CMMS, it is possible to define the preventive maintenance activity, cost it, and project the Stage II costs before they occur. In the site visit, it is also helpful if the site has a CMMS in place and copies of the data can be obtained for the machine.

The variable that must be projected is the planned use of the equipment since maintenance can be based on time or use. The "meter reading" approach is better since it reflects actual use since the last preventive maintenance activity as opposed to the calendar. In addition, there are often levels of mainte-

---

6. In one company, it was possible to make the same product on three different machines. On two of the three, the company lost money. The sales force, knowing this to be the case, took orders for that product only if they were assured the product would be produced on the machine that showed a per-unit profit, thus ensuring the stability of their commissions on the sale. The company solved the problem by raising prices by 7 percent—indeed, a large Band-Aid placed over the problem.

7. In the purchase order, the buyer specifies that all warranties from parts or component suppliers are automatically transferred to the buying company upon transfer of title on the equipment and the seller releases all claims to those warranties and guarantees their transferability. It is the seller's responsibility to gain that transferability clause from *his* sources.

nance that require different spare parts and different times. Going strictly by the calendar could cause maintenance to be performed when it is not needed due to a period of machine idleness. Both options should be reviewed by the buying team.

To project the cost of Stage II, it is also necessary to have an estimate of the period of service in either time units or output units. What levels of preventive maintenance will be undertaken, with what frequency, and thus how many treatments will the machine receive? What is the cost of each treatment in terms of consumable parts replaced and labor consumed? Are the parts expendable or capable of being repaired or reconditioned?

Stage II planned maintenance is treated on a case-by-case basis, and the maintenance plan is drawn up as part of the purchasing process, not as an afterthought. The planning process is crucial since not only does the planning occur, but also decision making on the level of maintenance. While the machine is down for maintenance, is it better to increase the level or depth of maintenance to avoid another teardown and the associated downtime?

There is no single answer, but these are factors to consider in planning the preventive maintenance effort. Counterbalancing that line of thought is the IR-OAN philosophy (Initiates Repair Only As Necessary): Maintenance takes place when maintenance is needed. The positions of heavy emphasis on the preventive side of maintenance versus doing it only when you have to may represent ends of the maintenance spectrum. What is needed is the proper balance between the costs. As the preventive maintenance level of effort increases, the costs rise. At the same time, the estimated costs of failure, principally downtime, decline. A balance is ideal; however, there are other factors to consider:

- Is the downtime cost real or illusory?
- Can the machine be taken out of service with little or no impact on output?
- Can scheduled production be changed to bypass the machine?
- Do alternatives exist in the form of standby equipment or other machines capable of carrying that workload?
- What are the other options, and what are their costs relative to the downtime costs?

Answering all these questions may not be easy but is necessary to establish a program that minimizes the total cost of maintenance and downtime and still maintains a reasonable level of equipment availability. The final approach would be to visit an installation to see the types of data generated in Stage II by a user. This will define a point on the spectrum.

Stage III: Disposal

Eventually the equipment enters Stage III, the disposal stage. Prior to considering the activities and costs associated with this stage, it is important to understand the entry point into this stage. What brings the organization to make the decision that a piece of equipment is ready to be removed from service and replaced? There are both qualitative and quantitative determinations regarding reaching this point.

Following are some qualitative criteria:

- The equipment has become a bottleneck in the operation. Inventory is building up while waiting for access to the machine, and its speed is starving operations after it.
- The quality of output is below requirements, and waste or rework is excessive.
- There is a safety problem associated with the equipment that cannot be addressed.
- It lacks flexibility or the cost of setup is excessive.
- Its downtime due to breakdowns is excessive and disrupts schedules.
- It consumes excessive energy relative to similar equipment.
- It is worn out and incapable of being brought back to any reasonable condition relative to its original state.
- The technological advances in the field have rendered it obsolete and relatively useless. It does not meet today's environmental standards and regulations.
- It is no longer possible to get spare parts, making it impossible to maintain it except at extremely high cost.

Qualitative criteria are just that—based on observations, perceptions, and experiences. They also may be biased or skewed. They may be emphasized to reach a distinct conclusion. For these reasons, we try to generate some quantitative measures that point the way to options without having to contend with the bias.

The equipment has reached the end of its service life. It may still be capable of producing output, but it is a marginal proposition. All the reasons are qualitative as expressed. Yet there are decision rules that can be structured to determine when the equipment moves to the disposal stage:

- *The estimated cost of the next repair is 65 percent of the current estimated market value of the equipment.* Sixty-five percent is simply an illustration value. It could be 60 percent or 70 percent, but using a percentage can avoid putting good money into a machine and never recovering a fraction of it. The main issue becomes how much the continued maintenance really buys. Is the service life extended to the point where it is justifiable to put more money into the equipment? Will that expenditure extend the service life sufficiently to make the decision viable?

This rule can lead in two directions. If the machine can still produce 10,000 units after overhaul and it costs $10,000 to overhaul it, then the marginal cost of those 10,000 units is $1 per unit. If the option is buying a new machine for $100,000, the new machine must have a projected life of better than 100,000 units. Watch these rules carefully. There must be an underlying philosophy that says to operate the machine to where it cannot be repaired and must be replaced or to replace it after so many years or units of output.

• *When the cumulative maintenance cost has reached 150 percent of the original cost of the equipment.* Again 150 percent is not a magic number, but by setting the decision rule, candidates for replacement can be picked up by the CMMS as it accumulates the maintenance cost of individual pieces of equipment. This does not say the equipment will be replaced, but such a decision rule does flag potential replacements.

• *When the cumulative maintenance cost has reached 100 percent of the current value of the equipment.* Some of these data come from the CMMS, and the remaining segment can be added into the CMMS as a schedule of value over time. This can be the depreciation schedule for the piece of equipment. Again it is candidate identification.

• *When the cost of repair exceeds 50 percent of the replacement cost of the equipment.* This rule must be applied carefully since replacement can be defined over a variety of options. The options can be new, used, or rebuilt (if the rebuild is a complete rebuild that essentially replaces the unit in all the key dynamic components).

The final decision will be based on both qualitative and quantitative factors. The quantitative elements will show costs of replacement as seen in Stage I analysis as well as the costs that will be avoided by replacement. The process is a continuous loop. The stumbling block in the decision process is the economic value of the equipment, as the following example shows.

The city of Frostbite Falls, Minnesota, has a fire truck that is 10 years old and in need of refurbishing. The estimated cost to repair and place it in workable condition is $15,000. Investing the money will provide an estimated 5 years of additional life with normal routine maintenance. That same vehicle may be sold for $7,000 with minor repair to place it in sellable operating condition with a 30-day limited warranty. The issue now becomes whether the city council approves investing $15,000 in a $7,000 vehicle.

Analysis: There is no single answer to the question. It may be argued from many perspectives, and each argument will have merits. One side will look at cost and another side functional use. Both sides are correct, and both sides are wrong. The cutoff decisions are not easy to make. In replacing the equipment, the options become clouded by the ability to trade in the old equipment, thereby getting rid of it and receiving some credit for the trade-in against the purchase of the new equipment. Volume and standardization are key elements here.

Let us say the decision has been made to replace the existing equipment. Now the disposal phase begins. There are numerous ways to dispose of equipment:

• Use the old equipment as trade-in for new equipment. The seller may allow some discount in the price of the new equipment if there is a ready market for the old equipment or as an inducement to make the purchase. The seller is simply reducing the profit on the sale of the new equipment. In some cases, the trade-in is honest; in some instances, it is just a convenient method of disposal for the buyer.[8]

• Move it to a standby status. This is really doing nothing with it except physically moving it to another part of the facility and using it in emergencies or special situations. In theory, this is a costless option, especially if accounting says the equipment is fully depreciated.

• Sell it outright to interested buyers. Recognize that there are costs associated with selling the equipment, and they rise if there is not a ready buyer for the equipment. One public utility allows employees to bid on company automobiles and pickup trucks. In this manner, they are sold on an as-is basis, and bidding keeps the employee from feeling the price is too high since the seller did not set it.

• Sell it to a used equipment dealer.

• Sell it at an equipment auction.[9]

• Cannibalize it for parts and sell the remainder as scrap metal.

• Donate it to some organization, such as a technical or vocational school, and collect any tax benefits.

• Pay to have it removed.

• Rebuild, recondition, or retrofit it.

• Assign it to other uses, such as apprentice training.

There is no one best option; rather, the selection of the option will depend on an array of factors. In some instances, the equipment can have little or no

8. The city of Kansas City recently purchased 44 new fire trucks from a single manufacturer. The city order varied in models, but by order consolidation and standardization, it was able to obtain a trade-in allowance on each vehicle being replaced. The trade-ins will be refurbished and sold to Third World countries.
9. It is sold as is, where is, with full disclaimer of any warranty provision both express or implied except the ability to pass clear title to the equipment. See Chapter 8 for a full discussion of auctions.

value, as in the case of some computers whose capability is so limited that it is impossible to use modern software on them. They are operational, but they are also technological dinosaurs. Other pieces of equipment bring premium prices. Buyers line up to buy used equipment.

Market forces determine price, and the scarcity of the item will influence that price. Model changes will affect the value of the used equipment. In some cases, the older models are superior in quality of materials, size, or design. Numerous examples exist to show the impact of regulation on the value of equipment. Older automobiles without catalytic converters rose in price since they could use cheaper unleaded fuel. Commodes using 5 gallons per flush were found to be highly superior to the resource-saving 1.6 gallon per flush models. Price is determined by the interaction of supply and demand.

Selling the equipment in any way, shape, or form other than as scrap does entail some legal factors and potential liability. The seller has to deal with the issue of implied warranty. The seller must either pass clear title or indicate the existence of any liens on the property. The seller warrants the equipment to be in average condition and capable of performing its intended purpose. To avoid the latter two warranty components, the seller sells the equipment as is, where is and disclaims all express or implied warranties as a condition of sale. Naturally, this has an impact on the price.

There are certain costs in the third stage, but they are directly related to the channel of disposal. They can range from simply disconnecting the utilities and unbolting the machine and moving it to the loading dock to cleaning, lubricating, painting, crating, and shipping the equipment to a buyer. The issue is what the condition of the equipment is at the time of sale. How much money does the seller wish to invest in the equipment to enhance its value in the marketplace? This can range from practically nothing to a significant investment. That investment decision is up to the organization selling the equipment. There are some common cost components that every sale will include:

• Removing the machine from its present site (disconnecting and shutting off utilities and moving the machine to another location).

• Clean-up and make-ready costs.

• Spare parts that have no further use when the machine is gone. These could have some value, and the buyer, who is now the seller, should investigate the market for those spares before disposing of them. Disposal of the spares can be accomplished in many ways: sold with the machine, sold as scrap, or possibly returned to the original source. If they have no further use to the selling company, they should be removed from the storeroom and the records purged of them. Their cost would be the difference between the original price and what they bring on the open market, assuming they have not been expensed. The tool crib can make up a list of spare parts for disposal. The buyer should contact sources to determine their value. Experience has shown that this may not be a fruitful area for savings or returns of parts to suppliers. These parts do not return to the supplier's shelf easily. They are usually old, and packaging has changed along with identification numbers and methods of identification (bar coding). The process of taking them back into a system may far exceed their value.

• Tooling, jigs, and fixtures associated with that machine that have no alternative uses. The buyer should consider selling the machine with tooling to a supplier who now has limited capability to supply parts formerly made on the machine. It is a second or standby source.

• Finding the appropriate channel of distribution for disposal. The income generated, if any, in the disposition is a function of that channel. The auctioneer charges a percentage, usually 10 to 25 percent, for conducting the auction and its associated costs. The used equipment dealer has to make a profit. Thus, there are channel costs that reduce the value of the equipment in the disposal phase.

• Transportation of displaced equipment. Equipment cannot be transported with any liquids, such as hydraulic oils, solvents, coolants, or cutting oils. It makes no difference if it is going to a scrap dealer or a used equipment buyer or a customer. Truck drivers are instructed to look for possible liquids in the equipment *before* they sign for and move the load.

With respect to the price received for the equipment, the seller can make a profit on the sales, with the profit being the difference between net price received and book value (depreciated value at time of sale) or sustain a loss where the net price received is less than book value. This is an accounting issue, and the buyer who is now disposing of the equipment should be in contact with the accountants as the option is explored to determine the desired price of the equipment.

Looking at Total Cost of Ownership

Initial cost is only a fraction of the cost picture. Ownership encompasses buying the equipment, operating it, maintaining it, logistically supporting it, and disposing of it. Admittedly, the buying process and the investment in the equipment may appear to be the biggest cost element because it occurs at one point in time. Yet if you look over the total life at the dollars expended for maintenance, operation, utilities, spare parts, and consumables, the second stage of ownership can be far more expensive if costs are properly tracked. Finally there comes a point of replacement. Costs here may be low, but the level of effort associated with disposal may be significant if a "reasonable" price is desired. All through the process, there must be good cost tracking and estimating. Estimation is important in the decision phase to make the best equipment selection. Tracking is important to validate the estimates in the buying phase as well as developing a database for future decisions. Accumulation of maintenance cost data is a vital component of the disposal decision process. It also has value in the selling phase by providing the potential buyer with the information on the maintenance history of the equipment. A buyer of previously owned equipment will feel much more confident about the value received if the maintenance history is available. It is not a guarantee that a failure will not occur, but it does indicate the care the equipment received from its previous owner.

Total cost of ownership is important from two perspectives. Initially, all the costs discussed in this chapter are going to be incurred. Failing to capture them or ignoring them will not make them go away. Second, the issue is *cost per unit*. It may be cost per unit of product or cost per transaction in the service environment, but it is *cost per.* Looking only at the initial cost is totally myopic. The more expensive machine may be the best value. It may have lower operating costs and a higher end-of-life value. Failing to look at the total picture will always lead to the lowest initial price, and the savings on the purchase price can easily be dissipated in the latter stages. Initial cost is important, but it is scarcely the entire picture.

When all the costs are totaled, do not be surprised if the total cost of ownership is three to five times the original price paid for the item. Maintenance, operating costs, depreciation, taxes, and insurance all add to the original cost. This does not stop the sale of the equipment. It is essential for the business to have it, yet taking a total cost of ownership perspective gives the buyer a realistic overview and allows for consideration of expenditures that may seem more costly in initial cost but quickly take on a different meaning. Value is determined over the entire life of the equipment, not its initial price.

Checklist for Total Cost of Ownership

Have you:
- ☐ Checked production rates and made comparisons?
- ☐ Determined the capacity of the equipment and at what rate will it be operating?
- ☐ Evaluated operator selection procedures, costs of training, and assistance by the supplier in getting you up and running?
- ☐ Looked at how much scrap will be produced and how to dispose of it? (This includes scrap handling equipment such as a chip conveyor or a centrifuge.)
- ☐ Asked about repair accessibility in terms of time to gain access versus repair time or maintenance time?
- ☐ Inquired about energy consumption relative to price?
- ☐ Examined Environmental Protection Agency requirements before signing on the dotted line?
- ☐ Asked about trade-in values for failed components or modules?
- ☐ Developed an annual cost of operating supplies and maintenance parts based on information from the dealer?

☐ Calculated the costs of keeping spare parts on the shelf versus the availability and delivery from the supplier?

☐ Coordinated with accounting on depreciation, service life, and residual value so there is one set of numbers in the computations?

☐ Provided for the record keeping and documentation on maintenance activity, operating hours, and units produced?

☐ Involved the user?

☐ Set a figure for nonequipment-related expenses as part of the budget request?

☐ Included maintenance downtime as part of the total cost of ownership?

☐ Considered final disposition options and costs?

☐ Decided what type of total cost of ownership model to use?

☐ Planned the documentation of the costs to provide input into the next decision on buying this type of equipment?

☐ Shown management the advantage of using a total cost or life cycle cost approach in the costing of capital equipment?

12

Controlling the Acquisition of Capital Equipment

Perhaps the most thankless job is that of the project manager. To paraphrase the late Sir Winston Churchill, "Never has so much been asked of so few who were given so little." The project manager is like the gambler who never gets to deal, cut, or shuffle the deck. He or she must play the cards dealt. Most organizations are structured along functional lines with departments that perform business functions of accounting, marketing, engineering, and so on. Enter now the project, and both the organization structure and work flows are different. Exhibit 12-1 shows the difference between project work and mainstream or function work as viewed from an array of perspectives.

The perspective of many organizations is that a project orientation is not part of the organizational culture. The organization produces goods or services, and the processes of making, marketing, and invoicing for these efforts are the core of the business. These are repetitive activities, performed daily, to ensure the economic vitality of the organization. Lincoln Electric has been making arc welding equipment for generations. General Motors has delivered millions of cars to worldwide markets over the memory of most living people. Mainstream work is the essence of the enterprise. The project focus or orientation is present only in companies such as Black and Veatch, Burns and McDonald, Bechtel, and others whose core business is associated with projects themselves. Mainstream work is the area that has first claim on the resources of organizations, with the projects often taking a back seat. This is easily understandable because at the conclusion of the project, what happens to the resources on it? Can they be absorbed into the mainstream? Do they still possess the requisite skills to fit into the mainstream? Are they needed in the mainstream, or has their absence been compensated for by others in the organization? When the flag bearer is killed, there will always be someone who picks up the flag and carries it forward. So it is true in organizations. Gaps are filled as work is reallocated to those who remain. Not wanting to see the job disappear with the close

Exhibit 12-1. Orientation toward mainstream and project work.

Viewpoint/Orientation	Mainstream Work	Project Work
Timing	"Now," urgent and important," "routine"	Plenty of time, important but not urgent
Status quo	Constancy and consistency	Modify, new ground, unknowns, change
Contribution to the organization	Essential, basic, central	Fringe, extra, nice but not essential

of the project, the project leader and those chosen for the project effort try to keep feet in both camps with the project being "an extra assignment."

As the project manager "buys" the resources needed for the project, the mainstream work managers may resist the "purchase" of their good workers. After all, the organizational culture prizes mainstream work and tolerates the project. Mainstream work managers know they will be evaluated on how effective their staff were in performing essential tasks, not secondary or tertiary tasks. Therefore, the project manager must perform with a set of organizational perceptions about projects as well as the constraints of time and money. This is why the role of top management is critical. There must be a sponsor or *project champion* above the project manager who will signify the importance of the project, aid the project manager in securing the resources, and run interference for the project. Not an active member of the project, this person is the implied authority of the project manager and a measure of the importance of the project to top management.

Why all this information as a preface? Projects are often underrated in organizations. The impact of a project is not clear to many, especially in the capital equipment area. Buying capital equipment and adding or replacing capacity are the driving forces behind next year's operating, material, and maintenance budgets. Capital equipment is as much a contributor to the profits as the materials used on them. A well-managed capital equipment purchase project that buys the right machine at the right time, and is delivered, installed, tested, and accepted begins to return on that investment immediately. Reverse those elements of the purchase, and watch the costs increase with idle workers waiting for the equipment, overtime, and all sorts of unnecessary expenses being incurred.

In no other area is the domino effect more evident than the project. The inability to complete one activity may have all sorts of consequences downstream. Missing target dates in the manufacture of the capital equipment may require waivers on acceptance criteria and testing. The pressure of time to complete the project may cause shortcuts to be taken that have disastrous results. One has only to recall the Challenger space craft and the O ring problem. Not every purchase is going to be a disaster, yet there must be an element of control over the process.

The focus of this chapter is upon the tools useful in that control process and how they may be used, even if the project is viewed as a secondary contributor. It is evident in our experience that smoothly run projects are rarely applauded or heralded, but poorly managed ones are subjected to the harsh light of many and are twice damned since they also take time away from mainstream work. Given these organizational barriers, how does the project manager overcome these impediments?

Organizing for Project Management

Organizing for the process of project management can take many forms. It may be as simple as assigning one person to be the project manager to coordinate, supervise, and expedite a series of activities with the appropriate functional managers. A simple capital equipment acquisition may need only one person to develop the list of activities to accomplish the project and ensure they take place at the right time. It is a coordination process. The more complex the project, the greater the need for resources and some form of organization structure to manage those resources.

When the project becomes more complex and moves beyond the capacity of one person, additional resources are needed. The project manager then may become a purchaser of resources using a matrix organization. Functional organization charts, like the one shown in Exhibit 12-2, allow different functions to be displayed as vertical entities in the organization. The project moves across the organization, buying resources for specific tasks and specific periods in which to perform those tasks.

Exhibit 12-2. Matrix organization.

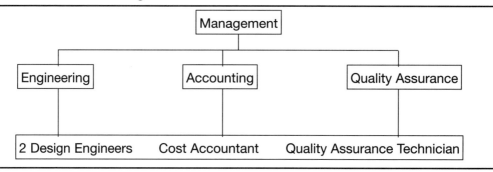

In Exhibit 12-2, the project spans the functional areas and draws resources from the functional areas as team members. The matrix organization, allowing people to remain in their mainstream work units and calling on them for limited periods, is the forerunner of today's popular teams.

Buying the resources and putting together the team for the project may have several distinct phases. The initial phase may be used to develop the work breakdown structure (WBS) of the project. Upon completion of the WBS and the development of the control device (such as a Gantt chart), specific duties can be assigned to individuals on the team. When the activity is over, the team members return to their functional assignments. In this manner, no new organization is created beyond the length of the project.

The Project Manager and Project Management

The role of the project manager is just that: the management of a complex project. Normally, the characteristics of the project type of activities include:

- One-time projects
- Large dollar-item projects
- Projects where increasing staff is not feasible

As examples, consider the following types of projects:

- Installing a new computer system
- Managing a new building under construction
- Planning for the addition of a new department

Any major project, beyond even the addition of a copier or small office machine, needs a degree of control over it to ensure it is done in a timely and effective manner. To establish control, it is necessary to understand the tools of control. They range from the very simple (in the case of WBS, a checklist of activities and tasks needed to perform the project), to the complex Program Evaluation Review Technique (PERT), which employs multiple time estimates for each activity. Selecting the method for control depends primarily on the complexity of the project and the resources available for project management and control. An elaborate control system for a simple project is as preposterous as trying to control the construction of a nuclear power plant with a Gantt chart. There are tools for each situation. Also, numerous software packages are available for conversion from the Gantt chart to the Critical Path Method (CPM) and to Program Evaluation Review Technique (PERT).

Essential Ingredients for Project Control

The project manager must know the activities that make up the project and how long each takes to accomplish. What is the starting date of an activity and what is the required completion date? Knowing this information as well as the relationship between activities ensures that purchased resources are bought when they are needed and for the proper duration. Buying resources that are going to be idle or waiting for the completion of earlier activities wastes those resources. Therefore, the project manager's planning is fundamental to the control process. The starting point is determining the tasks necessary to complete the project. This is the purpose of the **work breakdown structure** (WBS). As the name implies, WBS requires the project manager and team members to define the tasks and the sequence in which they are performed.

The team members continuously subdivide the project into smaller and smaller activities and tasks until individual responsibilities begin to appear. It is then possible to assign responsibilities for those tasks to individuals either directly or by giving them the "follow up and report back or updating" responsibility.

The process normally takes place in the beginning of the project, when the team is first formed and given its responsibility or charter by the project sponsor or champion. The sponsor, usually a member of top management, will provide a brief overview of the project, its time line and importance to the organization, and the expected financial impact. The project manager then takes over and explains the ground rules for defining the WBS. The project manager should not attempt too much in the initial meeting, but should focus on defining the phases of the projects and the activities in these phases. Time estimates are important. However, trying to move too quickly from macro to micro can lead to exclusion of key activities. Normally two to three sessions are sufficient to get the complete WBS for the project.

A rule of thumb in developing WBS phases and tasks is that every capital equipment project includes developing the appropriation request and the data needed to support it, selecting the equipment, deciding on how it will be paid for, qualifying it off site, bringing it in to the plant, setting it up, running it for acceptance and then for production, and disposing of the replaced equipment. This is not to say all projects are alike, yet there is a commonality of activities on the macro level that may help in developing the WBS. This commonality is important because it forces the project team to look at the notion of interdependencies within the project.[1]

The WBS phase of project control is the first step in the process. Once having moved to the point where individual or small-group responsibility can be assigned for certain activities, the project has begun. For some projects, the WBS may be the only tool needed. A relatively simple project made up of a number of independent activities, could be controlled with a simple WBS and assignments to individuals with individual deadlines. However, as projects become more complex, the need for more sophisticated control tools increases. Tasks are no longer independent of each other. The output of one task becomes the input to the next. Time relationships appear. Activities or tasks depend on

---

1. The term *precedence* will also be used in that it is impossible to carry on one activity until another activity has been completed. Personnel selection depends on interviewing personnel first, for example.

the completion of other tasks. The classic example is building the house. The roof must go on *after* the walls are completed.

The next set of tools introduces and incorporates the concept of time and dependency into the control process. Just because the person has been given the activity assignment, does *not* mean that assignment must be carried out today or tomorrow. The purpose of the time control tools of project management is to let individuals know *when* their respective contributions to the project must begin and must be completed. In fact, making contributions or carrying out work effort ahead of schedule can be detrimental to the success of the project. For example, a contractor orders sod when the house is complete. Putting in the lawn is one of the last activities in the construction WBS. Having a pallet of sod delivered when the foundation is being dug will result in reordering that sod some ninety days later. The *when* of the activity is just as important as the *what* of the activity.

Starting the Process: A Simple Example

Assuming the project manager can gather the necessary resources, what tools are available to help the manager assess progress in meeting the deadline? How can these tools warn the project manager of possibly missing the deadline? Let us illustrate using a simple example of a project.

A company has decided to set up a customer service department to handle customer complaints and do telemarketing. This project will become part of the order entry department once it has been set up and in operation. The setup portion is a project and must be completed in four months (sixteen weeks). There is insufficient workspace available at the present site, so a new space must be secured for the workforce. The company also feels the duration of the telemarketing and complaint management activity is long enough to justify hiring more people to staff the operation.

The first step in the project is to identify the major phases that must take place in order to accomplish the overall project. The process begins by defining what actions have to be taken. It is the WBS for the project. In this example, the new site is to be selected and new personnel hired, trained, and moved to the new site.

WBS starts at the macro level by considering the major phases of the assignment, and then progresses downward to the micro. The WBS table is shown in Exhibit 12-3.

On the macro level, the new office has two requirements: office space and people to staff the office. The exhibit lists the steps or activities necessary to meet those requirements and time estimates for each one. How long does it take to perform the activity? The time period may vary since both internal and external resources may be used. The project must consider external lead times

Exhibit 12-3. WBS for telemarketing and complaint management site.

Major Phase	Major Activity	Task	Time Estimate
Office space	Site location	Physical space, neighborhood, parking, rent, duration	8 weeks
	Renovation	Design, costs, codes	3 weeks
	Order furniture and phones	Selection	3 weeks
	Set up and move in	Uncrating, removal of packing, installation	1 week
Staffing	Interviewing	Scheduling, applications	2 weeks
	Selecting people	Notification, paperwork, physicals	1 week

as a critical element in the project. It is often possible to compress internal lead time at little cost, but the external lead times are often expensive to condense.

The steps in the project and their time estimates for the activities are contained in the WBS table. Simple addition of the times would show the project taking 18 weeks if done sequentially. This is two weeks beyond the deadline. Thus, some activities must be carried on concurrently.

The first step, beyond the WBS, is to realign the activities in such a way that *precedence* can be established. In addition, consider the connotation of independence of events versus interdependence. For example, the activities of site selection and personnel interviewing are independent of each other, so they may be carried on concurrently. Conversely, site renovation cannot be done until the site is selected. Thus, site selection must precede site renovation. In realigning, a table of precedence relationships shown in Exhibit 12-4 is developed. Activities are given letter designations.

Exhibit 12-4. Precedence relationships.

Activity	Designator	Duration (weeks)	Predecessor Activity
Site selection	a	8	—
Personnel interviews	b	2	—
Personnel selection	c	1	b
Site renovation	d	3	a
Order furniture and phones	e	3	a
Set up and move in	f	1	d, e

To organize the activity to ensure timely completion of the project, the project manager might choose the graphical approach using the Gantt chart. Developed by Henry Gantt in 1922, it is a chronological bar chart, showing activities against a time line. A sample chart is shown in Exhibit 12-5. The activities are taken from the WBS listing and placed on the vertical axis, and a time line or planning horizon or project duration is projected across the top horizontal axis. The activities from the WBS are now filled in the left-hand vertical cells, and their time lines are added in the appropriate units—in this case, weeks. The rule is quite simple: If there is no predecessor, there is no constraint on when the activity can begin; if there is a predecessor, the activity must wait until the predecessor is complete. The chart should include the project title and may also have a remarks section on the right-hand side.

The process of updating is important from a control perspective. Updating shows the movement through time and the completion of activities, as well as the time remaining in the project.

The chart provides a picture of the process, yet it lacks certain information that would be nice to know from the perspective of the project manager. It *does* say how long the project will take, by reading the axis or time line. It *does* tell how long the project manager can wait to commit resources to a particular activity in the project or how much slack time is present in the system. This information is vital to the project manager who is trying to manage the project successfully and still husband the correct resources to be applied only when needed. The difficulty lies in the interdependencies between activities and seeing them. The issues of interdependencies and driving activities are important to the project manager. Although the Gantt chart is still widely used in many companies, its shortcomings gave rise to another set of tools that are logic-based management of task interdependencies.

Do Not Forget the Obvious

In purchasing capital equipment, the control element is crucial. Capital investments often involve small items that may appear inconsequential, but can have serious ramifications if they are overlooked. The completeness of the WBS is essential not only in defining the tasks, but also understanding what is involved in the task itself. Such simple considerations such as access to the facility must be part of the process. It is the simple act of measuring the height and width of a door or dock or bay. Is access to the facility possible, given the size of the equipment?

Thirty years ago, the U.S. Army purchased forklift trucks for use in Southeast Asia. True to government purchases, they were designed to an array of specifications. Upon completion of this special order, it was determined they were too wide (by 1/2 inch) to be loaded into the cargo bays of the Air Force C-130s. They had to be shipped by more expensive means with a great deal of unused and underused cargo space on the larger aircraft.

There are thousands of examples of projects being slowed down or derailed by failure to include the activity in the WBS checklist, not monitoring

Exhibit 12-5. Gantt chart for opening office.

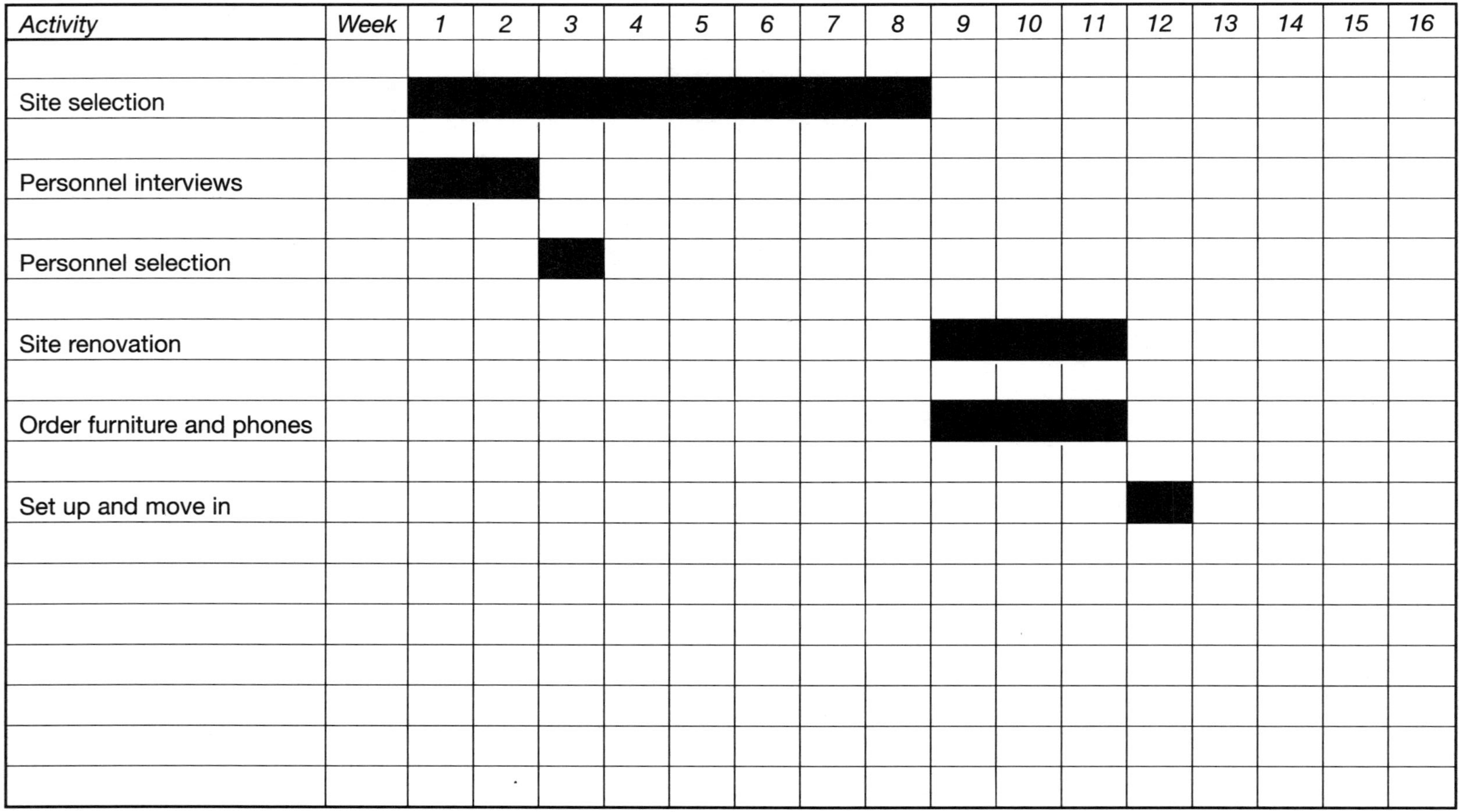

Activity	Week	1	2	3	4	5	6	7	8	9	10	11	12	13	14	15	16
Site selection		██	██	██	██	██	██	██	██								
Personnel interviews		██	██														
Personnel selection				██													
Site renovation										██	██	██					
Order furniture and phones										██	██	██					
Set up and move in													██				

closely enough, not recognizing the relative importance of the activity, or not fully understanding the nature of the task to be performed. Failing to order test equipment can slow or stop the acquisition of capital equipment. This was the case with one company that had dispatched an engineering team overseas to begin acceptance testing and validation on a piece of equipment. The test equipment, which was supposed to be on site upon their arrival, had never been ordered. They arrived with micrometers and calipers. The test instruments were actually incapable of performing the required measuring. Mistakes happen and will continue to happen, but many can be avoided by simply walking through the process and counting the steps.

A recent event in a major midwestern city found the school bus contractor short of drivers for the opening day of school. The contract was supposedly monitored by a department in the local school system. Someone had not put the WBS activity that required validation of the requisite number of drivers on the payroll by a certain date for the opening of school. Sometimes the obvious is *so* obvious, it is missed.

Good project managers learn not to assume anything. While tasks may appear to be repetitive or even rudimentary, failure to include them in the WBS can create all sorts of problems or inconveniences. As an adviser in a major physical move of a midwestern company to new headquarters, one of the authors saw the discontent created when the wastepaper baskets were not in the WBS list of office supplies. It was an inconvenience, but it created a fair amount of dissatisfaction, given the amount of funds spent on new furniture and carpeting. Control is essential.

The capital item may be a stand-alone item or it may be a key item in a larger project, such as the generator in a power plant or a key machine in a production line. Regardless of where it fits, there must be some element of control over the process. Remember that the investment in the equipment is not the only expense related to the purchase. There may be operator training involved, spare parts stocking, manufacturing schedules based on the new equipment being in place, or the reallocation of work efforts on the shop floor. In the area of training on the machine, the training is of little value if it takes place weeks before the arrival of the machine or too long after the arrival. If it takes place after the machine arrives, it may cause machine downtime.

A smart project manager will recognize opportunities to overlap activities or tasks. The scheduled runoff at the manufacturer's plant is a good time for training machine operators and maintenance personnel. Take them along to the runoff to observe, train, and possibly be part of the runoff. It is the closest experience they will receive before having to use the machine at their own plant. A change of venue can also strengthen the training by adding a sense of importance to that training. Selection to go to the supplier's site places a different perspective on the training. The operator is the first one on the new machine. This equates to a sense of ownership and a greater commitment to the equipment. It is simple pride.

Capital equipment arriving at the job site or installation late has the impact of making all the jobs or activities following the installation late. It is the traditional domino effect. The first impression is difficult to change. It may be viewed as a forerunner of things to come. Often the term is heard, "This machine has been nothing but trouble from the day it came." A way of avoiding lateness is treating the purchase as a project. In actuality, it *is* a project. It *does* qualify for that definition in these senses.

- Normally, it is a one-time expenditure of large proportions.
- It has a definite beginning and ending point or deadline when it must be completed.
- Typically, there is no organization structure strictly devoted to the project. One or more persons may be assigned the task of monitoring the effort and perhaps some resources for expediting and controlling.[2]
- The project itself consists of a set of clearly defined activities or tasks, and a relationship between tasks may be defined in that the precedence among tasks may be established—i.e., what task must precede another, as well as what tasks may be done in parallel.

Having these four characteristics, it is possible to employ one of two well-known and widely used project management tools: Critical Path Method (CPM) and Program Evaluation Review Technique (PERT). The Gantt chart, considered in the opening example, has a long history of use including being the planning tool used in the Soviet Union for many years. The Soviets claimed it was really invented over there. CPM and PERT are relative newcomers, appearing in 1956 and 1957 respectively. Developed independently of each other, they fulfill a need to effectively control large-scale, complex projects containing many activities. In fact, the initial PERT application was as a management tool for the U.S. Navy's Polaris missile project, composed of over 4,000 separate, yet interrelated activities. A project of such complexity could not be managed on a manual basis. The rapid acceptance of PERT positioned it as the leading project management tool within the Department of Defense as well as defense contractors. It is a complex technique that requires the proper training and experience. It also requires the use of statistical analysis as will be seen later in this chapter. It is a technique to be employed for control of larger-scale projects, where time is of the essence and management feels it must have probability estimates of completing the job at certain time intervals.

---

2. In some cases, the involvement is handed off at various stages of the acquisition process. This is perhaps the worst way of controlling the project or process, since there may have to be "re-learning" at several segments of the project. Continuity is a valuable resource, not to be squandered.

Some Basic Characteristics of CPM and PERT

Before getting into the examples of employing CPM and PERT, some basic background on the methods is helpful. Both are project managers' tools for controlling a project. Both begin with the same basic information found in the Gantt chart, namely, what activities are to be performed and what is the precedence relationship among the activities. Instead of a chart, the two tools require the development of a network diagram that shows the precedence relationships. Widely accepted for both tools is the Activity on Arrow convention (A-O-A) where an activity, such as site selection in the office moving example, is displayed as a circle (called a node) followed by an arrow (an activity) touching another node. Nodes represent the starting and ending point of an activity as shown in Exhibit 12-6.

Exhibit 12-6. Activity representation.

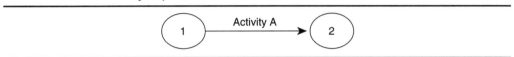

Activities are now added to the basic diagram to show precedence relationships as seen in Exhibit 12-7, illustrating the CPM diagram for the location of the complaint management center. The objective is successful project completion. Success is defined, in this case, as completing the project in sixteen weeks or less. Looking at the diagram, we see certain activities can be carried on concurrently. The WBS told us the two major activities were the site and personnel, and the precedence diagram shows this also. The diagram shows three paths from the left-hand nodes, 1 and 2 to node 7, the completion of the project. Moving from node to node defines a path. In this example there are three paths, A-D-F, A-E-Dummy-F, and B-C. The length of the first path or the number of weeks required to get from node 1 to node 7 is 8 + 3 + 1 or 12

Exhibit 12-7. CPM precedence network for complaint management facility.

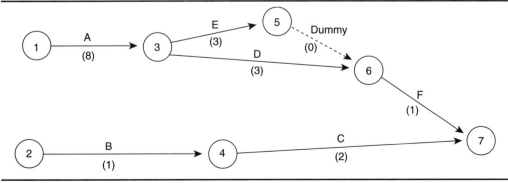

Numbers in parentheses indicate the number of time units needed to complete the individual activity.

weeks. The second path, A-E-Dummy-F is also 12 weeks, and the third path B-C is 3 weeks. What we are looking for is the time to complete the project. This is called the critical path. It is the longest path through the network. This simple example tells us to start with site selection. When that is completed, we should begin renovation and telephone installation. After renovation and telephone installation, we set up and move in. Meanwhile, personnel selection and interviews can be done at any time from the beginning of the site selection up to one week past the start of renovation and telephone installation. Interviewing and selection has nine weeks of slack in that path and as long as the personnel aspects begin three weeks before startup of the operation. They will not delay the project beyond its scheduled twelve-week duration.

CPM also tells us that any delay in any activity on the critical path will delay the completion of the overall project. If site selection took nine weeks, the project would take 13 weeks. If telephones took four weeks, the same would happen. Delays in events along the critical path delay the whole project, thus the name *critical path*. Notice the use of the dummy activity in the network. A dummy activity is used when two events or activities start at the same node and end on the same node. By convention, we insert a dummy activity represented by the dotted line and a node to branch off and then connect the dummy activity to our ending or terminating node. Dummy activities take zero time to complete. They are present to communicate with the computer programs used to solve larger-scale problems—to tell the computer that two events start and finish at the same node. Since a dummy has zero time duration, it will not affect its path. The CPM has one time estimate for each activity, and thus is limited to telling the project manager the duration of the critical path or project duration.

It is also possible to consider the likelihood or feasibility, from a planning perspective, of reducing the length of some of the activities on the critical path by expending more resources or literally trading dollars for time. Time can be reduced by adding more people to a project, working overtime, or adding a second shift. Suppliers can be given incentives to reduce the time required for the activities. While activities can be compressed, others take a finite period of time, regardless of the resources allocated to the activity. Compressing the time is known as crashing the project (i.e., completing the project either ahead of schedule or on time, but with the expenditure of additional resources). A distinction must be drawn between crashing the project and concurrent engineering, a popular term in industry for reducing the cycle time or critical path. In concurrent engineering, the organization changes the *relationship* between activities. In concurrent engineering, the company is changing the path by doing away with precedence relationships. As an example, consider the idea of a worldwide or global company with design engineers in three separate locations such that at the end of the work day in the United States, all the engineering work done on a project that day is transmitted by satellite to a location in Hong Kong to be worked on for eight hours, and then sent to France to another group of engineers who spend eight hours on the project, finally forwarding it to the United States in time for the U.S. engineers to start work. At the end of the engineering effort, the procurement of materials begins. Contrast this with changing the precedence relationship such that as soon as the design of the power plant's sub, sub basement is completed, the construction process begins. No longer does a precedence relationship exist between design and construction or production. They are now parallel or concurrent, not sequential. Concurrent engineering gains time, but also can add risk to the process. If an error is made in the design phase, it may be incorporated into the product before it is found and corrected. The same may be true of sequential activities, but compressing time can have its own set of risks. By way of example, a major steel company, in order to comply with an EPA order, built a water purification plant, and while the plant was being built, equipment, still in the experimental stage, was being installed. The normal testing time was omitted, and the equipment moved from prototype to installation. This was a very risky venture.

In crashing the project, the project manager adds more resources to an existing path or activities on the critical path to reduce the duration of the critical path.

With respect to crashing, compression of the schedule would require reduction of time of those activities on the critical path. One must exercise care, however, since the critical path is not constant and can be changed. For instance, a critical path is 12 weeks in duration, and the next longest path is 11 weeks. The critical path is crashed and reduced by 2 weeks, however, the activity(ies) that have been crashed are not part of the 11-week path or the next longest path, only on the critical path. The next longest path has not been affected by the crashing process, and it still remains 11 weeks. The old critical path is now 10 weeks, and is no longer the critical path in the network. The shifting of resources from a noncritical path to the critical path may cause the noncritical path to become critical or even lengthen the critical path. Remember, these are tools for managerial decisions and control over the project, not "iron clad" rules. Crashing should be done on the following bases:

- *The least cost-per-time unit principle.* Start by crashing an activity on the critical path that has the lowest cost-per-time unit to reduce that time. A $300 per day expenditure to reduce the activity is preferred to a $500 per day expenditure to reduce the time.

- *Reductions of time of activities must take place on the critical path.* It is desirable if these activities are also on paths whose total time are close to the critical path time. If the activity is on *both* the critical path and the next longest path, both paths are reduced in length as crashing takes place.

Program Evaluation Review Technique (PERT)

Before discussing PERT, remember that the techniques for control become more complex as the project complexity grows. PERT introduces features that provide more information, but also require more computation. Balance need for control with the cost of control. While very closely allied in terms of network design, terminology, and applicability, there are sufficient differences in data requirements to consider project size to differentiate between using CPM versus PERT.

A shortcoming of CPM is the single estimate of the time required to perform each activity. Single estimates are normally in error, especially if they are numerical. Estimating the activity times for hundreds or thousands of activities will result in some errors. In addition, a single point estimate does not allow the decision maker to infer the likelihood of completing the project within a certain period of time. To infer, it is necessary to have a measure of central tendency, the mean, and a measure or dispersion or variability about that mean—the standard deviation or variance. PERT fills that void in the following manner:

   • Three estimates of the time required to perform each activity are required. These are:
   t_o—The optimistic time; normally an optimistic time to complete the activity.
   Generally the chances of completing the activity in t_0 units is 1 in 100.
   t_1—The likely time; the expected time an activity should take to complete.
   t_p—The pessimistic time; normally the longest possible time for an activity—the chance of that taking so long is 1 in 100.

   • The next step is the computation of the mean or arithmetic average of the three time estimates and variance (a measure of dispersion around the average)[3] of each activity. Using the beta distribution (a probability distribution that approximates the normal curve), the mean and variance are computed using the following equations:

$$\text{Activity mean, } t_m = \frac{t_o + 4t_l + t_p}{6}$$

$$\text{Activity variance} = \frac{(t_p - t_o)^2}{36} \text{ or } \left(\frac{t_p - t_o}{6}\right)^2$$

---

3. This is a "red flag" area. If the variance or its square root, the standard deviation, is very large relative to the mean or arithmetic average, it is good to stop and reflect on the time estimates for the length of the activity. The estimates may not even be good guesses. It may be time to regroup.

• The critical path is found. Use the average (or mean) activity time for each activity in computing the length of the path.

• The variance of activities along the critical path is determined by adding the individual activity variances along the path. Since all have a common denominator, it is an easy task and:

$$\sigma_{cp}^2 = \sum \sigma_{1\ldots n \text{ activities}}^2$$

• The standard deviation is then calculated taking the square root of the variance:

$$\sigma_{cp} = (\sigma_{cp}^2)^{1/2}$$

At this point, the two necessary computations are complete, and inference statements can be made about the likelihood or probability of completing the project in any period of time. For example, if the office location problem were a PERT problem and had a critical path of 12 weeks, the standard deviation would have to be computed. Assume that value is 2 weeks. What is the probability of completing the project in 16 weeks, the maximum allowable time? Borrowing from basic statistics, we use the simple formula to convert the desired completion time to standard deviations.

$$Z = \frac{\text{Completion time } - \text{ critical path}}{\text{standard deviation along the critical path}}$$

or

$$Z = \frac{X - \text{C.P.}}{\sigma_{cp}}$$

In the example, $Z = \dfrac{16 - 12}{2} = 2.0$

Sixteen weeks represents two standard deviations beyond the duration of the critical path. Going to a normal distribution table, we see that 2.0 standard deviations beyond the mean encompasses 97.5% of the distribution.[4] This translates to a 97.5% likelihood of completing the project in 16 weeks. It is virtually certain the office will be operational in 16 weeks. If the question were posed as to the likelihood of completing the project in 10 weeks, the computation would be the same, except that 10 weeks is 2 weeks shorter than the critical path, and the value of Z would then be:

4. The beta distribution is a very close approximation to the normal distribution. This allows us to use the normal curve when computing the probability of project completion.

$$Z = \frac{10 - 12}{2} = -1$$

Z has a negative value. This presents no problem. Looking at a normal distribution table, one standard deviation to the left of the mean or critical path or C.P. $-1\sigma_{cp}$ means only 16% of the distribution is covered. This means the likelihood of successful completion is 16%. Remember that the critical path in PERT is the mean or average of the distribution, and the probability of completing in the mean or average time is 50 percent. Half of the time, it will take less time, and half the time, it will take more time. This is one of the reasons for using the normal curve. It is symmetrical about the mean. Thus, any time completion less than the critical path in duration will have less than a 50 percent chance of occurring, and any completion time larger than the critical path will have a greater than 50 percent chance of completion in the required time. To pinpoint the exact likelihood of completion, we need a measure of dispersion of completion time about each activity. The measure of dispersion, the variance, provides two important items of information: (1) the variability itself as measured by the variance, and (2) the inherent uncertainty connected with that event. For example, consider the following data, where there exists an optimistic, most likely, and pessimistic time estimate for the site selection activity. Applying the formulas for computing the mean for the activity, $t_m = (t_o + 4t_l + t_p)/6$ and the variance, $\sigma^2 = (t_p - t_o)^2/36$:

Activity	t_0	t_1	t_p	t_m	σ^2
Site selection	7	8	9	8	4/36
Personnel interviews	1	2	9	3	64/36

Notice that the pessimistic time estimate of 9 weeks for personal interviews has only raised the average slightly, but the variance is now rather large. A wide range between the optimistic and pessimistic time estimates is an indicator of the perceived risk in the activity or the reliance upon an outside supplier of product or services where the project manager has less control or influence. This issue is raised because every project has key activities along the critical path that are the linchpins of the project. Being late on the critical path delays the whole project from a mathematical perspective. From an operational perspective, the project manager must know these key activities and what resources are available to expedite the process if the activity slows down. In formulating the initial estimates of the time required for each activity, the project manager or sponsor must consider the degree of control over the activity. If no control is present or there are no sanctions, such as liquidated damages against the supplier, the project can be late and either tie up other resources or incur costs of expediting the completion of the activity.

The selection of the control mechanism is a decision for the project manager. We have seen very complex projects managed with a Gantt chart and reliance on experience in doing that type of project. Where the experience factor is high, the project manager may only need the broad overview afforded by the Gantt chart. Each of the activities may be a subproject in itself, yet experience in that field of endeavor gives the project manager the "feel" for the activities and the project progress.

Lacking the experience due to the infrequency of the project may dictate closer definition of the activities, time estimates, measures of risk, and more complex tools of analysis. The key issue is the availability of the tools and the selection of that tool best suited for the project. Selection of a simple tool may mean too much of the project is carried in the "hip pocket" or the head of the project manager and slippages may occur. Making the project more complex than it is may over-control the project, and valuable time can be wasted generating reports that no one uses.

The purpose behind the discussion of this material on the CPM and PERT, is to acquaint the reader with some of the instruments available for maintaining a degree of visibility over the project, and estimating the impact in schedule slippage before the slippage occurs. For example, consider the contractor who has purchased a load of sod and plans to install the lawn at a newly completed home. The sod company promises delivery at 7:00 AM. The contractor has a crew of four people and the equipment on the job site at 6:55 AM, ready to lay sod at 7:01 AM. The sod truck is one hour late. The cost is apparent: four hours times the labor rate plus any impact of not having the work crew available at the scheduled completion time, but one hour later. This information needs to be known "before the fact," not after. CPM and PERT provide that type of information by analyzing the project on a before-the-fact basis, looking at the total completion time of the project and the various trade-offs that can be made between types of resources. They are widely recognized as valid, and useful planning and control tools. This is especially true in the field of construction and complex projects. They are not limited to these areas, and have been used in process redesign, reorganizations, and to simply identify the sequential nature of the job. They can be invaluable communications devices when widely shared.

What the Techniques Tell Us

Often we think of projects as a series of sequential activities, being performed in a linear fashion. Complete task 1 and proceed to task 2. The result is the total task time or project time is the summation of the individual task times. Linear thinking is the enemy of project management. Independence between tasks is the essential ingredient for concurrence. For example, the electrical fixtures and plumbing fixtures can be installed in the new home simultaneously, yet the tiling of the bathroom must be done after the installation of the bathtub. This is the inherent secret to the successful use of any control technique. It is the logical subdivision of the total effort into independent and interdependent groups. If groups of activities must wait for the completion of some earlier activity group, they are interdependent. If they are "stand alone," they are independent. Independent activities should be nested (carried on simultaneously) with longer interdependent activities. The more sequentiality the precedence diagram contains, the longer the path to project completion. Time is money. Just a note at this juncture: Do not get frustrated at the complexity of the examples. They are real world examples and the type experienced in business every day. Ignoring them because they are complex is counterproductive. Ignoring complexity does not make it disappear. Consider the network in the same manner as the Work Breakdown Structure. It begins at the macro level and works its way down to the micro level. The most difficult part is the precedence diagram showing "what comes first." Failing to understand "what comes first" is more a matter of common sense than anything else. So begin with the major activities, and recognize that a major activity is the summation of smaller activities. Finding a site may be made up of many sub-activities that can also be networked. Develop the network with the major activities and then dissect the major activities into smaller activities and network the major activity.

Prior to the machine acquisition example, consider the use of both the Gantt chart and CPM in a reorganization situation. This example illustrates the flexibility of the tools. Consider the example of a major metropolitan city that has elected to reorganize or reengineer its purchasing processes. The project must be kept under control and completed within a year from the time the effort is given to the implementation team.

Exhibit 12-8 shows that some activities overlap and others start only when a predecessor is completed. This is the method of showing precedence. While easy to understand, it does not have the same visual impact as the precedence diagram or network commonly used in both CPM and PERT.

Controlling With CPM

The city has just completed a reengineering of its purchasing processes. Several major activities will be expanded, others will be moved, and the individual departments will be given procurement cards for very low dollar purchases as opposed to the traditional purchase order system. The system design team has passed the project to the implementation team, along with the recommendation to use either CPM or PERT as its project control method. The system design team has identified the following activities necessary for implementation of the proposed changes. They were:

Exhibit 12-8. Gantt chart for city purchasing reengineering.

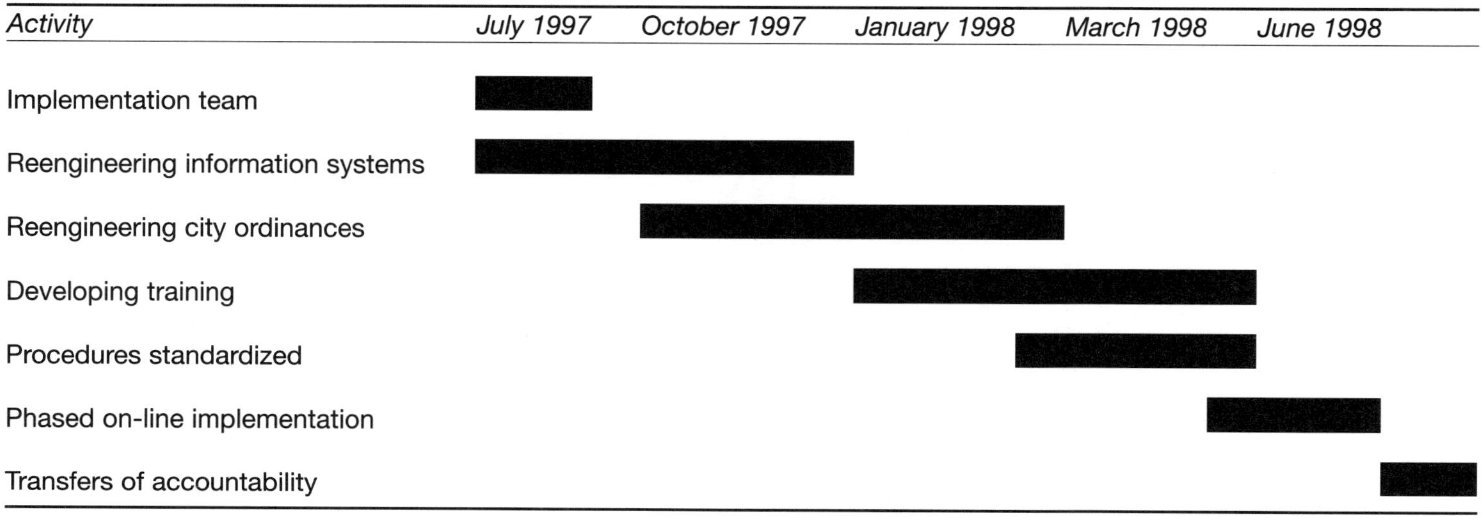

Activity	July 1997	October 1997	January 1998	March 1998	June 1998

Implementation team

Reengineering information systems

Reengineering city ordinances

Developing training

Procedures standardized

Phased on-line implementation

Transfers of accountability

- Develop the procurement card Request for Proposal.
- Develop the computer equipment Request for Proposal.
- Move the minority business enterprise/woman's business enterprise compliance team.
- Begin the computer system conversion.
- Change the city ordinances.

They can all be done concurrently since they are independent of each other. This then begins the development of the CPM chart. The initial inputs include the listing of the activities, the anticipated time for each activity, and the precedence relationship among the activities as seen in Exhibit 12-9. While the array of steps looks formidable, looking at the precedence relationship reveals many facts. Once the team is formed, five separate activities can begin. Thus, the starting point is setting up the implementing team and then beginning the activities B, C, D, E, and F.

The Network Diagram

The analyst begins by building a network based upon the precedence data provided. Convention used in CPM tells us that we begin on the left-hand-side of the paper with a small circle. This is the network itself, showing the precedence relationships. Look at Exhibit 12-10. Note that an activity G has been added. It goes from node 5 to node 6, and the connection is a dotted line. This activity is known as a dummy activity. A dummy or nonexistent activity is added to the network when two activities start at the same node and end at the same node. This has been done because activity D, Moving the Minority Business Enterprise/Woman Business Enterprise Compliance Office, and activity E, Computer system conversion, must *both* be completed before purchasing department procedures are rewritten. Procedures depend upon what the system does and who in the system does what. Procedures (activity J) depend on both D and E being completed. To avoid two activities starting at the same node and ending at the same node, we add a dummy activity and label it G.

Starting at the top of the network at node 3, upon completion of activity B, procurement card RFP and contract, the implementation of the procurement card is next undertaken. As the equipment RFP is completed and the contract is issued, the computer equipment is purchased and set up. Notice that the procurement card and the computer equipment paths show the activities can be performed concurrently. Concurrent activities compress the overall project completion time.

As the network is expanded, the same need for a dummy arises after J is completed. Here, activities K and M begin after J, and end before O can begin. Activities O and P start at the same node, and must be completed before activity R can begin. Again the dummy is needed. Notice the existence of a number of paths through the network to get from node 1 to node 13, the end of the

Exhibit 12-9. CPM data for city purchasing reorganization.

Activity	Description	Preceding Activity	Nodes*	Time (weeks)
A	Form implementation team	—	1→2	3.00
B	Develop procurement card RFP	A	2→3	6
C	Computer equipment RFP	A	2→4	6
D	Move Minority Business Enterprise/Woman's Business Enterprise Compliance Office	A	2→5	7
E	Computer system conversion	A	2→6	20
F	Change city ordinances	A	2→9	4
G	Dummy	D	5→6	0
H	Procurement card implementation	B	3→9	8
I	Computer equipment purchase and set up	C	4→9	4
J	Redesign purchasing department procedures	E	6→7	6
K	Redesign departmental requisitioning procedures	J	7→9	6
L	Dummy	J	7→8	0
M	Test and debug programs	L	8→9	6
N	Develop training materials	E	6→9	10
O	Present training	H,I,K,M,N	9→10	6
P	On-line testing	H,I,K,M,N	9→11	5
Q	Dummy	O	10→11	0
R	Procedure phase in	Q,P	11→12	4
S	Transfer accountability	R	12→13	4

*The column labeled "Nodes" now shows once the procurement card has been completed, the computer RFP, physical movement of the Minority Business Enterprise/Woman's Business Enterprise Compliance Office move, and the computer system conversion can be started. The way to begin is from node 1 to node 2. This is activity A. Once at node 2, activity B goes to node 3, activity C to node 4, activity D to node 5, and so on.

project. Obviously, that is the goal, reaching the end of the network and completing the project. Defining the network is nothing more than these steps:

1. Defining the phases in the WBS table.
2. Moving to the activities that make up the phases. They are the activities in the network.
3. Labelling each activity with a letter or number.
4. Looking for precedence relationships between activities.

Exhibit 12-10. CPM network for city purchasing reorganization.

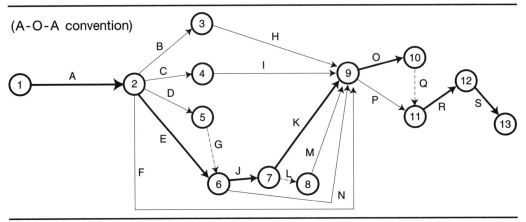

(A-O-A convention)

Activity Designation	Activity Description	Start Node	End Node	Time Estimate for Activity
A	Team formed	1	2	3.00
B	Procurement card RFP/ contract	2	3	6.00
C	Computer equipment RFP/ contract	2	4	6.00
D	Move compliance team	2	5	7.00
E	System conversion	2	6	20.00
F	Ordinances changes	2	9	4.00
G	Dummy	5	6	0.00
H	Procurement card implementation	3	9	8.00
I	Equipment purchase and setup	4	9	4.00
J	Purchasing department procedures	6	7	6.00
K	Redesign departmental procedures	7	9	6.00
L	Dummy	7	8	0.00
M	Test and debug programs	8	9	10.00
N	Develop training materials for using departments	6	9	6.00
O	Present training	9	10	5.00
P	On-line testing	9	11	0.00
Q	Dummy	10	11	0.00
R	Procedure phase-in	11	12	4.00
S	Transfer accountability	12	13	4.00

Critical Path Length   49 weeks
Critical Path Definition   A-E-J-K-O-Q-R-S

5. Stating those precedence relationships in the precedence table you develop.
6. Estimating the time required for each activity.

When the network is completed as seen in Exhibit 12-10, there are several paths from start (node 1) to finish (node 13). Each has its own length. What is sought is the critical path or longest path through the network as measured by the length of time for activities (i.e., days, weeks, or months). The critical path will be the project duration. Next comes the application of the method itself.

It is also possible to determine the amount of slack in the other paths. The slack in a path is length of the critical path minus the length of any path being considered. Consider the finished version of the project using CPM as seen in Exhibit 12-11. Activities are designated by letters of the alphabet and numbers.[5] This is the computer printout that defines the critical path and the amount of slack in the network. From the output, we determine two critical paths with a

Exhibit 12-11. Critical path for purchasing process reengineering.

Activity	Earliest Start (ES)	Earliest Finish (EF)	Latest Start (LS)	Latest Finish (LF)	Slack (LS-ES)
A (1)	0	3	0	3	0
B (2)	3	9	21	27	18
C (3)	3	9	25	31	22
D (4)	3	10	16	23	13
E (5)	3	23	3	23	0
F (6)	3	7	31	35	28
G (7)	10	10	23	23	13
H (8)	9	17	27	35	18
I (9)	9	13	31	35	22
J (10)	23	29	23	29	0
K (11)	29	35	29	35	0
L (12)	29	29	29	29	0
M (13)	29	35	29	35	0
N (14)	23	33	25	35	2
O (15)	35	41	35	41	0
P (16)	35	40	36	41	1
Q (17)	41	41	41	41	0
R (18)	41	45	41	45	0
S (19)	45	49	45	49	0

5. Normally, letters are used to define activities. The numbers have been included in the parentheses since the computer program output prints the results with numbers representing activities. This is simply an accommodation to make the results easier to read.

total length of 49 weeks for the project as seen in Exhibit 12-12. The observant reader will note the existence of two critical paths. They exist because the time required to go from node 7 to node 9 is the same regardless of the routes taken. Going from node 7 to node 9 by performing activity K takes the same 6 weeks as going from 7 to 8 to 9, and doing activities L and M. The answer to the length of the critical path is the same.

Exhibit 12-12. Path lengths for city purchasing reengineering.

Path #	Path	Length of Path
1	A-B-H-P-R-S	30 weeks
2	A-B-H-O-Q-R-S	31 weeks
3	A-C-I-P-R-S	26 weeks
4	A-C-I-O-Q-R-S	27 weeks
5	A-E-J-L-M-O-Q-R-S	49 weeks
6	A-E-J-L-M-P-R-S	48 weeks
7	A-E-J-K-O-Q-R-S	49 weeks

In addition, we are able to determine the amount of slack associated with each activity. To do so, we begin at the end of the network and work backwards along the critical path. Since the expected completion time is 49 weeks, activity S must begin in the 45th week. Activity R must begin at the beginning of the 41st week. Since the critical path includes activity O (which takes 6 weeks to complete) and activity P (which takes 5 weeks), activity P can begin one week after O commences or start at the same time as O and finish a week earlier. This translates into one week of slack for activity O. We can slip its start one week or finish a week ahead of activity P.

We may also begin at the front end of the project. Activity A begins the process. It consumes three weeks, and nothing can begin until activity A is finished. Activities B through F can only begin at the start of week 4. The length of the critical path at each point is obtained by simply adding up the CP values to that point. Looking back at the diagram, node 9 is the point where all the paths converge. Node 1 through node 9 encompasses activities A-E-J-K (forming the implementation team, computer system conversion, redesign purchasing department procedures, redesign using departmental procedures) for a total of 35 weeks. Next, look at the path A-B-H (forming the implementation team, develop the procurement card RFP, procurement card implementation). Its length is 17 weeks. Therefore, there are 18 weeks of slack in the B-H portion of the path since activity A is a common element to both paths. This means that the latest starting time for activity B would be 18 weeks after activity A was completed, or at the end of week 21. Since activity B takes 6 weeks, the latest completion date for B could be at the end of week 27. This assumes that activity H, consuming 8 weeks, would commence immediately and at the end of 35 weeks. The activities converge at node 9. Using the same logic for the slack in activity H (using 9 weeks for A and B, and needing 8 for activity H for a total of 17 weeks), the slack is 18 weeks for H. The concept is: Simply take the length of the critical path and subtract the length of every other path from that value. The resulting number will be the slack in that path. That slack can be applied to any activity in the noncritical path as long as the activity is *not* on the critical path. Eliminating the common elements from path 1 and the critical path, activities B, H, and P have 19 weeks of slack in total. Compare that with path 2 versus the critical path and eliminating the common elements, activities B and H have 18 weeks of slack between them, giving activity P one week of slack. Compare path 4 with the critical path, and activities C and I have 22 weeks of slack. Getting it down to the individual activity is simple. If, for example, activity B consumes all of the slack, there is none left for activity H. However, either can consume a part of the slack such that the total consumed does not exceed the value in the slack column for that activity.

Why the concern over the slack issue? Slack provides a breather in the process where activities can be dormant and resources not used or obligated as long as activities along the critical path are taking place. Delays, oversights, and errors occur and are part of the process. They may occur *after* the time estimates have been made, and slack may be the shock absorber to the system. It is nice to know where activities can slip without endangering the completion date of the project. Consider the house example. If the painters take eight hours to paint the house, and the sod people take four hours to lay the sod, the sod layers can begin *with* the painters, and finish four hours ahead, or start four hours *after* the painters, in which case both groups finish together. There is also an infinity of combinations in between the extremes. In using a team approach to buying capital equipment, the process will not translate to committing all the time of all the members to the project. A well-defined network will tell when the resources are needed and the degree of flexibility available by pointing to the slack in the network. Slack represents the time the team member will be addressing his or her normal duties. In addition, the network allows the project manager to more accurately measure the progress, keep focused on the critical path activities, and selectively manage, as opposed to trying to manage "the whole thing." There are numerous computer programs available to perform the computational aspects of the network analysis. The role of the planner or project manager is to establish the logic of the network and portray that as the precedence diagram or network, and secure the time estimate for each activity.

CPM networks are not static and are regenerated when a node is reached. This updating process may reveal a new critical path. The project manager always focuses on the critical path.

Revisiting the Network as a PERT Problem

Return now to the network with additional data as seen in Exhibit 12-13. Notice that there are now three time estimates for each activity. As a result of devel-

(*text continues on page 344*)

Exhibit 12-13. PERT network for purchasing reengineering implementation.

PERT Network
(A-O-A Convention)

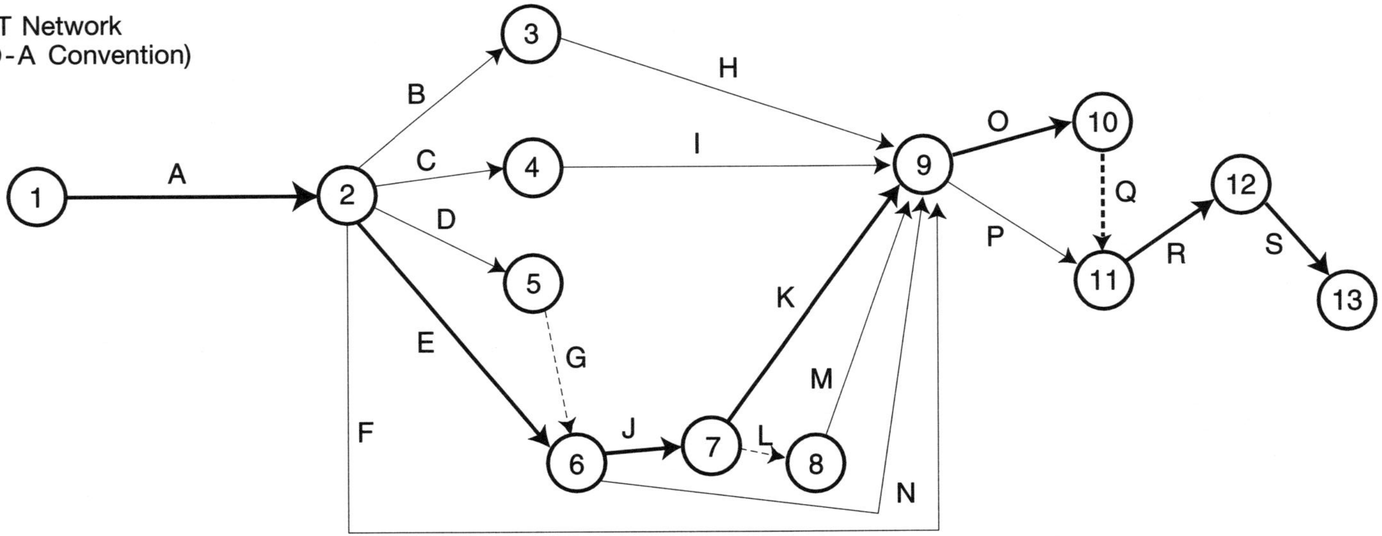

Time Estimates (Weeks)

Activity Designation	Activity Description	Start Node	End Node	Optimistic	Most Likely	Pessimistic	Mean	Variance
A	Team formed	1	2	2.00	3.00	4.00	3.00	0.111
B	Procurement card RFP/contract	2	3	4.00	6.00	8.00	6.00	0.444
C	Computer equipment RFP/contract	2	4	4.00	6.00	8.00	6.00	0.444
D	Move compliance team	2	5	4.00	7.00	10.00	7.00	1.000
E	System conversion	2	6	16.00	20.00	23.00	19.83	1.361
F	Ordinances changes	2	9	2.00	4.00	8.00	4.33	1.000
G	Dummy	5	6	0.00	0.00	0.00	0.00	0.000
H	Procurement card implementation	3	9	6.00	8.00	9.00	7.83	0.250
I	Equipment purchase and setup	4	9	3.00	4.00	5.00	4.00	0.111
J	Purchasing department procedures	6	7	4.00	6.00	8.00	6.00	0.444
K	Redesign departmental procedures	7	9	5.00	6.00	8.00	6.17	0.250
L	Dummy	7	8	0.00	0.00	0.00	0.00	0.000
M	Test and debug programs	8	9	4.00	6.00	8.00	6.00	0.444
N	Develop training materials for using departments	6	9	6.00	10.00	14.00	10.00	1.778
O	Present training	9	10	3.00	6.00	10.00	6.17	1.361
P	On-line testing	9	11	4.00	5.00	6.00	5.00	0.111
Q	Dummy	10	11	0.00	0.00	0.00	0.00	0.000
R	Procedure phase-in	11	12	2.00	4.00	6.00	4.00	0.444
S	Transfer accountability	12	13	3.00	4.00	5.00	4.00	0.111

Critical Path   49.167 weeks
Standard Deviation   2.02 weeks

Critical Path   A-E-J-K-O-Q-R-S

The critical path is the longest path through the network, and is therefore the project duration. The standard deviation along the critical path is a measure of dispersion or variation as to the time required to complete the project.

oping the three estimates, it is possible to compute the mean time for each activity, as seen in the next to last column and the variance. Again, the critical path is the longest path through the network, 49.167 weeks in this case.[6] Having determined the critical path as A-E-J-K-O-Q-R-S, the next step is the computation of the variance. This is simply the sum of the variances along the critical path and is 0.111 + 1.360 + 0.444 + 0.250 + 1.361 + 0.000 + 0.444 + 0.111, a total of 4.081. Taking the square root of the variance to determine the standard deviation, the value is computed to be 2.02 weeks. At this juncture, the question may arise, "So what's the big difference?" The difference is important. It is now possible to make inference or likelihood statements about project completion in any period of time based on the two statistical measures needed: the mean and standard deviation.

Measuring the Likelihood

Having the capability to infer completion time of the project, a question is asked, "What are the chances of completing the project in 52 weeks?" To obtain the answer, one simply subtracts the critical path length from the asking date, and divides by the standard deviation. Thus, 52 less 49.167 = 2.83 weeks. The asking date is longer than the critical path. If this is the case, immediately one knows the probability of completing the project in 52 weeks is going to be higher than 50 percent. If the critical path is 49.167 weeks, there is a 50 percent chance of finish before 49.167 weeks, and a 50 percent chance of taking longer than 49.167 weeks.[7] As we raise the amount of time above the length of the critical path, the probability of completing the project in that raised or increased time should go up. And indeed, it does. How much higher is determined by that difference between the allowed time and the length of the critical path (52 weeks minus 49.167 weeks, or 2.83 weeks) divided by the standard deviation. This figure, 2.83 ÷ by 2.02, or 1.400, tells us the number of standard deviations beyond the critical path length of mean or average. Fifty-two weeks goes 1.400 standard deviations beyond the mean. Fifty-two weeks equals the critical path + 1.400 standard deviations. Referring to Appendix E, the area under the normal curve table, Z has a value of 1.400. Going down the extreme left-hand column to 1.400, the value of 0.9192 appears. Now the probability of completing the project in 52 weeks is 91.92 or 92%. It is almost a probabilistic certainty that, given the validity of the time estimates, the project will be completed in the 52-week time frame.

Consider now the mirror image of the request. What is the likelihood of

6. The reader may wonder why the path length differs from the previous problem, and why there are not two identical length critical paths. The answer is in activity K. It was 6.00 weeks in the single estimate CPM technique. It now *averages* 6.17 weeks in the PERT version of the problem.
7. Since the β distribution is relatively close to the normal distribution, it is allowable to use area under the normal curve for inference purposes.

completing the project in 46 weeks? Immediately, since the completion time is less than the critical path, the probability is going to be less than 50 percent. How much less is going to be determined in the same manner. Again, subtract the critical path from the requested date, or 46 minus 49.167 equals negative 3.167 weeks. This is again divided by the standard deviation or $-3.167 \div 2.02 = -1.567$. Again refer to Appendix E, this time looking at the negative values for Z. Again, going down the extreme left-hand column, reaching a -1.5 and moving across the row to 0.07 for a total of -1.57, the value 0.0582 appears. This says the probability of completing the project in 46 weeks is slightly under 6 percent, or not very likely. Again remember the caveat with respect to the time estimates.[8]

At this point, it is appropriate to briefly discuss the integrity of the time estimates for each activity. They are the building blocks of the control process. If they are inaccurate, the Gantt chart, PERT, or CPM will not make them valid. Several possible problems arise in the estimating process that must be addressed. They include:

1. *Padding the estimates.* One way to minimize the risk of "being late" on the project is the padding of the estimates. This is simply overestimating the time required to perform an activity. Detection of padding is difficult if the person padding knows how to do it. To pad properly, all three of the PERT estimates must be padded. Simply padding the pessimistic estimate will cause the variance to increase significantly. The variance is a measure of the risk in the activity. Smaller variances are caused by less dispersion about the most likely time required to complete the activity. The more confidence in completing the activity in the most likely time, the less dispersion about that estimate, especially on the pessimistic estimate. Watch the variation; it is the indicator.

2. *The problem of control when true control lies beyond the capability of the buyer.* Not all elements in a project are under the project manager's hands. This is especially true in buying capital equipment. Once the order has left the buyer's control and goes to the supplier, control is limited. If there is slippage in the manufacturing schedule at the supplier's facility, that slippage is going to appear in the overall project schedule and have an effect on that completion date. What are the options open to the project manager? There are several including:

• Having more funds available to expedite or crash certain segments of the *supplier's processes.*

• Insisting on liquidated damages or penalty clauses in the contract for late delivery as per schedule. Recognize that these clauses in the contract must be agreed to by both parties. They must be sufficiently substantial to deter

---

8. For the equation hounds, the value of Z is based on the normal deviate equation, $Z = (X - \mu)/\sigma$, where X is the desired completion date, μ is the length of the critical path, and σ is the standard deviation.

lateness.[9] There will also be issues of proof that the delays were not force majeure events.

• Building in the contingency factor on the original time estimates to allow for slippage on the part of any activity that could have slippage or any activity beyond the normal control of the project manager, such as buying from outside suppliers. The origin of the contingency data would be from calling other suppliers' customers to obtain performance history. This must also be tempered with information from the supplier on his backlog. One simplistic indicator is a measure of the backlog and converting that backlog to days of effort. Assuming the company sells at the rate of $1,000,000 per day, and the backlog is $60,000,000, then it is logical to assume they have 60 days of sales in house and will meet those commitments on a first-come/first-served basis. Thus, any promise made short of the 60 days plus the manufacturing leadtime may be viewed as either giving the order priority in the schedule or making a promise that will be difficult to keep. This is one of the indicators that can be used to spot problems before they occur.

Again, recognize the technique is only as good as the data going into it and the technique will not purify polluted data.

3. *Failing to understand what goes on outside the organization in terms of the supplier's commitment to the project.* Often the purchasing portion of the capital equipment acquisition is not complex as a process, yet there must be a good understanding of what is involved from the supplier's perspective. Does the supplier have the capability to perform and meet delivery dates and milestones? How much of the purchase is coming from subcontractors? It is essential to keep track of the deliveries of the components such as electronics, valves, and tooling that can delay the project. What type of equipment is being purchased? Is it "off-the-shelf" or custom-built? Is it a design-and-build contract or a build-only contract? Custom-building and design-and-builds are normally more risky and should be given more time in the schedule to compensate for that risk.

Monitoring the Project

Once the network and its accompanying computations are complete, the project is really just beginning. Monitoring and updating are just as important as proper project definition. A project is a dynamic entity. As activities are completed, the chart or the network is updated to reflect that completion, and attention is kept on the critical path. Noncritical path activities can expand to

---

9. In one contract the penalty clause was $1,000 per day for a late delivery up to a maximum of 30 days. The value of the order was $750,000. The penalty was less than 5% of the order size. It had little impact on the supplier.

consume their slack. When this happens, there is no more time for anything to go wrong. Expanding beyond that time line would cause the activity to become part of a new critical path, all other activity times staying the same. In the monitoring process, there are some general guidelines that may be followed. They include:

- Focus attention on the long-time activities.
- Focus attention on the activities having the largest variances.
- Focus attention on the outside activities, those not directly under control and requiring progress reports from the supplier as compared to his PERT network or schedule.

Data from progress reports are direct feeds into the PERT network. This can be a stipulation in the contract as to the reporting responsibility of contractors. The frequency of these reports should be specified before the purchase order is written. If this is determined, make the reporting simple and straightforward for the supplier. Do not compound the process with excessive reporting requirements. This simply adds costs to the project. Careful planning at the outset will streamline and simplify the control process. Simple follow up by fax or telephone to suppliers before their activity is scheduled to take place can be of immense help.

A Capital Equipment Example

The scenario: Press Industrial Products has need of a CNC blank machine. The purchase itself is not overly complex, but there are a number of steps in the process that must be accomplished as seen in Exhibit 12-14. This is a real situation with the names of the buying and selling company changed. The machine cost was $125,000.

A total of 33 activities are needed, including dummies. There are two options open in controlling the project. They are the Gantt chart, shown in Exhibit 12-15, and CPM.

The Gantt chart supplies the viewer with much good information:

- It indicates the activities needed to purchase and install the machine.

- It provides a time line with project completion in approximately nine months from approval of the requisition to buy the CNC blank machine.

- It measures progress on the time line. A person selecting the date of December 20 would expect to see the transformer for the CNC machine at the plant and the CNC training program in progress, plus completion of an array of activities such as factory rearrangement, purchase orders issued for installation of the machine, and the shipment of pre-blanks or raw materials to the machine manufacturer for supplier testing prior to runoff and shipment of the

(*text continues on page 351*)

Exhibit 12-14. Activities involved in the purchase and installation on CNC blank machine.

Activity	Designated	Time Required (weeks)	Predecessor
CNC Blank Machine Purchase Approved	A	2	—
Vendor Quotes In	B	6	A
Vendor Selection	C	2	B
Purchase CNC Machine	D	1	C
Tooling for CNC Runoff	E	2	D
Transformer Order for CNC Machine	F	7.5	D
Factory Layout and Approval	G	3.5	C
Factory Rearrangement	H	1	G
Vendor Quotes to Install Machine	I	1	G
Finalize CNC Rigging Details	J	2.5	I
Run Preblanks off RisMatic #2	K	1	I
Inspect Preblanks	L	.2	K
Ship Preblanks to Vendor	M	.2	L
Issue P.O. for CNC Machine Rigging	N	1	J
CNC Program Training	O	1	M
CNC Runoff at Vendor	P	1	M
Run CNC Electrical and Air Drops	Q	4	F
CNC Ship to Buyer	R	1.5	H,N,P
Riggers Install CNC	S	.2	R
CNC Hookup and Debug	T	.4	S
Final Runoff on Site	U	1	T
Final Acceptance Meeting	V	.2	U
Old Machine Phase-Out	W	10	V
CNC Programming for New Machine	X	12.5	V
Finalize Tooling for Product	Y	6	V
Machine Operator Procedure Setup	Z	4.5	V
Disconnect Old Machine and Prepare for Sale	AA	1.5	X

Exhibit 12-15. Gantt chart for purchase of CNC blank machine.

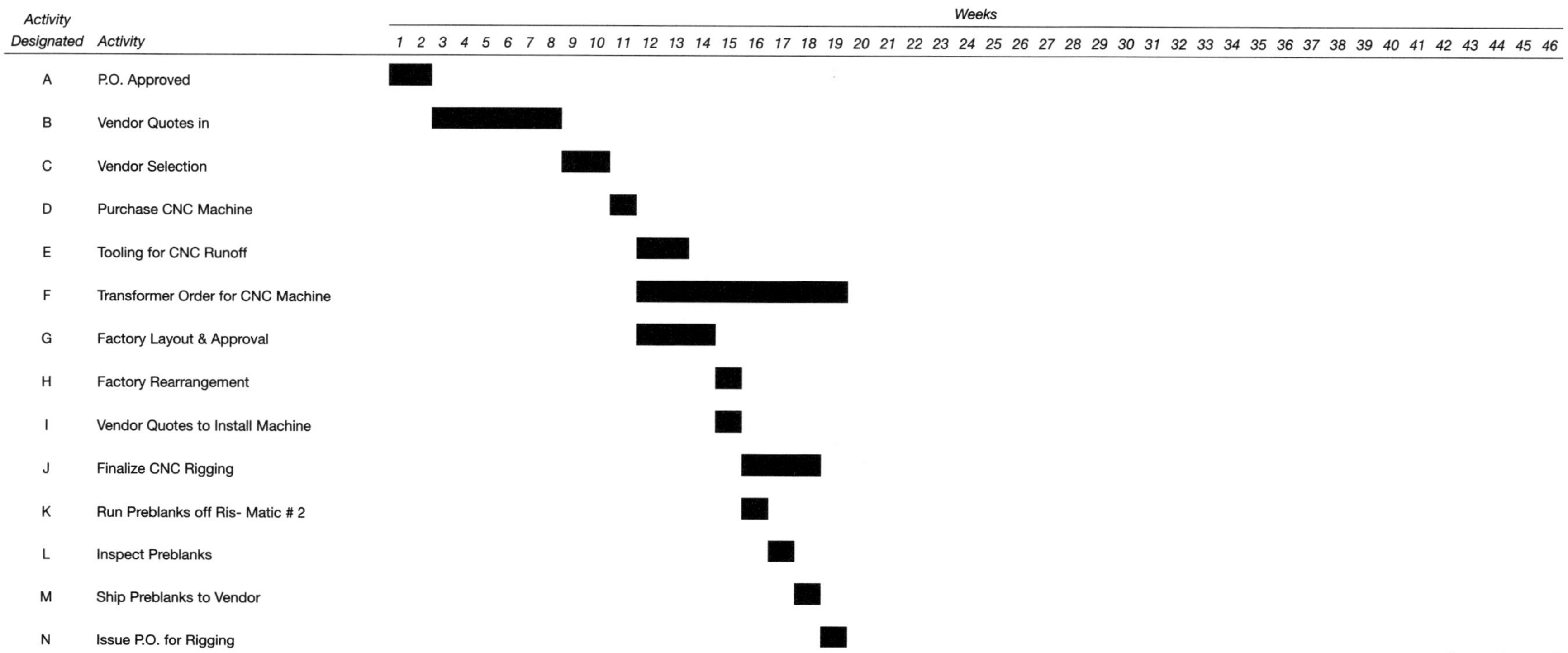

Weeks

Activity Designated	Activity	1 2 3 4 5 6 7 8 9 10 11 12 13 14 15 16 17 18 19 20 21 22 23 24 25 26 27 28 29 30 31 32 33 34 35 36 37 38 39 40 41 42 43 44 45 46
A	P.O. Approved	
B	Vendor Quotes in	
C	Vendor Selection	
D	Purchase CNC Machine	
E	Tooling for CNC Runoff	
F	Transformer Order for CNC Machine	
G	Factory Layout & Approval	
H	Factory Rearrangement	
I	Vendor Quotes to Install Machine	
J	Finalize CNC Rigging	
K	Run Preblanks off Ris- Matic # 2	
L	Inspect Preblanks	
M	Ship Preblanks to Vendor	
N	Issue P.O. for Rigging	

(continues)

Exhibit 12-15. *Continued*

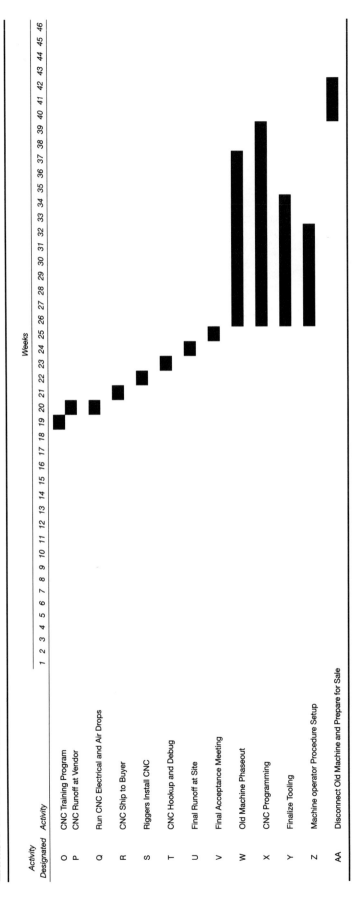

machine to the customer. With respect to factory rearrangement, the supplier should be able to provide a *footprint* of the machine indicating floor dimensionsas well as drop positions/hookups for air, water, or electricity.

• It shows the skill of the project manager in terms of scheduling of activities from two perspectives:

1. Look at the activities that take place while the transformer is on order. These activities are "nested" under the longer lead time item as they should be.
2. Are the times realistic for activities performed by the supplier such as machine construction, supplier testing, rigger installation, hookup and debug, and final runoff? The good project manager will get the best possible information, from the person who would normally perform the task, or have it written into the purchase order or contract as to the allowable time for the activity.

• It shows the sensitive or "dominoes" of the project, such as the transformer being late in terms of delivery would throw the entire schedule off. It is a critical event.

Notice several additional characteristics of the Gantt chart in this example:

• Different symbols can be used to denote different situations as to the activity status, the criticality of the activity, and the actual time spent having the task being performed. For some people, the Gantt chart is sufficient as a visual to control the project. Even the number of symbols allows each symbol, + or =, to represent one full day. The Gantt chart is a simple visual that allows for a somewhat micro control process. A vertical hatched line is sometimes used to depict a "moving calendar" approach to project control. The analyst can see progress on a "day by day" basis and can "look ahead" to some degree to foresee bottlenecks.

• A view of the chart gives the reader an overall feel for the project and the role of secondary activities in successful project completion.

Dissecting the Project

It is often useful to look first at the macro segments or sectors of the project, breaking the whole first in large parts, and then dissecting each of the large parts into smaller parts or activities. This approach affords the opportunity to identify key project activities that drive that macro part or sub-project. It also allows for consideration of the tradeoffs that may take place.

Looking at the chart reveals four major sub-projects that make up the project itself. They are:

1. *Selection of the supplier and purchase of:*

- The machine itself
- The transformers
- The transportation
- The installation

2. *The make-ready activities of the plant prior to the arrival of the equipment including factory arrangement, runoffs at the supplier's facility, and electrical testing.*

3. *Shipment, installation, hookup, acceptance, programming, and tooling of the CNC blank machine.*

4. *Phase-out of the old machine and its preparation for sale.*

This is where the issue of independence and interdependency should be addressed. As seen in the Gantt chart, there are distinct groups of activities. In group # 1 (supplier selection and purchase), the equipment and its power supply are going to be several months in the ordering process along with the transformer. Therefore, the activity of factory layout and approval and arrangement really need not take place until the equipment arrives. Notice the second group of activities, which include testing the machine at the supplier's facility. Once the machine is completed at the supplier's facility, on-site testing is ready to be conducted. It is independent of the installation, allowing us to "nest" the testing in those weeks waiting for the transformer to arrive.

The installation process, from shipping to the day before final acceptance, is accomplished *while* the electrical system and air drops are being tested. Note that final acceptance is scheduled for *after* all parts of the system are working to the satisfaction of the buyer and *before* the expenditure of time and money on programming and *before* the phase-out of the old machine. From the legal perspective, once final acceptance is accomplished, the buyer owns the machine, and with the exception of warranty claims, the buyer has little or no leverage over the supplier if the machine fails to deliver the goods. The careful planner attempts to avoid being "caught in the middle" with no capacity or having expended funds that must be "re-spent" to do the job properly. This part of the Gantt chart illustrates the hedging that is often done with respect to new equipment. Keep the old in place until the new one works. Allow two or three or four months for keeping the old machine around. Its value is not going to disappear in that period of time, and the security of having it there more than compensates for possible differences in resale value. The difference in selling value of the old based on a 10-week phase-out is minuscule in comparison to not having the capacity. Systems often run in parallel before sufficient confidence is developed in the new system to abandon the old one. When the old machine is sold, make the tooling part of the resale package, just in case you need to have the buyer of the machine make some parts for you in an emergency. The tooling is free.

The only issue that might be addressed in this case is the CNC programming. Could it have begun somewhat earlier? In all likelihood, the answer is no. The initial reason is one of acceptance of the machine. It was not the property of the buyer until final acceptance. Second, there would be significant questions if the equipment did not operate correctly as to the program validity. As in the case of most machines of this type, they are purchased to produce a variety of parts. It should be programmed to run a reasonable sample of the same parts to be run in production.

It was a wise decision to postpone or schedule the majority of programming after final acceptance. If time were an issue, the whole process should have been "backed off" the expected completion date to ensure meeting a deadline.

It is interesting to note the purchase of the machine was simply a part of the process. Secondary or support activities are often as important as main activities in successful project completion. The Gantt chart provides much to allow a picture of the process, yet there is more to be considered. Even this Gantt chart is incomplete, for there is no indication of the financial considerations of the project, the spares issues, and the supplier support of the equipment as it relates to warranty. This is but a small part of the overall picture, focusing on the operational steps involved in getting the equipment in, up, and going. It *does* illustrate nesting when looking at the testing at the supplier's site.

What advantage, if any, does the PERT or CPM approach offer over the Gantt chart? Notice on the Gantt chart many of the items were indicated as critical, yet the process appeared to be rather sequential. It is really a matter of preference with respect to use of either technique. The computer advocates will probably select the CPM or PERT technique while others may feel the visual capability of the Gantt chart offers a more rapid reading of the progress on the project. The authors say, "Either one is good, but be sure to use something to control the project or it will slip away from you."

The CPM Network

Consider now the transformation of the data from the Gantt chart to the Critical Path Method format. In order to make this transformation easy as possible, the activities will be relisted with the appropriate dummy activities.[10] The activities are shown in Exhibit 12-16.

With the data provided, it is possible to now develop the network and its solution. Note that the network requires the inclusion of six dummy activities, are seen in Exhibit 12-17.

The results of the computer program used to solve the problem showed

10. Remember that dummy activities are used when two activities start and finish at the same node. They take zero time to complete, but to avoid cluttering the chart, they will be placed at the end of the table.

Exhibit 12-16. Data for development of CPM network for purchase of CNC blank machine.

Activity	Description	Start Node	End Node	Time
A(1)	Purchase Approved	1	2	2
B(2)	Vendor Quotes In	2	3	6
C(3)	Vendor Selection	3	4	2
D(4)	Purchase Machine	4	5	1
E(5)	Tooling for CNC Runoff	5	6	2
F(6)	Transformer Order for CNC Machine	5	7	7.5
G(7)	Factory Layout and Approval	4	8	3.5
H(8)	Factory Rearrangement	8	9	1
I(9)	Vendor Quotes to Install Machine	8	10	1
J(10)	Finalize CNC Rigging Details	10	11	2.5
K(11)	Run Preblanks off Ris- #2	10	12	1
L(12)	Inspect Preblanks	12	13	0.2
M(13)	Ship Preblanks to Vendor	13	14	0.2
N(14)	Issue P.O. for CNC Machine Rigging	11	16	1
O(15)	CNC Training Program	14	15	1
P(16)	CNC Runoff at Vendor	15	16	1
Q(17)	Run CNC Electrical and Air Drops	7	17	4
R(18)	CNC Ship to Buyer	16	17	1.5
S(19)	Rigger Install CNC	17	18	0.2
T(20)	CNC Hookup and Debug	18	19	0.4
U(21)	Final Runoff On Site	19	20	1
V(22)	Final Acceptance Meeting	20	21	.2
W(23)	Old Machine Phase-out	21	22	10
X(24)	CNC Programming for New Machine	21	23	12.5
Y(25)	Finalize Tooling	22	24	6
Z(26)	Machine Operator Procedure Setup	22	25	4.5
AA(27)	Disconnect Old Machine and Prepare for Sale	23	25	1.5
D_1	Dummy 1	6	9	0
D_2	Dummy 2	9	11	0
D_3	Dummy 3	23	26	0
D_4	Dummy 4	24	26	0
D_5	Dummy 5	25	26	0

Note the numbers in the parentheses in the activity column are used to aid in the identification of activities in the solution to the problem. Computer systems will require the numbering of the activities.

the network to have a critical path of 38.3 weeks in duration. The output data are seen in Exhibit 12-18.

The critical activities include:

- Purchase approval
- Vendor quotes in
- Vendor selection
- Purchase machine
- Transformer order
- Running CNC electrical and air drops
- Rigger installation of CNC
- CNC hookup and debugging
- Final runoff at site
- Final acceptance meeting
- CNC programming
- Disconnecting and preparing old machine for sale

Looking at the results reveals the existence of slack in the system and also the possibilities of compressing the network, if necessary. In addition, if the need became critical to bring the machine on-line earlier, what activities could be compressed? Where does the vendor fit into the scheme of things? Notice the five-week lead time afforded to the vendor from the time of purchase to shipment of the machine, and four weeks between purchase and machine run-off at the vendor's facility. It had to be an "off the shelf" machine to be available in that short a time frame. A unique feature of the machine and one of its "selling points" was the robotic arm, which inserted blanks and removed finished parts. The robotic arm was made by the machine manufacturer and mated to the base machine. Having one company do "all the work" pinpoints responsibility and eliminates a good deal of "finger pointing" if something does not operate properly. The robotic arm was also cost-effective and safety-oriented.

In addition, the schematic, either CPM or Gantt chart, tells us that CNC programming will begin after arrival and acceptance, and the machine replaced will not be phased out until the new machine has arrived, however without finalization of programming and tooling requirements for the product.

Obviously, the results of CPM analysis and the Gantt chart are close in terms of total time of project. CPM data shown in Exhibit 12-18 indicate a critical path of 38.3 weeks. The Gantt chart shows more than 40 weeks.[11] The results are quite close, but the time line does not tell the whole story. In terms of seeing problems before they occur, the moving calendar line on the Gantt chart can

---

11. Part of the reason for the difference is the scaling on the Gantt chart. All activities are expressed in weeks of effort, and many of the activities are small fractions of a week. Exercise care in drawing the Gantt chart.

Exhibit 12-17. CPM network for CNC blank machine.

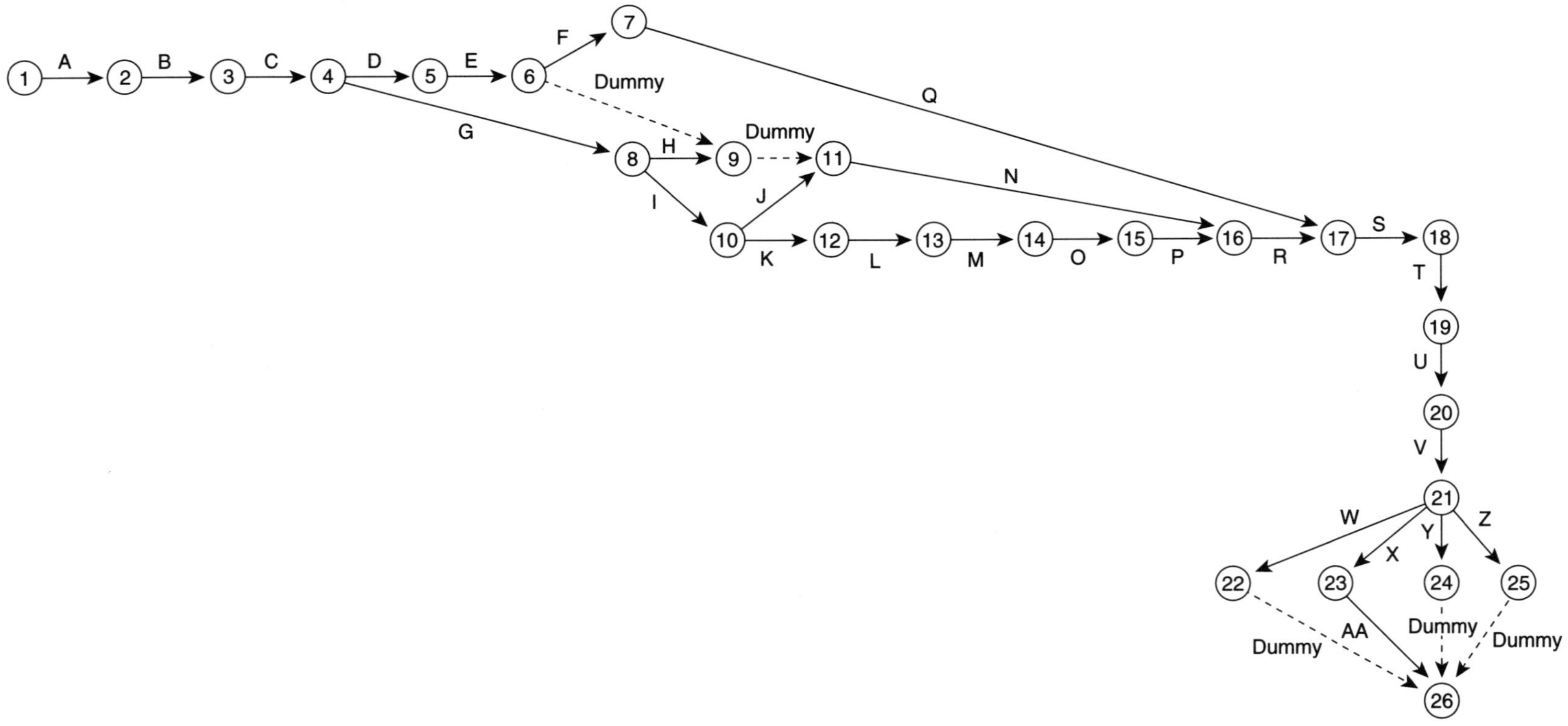

Exhibit 12-18. Program output for CPM on blank machine purchase.

Activity	Earliest Start	Earliest Finish	Latest Start	Latest Finish	Slack
1*	0	2	0	2	0
2*	2	8	2	8	0
3*	8	10	8	10	0
4*	10	11	10	11	0
5	11	13	18	20	7
6*	11	18.5	11	18.5	0
7	10	13.5	13	16.5	3
8	13.5	14.5	19	20	5.5
9	13.5	14.5	16.5	17.5	3
10	14.5	17	17.5	20	3
11	14.5	15.5	17.6	18.6	3.1
12	15.5	15.7	18.6	18.8	3.1
13	15.7	15.9	18.8	19.0	3.1
14	17.0	18.0	20.0	21.0	3.0
15	15.9	16.9	19.0	20.0	3.1
16	16.9	17.9	20.0	21.0	3.1
17*	18.5	22.5	18.5	22.5	0
18	18	19.5	21.0	22.5	3
19*	22.5	22.7	22.5	22.7	0
20*	22.7	23.1	22.7	23.1	0
21*	23.1	24.1	23.1	24.1	0
22*	23.1	24.1	23.1	24.1	0
23	24.3	34.3	28.3	38.3	4.0
24*	24.3	36.8	24.3	36.8	0
25	24.3	30.3	32.3	38.3	8
26	24.3	28.3	32.8	38.3	9.5
27*	36.8	38.3	36.8	38.3	0
28	13.0	13.0	20.0	20.0	7.0
29	14.5	14.5	20.0	20.0	5.5
30	24.3	34.3	38.3	38.3	4.0
31	30.3	30.3	38.3	38.3	8.0
32*	38.3	38.3	38.3	38.3	0.0

*Denotes the elements in the critical path.

provide some insights, but the key issue is the critical path. What activities are the drivers of the purchase? Delays in any one of those activities will delay completion of the entire project. They should be the focal points of the project management effort. This is not to say other activities are not important. They are, but they have some slack in the network as seen in the results of the CPM analysis. The activities with slack must also be watched, but not as closely as the critical path where there is no slack. Now the project manager focuses on activities in the critical path, and by management or oversight on those activities, he or she sees the project coming to a successful conclusion, success being defined in terms of time and cost.

The fact that the critical path encompasses less than one third of the activities shows a reasonable job of nesting the shorter activities under the umbrella of longer activities. This is reinforced by relatively small quantities of slack in the system. In the company where this purchase took place, the project came off well and on schedule. The control was present, and the ability to gain visibility over the purchase was established before the purchase was made. Accomplishment is the ability of all the parts to come together at the right time and place. The final issue in the case was "Who will run the machine?" Recognize in a union environment, the basis of selection may be seniority, and the bidding process for the job, especially if it pays more, may affect who will be entrusted with the responsibility of being the operator. Keep this in mind in the training portion of the network. That slack may come in handy.

Lessons Learned—A Summary

What does the CPM method tell us? Looking at the printout, there is not much slack in the system. There are several key events such as:

- Ordering the transformer for the machine
- CNC programming on the new machine
- Developing setup procedures
- Sourcing and buying the machine

Several interesting observations and generalities may be drawn from this example. They include:

- A well defined and developed Gantt chart can be equally useful as a CPM chart when the project has certain characteristics such as being rather linear with a small number of key activities that take up significant blocks of time.

- Watch out for activities that either lie beyond the control of the buyer as vendor-performed activities such as in-process testing or prototyping or activities that can only be performed after the machine arrives, such as the CNC programming on the machine and the ordering and/or fabrication of tooling for the product.

- Recognize the parts of the buying cycle, such as transportation, installation, and debugging as separate segments of the contract. These activities may be included in the price quoted by the suppliers or may have to be covered by a purchase order. What is covered or excluded depends on the manner in which the RFQ was structured *and* how the vendors responded. With respect to the CNC program training: Is it part of the overall agreement or a separate activity? Where will it be conducted, by whom, and what are the qualifications of both the trainer and trainee(s)? It is not uncommon to get a variety of responses to the RFQ. Each must be read carefully to see if the supplier is responding to the request or making a new offer. Strive to clarify your quotes with the various potential suppliers so that the comparisons are "apples to apples." This has the added benefit of being fair to suppliers with no one getting the edge up on the business.

• Recognize that ancillary activities often take the most time, and the procurement of the machine itself may be a relatively simple process. Having the machine sitting at the plant, uninstalled or installed but idle, raises costs. This will happen when a contingent part of the project has not been completed. Consider the case of the piece of equipment, ordered, delivered, and accepted. It could not be set in place because an automated parts storage system was late. When the system arrived, it malfunctioned and had to be redesigned and rebuilt. Manufacturing had to continue to use the old equipment for nine months before the new machine was installed. The supplier is not going to wait until product is produced and sold to ask for payment.

• Recognize the final acceptance meeting is the last point in time to raise issues relative to the machine. This means the final runoff at the buyer's site should be sufficiently complex and lengthy as to satisfy all concerned. According to the schedule, the final acceptance meeting takes place at the end of the final runoff at the buyer's plant. This is the *moment of truth* in the process. The preparation for the acceptance should cast aside any doubts and prove the decision was correct. If there are any doubts, this is the last chance to clear them up before you inherit the problems. This includes the physical process of acceptance as well as the definition of acceptance. This can be softened by a good warranty and a good relationship with the supplier, but it should be planned in detail to be a positive finale to the purchase.

• Consider what will be done with the old machine whose place the CNC blank machine has taken. According to the schedule, there is a twelve-week period of time in which resources will be devoted to the phase-out and disconnecting of the old machine. During part of this period, the phased-out equipment will probably be producing product and therefore contributing to revenue. However, there will be periods of time where the process of phase-out will be labor consuming. Where are these costs going to be charged? Will they represent costs against the money earned from the sale of the old equipment or charged against the new machine as part of the setup and installation of the blank machine?

• An important factor is the integration of the new machine into its work environment, and this is reflected in the activity of factory rearrangement. Failure to carefully consider integration can lead to added expense of material-handling equipment and reduced productivity of the workforce. One of the reasons the Japanese specify container size in automotive assembly plants is to ensure the assembly-line worker does not perform extra motions, thereby lowering productivity. Too many steps taken to select material for a product moving down an assembly line can be a waste of motion, source of fatigue, and unproductive activity. It is essential to take the perspective that the machine is part of the system and must be integrated in a physical sense as well as system sense.

• The actual purchase took a relatively small portion of the total time. Seeing that the buyer got what was needed, verifying, testing, delivering, installing, testing, and making the machine ready for productive use represented the largest portion of time in the schedule. Who paid for that time? Was it included in the purchase price or carried as a cost of doing business or overhead? Most likely, it is considered overhead and will be absorbed in that account or those accounts. Yet the cost is still there, and in looking at total cost, it should be present as part of the overall cost of the machine.

• Use the Gantt chart of the CPM network to monitor responsibilities as far as personnel are concerned. The project manager can identify the key team members and can manage on an exception basis. Milestones (activities on the critical path) are those that must be managed and coordinated. Noncritical activities can be monitored with less rigor. All that needs to be known is the starting date and the progress. Slack shows us the slippage in the system.

Chapter Checklist—The "Have You" List

- [ ] Fully defined the project? Included all the steps by having different people participate in the WBS sessions?
- [ ] Got some preliminary quotes to determine the money involved and the lead times?
- [ ] Established a realistic completion date based on simple statistical analysis and the experience of others?
- [ ] Selected a team with the various disciplines needed to get the job done from beginning to end?
- [ ] Have all the funds been provided for tooling, installation, start up, travel, and unanticipated expenses?
- [ ] Checked the supplier's performance by asking for customer names and business done with that customer similar to the work the supplier is going to perform for you?
- [ ] Contact those customers and plan on at least two visits to see the same piece of equipment running? Make sure the sites are willing to provide information on the smoothness of the overall process, the integrity of the supplier's promises, and the after-installed performance and costs.
- [ ] Asked for a "footprint" on machine dimensions and hookup positions?

☐ Put together a Gantt Chart, CPM, or PERT network and are using it? Update it as needed and keep control of the project.

☐ Remember the importance of acceptance testing, and involve all the people who need to be in the loop on acceptance testing. Use acceptance testing and pre-testing at the supplier's site for determining the Process Capability Index for the machine on specific parts.

13

Some Closing
Observations

We have come to the end of the book, and if the process were to follow the normal pattern, it would mean a summary of what has been written, or as the army taught, "Tell 'em what you're going to say, say it, and tell 'em what you said." Were it that simple, it would be easy. What this handbook has done is raise more questions than it has answered. This, however, is useful; the size of the capital investment and its organizational ramifications caution us to err on the side of being too conscientious in our evaluation as opposed to making the decision too quickly.

The issue of using the team approach in the decision making still has merit, although the level of frustration can be high. Teams tend toward consensus decision making and there are arguments pro and con. With teams, there is at least a hearing on the areas of concern. Not everyone can win in the team process, but at least the concerns are aired and the trade-offs discussed. The key here is to avoid a situation that compromises to keep people happy. The end result is the camel: a horse designed by a committee. There are clearly going to be parts of the organization that are better represented than others. These are simply greater stakeholders in the process. Engineering will probably emerge as the winner since there are few who can question the technical segment of the purchase. Often those aspects are givens.[1] Finance will also be a winner because these are essentially financial decisions with criteria finely honed, even if the data used have all the solidarity of cotton candy. Shaky estimates of savings, revenue projections over two decades, and assumptions on tax rates projected into the next decade have never deterred the financial

---

1. In dealing with a major contractor building a multimillion-dollar turnkey operation, the contractor was asked to list the areas open to negotiation. As the list grew, it became evident that everything on the list was business oriented and nothing was of a technical nature. When asked about this, the contractor replied that "everyone knew what was wanted and how to build it." The question was whether all the parties could cooperate in the business sense long enough to complete the project. The negotiation became a process of dividing risk and rewards.

analyst from computing to the fourth decimal place. It is often a case of analysis firmly founded on quicksand. Other winners may be quality assurance staff who raise the specter of rejects and rework that escalates costs and deprives the company of sales revenues. If marketing has done its work correctly, a new or improved product has been added to its line.

There are also those who will have to hustle to stay in the same place and act as the bearers of bad tidings. Often this is purchasing, which must view the terms and conditions of the seller's offer and reject them when the enthusiasm of the rest of the team is high as the process nears completion. Purchasing often adds a sense of reality to the total cost of ownership calculation by reminding the team that the equipment must be transported, installed, tested, and accepted before payment is made. Other costs have to be added to the asking price, and a postpurchase audit must be conducted to verify the original numbers used in the calculations.

Still, even with the negatives, the team approach is best. If nothing else, the issues are aired and at least considered before the purchase is made. The team approach tends to minimize the surprises that often accompany the arrival and performance of the capital equipment. Perhaps the most important aspect of the team approach is the communication that the equipment is coming. The preceding statement may appear rather simplistic, but the arrival of the equipment must be properly planned. The footprint must be known to allow for installation and hooking up necessary utilities. The space must be available. Normally installation equates to a representative of the seller's being on site to aid in the process. If the site is not ready, the seller is under no obligation to extend or reschedule the visit. Leaving aside all of the details for a moment, lack of preparation equates to the equipment *not* in operation. Nonoperating equipment generates no output, and no output equates to costs only. Having a team generates a network of individuals who are going to have some role to play in the installation, acceptance, operation, and maintenance of that equipment. The network carries the information on the arrival and coordinates the various activities needed for a successful start-up.

The initial issue lies with top management. They have the responsibility of selecting a team leader who has the right credentials to fit the project at hand. This cannot be an added responsibility for the individual. It must be an assignment with the authority, responsibility, and time to perform it correctly. If the people at the top of the organization do not feel the leadership issue is important, what message does that send to the team?

The team faces a myriad of questions. The gut issues in the selection process are endless, including new versus used, lease versus buy, retrofit versus used versus new, spares options, and all forms of measurement. What shall be the decision criteria? How much weight will be given each criterion? How accurate are the forecasts? What is the position on residual value of the equipment? How shall the costs be tracked? How shall the equipment be maintained? Yet when one analyzes all the issues, one glaring fact emerges: There are more policy decisions than technical considerations. One of the most important considerations is the case of balance. Looking at the Stage I costs in Chapter 11, simple computation of equipment cost to total cost was made for a reason. Is the team focusing on the tail of the dog? Is the important cost area, the cost of the equipment, being given its due consideration, or is it assumed to be correct and much of the emphasis placed on the other elements? It is as if the technology was accepted as a given, and all the other issues of legal, financial, testing, installation, acceptance, and disposal took center stage. Somehow the technical aspect is left to the technical personnel, and technical almost becomes a given with all the emphasis on making the right remainder of the decision. This means that much of the decision process is focusing on the fringe of the decision, with about 75 to 85 percent of the decision locked in by the technical selection. It is analogous to the product design issue. Once the engineering design is finalized, 75 percent of the costs are embedded in the design. The fact that most of the cost is in the equipment itself is a fact, yet do not accept that as a given.

Is this necessarily bad? The search for an answer comes back to the issue of buying by brand name or manufacturing reputation and the relevant arguments for that decision versus the decision to buy for intended use of the equipment. Much of the answer lies in policy formulation. What is the company or organizational policy on such issues? Part of the process may be to question the technical aspects of the equipment and look at options that encompass lower, but more proved and reliable, technology as opposed to the "newest" technology. What is the price of the new technology, and what is to be gained by using it? One company purchased a machine and allowed the seller to convince the buyer that the auto-loader was really necessary. It was a new device, relatively unproved in the industry. In addition to being expensive relative to the machine cost, it did not work well and was the principal reason for low machine productivity. Perhaps a team looking at that purchase would have seen the problem and delayed the purchase of the auto-loader until some later date or never. The basic question that was not addressed was what the real contribution of that auto-loader was. Did it increase productivity? Would it allow the machine to operate at a faster rate? Did it improve quality? Is there a matching process of the equipment design to existing components where there can be the use of already owned spare parts from similar machines? To illustrate this, a major auto assembler insists that suppliers freeze the component design for five years. Body styles may change, additions made in the form of customer conveniences, but basic "fit-together" components stay the same. Components must fit together, and changing one component may trigger a domino effect in form and fit. The company wants no unplanned product re-engineering over the five-year cycle. Another, simpler case is standardization.

What is the focus of the company? Lower technology is not a bad idea if its productivity is competitive. Lower technology may translate to lower maintenance costs, higher reliability, lower spare parts costs, simpler repairs, and reduced downtime. Retrofitting may reduce learning time for operation while being less expensive in Stage I costs. If the policy is focused toward standardization and reaping the benefits of uniformity, then buying all Clark forklifts or all Hyster forklifts makes sense. Splitting orders simply raises costs and complicates the issue of spare parts and maintenance. Being focused on the task being performed and not wanting to buy above the use could lead to a mix of models, which may not be economical. Compound this with the issue of new versus previously owned equipment and the associated attitudes toward previously owned equipment, and the decision takes on many more variables. The issue is one of laying the ground rules for the acquisition process and following those rules in a consistent manner. Once the rules or operating principles are established, much of the decision process can be structured and a better decision can be made. The quality of the decision is enhanced because there is a sense of direction or focus with respect to key variables and the process is not window dressing to enhance or aggrandize a decision that has been made already. This is the process of having the acceptable answer and figuring out how to make it look correct.

Top Management's Role

Top management in the decision-making environment is like that of the search engine on the Internet. It allows the answers or alternatives to be generated. As in the case of the search engine, it defines the policies, which act to limit options. Reducing the options leaves fewer choices and therefore less evaluation. It is the process of defining the rules of selection and asking what fits under those rules. Once the selection is made, much of the remaining decision making becomes standardized, with certain activities always being associated with the purchasing process. Top management provides the vision with respect to rules or policies, and it delineates the scope of decision making. What class of equipment can be used or previously owned versus what must be new? How will the residual value of the equipment be treated? Does the company concern itself with a value 10 years into the future or simply assume zero residual value and allow for equipment modification to meet changing or expanding needs? What will be the maintenance policy, and how will the equipment be tracked? Adding another machine to an on-line computerized maintenance management system (CMMS) benefits all parties. The crucial role of top management is to spell out the capital equipment philosophy and adhere to it. The issue of buying is complex enough, without having to contend with the shifting sands of indecision on technology issues.

Since this book addresses these issues individually, there is no reason to dwell on them, but the part top management plays in defining policy and guidelines spells the difference between a seamless decision process and one that may appear to be a Gordian knot. It is management's responsibility to define the model or schematic to be used. Definition can be via a formal model or guidelines with flexible parameters or strict limitations. Expenditure evaluation can be broadly focused with significant latitude in trade-offs or be the single-value process. In the latter case, all projects coming in above the magic number are still under consideration, while those falling below are also rans. In this situation, much effort is expended in creatively getting the right number in the correct place on the appropriation request. A great deal of energy is expended on a rather useless or myopic task.

It is top management's responsibility to define how a project will be approved and what the criteria are for project selection, as well as how the project is to be presented. It is their responsibility to develop these criteria, communicate them, and stay with them in the decision process. The modeling process may simply be a list, a schematic, or a series of statements in the "how we do it at XYZ Company" book.

The important point is that something is in place to guide the process. The something should be the capital investment analysis manual for the company, defining philosophy, policy, rules, laws, and practices and heavily saturated with examples. The manual also sets out the responsibilities of the team members, defines the approval processes, and generally guides all those responsible for the preparation of requests through the process. It should establish the postpurchase audit process to verify that the data going into the decision to buy were valid and the numbers claimed before the fact did occur after the fact. It does little good to go through the entire process and never evaluate its accuracy. Accountants play a vital role in accurately measuring the results and feeding this information back to the top management. It is important to learn how well the project has done and if the yardsticks are valid.

Without the postpurchase audit and response, the process will never improve. It will remain stagnant since there is no motivation to improve the reliability of the data going into the request. If no one looks at it after the purchase, what difference does it make what it says going into the purchase? Without monitoring for accuracy, any lies can be told without fear of being uncovered. Developing the proposal becomes an exercise in manipulating numbers to reach an answer in such a way the numbers look reasonable or plausible. It is a matter of how the counting took place. It can be done in the same manner that casinos count winnings and losings. A slot machine player who starts with $20 and loses it all has intermediate winnings counted, but losing them does not count in losses. If a player wins $100 and loses it all plus the $20 original stake, the count becomes "won $100, lost $20." The rationale is simple: The loss is the original $20 but not the $100, since the player did not have that with him upon entry into the game. Figures lie, and liars figure. Without some follow-up procedure, there is no motivation to remain honest. Honesty in the capital equipment appropriation arena is a difficult trait. If the numbers are fudged in the appropriation request, in all likelihood it will be discovered and credibility will be lost.[2] Capital is not unlimited, and not all projects will be funded. Only the most promising or badly needed make the cut. Ensuring the project proposal will clear the hurdle is itself a victory of sorts. It is analogous to the statement in the chapter on leasing where the down payment was questioned in leasing. A down payment or cost capitalization reduction (to obscure) makes a bad lease look good. Hiding or obscuring costs through budgetary transfers or inclusions in different budgets hides costs and makes a bad project look better.

Therefore, an element essential to the integrity of the process is the acceptance of the philosophy of life cycle costing or total cost of ownership. Only by embracing the concept of cradle-to-grave ownership can accurate comparisons be made using true costs. Initial cost is only one part of the picture, and often a very small part. Any company that looks at the initial cost is taking a very myopic perspective. It is always cost per.

Putting the Manual Together

If the capital investment process is important to the company, then the manual is an indispensable guide for those concerned with the process. The manual should be composed of seven major sections.

Corporate Philosophy on Capital Investment

This section clearly defines the position of the company as it relates to capital investments. Is the focus of the company toward the cutting edge of technology in buying equipment for production and "nearly" state of the art on support equipment? Is the focus toward standardization, with the purchase of the outlier discouraged? Has the product design been reviewed to eliminate oddball dimensions and tolerances that may add cost to the product but not value? Having those tolerances may raise the cost of the capital equipment without really imparting any more value to the product.[3] Does the company want to replace the equipment over some defined period, thereby giving it a very definite service life, or run it until the wheels fall off and keep repairing it theoretically forever? Is the service life equal to the depreciation schedule in years? If this is the case, the real measure of use may not even be counted. What is the

---

2. The classic case is the federal government's estimates of the cost of a program. Multiply them by 6, 10, or 50 to get closer to the real answer. This is part of the reason the trust level is so low between government and its citizens, who have to pay for the mistakes.
3. By way of example, a medical device for closing incisions during surgery had a print tolerance on the size of the letters telling the company name on the device. That tolerance was ±0.0001 inch. This required a very precise printing machine to imprint on the device. It looked great but did nothing as to the functional use of the device.

policy on residual value? Are all residual values equal to zero and will the equipment sale at the end of the service life be treated by accounting as a sales of assets for tax purposes? How much can be spent on getting the equipment ready for sale?

This section provides the overall guidance as to the attitude of the company toward the purchase in a written and consistent presentation. It is the initial road map for the buyer in preparing the justification for the purchase, and it provides the requestor with a specific path to follow. It does little good to prepare a justification for a $500,000 machine encompassing the state of the art if the company philosophy is to be a follower in the field of technology. There is nothing wrong with being a follower when there can be only one leader. If the company position is to buy previously owned equipment for non-production applications, forget the brand-new forklift truck. Providing this guidance early in the manual sets the stage for the appropriation request.

In addition, the company can set out its philosophy of evaluation and project selection, stating the criteria on which a project will be viewed plus the depth of information required so the project may be considered fairly. How much subjectivity is allowed compared to quantitative data? How much does the company want to see with respect to other user information? What is the depth of analysis required? All projects are not going to require the same scope of coverage, yet there must be some minimum baseline to be met. That baseline need not be the same for all classes of equipment since the "one size fits all" mentality is dangerous here. Using a single criterion, such as a required return on investment (ROI), for all investments may cause the team to generate questionable or spurious data to gain that ROI. There is no single yardstick to employ, and the sooner top management communicates that understanding, the less time will be spent proving the impossible or quantifying the unquantifiable. Communicating these differences and understanding that they will occur with different types of equipment will result in better time allocation among the team members, who no longer seek the impossible.

Representation in the Process

Who sits on the committee or team, and who will be the team leader or project manager? What will be the charge to the team in both specifics and general responsibilities? Saying that a member of the team from quality assurance (QA) will be responsible for all quality issues is a rather empty statement that conveys little. Compare that with the statement saying, "The role of quality assurance is the preparation of the QA plan for acceptance of the equipment, including (1) acceptance testing at the supplier's site, (2) determination of the testing size and procedures for determining the process capability index for the machine, (3) representing the QA in visits to installed sites and providing QA input into the decision process, and (4) design of QA inspection tools."

The manual will indicate team membership and may specify the size of the team by type of equipment. Representation for production of new or existing products may be totally different from the team for buying transfer equipment or vehicles. Again, a balance must be struck on use of the correct team members versus the scale of the project.

The manual should also address the issue of the hand-off of the equipment from the team to manufacturing or the user. This can be a sticky issue. If manufacturing is not satisfied with the equipment, it may be hesitant to accept it. If manufacturing is anxious to get the equipment, there may be an effort to secure control before final acceptance has taken place. This too can present problems.

In addition, it is necessary to define the duties and responsibilities of the project manager. What will that person do? What information will be collected, and what type of documentation is necessary, such as sign-offs by appropriate personnel? (See Chapter 12 for a more detailed discussion of this approach to project documentation.) In addition, what are the responsibilities of each of the team members? Where does their contribution come into play, and what is the weight of that contribution? The decision is not one of consensus to keep the team members satisfied. It is the best possible decision for the company. The project manager is probably the one to make the final recommendation to move the project along for higher approval. In the approval process, the decision comes down to a yes or no, not looking at additional options. Those options should have been discussed and analyzed by the team members. The final approval is placing that request on the approved list and appropriating the funds, not rehashing the team efforts.

Technical Guidelines

What are the technical guidelines that must be followed? Buying capital equipment or leasing has tax ramifications. There are approved periods of time for depreciation of the capital equipment ranging from 3 to 40 years, depending on the type and nature of the equipment. Naturally, accounting would like the shortest depreciation schedule possible, writing off the equipment as quickly as possible, yet the rules must be followed. This information and the guidance provided by accounting or finance can have an impact on the decision and should be clearly provided in the manual. These are the rules over which the company has no control. The Internal Revenue Service sets many of them and they must be followed.

Data in this part of the manual are for guidance and determination of possible courses of action. For example, the vehicle may be fully depreciated over three years. Does this mean the company changes vehicles every three years? Not necessarily. The most cost-effective approach may be to keep the vehicle for five years and when it is sold or otherwise disposed of, handle that as the sale of an asset for tax purposes. The tax liability that is created by the sale would have to be considered in the computation of the total cost of ownership.

How the project is to be evaluated is another set of policies. What methods will be used? What are the relevant interest rates or ROI that will be used in the computations? What tools will be used to evaluate? Is the payback period acceptable, or is net present value analysis or internal rate of return needed? How valid are revenue estimates in the future? Does the company want to minimize total costs by simply adding up all the costs in all stages of the life cycle and dividing by some factor to get cost per and looking at that number associated with alternative investment options or different pieces of equipment?[4] If there is agreement on the methodology and all options are measured with the same yardstick, the consistency factor will override the lack of sophistication of the tools used. There is no point in using a highly mathematical model with bogus or bad data. Models do not correct spurious data.

The Presentation

Guidance on the presentation is important for the team. What does top management want to see in the presentation? Closely related to this question is the matter of process. What is the approval process, and what is to be presented at each level of it? Is there a series of reviews and sign-offs by various levels of management? Does approval vary with levels of authority? Perhaps the forklift can be signed off at the plant manager level, while the CNC machine must go to the vice presidential level. Here is where the schematic of the process is very useful for the team. It shows the gatekeepers in the process or the hurdles that must be overcome for project approval, plus the documentation required at each level. In addition, it should specify the postpurchase audit procedure and the information required to validate the audit.

Examples

The adage of the value of the picture versus words is still as valid today as it was centuries ago. The manual should contain a set of examples of various types of proposals to serve as models or reference points for the team. A com-

---

4. Using the cost approach is an excellent method of shooting one of the sacred cows of financial analysis: the concept of present value. Most present value approaches require the analyst to discount future earnings at the appropriate discount rate and then subtract the initial cost (adjusted for the projected salvage value) from the summation of the earnings. A positive value shows future discounted revenues cover present costs if the result is positive. The problem is that the whole process is based on estimates. Why not simply add all of the current costs (Stage I) in the life cycle and all Stage II preventive maintenance costs and estimated disposal costs plus an estimate of disposal costs? Do not worry about the discounting process since the future cost of maintenance labor and spare parts will rise to approximate the discount rate, thereby canceling the discounting process. All the fancy manipulation of the data is excellent if one can rely on their accuracy. Costs are far easier to project than revenues. In addition, how one projects the revenues from the CNC machine that is part of a production line is questionable. Keep the evaluation process simple. Clarity of method pays for itself.

pleted proposal with all the detail can serve as a useful guide. In addition, the company may wish to define dollar levels and the extent of documentation needed at each level. A request for $25,000 to purchase a piece of equipment may require significantly less documentation than a $250,000 request. This information can best be consolidated in a table or matrix format. In addition, the company guidelines are essential on certain key points. For example, what is the company position on cost overruns? Is the price firm, or is there some level of variation that can be approved by the project manager without going through an approval process? How much latitude is allowed the project manager? Where is the point where the process or segments of the process must be repeated? An example of the process adds immeasurably to uniformity of presentation and ensures the key points of the analysis are present.

Directory of Information

Time is a key commodity for all members of organizations today. It is not something to be wasted. Any organization that has undergone downsizing, reinvention, refocusing, or any of the other popular terms knows the end product is that fewer people do the work. The project team is no exception. Anything that can be done to take the "grunt work" out of the process is important and useful. One method is that of having appropriate computer programs on the network, available to the team for some of the number crunching associated with the project. These can be standard programs normally associated with spreadsheets or word processing, or they may be programs that have been written by individuals especially for this process. Regardless of the source, the availability of this information can be a significant plus for the team. It is basically a "where it's located" directory of information, programs, and brief descriptions of what the program will do, plus where it fits in the evaluation process. These can be standardized and available on a network. Many of these programs are standard to the spreadsheets as financial functions; others may be historical data from the existing company records. If one is seeking a method of justification of replacing one machine with another, more advanced and more cost-effective, the **challenger-defender approach** is useful. The existing machine is the defender, defending its position; it is challenged for its space. Defender data should be available from the records of the purchase (Stage I data) and the CMMS system (Stage II data) as well as the operating costs.[5] All that needs to be done is the evaluation of Stage III or disposition or disposal analysis. This provides the defender position. The challenger must have the work-up for all stages. To simplify the process, drop Stage III from both computations and

5. Be sure to draw the distinction between maintaining the equipment (CMMS data) and operating the equipment (power, lubrication, setup, scrap, quality, time down, other costs associated with the equipment) in coming up with a cost per unit. Assuming labor cost to be equal on both machines on a cost per hour basis, the challenger machine must do better in costs than the defender.

assume zero disposal or residual value or a net zero value.[6] At this point the defender costs become the target. If the challenger can do better than the defender, then it deserves to be purchased or leased.

This approach has merit from the perspective of avoiding the sometimes spurious cost savings estimated in analysis of options. Again, cost savings are reductions in actual expenditures from budgeted or planned spending. They are positive variances where actual is less than planned. They are valid only for the period of that forecast or budget. Beyond that, they are figments of the imagination. For example, if the operating expenses for producing 100,000 units on a machine were budgeted at $50,000 for the current year and at the end of the year it was determined that the actual expense was $45,000, it would be very difficult to convince someone to allow the $50,000 again next year in the budget. The $45,000 figure would be more realistic. Therefore in the second year, the target or budget would be $45,000 and any "savings" would have to be on that basis. Thus comparisons made on project costs are much more realistic than numbers based on so-called savings. If savings are to be used in the calculations, they are valid for budget period by period and therefore have to be adjusted on an annual basis. In this case the comparisons come down to comparing two numbers: the cost per of the defender and the cost per of the challenger.

Checklist

Last in the manual is the Checklist. This can range from a simple list of the activities that must be accomplished to a more elaborate listing of activities plus the date of assignment, due date, and action person as seen in Exhibit 13-1.

The purpose of developing the checklist for the project is to ensure all the critical aspects of the process have been covered. Has all the information· been generated, analyzed, and put into the report? Are there any gaps in the analysis, and have they been recognized and explained? Are the right parties included in the flow of information? Is the process ready to move forward after approval?[7]

The checklist should be subdivided into project phases to force the project manager into looking beyond the approval process to the acquisition, installation, and acceptance of the equipment. In addition, it is useful to look at team membership as it relates to phases of the project. As a phased effort, certain persons may no longer be needed on the team. Like any other project, the time spent is over and above the everyday workload. This means the normal job activities must be accomplished as well. Once efforts have been accomplished,

6. A net zero value would mean there is no cost of disposal and no revenue from it. The scrap dealer disconnects it and hauls it away for free.
7. A significant problem can occur in project types of activities. The presentation of results becomes an end in itself. The project lacks the implementation segment, and approval of the project is the "end product." Approval is simply a stage in the process.

Exhibit 13-1. Suggested format for manual checklist.

| Project # _____ | Project Leader _____ |
| Inception Date _____ | Completion Date _____ |

Project Description

_____

_____

_____

Activity	Responsible Party (ies)	Start Date	Completion Date	Comments/ Coordination
Team Selection				
Scheduling				
Meetings				
Budget				
Preparation				

the project manager should have the authority to release members from the team to allow them to return to normal job responsibilities.

Role of the Manual

The purpose of the manual is not to micromanage the process but to be sufficiently clear on duties and responsibilities to allow for good input into the decision process as well as to point out potential shortcomings and problems. Smaller companies may not have a manual. Nevertheless, it is important for everyone to have a complete awareness of all the details that go into the capital equipment purchase. Small companies are in less of a position to make financial mistakes. The manual may also stipulate the need to write up the project as a historical document with lessons learned from the project. Often in organizations there are projects undertaken where an abundance of information is obtained during the project that may be useful later. Typically it is lost since it is never documented or captured anywhere in the organization. The next project manager must spend time learning the same thing that has been learned before. Reinventing the wheel can be a costly process.

Some Final Considerations

We have discussed a wide range of activities connected with the process of obtaining capital equipment. There is no one perfect method of performing this process. Needs differ, as do space available and capital requirements. The team making the analysis, the project manager directing the purchase, and the upper echelons making the final decision should all keep certain principles in mind:

1. *Remember the concept of balance.* Replacing the 60-unit-per-hour machine with the 120-unit-per-hour machine when all the other machines in the line are geared to 60 units per hour will simply create bottlenecks in the process.

2. *Projecting savings into the future is introducing fiction into a fact-based world.* Fallacious savings are nothing more than tools to skew a decision in one direction. It is a method of starting with the answer and working back to the question.

3. *Recognize the difference between basic functions and secondary or supporting functions.* Basic functions do the job intended. Cutting grass is the basic function of a lawn mower. Catching grass is a secondary function. So is starting with a push button ignition. Secondary functions satisfy the user or supply convenience. Learn to separate the primary from the secondary and analyze what you are paying for convenience and satisfaction versus performance of the primary function.

4. *Record keeping is a key element of analysis.* Most people are lousy record keepers. If the equipment is important to the organization, the records are also important. Look for a system that is user friendly, captures needed data, and allows for more wrench time on the part of maintenance people. That is what they are paid for.

5. *Cheaper options usually aren't.* Look at the total cost of ownership from the inception of the need to the passing of title to another party. What may be inexpensive at the time of purchase can be very expensive to operate and maintain later. Look at cost per regardless of what the per happens to be. Realize that you are comparing relatives, not absolutes, and if the basis of comparison is valid for all options, you are going to be able to make comparisons. Make the comparisons on meter readings or units of output, not time. Idle equipment does not deteriorate, even though clock hours are passing.

6. *Make your supplier a part of the process.* Your supplier should be able to provide a good deal of data on the equipment. Do not stop at that source. Make visits to installations and watch the equipment operate. Watch it being maintained, and solicit information before you buy.

7. *Realize that everyone in business must make a profit to survive.* It is the reward for risk taking. The only time this is not true is at a bankruptcy sale. If the deal is too good to be true, it probably is. There are bargains in the used equipment market or at auctions, but they must be searched for. Remember that often the purchase is as is, where is, and clear title is about all you can expect.

8. *Discuss the warranty very carefully with the supplier.* Get agreement on the terms of that warranty, especially as they relate to safety issues or employee

health. The seller's interpretation of safety requirements and the buyer's may differ considerably. The seller will probably want to be relieved of any liability for accidents, even during the warranty period.

9. *Make sure other terms and conditions are understood and acceptable to both parties.* Clarify the role of the supplier in testing, shipping, installation, and acceptance of the equipment. Will the supplier stand behind the equipment—and how far behind in the case of foreign suppliers? What is the relationship between the foreign supplier and the domestic representative? What would have to be done to alter the equipment to meet U.S. requirements? Who supports the warranty in this country? Have all the physical characteristics been considered, including size, footprint, weight, and specifications (metric vs. English)?

10. *Forgiveness may not be present in the equipment purchase.* A bad role of tape is thrown away. A bad coil of steel is returned to the supplier for credit or replacement. Incidents such as these are soon forgotten if they are not repeated. The equipment is present and serves as a constant visual reminder of a bad choice. The decision is one that will have to be lived with for years. Therefore, buy in haste and regret in leisure.

The elephant has many parts as viewed by the blind men. It is a tree, a snake, a wall, a rope, and many other things. We all tend to view the elephants from our own perspectives. Failing to notice the other person's perspective can be dangerous to the health of the organization and expensive in the buying process. If the talent is present in buying the equipment, use it—all of it. This goes all the way down to the operator and the person who maintains the equipment. These are the people who are going to live the decision on a daily basis. They can make that decision look terrific or terrible. Keep them in the dark, and you ask for problems. Involve them, and they become stakeholders in the process. Finally, always strive to stay in front of the elephant. Don't get caught in back.

Good luck on the next purchase, and keep records.

Appendix A
Process Capability Index: An Overview

Variation is the enemy of quality. Quality has been defined as the adherence to specifications. How closely does the product meet the design created by the design engineer? Designing a part is one thing; building it is another. The designer can be unhindered by the limitations of technology or the lack of it. Surviving for three decades and numerous spinoffs, *Star Trek* still portrays technology that may be generations into the future. The reality of producing the part comes down to the minimization of the variation in the production of the part. Since the machine is a possible source of variation, there must be adequate measures of the capability of the machine to produce acceptable-quality product on a consistent and predictable basis. The impossibility of predicting with 100 percent accuracy when a defective product will come off the machine forces us to retreat and look at what can be predicted as likely to occur and the actions that may be taken if that event takes place.

With the machine as a source of variation, it must be qualified as being capable of producing the part correctly. *Correctly* must be defined in statistical terms to mean so many parts per thousand defective on a random basis or nonassignable basis. Defects coming off the machine are either random, and therefore have no explanation as to why they were defective, or they are defective and some cause can be found. The key is knowing how many to expect on a random basis. If that number is exceeded, then there is a probabilistic expectation of an assignable cause of variation. It is almost a problem in logic. Defects must be assignable because they are not expected to be random. Having reached this stage, the next step is fault analysis or cause and effect diagrams (which are beyond the scope of this appendix).

The common measure is the **process capability index,** C_p. This value is defined in two ways:

$$C_p = \frac{\text{Upper specification limit} - \text{lower specification limit}}{6\sigma}$$

$$C_{pk} = \frac{\text{Mean} - \text{lower specification limit}}{3\sigma}$$

or

$$\frac{\text{Upper specification limit} - \text{mean}}{3\sigma}$$

The upper and lower specification limits are often called the **tolerances** and represent the maximum physical variation that may be allowed for the particular specification and still have the part perform its intended function. It is allowable variation. Products must be produced within those tolerances, or they will not work. The difference between the two measures C_p and C_{pk} can be seen by looking at the equations. C_p is concerned with the relationship between actual process variations and specifications. The smaller the actual variation as measured by the standard deviation, the higher the value of the index. This would show the process consistently producing product inside the allowable variation on a repeated basis.

In the case of the C_{pk}, the attention is given to the process variation by considering the relationship between the process average and the lower or upper specification. The numerator of the equation is a measure of the average variation from either specification. If the machine is producing close to either the upper or lower specification limit, the chances for the machine to be process capable diminish significantly. The numerator must be at least equal numerically to the denominator.

As the mean value of observed output tends toward the lower specification limit or lower tolerance ($\overline{X} \rightarrow \text{LSL}$), the size of the dispersion increases in the denominator. The variation between the actual versus the specification becomes larger. As the denominator increases, holding the numerator constant, the value of C_{pk} will decline. The same relationship will hold true for dealing with the upper specification limit or tolerance. Since the denominator of the equation is computed on the basis of variation between the specification and the means of small samples, any drift toward either specification limit would raise that variation, raising the denominator and reducing the value of C_{pk}.

Sigma (σ) is the Greek letter used for the **standard deviation,** a measure of dispersion around a probability distribution. It is the measure used to convey the distance between the mean or average value of a probability distribution and any point on that distribution. For example, a normal distribution has a mean or average of 100. It has a standard deviation, which is the square root of the sum of squared distances from the mean divided by the number of observations:

$$\sigma = \left(\frac{(x_i - \bar{x})^2}{n} \right)^{\frac{1}{2}}$$

From an algebraic view, quality assurance may specify a value for the specification as being 100 pounds with a standard deviation of 10 pounds. It is possible to determine how far from the mean any single value will be in standard deviations and through the use of a normal distribution table the probability of getting that observation or value as a possible reading or unit of output. Using the normal table (Appendix E), it is easily seen that if one goes plus or minus one standard deviation ($\pm 1.00\sigma$), then there is a 68 percent probability that an observation will fall into that range or between 90 and 110 pounds. Going out two standard deviations, there is a 95 percent probability that an observation or unit of output will fall within 80 to 120 pounds. Taking it to the three-standard-deviation level, the probability increases to 99.7 that a unit of output will be between 70 and 130 pounds. Thus, there are three chances in 1,000 that a unit of product will weigh less than 70 or more than 130 pounds, strictly on a random or nonassignable basis. By setting the denominator of the process capability index as 6σ or $\pm 3\sigma$, the chance of a single unit of output exceeding that range is 3 out of 1,000 on a random basis. The expectation is that 997 of 1,000 produced will fall inside that range. The minimum value for the process capability index is 1.00. This means the range between the upper and lower specification limits equals six standard deviations. This translates to the likelihood that getting a unit of output that exceeds either the lower or upper tolerance on a random basis is 3 out of 1,000.[1]

Now an expectation has been developed as to what percentage or number of defects would begin to signal a problem with the equipment. Yet there is not one single value for C_p. There are many values, with each value associated with every specification that appears on the drawing or print for the item. If failing to meet the specification or fall within the tolerances for the part translates to rejecting that part, then every specification must have a C_p value of 1.00 or greater. Thus, there is now $C_p s$, the term used to represent the process capability index for each specification selected. This now means multiple measurements of each unit coming off the machine in the supplier site machine evaluation phase. Exhibit A-1 is a sample chart.

A general rule for the sample size is based on at least 20 samples of 2 to 5 units that would be taken, and the grand mean or mean of sample means would be computed as well as the standard deviation of the individual sample

1. It is essential to understand the difference between random variation and assignable variation. I cannot cure random variation. Assignable variation can be traced and perhaps eliminated. The distinction is critical.

Exhibit A-1. Data for process capability determination: supplier site run.

Variable	Specification	± Tolerance	Sample Size = 5	Reading
Weight	100	+2, −2	1	101.2
			2	100.5
			3	101
			4	102
			5	99

means versus the grand mean.[2] Companies may base the sample size on the number of holding stations that the part passes through in the course of production. One company uses the decision rule of 50 units plus the square root of 4 hours of anticipated production. A production rate of 225 units per hour with 1 to 4 holding stations would equate to 50 plus the square root of 4 times $225(4 * 225)^{1/2}$ or $50 + 30$, or 80 pieces. They add 25 units for 5 to 9 holding stations and 50 for machines with 9 to 12 holding stations or fixtures. The more complex the product, the larger the sample. The samples are now measured against the specifications of interest. This means the same unit can have anywhere from 1 to n measurements associated with it.

The computation of the standard deviation can be done using the formula for the standard deviation or using the formula shown below if the sample size is 5. Since the range is also a measure of dispersion, its use should not be ignored in computation of the standard deviation:

$$\sigma = \frac{\overline{R}}{2.334}$$

The process capability index for this specification would be 4 (−2 to +2) divided by 6 times the standard deviation computed from the small samples. For purposes of illustration, assume the average range of the 20 samples was 2 pounds. If the range were used, the standard deviation for this situation would be:

$$\sigma = \frac{2}{2.334}$$
$$= 0.857$$

The process capability index for weight would be:

---

2. For a good discussion of process control charts and the underlying concept of this material, see J. Cryer and R. B. Miller, *Statistics for Business* (Boston: PWS-Kent, 1991), pp. 249–270.

$$C_p w = \frac{4}{6 * 0.857}$$
$$= 0.779$$

This machine would be process incapable for this process.

To be process capable, the average range of underweights and overweights must be no more than 1.56 pounds. This is computed by working backward through the equations by setting $C_p w = 1.00$, which means $4/(6 * x) = 1$. The standard deviation is the unknown, and solving for σ, a value of 0.667 is obtained. If σ is 0.667, then:

$$0.667 = \frac{\overline{R}}{2.334} \text{ and } \overline{R} = 1.56 \text{ pounds}$$

The purpose of working backward through the equations is to spot possible problems before they occur. If quality assurance knows the average range needed to meet the minimum process capability before the supplier site tests begin, then it is possible to monitor the testing in progress. This sequential approach can look ahead. If the average range is going beyond the maximum allowable range in the beginning samples, then it would be possible to conclude that the machine is failing the on-site test. This is simply a case of knowing what the answer has to be before the question is asked.

This would be the process capability index for the variable weight. Add up the number of variables that are considered important, and this will indicate the number of measurements to be taken for each product produced on the machine.

When products are designed, that issue of who is going to measure what is not always considered. This does not mean measurement does not take place. It must. If it does not, there is no such thing as quality of output, and quality is now a random event, unpredictable and uncorrectable.

What Does 1.00 Really Mean?

Earlier it was assumed that a value for C_p equal to 1.00 is adequate at the three-standard-deviation level. In many cases it is; however, the expectation is 3 defects per 1,000 on a random basis with no ability to assign a cause to these defects. In some companies, that percentage is considered unacceptable. Motorola and its famous "six sigma" concept set the denominator at $\pm 6\sigma$ level. Keeping the value for the process capability index at 1.00 with this approach means the stacked or added print tolerances would equal the area encompassed by a total of 12 standard deviations. Going well beyond the tabular ranges of most statistics books, this translates into the probability of a random defect being produced as measured in units per million. It is analogous to winning the lottery on a single ticket. Getting a ratio of 1.00 is a simple process. It is a number divided by itself. Encompassing a greater number of standard deviations or reducing the chances for a random defect is a management decision.

It is possible to achieve parts per million defective rates by the utilization of very high-quality machines, carefully calibrated and maintained with clocklike precision. It is possible to do this if cost is not a consideration or the product is known for that level of quality. In many instances, the level of quality is a competitive advantage, but quality of output is not free, and the cost of reaching that quality from the machine or equipment perspective may be very high. It then becomes a balance between the need for high-quality output and the cost of achieving that quality. If the quality is necessary, then the expenditure on process-capable equipment with the ability to provide quality output defined as minimum variability is justified. If there is an allowable variation, then dispersion is not an issue. The important consideration is what is to be measured. This appendix indicates approximately 100 observations of each specification of interest. This incurs cost and may cause people to reflect on what are the important specifications as opposed to proliferations on a drawing.

There are different approaches to expressing the process capability index to draw distinctions between different pieces of equipment. One may hold the $\pm 3\sigma$ denominator as constant and set the index at 2.0. This would mean the stacked tolerances would equate to twice the denominator and be the same as the six sigma case, but by holding the denominator at the $\pm 3\sigma$ level, a relative measure allowing comparisons can be made. When the C_p is specified, it must be stated at what level of standard deviations a value of 1.00 is acceptable. Thus, the quality assurance specification of a process capability index of 1.0 is meaningless unless accompanied by a statement such as "$C_p = 1.00$ at the $\pm 3\sigma$ level." Anything less is an incomplete specification.

What, then, is the overall process capability index for the machine? *It is the lowest acceptable index for any single critical specification.* This is not a place for averaging. The index for each and every critical specification should be at least 1.00 at the desired number of standard deviations regardless if the value is ± 3, ± 3.5, or ± 4 standard deviations. Do not average since averaging will mask extreme values. For example, the index values for four critical specifications were 1, 2, 2, and 1 or an average of 1.5, but 50 percent of the indexes barely met the minimum criteria. Four others could be 1, 0.5, 0.5, and 4. That also averages 1.5, but 50 percent of the indexes show process-incapable equipment on those specifications. There is an overall floor of 1.0. No index for a specification should be allowed to go below that value.

Be sure the testing at the supplier's site gains the greatest overall value and information for the buyer. Use it for training the operator(s). Use it to determine if the intended process capability indexes are met or exceeded and by how much or if deficiencies are present in the machine that may be corrected before the machine is shipped. The act of shipping can create problems, but rarely does it solve them. Gain the maximum value from the testing and use the talents of another team member: the quality assurance specialist.

Who are the responsible parties in this process? A minimum of four people are going to be involved in determining the process capability indexes. It is initially a top management decision to make the determination for all capital projects involved in the production of goods by the company. Without the indexes, any attempt at statistical process control is useless charting. Problems can be identified but not assigned. With respect to the knowledge of the procedures, sample sizes, and forms, this is an area of quality assurance expertise. They may also do the actual measurements, or that may be left to manufacturing engineering supported by quality assurance. The analysis is a QA function. Purchasing has the responsibility of incorporating the appropriate information about the testing process or program into the purchase order before it leaves the buyer's department.

As to the actual measurement by inspection, the supplier may do that in the presence of an engineering or quality team member, prior to shipment, to demonstrate the acceptability of the equipment. This is verified upon delivery of the equipment by completing the necessary tests. The test is done twice: once at the source and once at the destination. It is always completed prior to release of the equipment to production.

Some Final Thoughts

It is the simple things that often trip us up, and the process capability index testing is no different. A few simple procedures are helpful:

1. Number the pieces as they come off the machine during the test.

2. Note when a machine adjustment was made in the test run. What was the last piece before the adjustment, and what was the first piece before it?

3. Number in such a way that fixtures holding the part can be identified if there is more than one fixture holding the part.

4. Make the run without tool adjustments if possible.

5. Make a pretest run to check the setup of the machine.

6. Verify machine feeds, speeds, and tooling before the pretest run.

7. Define the characteristics for acceptance in terms of the index or the proportion of the output that must lie with a certain percentage of the tolerances. For example, one company says that all parts within the sample average, $\overline{X} \pm 3\sigma$, must not exceed 75 percent of the tolerances. This would give a process capability index of 1.33, since the denominator of the equation is equal to .75

times $\pm 3\sigma$. This would give a value of 1/.75, or 1.333, excellent for a process capability index.

8. This is the final opportunity to prevent future production problems. Use it accordingly.

9. Get the statistical process control information on the machine from the supplier before the computations are made or even before the test plan is developed for the parts coming off the machine, at both the supplier's site and when the equipment arrives and is installed.

10. Document everything. You may need it someday.

Remember, process capability standards should be set in relation to the tolerances of other equipment in the manufacturing process. Automated assembly relies on the uniformity of parts being fed into it. Set the standards too low, and machine jam-ups are sure to follow.

Appendix B
Reliability Analysis

When the issue of reliability is discussed, it is sometimes considered a part of quality and in some cases as a separate topic. For the purposes of this appendix, consider reliability to be stand-alone. If quality is defined as adherence to specifications, reliability is concerned with the duration of time the product will adhere to those specifications. It is best illustrated by the familiar task of checking ornamental tree lights at the holiday season. The string in series is dependent on the weakest bulb. It is *always* the last bulb replaced before the string lights. Investing a little more in a parallel strung set ensures all the lights will function independently of each other. Replacement is limited to the defective ones, which are significantly easier to identify.

Carrying the illustration to the machine, reliability is a critical dimension in machine design. Does the equipment have the capability to sustain a failure or a slowdown and still operate? Jet aircraft are often capable of flying on fewer than the number of engines normally found on the aircraft. This is especially useful in the case of international travel where the proximity to an airfield may be measured in hours or hundreds of miles. For capital equipment, there are many reliability issues that are important to the spare parts stocking program and maintenance activities. These activities compound the picture by affecting the record keeping associated with the machine.[1] Ensuring reliability can be accomplished by designing in the reliability through redundant systems. This is simply providing a backup system or secondary system to take over if the primary system fails. Hospitals have fossil fuel generators or battery power to provide electricity in case of emergency power losses. Garage door openers have manual controls in the event of a motor burnout or power loss. Secondary systems are common. A second way to ensure reliability is by maintaining the equipment in such a manner that significantly reduces the likelihood of machine failure. This is done with preventive maintenance or periodic or sched-

---

1. Throughout this book, the issue of keeping good records on the equipment arises. This appendix is no exception. Failure to maintain good records can result in unnecessary expenditures of money and time and the possible disposal of useful parts.

Exhibit B-1. Sequential reliability.

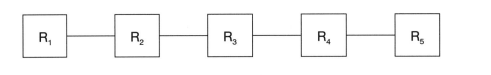

uled maintenance programs where replacement of parts with finite service lives is accomplished before the part or component fails.

System reliability itself is a rather simple concept. It is based on the weakest link premise. The system in serial format depends on the least reliable component. Link the components together so the operation of the system depends on a sequence of parts working, and the overall system reliability drops dramatically. System reliability is the product of the linked component reliability. A system is composed of five sequential parts, as seen in Exhibit B-1. The reliability of each part is 0.99. This means there is a 99 percent probability that the part or component will last to its expected service life. The system reliability is:

$$R_1 \times R_2 \times R_3 \times R_4 \times R_5 = 0.99^5 = 0.95$$

Add another part with the same reliability and the system number drops to 0.94. Add another part that has a lower reliability, say 0.8, and the system reliability drops to 0.76. The chain is truly as strong as the weakest link.

In order to prevent failures, several approaches are possible. The most common is building redundancy into the system. If the part fails, there is a backup capability to take over and perform the same function. This, in effect, allows the second part to take the place of the first part and significantly alters the overall system reliability.

Consider the example with the five components. All components having the same reliability resulted in a system reliability of 0.95. The addition of the sixth component with a reliability of 0.8 lowers the overall reliability to 0.76. That lower-reliability component should be the one having the backup or redundant system. The system now appears as shown in Exhibit B-2.

The impact of adding the redundant system is computed by using the equation:

$$P_{1w} + (P_{1w} * P_{2n})$$

where

P_{1w} = the probability of the basic components working
P_{2n} = the probability that the second component is needed. This term is nothing more than $1 - P_{1w}$.

Exhibit B-2. Series of components with backup.

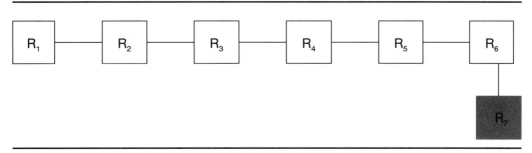

Consider the results. Adding the redundant component R_7 gives that sector (R_6 and R_7) of the system a reliability of

$$0.8 + (0.8 * (1 - 0.8)) \text{ or } 0.8 + 0.16 = 0.96$$

Now the system reliability is $0.99^5 * 0.96$, or 0.913. The probability of operating for a certain period of time has been raised from 76 to 91 percent by the addition of a unit that has no greater reliability than the weakest link, the least reliable component. The value of the system reliability will change as the redundant component is upgraded, yet the same unit as backup was used because sometimes it is impossible to go beyond a certain point in terms of reliability. If component 6 could achieve a reliability of only 0.8, then that is what must be used. The point is that reliability can be enhanced with the addition of redundancy. Now the issue is reliability versus cost.

For the equipment buyer, reliability is a decision criterion. It can be accomplished in three ways:

1. *Improved design* to build in reliability as part of the rationale for buying this particular model. An interesting situation often develops where the upgrading of the equipment can be done quite reasonably. Normally, it is not the expensive components that fail. It is the less expensive ones that may cause the machine problems. A slight increase in expenses for certain dynamic components can save maintenance costs in the future.

2. *A preventive maintenance program* that addresses the reliability issue. This is a trade-off issue: the expenditure of maintenance dollars in the form of prevention, thereby enhancing the reliability or decreasing the likelihood of failure while "scrapping" good parts versus the cost of failure maintenance and its accompanying downtime.

3. *Redundant systems in areas of lower component reliability.*

The answer can be the use of only highly reliable parts and components on the system. This can be deceptive also since all parts on a machine are not subject to failure and failure can occur in several ways. An automobile tire, for example, fails due to contact with a foreign object such as a nail or broken glass. It fails due to wear and reaching the end of the service life. Therefore the first issue to address is the definition of the possible failure-prone parts. Once having identified the candidates, what reliability data are available on those parts? Typically, failures of parts follow the traditional bathtub curve in Exhibit B-3.

Exhibit B-3. Bathtub failure curve.

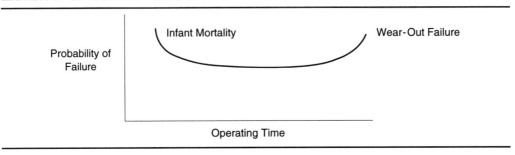

The curve shows the early failures as infant mortality failures, normally the result of improper manufacture or poor materials. As time progresses, the probability of failure stabilizes and centers about a long-term average. As time accumulates on the part, the probability of failure increases as wear-out begins. Although there are other possibilities as far as the failure distribution is concerned, this is the most common. With increased quality in the manufacturing process, the Weibull Distribution is seen.[2] In this case, the early failures are minimal and increase until the period of stabilization is reached. This period continues until "old age" is reached and wear-out failures begin, raising the likelihood of failure. This distribution is shown in Exhibit B-4.

This function allows prediction of failure based on knowledge of failure rates. If a theoretical probability distribution is deemed inappropriate or does not appear to be relevant, the other possibility is obtaining failure information from the supplier by parts using the failure frequency as a substitute for the probability distribution. The failure curve is based on experience with the part and may be gathered from the supplier or user (other machine owners) experience. This would mean getting historical data to determine the mean time between failure (MTBF) or getting the data from the supplier as to the MTBF or in the form of failure curves to evaluate the best possible maintenance policy. All this information should be incorporated into the manufacturer's suggested

2. With increased emphasis on defect prevention in the manufacturing processes, the traditional bathtub curve may no longer be appropriate as the failure curve. The Weibull Probability Distribution may be more appropriate. In the Weibull Distribution, infant mortality is low and increases until the long-run failure rate is reached. The constant failure rate continues until "old age" is reached and wear-out failures begin.

Exhibit B-4. Weibull failure curve.

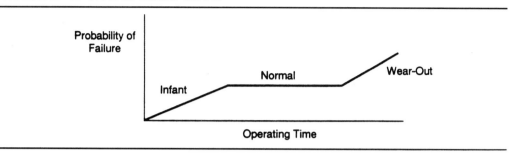

spare parts list. A typical failure curve, shown in Exhibit B-5, plots the cumulative frequency of failure as a function of operating time.

Using failure curve data, it is possible to simulate the failures of components and evaluate alternative maintenance policies. This approach is especially helpful when the teardown process is expensive. If teardown is expensive or accessibility is difficult, the policy of repairing and replacing parts on an as-needed basis may not be practical. The cost of the replacements may be small relative to the make-ready and reassemble costs. If teardown and reassembly costs are negligible, there is no point in throwing away good parts. Thus, the first element to understand in defining a policy is the maintainability of the equipment. Designing the equipment to be accessible to maintenance can command a slightly higher price in the market. High reliability and maintainability can command a premium price, with the added costs being offset by savings in the future from not having to spend dollars on spare parts and maintenance. Consumer examples are Maytag Products and the Kirby Vacuum Cleaner.

A series of decision rules can be developed to guide the maintenance ac-

Exhibit B-5. Failure curve.

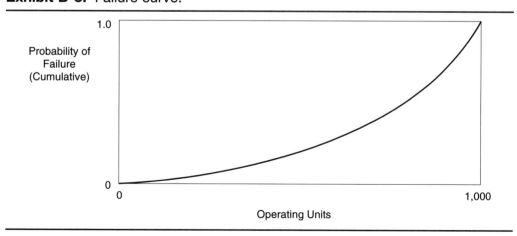

tivity in any policy route other than initiating repair as needed. These decision rules are needed for two major purposes:

1. When the machine is down for maintenance, what will the maintenance encompass?
2. When has the machine reached the end of its service life from a maintenance perspective?

In the first issue, it is often difficult to know the extent of the maintenance that will be needed until the machine is torn down or disassembled and maintenance personnel have an opportunity to go over it. Yet from a practical perspective, a teardown would encompass certain kinds of activities. Routine items such as gaskets, lubricants, and filters are routinely replaced. Thus, planning for the maintenance should include a factor to cover these costs. This is the first echelon of maintenance. Decision rules can be formulated to include a wide variety of items in this classification of first-echelon or routine maintenance, plus adding items to the list based on maintainability. There is little to be saved by not replacing a V belt to save a few dollars and having to spend 5 or 10 times that figure to replace it when it fails. Sparkplugs are not replaced on a single plug basis.

The second issue is more complex. When does the cost of maintaining the equipment start to become prohibitive? One could, in theory, keep a Model T automobile running forever by periodic replacement of all of the parts, yet the cost would be prohibitive and eventually the automobile would be totally replaced. What is the decision rule for saying "no more repair" on the machine and begin casting about for its replacement? Some heuristics are based on cost such as, "When the cost to repair equates to 50 percent of the present value of the machine, replace the machine."

Other rules look at service life extended on an incremental basis. A repair or overhaul extends the service life by some percentage or factor. It may never bring it back to its zero hour service life, but it may add 50 or 75 percent to the projected service life. Associated with that service life is an incremental cost required to achieve that addition. By way of example, consider that a complete repair and replacement on a machine costs $10,000. By performing this extensive maintenance on the machine, the service life can be extended by 2,000 operating hours. This means the incremental or added cost of extending the service life is $5 per hour to be added to its operating cost per hour. From a costing perspective, at the end of 2,000 hours, the cost returns to its former level if no other costs have occurred to raise that cost. What is sought is some measure to tell if continued repair is worth expending the dollars to extend the life of the machine.

This decision should be made in the design stage or the equipment selection phase. How closely does the maintenance service life parallel the financial service life? Are the financial numbers realistic in the light of the MTBF data and reliability information known about the equipment, or must the financial life be accomplished or achieved only with large expenditures to replace parts and components, amounting to "maintenance replacement" of the equipment?

The actual operational policy might be to initiate repairs and replacement when the teardown occurs, even if the parts are still usable. A policy would be to replace all defective parts and those having a 50 percent or greater probability of failure. Using the failure curve, the 50 percent probability would equate to 700 hours of operation. Thus, the maintenance policy would be to replace all defectives and all units of that part having 700 hours of accumulated operating time on them. This would be costed out in terms of the following elements:

1. Cost to tear down in maintenance dollars
2. Cost to replace in time and materials
3. Cost to rebuild in maintenance dollars
4. Downtime cost
5. Remaining service life in replaced parts

Is this the best policy? At this point it is unknown, and actual experimentation may be a costly way of determining the best policy. This is the reason to turn to simulation. Simulation of failures of key parts using failure curves allows the evaluation of several different policies. Initiating a repair will give rise to a fixed cost in simply diagnosing that problem. There will be a repair cost that is variable. It depends on the type of repair and its scope. There will be a reassembly cost that is probably fairly predictable, and there will be downtime associated with all the cost generators. Thus, with a fixed and variable element associated with the maintenance activity and a gain associated with the maintenance activity, it is possible to employ a form of break-even analysis or look at marginal costs versus marginal revenues to determine the best overall strategy as well as looking at the expenditures now for increased reliability in the design stage versus maintenance costs in the future. This policy would then be evaluated against other candidate policies and the most cost-effective policy selected.

Setting the Limits

Addressing the issue of reliability in the design stage is perhaps the most proactive approach the buyer can take. In this stage, when the paper is blank, it is possible to design the equipment or develop the specifications with reliability as one of the prime criteria. The task is not insurmountable. Certain parts are subject to failure, while others will operate for years without even a hint of trouble. Ideally, all parts would fail at the same time. This would allow for complete replacement of all failed parts. Unfortunately, machines are not so constructed. Having selected the most cost-effective method of maintaining the equipment, use the data to determine the total cost of maintenance. Again take a total cost approach.

Appendix C

Collecting Relevant Data on Prices From the Internet

All analysis has a data-collection component to it, and price analysis depends on doing the best possible job of data collection. This starts with some of the basics, such as the company data from the annual report, and periodic reports required by the Securities and Exchange Commission (SEC). Then, there are various government reports and data that should be amassed. Exhibit C-1 gives the sources that may be used to get this information.

To get PPI data, first, log on the Internet via our on-line service. Begin with the producer price index. Once ready to search, type BLS home page into the search box, and click the search button. This will bring you to a request page, where the Series Report page will ask for a series ID format (see last page of this Appendix for sample). In the box labeled series ID formats, you tell the system what series you want. For example, the following is a request for the PPI for single-sided, PC boards, and glass substrate. The series would be:

PCU3672#111

This tells the search engine exactly what you are seeking since:

Positions	Value	Field Name
1–2	PC	Series Prefix—PC is code for the Producer Price Index. The first set of letters define the BLS series desired.
3	U	Seasonal Adjustment Code—this indicates if the data is to be seasonally unadjusted or adjusted.
4–7	3672	Standard Industrial Classification (Industry) Code. This is the four-digit code for that SIC number.
#		The presence of this symbol tells the searcher that you will be going into a subset of the SIC code. In this example, 3672 is the code for Printed Circuit Boards.
8–11	111	Product Code—This tells the searcher that you are looking for a category or particular type of circuit board, in this case single-side, glass substrate, PC boards.

Exhibit C-1. Some Internet sources of information.

Information Needed	Source of Information	Available on Internet
Producer Price Index Data	Bureau of Labor Statistics Data by Standard Industrial Classification Codes (4 Digits)	Yes—BLS Home Page and Data Request Page
Wage Rate Data	BLS Data by State and Region	Yes—Same as Above
Annual Report	Company or Hoover Business Resources	Normally, Yes
10K	Company or Electronic Data Gathering Analysis Retrieval (EDGAR) Access	Yes, Also Try Company Home Page
SIC codes (4 digit). To get 7 digit, you must go to BLS series—192 pages—see LABSTAT.	Listing by U.S. Treasury	Yes—www.ustreas. home page or try the home page of the Census Bureau, www.census.gov. Another way is to search for SIC codes. Many sources, be sure to visit Cal Poly Pamona Library.
Economic Overview by SIC Code	U.S. Industrial Outlook Published Annually by Department of Commerce	Not Yet
Material to Labor Ratios	Census of Manufactures by SIC Code (4 digit)	www.census.gov or try www.lib.umich/lib.home/ Documents.center/ stats.html
Labor Rates by SIC Code	Census of Manufactures, U.S. Department of Commerce	Same as Above
Price Structure Data	Dun & Bradstreet, *Key Ratios & Industry Norms*	Yes, Available at a Cost
10Q	Individual Company or Electronic Data Gathering Analysis Retrieval (EDGAR)	Yes—Business Section, Then Hoover Business Resources or EDGAR Access

See Exhibit C-2 for the actual page as it appears on your screen.

Moving down the rest of the Series Report page, you are asked how many years of data you need and the format of the data. I suggest column data as opposed to table. At the bottom of the request page is a retrieve data button. Click on it with your mouse. When it comes up on the screen, it will look like the following pages. You may wish to print it or download it into a directory for direct use by your computer. Remember to download it as an .XLS file for excel.[1] If you download the file, it will probably come out under your Internet connector as a subfile. Before you use the data for analysis, make sure you view it to see how the data line up by columns.

Your next data requirement may be the annual report of the supplier. Here you have an array of options. Take the easiest one. This is usually Hoover Business Resources. One has only to select Hoover from the business menu and follow the instructions on the screen for getting the financials. It is really simple. Ten minutes of practice can save a good deal of time and effort in extracting data and knowing what to look for in the future.

If you are a heavy user of the PPI data, two suggestions are offered. Go to the BLS home page, point and click on the Data box, and get an overview of the whole process of getting information by going to the Gopher box. This will bring up the LABSTAT menu. Spend some time reading it. You may wish to extract all 121,000+ titles for the seven-digit SIC codes. The total printout is 192 pages. A worthwhile approach is first obtaining a listing of four-digit SIC codes in both numeric and alphabetic order. The second step is printing all of the seven-digit code listings, and placing the information in a three-hole binder for ready reference. Thus, when looking up a commodity, the first step is the four-digit SIC code and then going into the subcategories of that code for a more detailed search.

Changes Upon Us

On April 9, 1997, a new classification system was unveiled as the North American Industry Classification System (NAICS). It will replace the SIC codes with the first set of data appearing early in 1999. Estimates are that 34 percent of the direct comparisons between SIC and NAICS will not be possible. To see the new codes and how this may affect any code you may wish to use, obtain a free comparison table from www.census.gov. It is also recommended that users visit the Cal Poly Pamona home page and the NAICS home page at www.naics.com. The Cal Poly Pamona library maintains extensive links on the issue of SIC and NAICS issues with a five-page bibliography on the subject. About 60 percent of the articles can be accessed on the Internet.

---

1. For those of you who prefer phones and faxes to computers, you may call the Bureau of Labor Statistics at 202–606–7705, tell them the SIC code you need and the years you want and your fax number, and they will fax it that same day or the next day. If you're interested in data disks, call 202-606-7728.

Exhibit C-2. BLS Series Report Web page.

Series Report ⓑⓁⓈ

Information and Help

⚠ BLS Program and Survey Special Notices

Series ID Formats

Enter series id(s) below:

Years(s) to report for:
```
1996–199
1995–199
1994–199
1987–199
```

Format:

○ 1. Column
◉ 2. Table (Rows: *Year*, Columns: *Period*)
○ 3. Table (Rows: *Series ID*, Columns: *Period/Year*, Optional: *Net & % Change*)
○ 4. Table (Rows: *Survey Characteristics*, Columns: *Period/Year*, Optional: *Net & % Change*)

HTML Tables: ◉ Yes ○ No
Catalog: ◉ Yes ○ No
Delimiter: ○ Tab ◉ Space ○ Comma (Note: Tab delimited works for Mosaic 2.0 or better.)

Number of Characters Per Line: `400`

[Retrieve data] [Reset form]

 Data Home Page

Appendix D

Discounting Values for Select Interest Rates

Interest Rate

Year	5.00%	7.00%	8.00%	9.00%	10.00%	11.00%	12.00%	14.00%	15.00%	16.00%	17.00%	18.00%	19.00%	20.00%	25.00%	30.00%	35.00%	40.00%	45.00%	50.00%
1	0.9524	0.9346	0.9259	0.9174	0.9091	0.9009	0.8929	0.8772	0.8696	0.8621	0.8547	0.8475	0.8403	0.8333	0.8000	0.7692	0.7407	0.7143	0.6897	0.6667
2	0.9070	0.8734	0.8573	0.8417	0.8264	0.8116	0.7972	0.7695	0.7561	0.7432	0.7305	0.7182	0.7062	0.6944	0.6400	0.5917	0.5487	0.5102	0.4756	0.4444
3	0.8638	0.8163	0.7938	0.7722	0.7513	0.7312	0.7118	0.6750	0.6575	0.6407	0.6244	0.6086	0.5934	0.5787	0.5120	0.4552	0.4064	0.3644	0.3280	0.2963
4	0.8227	0.7629	0.7350	0.7084	0.6830	0.6587	0.6355	0.5921	0.5718	0.5523	0.5337	0.5158	0.4987	0.4823	0.4096	0.3501	0.3011	0.2603	0.2262	0.1975
5	0.7835	0.7130	0.6806	0.6499	0.6209	0.5935	0.5674	0.5194	0.4972	0.4761	0.4561	0.4371	0.4190	0.4019	0.3277	0.2693	0.2230	0.1859	0.1560	0.1317
6	0.7462	0.6663	0.6302	0.5963	0.5645	0.5346	0.5066	0.4556	0.4323	0.4104	0.3898	0.3704	0.3521	0.3349	0.2621	0.2072	0.1652	0.1328	0.1076	0.0878
7	0.7107	0.6227	0.5835	0.5470	0.5132	0.4817	0.4523	0.3996	0.3759	0.3538	0.3332	0.3139	0.2959	0.2791	0.2097	0.1594	0.1224	0.0949	0.0742	0.0585
8	0.6768	0.5820	0.5403	0.5019	0.4665	0.4339	0.4039	0.3506	0.3269	0.3050	0.2848	0.2660	0.2487	0.2326	0.1678	0.1226	0.0906	0.0678	0.0512	0.0390
9	0.6446	0.5439	0.5002	0.4604	0.4241	0.3909	0.3606	0.3075	0.2843	0.2630	0.2434	0.2255	0.2090	0.1938	0.1342	0.0943	0.0671	0.0484	0.0353	0.0260
10	0.6139	0.5083	0.4632	0.4224	0.3855	0.3522	0.3220	0.2697	0.2472	0.2267	0.2080	0.1911	0.1756	0.1615	0.1074	0.0725	0.0497	0.0346	0.0243	0.0173
11	0.5847	0.4751	0.4289	0.3875	0.3505	0.3173	0.2875	0.2366	0.2149	0.1954	0.1778	0.1619	0.1476	0.1346	0.0859	0.0558	0.0368	0.0247	0.0168	0.0116
12	0.5568	0.4440	0.3971	0.3555	0.3186	0.2858	0.2567	0.2076	0.1869	0.1685	0.1520	0.1372	0.1240	0.1122	0.0687	0.0429	0.0273	0.0176	0.0116	0.0077
13	0.5303	0.4150	0.3677	0.3262	0.2897	0.2575	0.2292	0.1821	0.1625	0.1452	0.1299	0.1163	0.1042	0.0935	0.0550	0.0330	0.0202	0.0126	0.0080	0.0051
14	0.5051	0.3878	0.3405	0.2992	0.2633	0.2320	0.2046	0.1597	0.1413	0.1252	0.1110	0.0985	0.0876	0.0779	0.0440	0.0254	0.0150	0.0090	0.0055	0.0034
15	0.4810	0.3624	0.3152	0.2745	0.2394	0.2090	0.1827	0.1401	0.1229	0.1079	0.0949	0.0835	0.0736	0.0649	0.0352	0.0195	0.0111	0.0064	0.0038	0.0023
16	0.4581	0.3387	0.2919	0.2519	0.2176	0.1883	0.1631	0.1229	0.1069	0.0930	0.0811	0.0708	0.0618	0.0541	0.0281	0.0150	0.0082	0.0046	0.0026	0.0015
17	0.4363	0.3166	0.2703	0.2311	0.1978	0.1696	0.1456	0.1078	0.0929	0.0802	0.0693	0.0600	0.0520	0.0451	0.0225	0.0116	0.0061	0.0033	0.0018	0.0010
18	0.4155	0.2959	0.2502	0.2120	0.1799	0.1528	0.1300	0.0946	0.0808	0.0691	0.0592	0.0508	0.0437	0.0376	0.0180	0.0089	0.0045	0.0023	0.0012	0.0007
19	0.3957	0.2765	0.2317	0.1945	0.1635	0.1377	0.1161	0.0829	0.0703	0.0596	0.0506	0.0431	0.0367	0.0313	0.0144	0.0068	0.0033	0.0017	0.0009	0.0005
20	0.3769	0.2584	0.2145	0.1784	0.1486	0.1240	0.1037	0.0728	0.0611	0.0514	0.0433	0.0365	0.0308	0.0261	0.0115	0.0053	0.0025	0.0012	0.0006	0.0003

21	0.3589	0.2415	0.1987	0.1637	0.1351	0.1117	0.0926	0.0638	0.0531	0.0443	0.0370	0.0309	0.0259	0.0217	0.0092	0.0040	0.0018	0.0009	0.0004	0.0002
22	0.3418	0.2257	0.1839	0.1502	0.1228	0.1007	0.0826	0.0560	0.0462	0.0382	0.0316	0.0262	0.0218	0.0181	0.0074	0.0031	0.0014	0.0006	0.0003	0.0001
23	0.3256	0.2109	0.1703	0.1378	0.1117	0.0907	0.0738	0.0491	0.0402	0.0329	0.0270	0.0222	0.0183	0.0151	0.0059	0.0024	0.0010	0.0004	0.0002	0.0001
24	0.3101	0.1971	0.1577	0.1264	0.1015	0.0817	0.0659	0.0431	0.0349	0.0284	0.0231	0.0188	0.0154	0.0126	0.0047	0.0018	0.0007	0.0003	0.0001	0.0001
25	0.2953	0.1842	0.1460	0.1160	0.0923	0.0736	0.0588	0.0378	0.0304	0.0245	0.0197	0.0160	0.0129	0.0105	0.0038	0.0014	0.0006	0.0002	0.0001	0.0000
26	0.2812	0.1722	0.1352	0.1064	0.0839	0.0663	0.0525	0.0331	0.0264	0.0211	0.0169	0.0135	0.0109	0.0087	0.0030	0.0011	0.0004	0.0002	0.0001	0.0000
27	0.2678	0.1609	0.1252	0.0976	0.0763	0.0597	0.0469	0.0291	0.0230	0.0182	0.0144	0.0115	0.0091	0.0073	0.0024	0.0008	0.0003	0.0001	0.0001	0.0000
28	0.2551	0.1504	0.1159	0.0895	0.0693	0.0538	0.0419	0.0255	0.0200	0.0157	0.0123	0.0097	0.0077	0.0061	0.0019	0.0006	0.0002	0.0001	0.0000	0.0000
29	0.2429	0.1406	0.1073	0.0822	0.0630	0.0485	0.0374	0.0224	0.0174	0.0135	0.0105	0.0082	0.0064	0.0051	0.0015	0.0005	0.0002	0.0001	0.0000	0.0000
30	0.2314	0.1314	0.0994	0.0754	0.0573	0.0437	0.0334	0.0196	0.0151	0.0116	0.0090	0.0070	0.0054	0.0042	0.0012	0.0004	0.0001	0.0000	0.0000	0.0000
35	0.1813	0.0937	0.0676	0.0490	0.0356	0.0259	0.0189	0.0102	0.0075	0.0055	0.0041	0.0030	0.0023	0.0017	0.0004	0.0001	0.0000	0.0000	0.0000	0.0000
40	0.1420	0.0668	0.0460	0.0318	0.0221	0.0154	0.0107	0.0053	0.0037	0.0026	0.0019	0.0013	0.0010	0.0007	0.0001	0.0000	0.0000	0.0000	0.0000	0.0000
45	0.1113	0.0476	0.0313	0.0207	0.0137	0.0091	0.0061	0.0027	0.0019	0.0013	0.0009	0.0006	0.0004	0.0003	0.0000	0.0000	0.0000	0.0000	0.0000	0.0000
50	0.0872	0.0339	0.0213	0.0134	0.0085	0.0054	0.0035	0.0014	0.0009	0.0006	0.0004	0.0003	0.0002	0.0001	0.0000	0.0000	0.0000	0.0000	0.0000	0.0000

To determine a value not in the table use the formula P.V. = 1/(1+i)^n, where i = the interest rate and n = the year. For example, the value of $1.00, six years from now at 6% is: /(1.06)^6 or 0.7050 or $0.71.

Appendix E

Area Under the Normal Curve

Z value	0.00	0.01	0.02	0.03	0.04	0.05	0.06	0.07	0.08	0.09
0.0	0.0000	0.0040	0.0080	0.0123	0.0160	0.0199	0.0239	0.0279	0.0319	0.0359
0.1	0.0398	0.0438	0.0478	0.0517	0.0557	0.0596	0.0636	0.0675	0.0714	0.0753
0.2	0.0793	0.0832	0.0871	0.0910	0.0948	0.0987	0.1026	0.1064	0.1103	0.1141
0.3	0.1179	0.1217	0.1255	0.1293	0.1331	0.1368	0.1406	0.1443	0.148	0.1517
0.4	0.1554	0.1591	0.1628	0.1664	0.1700	0.1736	0.1772	0.1808	0.1844	0.1879
0.5	0.1915	0.1950	0.1985	0.2019	0.2054	0.2088	0.2123	0.2157	0.2190	0.2224
0.6	0.2257	0.2291	0.2324	0.2357	0.2389	0.2422	0.2454	0.2486	0.2517	0.2549
0.7	0.2480	0.2611	0.2642	0.2673	0.2704	0.2735	0.2764	0.2794	0.2824	0.2852
0.8	0.2881	0.2910	0.2939	0.2967	0.2995	0.3023	0.3051	0.3078	0.3106	0.3133
0.9	0.3159	0.3186	0.3212	0.3238	0.3264	0.3289	0.3315	0.3340	0.3365	0.3389
1.0	0.3413	0.3438	0.3461	0.3485	0.3508	0.3531	0.3554	0.3577	0.3599	0.3621
1.1	0.3643	0.3665	0.3686	0.3708	0.3729	0.3749	0.3770	0.3790	0.381	0.383
1.2	0.3849	0.3869	0.3888	0.3907	0.3925	0.3944	0.3962	0.3980	0.3997	0.4015
1.3	0.4032	0.4049	0.4066	0.4082	0.4099	0.4115	0.4131	0.4147	0.4162	0.4177
1.4	0.4192	0.4207	0.4222	0.4236	0.4251	0.4265	0.4279	0.4292	0.4306	0.4319
1.5	0.4332	0.4345	0.4357	0.4370	0.4382	0.4394	0.4406	0.4418	0.4429	0.4441
1.6	0.4452	0.4463	0.4474	0.4484	0.4495	0.4505	0.4515	0.4525	0.4535	0.4645
1.7	0.4554	0.4564	0.4573	0.4582	0.4591	0.4599	0.4608	0.4616	0.4635	0.4633
1.8	0.4641	0.4649	0.4656	0.4664	0.4671	0.4678	0.4686	0.4693	0.4699	0.4706
1.9	0.4713	0.4719	0.4726	0.4732	0.4738	0.4744	0.4750	0.4756	0.4761	0.4767

Z value	0.00	0.01	0.02	0.03	0.04	0.05	0.06	0.07	0.08	0.09
2.0	0.4772	0.4778	0.4783	0.4788	0.4793	0.4798	0.4803	0.4808	0.4812	0.4817
2.1	0.4821	0.4826	0.4830	0.4834	0.4838	0.4842	0.4846	0.4850	0.4854	0.4857
2.2	0.4861	0.4864	0.4868	0.4871	0.4875	0.4878	0.4881	0.4881	0.4884	0.489
2.3	0.4893	0.4896	0.4898	0.4901	0.4904	0.4906	0.4909	0.4911	0.4913	0.4916
2.4	0.4918	0.4920	0.4922	0.4925	0.4927	0.4929	0.4931	0.4932	0.4934	0.4936
2.5	0.4938	0.4940	0.4941	0.4943	0.4945	0.4946	0.4948	0.4949	0.4951	0.4952
2.6	0.4953	0.4955	0.4956	0.4957	0.4959	0.4960	0.4961	0.4962	0.4963	0.4964
2.7	0.4965	0.4966	0.4967	0.4968	0.4969	0.4970	0.4971	0.4972	0.4973	0.4974
2.8	0.4974	0.4975	0.4976	0.4977	0.4977	0.4978	0.4979	0.4979	0.498	0.4981
2.9	0.4981	0.4982	0.4982	0.4983	0.4984	0.4984	0.4985	0.4985	0.4986	0.4986
3.0	0.4987	0.4987	0.4987	0.4988	0.4988	0.4989	0.4989	0.4989	0.499	0.499

To compute the probability of completing the project in a certain period of time, take the time period minus the critical path and divide the result by the standard deviation along the critical path. This will give you a value for Z.
Simply consult the table for the probability of completion.
Example — Critical path = 20 weeks, standard deviation = 2 weeks
Probability of completing in 23 weeks?
23 weeks is three weeks beyond critical path or 1.5 standard deviations.
23 weeks = critical path + 1.5 standard deviations.
Z value for 1.5 standard deviations = .4332; Probability is 0.5 + 0.4332 or .9332 or 93.32%. The value of 0.5 comes from the fact that the probability of completion in 20 weeks is 0.5.

Appendix F
Some Useful Web Sites

It would be impossible and counterproductive to try and list all the helpful Web sites that exist. Some useful sites are listed in Exhibit F-1. In addition, the list would be obsolete before it were printed due to the dynamic nature of the Internet. What we are attempting to do is look at the capital equipment buying process and identify several useful sources of information for the buyer. Some have been identified in the body of the handbook and these will be supplemented by a few more that will provide useful data or information to the buyer.

In going to the Internet, there are two distinct approaches. In the first case, we put in the term of interest and see what comes up on the screen. While this is time consuming, it is not that unproductive. Sometimes the broad search turns up useful data. The second case is going directly to the site and getting the information directly. This is more time effective, but hinges on knowing exactly where to go. Both approaches are useful. In addition, do not neglect software evaluations by users. Normally, these are rather interesting exchanges between users and potential users of software. They are insightful and allow you to have some point of contact on the Internet with someone who has "been down the road."

The Internet is an excellent source of information and a low-cost contact with a wide variety of products and services. Its value should not be ignored.

Exhibit F-1. Some useful Web sites.

Address	Provider	Information
www.census.gov	U.S. Department of Commerce	Wide range of data and statistics
www.bls	Bureau of Labor Statistics	Data on prices and wages at retail, wholesale and raw materials—a "must" for analysis
www.surplusrecord.com	The Surplus Record	Browse the previously owned equipment market
www.thomaspublishing	Thomas Publishing	A wide array of information on all Thomas Publishing goods and services
www.mdna@his.com	Machinery Dealers National Association	An opportunity to get a good booklet on purchasing previously owned equipment
www.lib.utulsa.edu/netref/ sic 2.htm	University of Tulsa	Wide range of information on SIC codes.
www.elaonline.com	Equipment Leasing Association	An excellent background on leasing capital equipment
www.alci.com	ALCI—commercial leasing	Application on the Internet, commercial leasing
www.nacis.com	Department of Commerce	Information on North American Industry Classification System
www.dbisna.com	Dun & Bradstreet	A significant amount of information on sources of supply
www.industry.net		A wide range of information on sources, industry data and the 100 top Web sites
www.reliability-magazine	Reliability Magazine	Articles on CMMS, maintenance planning, and maintenance prediction modeling

Appendix G
Selected Bibliography

The purpose of the bibliography is to provide references for the reader to gain more insight into the subject matter. One problem that arises with a bibliography is that often it contains so many references that the reader does not know where to begin. This bibliography is limited to a few of the "best in class" books. Its brevity should not hinder the reader from looking elsewhere, but given the pressures on time, one good reference can be worth many average ones. After each book will be a word or two about the coverage of the text.

Auer, Joseph and Harris, and Charles Edison. *Major Equipment Procurement.* New York: Van Nostrand, Reinhold, Inc., 1983.

Burt, David N. and Richard L. Pinkerton. *A Purchasing Manager's Guide to Strategic Proactive Procurement.* New York: AMACOM, 1996. This is a "must read" book for the Purchasing Manager. Keep it on the desk for reference.

Contino, Richard M. *Handbook of Equipment Leasing—A Deal Maker's Guide*, Second Edition. New York: AMACOM, 1996. An excellent book in the field of leasing.

———. *Negotiating Business Equipment Leases—Insider Strategies for Getting the Best Deal.* New York: McGraw-Hill, 1995. Another excellent book in the field of leasing.

Dixon, Robert L. *The Executive's Accounting Primer*, 2nd Edition. New York: McGraw-Hill, 1982. An older, but still useful book.

Held, Gilbert. *The Equipment Acquisition Book: What, When, Where and How to Buy.* New York: Van Nostrand, Reinhold, Inc., 1991.

Hirsch, William. *The Contracts Management Deskbook.* New York: American Management Association, 1983. Good information on negotiation.

King, Donald B., and J. J. Ritterskamp. *The Purchasing Manager's Desk Book of Purchasing Law,* 2nd edition. Englewood Cliffs, N.J.: Prentice Hall, Inc., 1995. Another important part of the library. A readable law book, designed to be understood.

Leeser, Robert C. *Engineer's Procurement Manual for Major Plant Equipment: A Guide to Principles and Procedures, Planning, Specifications, Bidding, and Evaluation.* Englewood Cliffs, N.J.: Prentice-Hall, Inc., 1996.

Mahoney, Francis X., and Carl G. Thor. *The TQM Trilogy: Using ISO 9000, the Deming Prize and the Baldridge Award.* New York: AMACOM, 1994.

Montgomery, Douglas C. *Introduction to Statistical Quality Control.* New York: John Wiley & Sons, 1996. A basic understanding of quality control is a must for the equipment purchaser.

Parker, Glenn M. *Cross Functional Teams: Working With Allies, Enemies and Other Strangers.* San Francisco: Jossey Bass, Inc., 1994. A primer on the issues of teams and teaming. A starting point for team formation.

Spenolini, Michael J. *The Benchmarking Book.* New York: AMACOM, 1992. An important work when looking at best practices.

Williams, Robert, Mark Teagan, and Jose Beneyto. *The World's Largest Market: A Business Guide to Europe 1992.* New York: AMACOM, 1992. Europe is a prime source of capital equipment.

Relevant publications from professional associations such as Machinery Dealers Equipment Association on "Buying Previously Owned Equipment."

The Federal Government is a treasure trove of good information. This is especially true of the *U.S. Industrial Outlook.* Published by the Bureau of Industrial Economics, U.S. Department of Commerce, this annual publication is an essential source of information on key domestic industries.

Index